Lightfoot Guide to the Via Francigena

Edition 9

The Great Saint Bernard Pass to Saint Peter's Square, Rome

1028 kilometres

www.pilgrimagepublications.com
Copyright 2023 Pilgrimage Publications All rights reserved.
ISBN: 978-2-917183-41-0

The authors have done their best to ensure the accuracy and currency of the information in this Lightfoot Guide to the Via Francigena, however they can accept no responsibility for any loss, injury or inconvenience sustained by any traveller as a result of information contained in the guide. Changes will inevitably occur within the life-span of this edition and the authors welcome notification of such changes and any other feedback that will enable them to enhance the quality of the guide.

The Modern via Francigena Sigerico

The Lightfoot Guide to the via Francigena, written by Paul Chinn and Babette Gallard presents, in great detail, the official route for walkers from Canterbury Cathedral to Saint Peter's Square in Rome, as endorsed by the European Association of Via Francigena.
The European Association of Via Francigena (AEVF), founded in 2001, is the custodian of the Cultural Route of the via Francigena. In 2006 it became the official body recognised by the Council of Europe for supporting, promoting and developing the route.
However, the route would not exist without the enormous support of the communities along its length and the many associations that have participated in its mapping and signposting and giving encouragement and support to those setting foot on the route.
In France the via Francigena has been adopted by the Fédération Française de la Randonnée Pédestre (FFRP) as the GR®145. GR® is a registered trademark of the FFRP.
About the Authors:
We are two very ordinary people who quit the world of business and stumbled on the St James Way during our search for a more viable, rewarding alternative to our previous lifestyle. Since then we have completed numerous pilgrimages, one of which was particularly tough and finally prompted us to create Pilgrimage Publications and the Lightfoot Guide series in 2006. We have no religious beliefs, but share a 'wanderlust' and need to know about and contribute to the world we occupy.
Pilgrimage Publications has 4 very basic aims:
To enable those who share our 'wanderlust' to follow pilgrim routes all over the world.
To ensure Lightfoot Guides are as current and accurate as possible, using pilgrim feedback as a major source of information.
To use eco-friendly materials and methods for the publication of Lightfoot Guides and travel books.
To promote eco-friendly travel.

Also by Lightfoot Guides:
Lightfoot Guide to the via Francigena:
Canterbury to The Great Saint Bernard Pass
Lightfoot Guide to the via Podiensis
Lightfoot Guide to the Three Saints Way:
Winchester to Mont St Michel
Mont St Michel to St Jean d'Angely
Lightfoot Guide to the via Domitia:
Arles to Vercelli
Lightfoot Companion:
to the via Francigena–Canterbury to The Grand Saint Bernard Pass
to the via Francigena–The Grand Saint Bernard Pass to Saint Peter's Square
to the via Domitia
Lightfoot Guide to Foraging–Wild Foods by the Wayside
A guide to over 130 of the most common edible and medicinal plants in Western Europe
Your Camino
A guide to assist in preparation for a pilgrimage to Santiago de Compostela
Slackpacking the Camino Frances
Taking (some of) the pain out of you pilgrimage to Santiago de Compostela
Camino Lingo
A cheats' guide to speaking Spanish on the Camino English/Spanish and Dutch/Spanish
Cover: Fortified Abbey of Abbadia a'Isola –watercolour by Jannina Veit Teuten
jannina.net

By offering choices of route, stopping places and accommodation styles the Lightfoot Guides are designed to enable everyone to meet their personal goals and enjoy the best, whilst avoiding the worst, of following the ancient pilgrimage routes.

The authors would like to emphasise that they have made great efforts to use only public footpaths and to respect private property. Historically, pilgrims may not have been so severely restricted by ownership rights and the pressures of expanding populations, but unfortunately this is no longer the case. Today, even the most free-spirited traveller must adhere to commonly accepted routes. Failure to do so will only antagonise local residents, encourage the closure of routes and inhibit pilgrims following on behind.

Please let us know about any changes to the route or inaccuracies within this guide book. Email us at mail@pilgrimagepublications.com

Our special thanks go to:
The many pilgrims who have willing shared information on their journeys.
Sylvia Nilsen, Jonas Ewe and the Confraternity of Pilgrims to Rome for their support of the invaluable facebook group web.facebook.com/groups/19899007360
The late Francis Geere for his tireless dedication to the route and those that pass along it.
Adelaide Trezzini for her contribution to the development and mapping of the via Francigena route www.francigena-international.org
Openstreetmap: The maps in this book are derived from data provided by © OpenStreetMap contributors (www.openstreetmap.org) and the cartography is licensed under the Creative Commons Attribution-ShareAlike 2.0 license (CC BY-SA).
The many contributors to open source software that brings high quality tools to us all.
Wiki Commons for providing photos licensed and attributed under the Creative Commons Attribution-Share Alike 4.0 International license.
The many associations that have cleared and signposted the way.
The families along the route that have willingly opened their homes to countless strangers.
Jannina Veit Teuten for her contribution to reawakening knowledge of the via Francigena in the many communities that straddle the route and for allowing the use of her watercolours in this book–jannina.net

This work is dedicated to the many unsung heroes that have toiled to make this wonderful route accessible to the world at large - *mille grazie*

Contents

Introduction:
The via Francigena Pilgrimage	1
Using Your Lightfoot Guide	2
Finding Your Way	6
The Basics	8
Resources	10
What to Take	11

Via Francigena di Sigerico:

No.	km	Stage	
49	30.9	Col-Grand-Saint-Bernard to Aosta	14
50	29.1	Aosta to Châtillon	19
51	20.2	Châtillon to Verrès	23
52	15.0	Verrès to Pont-Saint-Martin	27
53	22.1	Pont-Saint-Martin to Ivrea	30
54	36.9	Ivrea to Santhià	34
55	29.1	Santhià to Vercelli	39
56	33.4	Vercelli to Mortara	44
57	20.7	Mortara to Garlasco	48
58	24.6	Garlasco to Pavia	51
59	28.0	Pavia to Santa Cristina	54
60	16.3	Santa Cristina to Orio Litta	57
61	24.0	Orio Litta to Piacenza	60
62	31.5	Piacenza to Fiorenzuola-d'Arda	64
63	22.3	Fiorenzuola-d'Arda to Fidenza	67
64	34.0	Fidenza to Fornovo-di-Taro	70
65	21.5	Fornovo-di-Taro to Cassio	75
66	20.1	Cassio to the Cisa Pass Summit	79
67	20.0	Cisa Pass Summit to Pontremoli	83
68	32.4	Pontremoli to Aulla	87
69	18.2	Aulla to Sarzanna	92
70	29.1	Sarzana to Massa	97
71	25.9	Massa to Camaiore	102
72	26.7	Camaiore to Lucca	105
73	18.5	Lucca to Altopascio	109
74	29.3	Altopascio to San-Miniato-Alto	113
75	23.8	San-Miniato-Alto to Gambassi-Terme	118
76	14.0	Gambassi-Terme to San-Gimignano	121
77	27.2	San-Gimignano to Abbadia-a-Isola	124
78	24.5	Abbadia-a-Isola to Siena	129
79	25.9	Siena to Ponte-d'Arbia	133
80	26.3	Ponte-d'Arbia to San-Quirico-d'Orcia	136
81	33.4	San-Quirico-d'Orcia to Radicofani	139
82	23.9	Radicofani to Acquapendente	146
83	23.0	Acquapendente to Bolsena	150
84	16.5	Bolsena to Montefiascone	153
85	17.9	Montefiascone to Viterbo	157
86	22.0	Viterbo to Vetralla	160
87	23.3	Vetralla to Sutri	164
88	24.3	Sutri to Campagnano-di-Roma	168
89	23.1	Campagnano-di-Roma to La Storta	171
90	19.2	La-Storta to Saint Peter's Square	174

Via degli Abati:

59a	19.9	Pavia to Colombarone	180
59b	16.9	Colombarone to Pometo	184
59c	30.4	Pometo to Bobbio	188
59d	20.1	Bobbio to Nicelli	192
59e	13.2	Nicelli to Groppallo	196
59f	21.8	Groppallo to Bardi	200
59g	28.8	Bardi to Borgo-Val-di-Taro	204
59h	33.7	Borgo-Val-di-Taro to Pontremoli	208

Introduction

Traveller, there is no path, paths are made by walking.
Antonio Machado

The via Francigena Pilgrimage

The epitome of the medieval travelling man, the *homoviator,* was the pilgrim who embarked on a journey towards one of Christianity's holy destinations. The practice of peregrination was presented as an example of faith and charity, linked to the metaphor of our journey towards the ultimate spiritual and heavenly goal.
The main destinations were Rome, Jerusalem and Santiago de Compostela, carried out on foot, with the help of nothing more than a *burdon*–a pilgrim staff.
The routes to the holy destinations were of course not a single road but a network connecting many starting points and adapting to avoid both physical and human barriers en route.

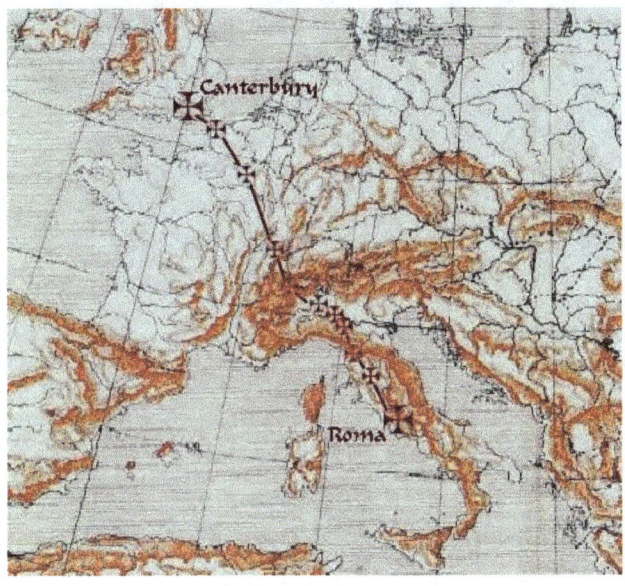

The via Francigena, connecting northern Europe to Rome, was also not a single road, but a collection of several possible routes, which changed over the centuries as trade and the pilgrimage culture developed and then waned. Depending on the time of year, political situation, and relative popularity of the shrines of saints along the route, travellers may have used any of three or four crossings over the Alps and the Apennines.
First documented as the Lombard Way and later the Iter Francorum. The via Francigena was only mentioned as such in the Actum Clusi, a parchment produced in 876 in the Abbey of San Salvatore al Monte Amiata (Tuscany).
Then, at the end of the 10th century, Sigeric the Serious, Archbishop of Canterbury, used the via Francigena to travel to Rome for his consecration by Pope John XV. He recorded his return journey, and the places where he stopped, in a document which is now held in the British Library, but nothing in it suggests that the route was new or unique. His itinerary lists the seventy-nine *submansiones*, which have formed the basis of the via Francigena Sigerico as we know it today.
Not surprisingly the *submansiones* typically lie on the vestiges of the Roman road network that was constructed to facilitate trade, conquest and occupation of Britain and Gaul. These roads offer the shortest route from the Channel coast to Rome and even 1100 years after Sigeric's journey they are clearly identifiable features of the landscape.
This book traces the modern via Francigena from the summit of the Great Saint Bernard Pass–*Col du Grand Saint Bernard/ Colle del Gran San Bernardo*–to Saint Peter's Square–*Pi-*

Using Your Lightfoot Guide

Sigeric's Chronicle

azza San Pietro–Rome. Volume 1 of the series covers the journey from Canterbury Cathedral to the Great Saint Bernard Pass. The Lightfoot Companions provide more information on the culture and history of the places that you will encounter on the way.

Layout

You will find an introductory section followed by 42 chapters, each of which covers a segment or stage of the "Official Route" and 8 chapters describing the stages of the via degli Abati. Each chapter contains:

- A stage summary
- Cultural highlights
- Detailed instructions
- One or more maps
- An altitude profile
- Route alternatives
- Addresses and contact information for accommodation and tourist information points

Accommodation is not only listed for the stage ends but for the entire length of the stage so that is up to you and your body where you decide to stop.

The book charts the "Official Route" for the via Francigena as endorsed by the AEVF. However, over the years this has grown substantially for reasons of safety, tourism and expediency adding as much as 700 kilometres to the route followed by Archbishop Sigeric.

Where available Alternate Routes are also provided that will reduce the length of your journey, take you to places of interest or provide the possibility of travelling more closely in Sigeric's footsteps or more likely hoof-prints. The shorter routes are titled "Direct Route". You will note that stage lengths vary considerably. Many factors influence this, including the availability of accommodation, the difficulty of the stage or perhaps that of prior or subsequent stages.

Using Your Lightfoot Guide

Stages
The stages in this book should not be thought of as definitive, but an initial planning guide. The distances can be covered by an average physically fit walker with a moderately loaded pack in fair weather conditions. They are of course influenced by availability of accommodation and points of interest while also recognising that many readers of this book will be constrained by Schengen visa restrictions. As a result of striving to achieve these goals the stages do not always conform to the stages suggested by the European Association of the via Francigena (AEVF). but you must decide both in the planning stage and when walking just where to break your journey.

Chapter contents:
Summary
The summary provides distance and ascent and descent details as well as overall progress statistics. It will describe the conditions that you can expect to encounter during the stage. In planning your day, 4 km/hour is the usual rate of progress for a hiker over level ground, falling to 3 km/hour or less on steep ascents and descents.

Cultural Highlights
A cultural perspective on the area is provided to prepare the mind as well as the body for the day ahead. More historical and cultural information can be found in the Lightfoot Companion to this guide.

Instructions
The entire route has been GPS traced in detail and every significant intersection logged using GPS co-ordinates and a way point description. Each instruction is identified by its distance from the start of a stage or the alternate route in tenths of kilometres.
Altitudes have been obtained from the best currently available satellite radar data.
It is very likely that you will use a GPS enabled smartphone or sports watch to keep track of your distance. While these devices are very useful their accuracy can be affected by both the environment and the way they are used. In deep valleys and thick woodland satellite signals will be subject to reflections leading to more apparent movement. Military advice is to allow for a 6-7% over estimate of distance travelled under these conditions. When a device is stationary for long periods reflections will again create apparent movement leading to an increased estimate of distance travelled. It is good practice to pause device logging when you are stationary for more than a few minutes.
In addition to the basic instruction, where necessary a visual confirmation is included in [].
The GPS coordinates of each way point can be downloaded from the "GPS Download" tab at the foot the book description page at www.pilgrimagepublications.com
The route signposting has improved dramatically since our first edition and we hope that you will only need the instructions where there are missing signs, doubt over the intended direction or where you choose to use one of the many Alternate Routes.

Maps
The maps provide a north-up visual representation of the route. To reduce clutter on the maps, way points are only shown with a minimum of a 1 km separation. However, all way points and their descriptions are presented in the text. The maps also show the location of each listed accommodation option and information point.
To optimise space within the book the scale varies from map to map but way point distance identifiers and the scale bar allow you to quickly assess your progress and route options.

Altitude Profile
The profiles provide both a rapid visual assessment of the difficulty of each stage with the altitude variations and distance to intermediate towns. Both vertical and horizontal scales are adjusted by stage.
Where alternate routes offer a distance advantage over the "Official Route" then a contrasting profile for the shorter route will also be shown. This may span several stages.
At the end of the book you will find altitude/distance profiles of the entire route from the

Using Your Lightfoot Guide

Col Grand Saint Bernard to Saint Peter's Square contrasted with a shorter route taking advantage of the alternate trails that follow more closely the path of Sigeric.

While the time and distance savings in Italy are rather less than are possible in France and Switzerland they may still save 2 or 3 hiking days or take the sting from some of the more challenging days.

The *Francigena di Montagna* or *via degli Abati* (Abbots Way) that joins Pavia with Pontremoli is described in detail in the rear of the book as stages 59a-h. This mountain route allows an early exit from the Po valley and follows in the footsteps of those pilgrims that chose to include the resting place of Saint Columban in their journey to Rome.

Accommodation Listings

A price banding is used based on the least expensive mid-season option for two people in each establishment–accurate at the time of entry, but of course subject to change. For simplicity, the listing is divided into 4 price bands:

A > (€) 75 B = (€) 40–75 C = (€) 0–40 D = Donation

A range of options is provided where they are available. Prices may or may not include breakfast and some establishments make a supplementary charge for pets. In general, dogs are not welcome in Commercial or Religious Hostels. The general rule for accommodation in Religious Houses is that reservations must be made 24 hours ahead of arrival.

Each listing has been verified before publication of this guide and while in general the accommodation along the route is rarely full, seasonality and increasing popularity of the route mean this cannot be guaranteed. Commercial pressures may also lead to closure or change of ownership between publication and when you travel. We therefore recommend a general rule of where possible booking 48 hours in advance providing enough time for you to find alternatives if your first choice is not available. Longer range planning is possible, but will create pressures to meet a schedule that may prove impossible in the light of weather or injury. In the eBook edition of this guide phone numbers, email and web addresses are presented as active links. There is an inevitable churn in mobile phone numbers, email and web addresses as staff change, technology is updated or cost savings sought. While all the listing data is believed accurate at the time of writing, change will occur and so if you do not receive a response or your messages are rejected then make a web search on the name of the establishment and double check the details.

Donation means just that, you are expected to give what you can and think the accommodation warrants, but remember nothing is free. The hostels require heating, cleaning and maintenance and if you do not pay then someone else must. As a guide 15€ or 20€ per person is normal without an evening meal for which you should expect to pay a similar amount again.

PR–indicates accommodation on which we have received a positive pilgrim recommendation.

Accommodation is classified as:

 Pilgrim Hostel

Hostels that principally accommodate via Francigena pilgrims. Usually with dormitory accommodation, kitchen and shared bathrooms. The hostels may be run by commercial, municipal or religious authorities and may require to see your pilgrim credentials.

 Religious Hostel

A facility with accommodation managed by a religious group which may have space for via Francigena pilgrims. Usually with dormitory accommodation, shared bathrooms and kitchen facilities or the possibility of prepared meals. Credentials will be required. You may

Using Your Lightfoot Guide

find that priority has been given to increasing numbers of homeless refugees.

 Commercial Hostel
Commercial or municipal hostel including youth hostels and gîte d'etape in France. Usually with dormitory accommodation, kitchen facilities and shared bathrooms.

 Church or Religious Organisation
Places where limited, basic accommodation or assistance may be offered. Credentials will be required.

 Pilgrim Hosts
Families or secular organisations that wish to support pilgrims by offering limited accommodation in their homes. Credentials will be required.

 Bed and Breakfast
More expensive commercial home accommodation including chambres d'hôtes in France and agriturismos in Italy which may charge by room or by person. There are usually double or family sized rooms with the possibility of a private bathroom. Bed and Breakfasts and agriturismos may be isolated from shops and restaurants. Often dinner can be provided if requested in advance. Kitchen access may also be possible.

 Hotel
Hotels normally are priced by room. Where there is a choice of room types the price band is given for the room type with the lowest price. In some situations there may be seasonal premiums. Many of the hotel chains and booking sites use similar pricing principles to airlines and vary their prices by both time of day of your booking and room availability.

 Room, apartment or whole house rental
Self catering accommodation including *affittacamere*. Multi-room or whole house rentals may have a minimum stay of more than 1 night. Beware of additional costs for cleaning and utilities and tourist taxes.

 Camp-grounds
Generally well equipped camp-sites with showers, laundry facilities and mini-markets. Some will also have a bar/restaurant. In addition to offering sites for tents most offer pre-erected tent, mobile home or chalet rental. They are normally open from early April to late October. While "wild" camping does take place along the route it is illegal in Italy.

 Information Points
Tourist offices and town halls where information can be found on accommodation and services in the community. They may also be willing to assist with making forward bookings. Hours can be erratic, particularly in the low season.

Accommodation booking sites such as booking.com, agoda.com and airbnb.com offer a vast array of options. However, many of the addresses listed in the guide do not have a presence on these sites and the prices offered by direct booking and the booking sites may also differ. It is wise to compare.

Finding Your Way

In Italy you will find many signs to help you on your way. The European Association for the via Francgena (AEVF) has toiled for many years to have the route signposted and to sponsor improvements to pathway safety. These efforts have been supported by many local groups that have added additional signposting and initiated local improvements.

The dominant signposting therefore may change from region to region and occasionally be in conflict with the "Official Route". This can be particularly difficult where signs relating to an older version of the route have not been removed or a new improvement has been started but not completed. Be also aware that other *vie Francigene* exist in some provinces that view the "Official Route" as just the *via Francigena di Sigerico*.

Ultimately the routing decisions will be yours, but beware following signs that appear to deviate from the route as described in this guide.

This AEVF sign is normally only found on the current "Official Route".

It will be seen both in towns and mounted on poles in the heart of the countryside. The arrow/chevron indicates the direction to Rome.

The large brown signs are typically found on or close to roadways and either show the yellow pilgrim or hikers (for a walking route); a bike (for a cycling route) or a car (for a motoring route).

Some signs are also bidirectional. The convention is that if there is both a white and a yellow arrow then the white arrow indicates Rome and the yellow Canterbury or sometimes Santiago de Compostela.

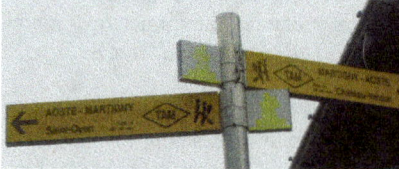

In the Aosta Valley the ever present yellow pilgrim is attached to signs giving the names of pathways and intermediate towns and villages.

The intensive farming of the Po valley often leads to flattening of the official signs, which can reemerge in hand painted forms such as these.

Finding Your Way

You will also see souvenirs from the passage of many via Francigena related associations stretching over the years, but beware that they may have followed a version of the trail that is not the current "Official Route".

In the Tuscany you may encounter the via Francigena mileposts with the attractive terracotta pilgrim, but sadly these have frequently become the target of souvenir collectors. You will also see the red and white signs of the Club Alpino Italiano. As the club signposts many different paths, they distinguish the via Francigena by including a small black pilgrim or the name of the route and sometimes the upcoming towns, in Lazio you will also find milestones with a red pilgrim, but of course there are all the combinations, and each community will add its own flourish.

The Basics

The Basics in Italy

Currency:
Euro–€. Standard banking hours: Monday-Friday 08.30-13.30 and 14.30-16.00. Generally closed on weekends and holidays ATMs or *Bancomats* are available at most banks, post offices and in larger supermarkets.

Emergencies
112–Carabinieri (national-level police who also perform military police duties)
113–Emergency Police Help Number (also ambulance and fire)
115–Fire Department
116–A.C.I. (Italian Automobile Club) road assistance.
118–Medical Emergencies

Post Offices (Poste Italiane)
Standard Opening Hours: 08.30-19.30 and 13.45-18.30, Monday to Friday. Branches in smaller towns and villages close for an hour, 13.00-14.00.
Stamps can be purchased at post offices–*uffici postali*–or licensed tobacconists–*tabacchi*.
Post restante services–*Fermoposta*–are available in many post offices. Mail is retained for 30 days before being returned to the sender. You will need to provide adequate identification to retrieve your mail. The envelopes should be marked with your full name, the exact address of the post office and the word "*Fermoposta*". A small charge is made for each item. www.poste.it provides a full list of post office locations.

Telephone
Phone booths that still accept coins are hard find. If you're planning to use a public phone purchase of a telephone card is recommended.
Numbers beginning with 800 are free.
170–English-speaking operator.
176–International Directory Enquires.
12–Telephone Directory Assistance Number
Note: Italian telephone numbers have between 6 and 11 digits, so don't automatically assume you have the wrong number if it looks strange. Since December 1998, calls to land lines in most cities, but not all, and all other points in Italy must include a leading '0' regardless of whether the call originates within or outside of Italy. However, the leading '0' is not required with mobile phones.
The main mobile phone operators in Italy are TIM, Vodaphone and Wind Tre. If you already have a mobile phone contract from an EU country then you can "roam" in Italy without extra charges. If you would like to buy a pre-paid SIM then this can be done at a phone store, but you will need to provide your identity documents to complete the paperwork
Pre-paid SIMs can be topped up at most supermarkets or online.

Basic Business Hours
08.00-13.00 and 16.00-19.00, Monday to Friday. Shops in smaller towns may close on Saturday afternoons and Monday mornings.
Italy observes the standard European holidays but also adds a few religious and national days. *Ferragosto*, August 15, marks the start of the summer vacation for many Italians when you may find some shops, restaurants and even hotels close for 2 or even 3 weeks.

Health Care
All EU citizens are eligible for free health care in Italy, if they have the correct documentation. UK citizens can apply for a Global Health Insurance Card that will allow access to state

The Basics

healthcare in Italy and other EU countries for free or reduced rates. Non EU Citizens must arrange personal health insurance.

Food

Pizza is now a worldwide phenomenon, but Italy remains the best place to eat it. Italian ice cream (*gelato*) is justifiably famous and available in every conceivable flavour. Traditionally Italian food consists of lunch (*pranzo*) and dinner (*cena*) starting with *antipasto* (literally before the meal), a course consisting of cold meats, seafood and vegetables. The next course, *primo*, involves soup, risotto or pasta, followed by *secondo*–the meat or fish course, usually served alone. Vegetables–*contorni*–are ordered and served separately.

Breakfast (*calazione*) tends to be small–typically a pastry (*brioche* or *brioscia*) and coffee. As in France the workers lunch–*Pranza do Lavoro*–offers a generous meal at a low price.

Accommodation

Italian hotels fall into a number of categories, though the difference between each is gradually decreasing and prices increasing. Virtually all hostels–*ostelli*–excepting Religious Hostels) are members of the International Youth Hostel Association.

Agritourismi are basically an upmarket B&B in a rural area and usually on a working farm. *Affittacamere*–rooms to rent–can be an economical option, typically comparable to Air BnB.

Campeggi–camping in Italy is popular and the sites are generally well equipped.

Public Transport

Italy has a good range of bus and rail services. For buses you will need to buy your ticket at a local store or *tabacchi* before the journey. There is a comprehensive and affordable regional train network, tickets are normally purchased though machines or cafés located beside the stations. Bikes can be taken on those regional trains that carry the bike symbol for a small supplementary daily charge. High speed trains–*Frecciarossa, Frecciargento* and *Frecciabianca* -are more expensive, with pricing structures that escalate close to departure time, so it is a good idea to buy ahead using www.trenitalia.it. Unless dismantled and packed, bikes are not allowed on the high speed trains.

Resources

Useful Links
www.viefrancigene.org-the official website of the European Association of the via Francigena (AEVF) and source for pilgrim credentials
www.pilgrimstorome.org.uk-practical information for the pilgrimage and credentials.
www.viadegliabati.com - history, details and credentials for the via degli Abati.
www.francigena-international.org-International Association for the via Francigena-publishes maps of the route in walking stages as well as route instructions and accommodation lists
www.viefrancigene.com-Italian site providing information and credentials.
gronze.com-maps and accommodation lists
pelgrimswegen.nl-pilgrims association in the Netherlands
www.eurovia.tv-German language site with information on European pilgrim trails
www.camminideuropageie.com-an Italian, Spanish, French collaboration to promote cultural tourism in Europe
www.csj.org.uk-the Confraternity of Saint James UK chapter, providing a wealth of information about the many pilgrim routes to Santiago de Compostela in Spain as well as general guidance and advice to pilgrims and an online bookstore. It is well worth visiting if this is your first pilgrimage.
www.caminoways.com-provides fully organised tours of the via Francigena
www.sloways.eu-provides tours on foot or bike, also can arrange baggage transport
www.tuscanbike.it-bike tours and rental
bags-free.com-baggage transport
www.pilgrimstales.com-Pilgrims Tales Publishing is passionate about inspiring others with the possibility of discovery, understanding and peace through travel.
www.italia.it-Italian tourism official website
www.museivaticani.va-information and tickets for the Vatican city museums.

Facebook:
web.facebook.com/groups/amicidellaviafrancigena-amici della via francigena
web.facebook.com/groups/2141771089468226-via Francigena Italia
web.facebook.com/groups/19899007360 - multilingual group for all with a valid interest in the route
web.facebook.com/groups/65535048915186a-via Francigena Road to Rome-large international group
web.facebook.com/groups/201103184657309-via Francigena: Australian and New Zealand Walkers and Friends
web.facebook.com/groups/377106036592365-Dormire sulla via Francigena, information on accommodation in Italy
web.facebook.com/francigenatoscana-the via Francigena in Tuscany
web.facebook.com/groups/251274001687610 - Spanish language group

Recommended Reading
The Art of Pilgrimage-Phil Cousineau
The Essential Walker's Journal-Leslie Sansone
Along the Templar Trail-Brandon Wilson
Rome: A Pilgrim's Companion-David Baldwin
The Age of Pilgrimage: The Medieval Journey to God-Jonathan Sumption
In Search of a Way: two journeys of spiritual discovery-Gerard Hughes
Traveling Souls: Contemporary Pilgrimage Stories -Brian Bouldrey (Editor)

What to Take

It is said that your backpack should weigh no more than 10% of your body weight. If you weigh 75 kg (165 pounds), your backpack should not weigh more than 7.5 kg (16.5 pounds). You will also have to allow for the weight of water (up to 2 litres or 2 kg.)
Mental preparation for your trip begins when reflecting on what is truly essential to take. The more weight, the tougher the walk. You might want to follow this tried and tested maxim:
1. Make a list of only essential items
2. Tear the list in half.
3. Pack your bag
4. Throw half of its contents away

It is wiser to have to buy something en route than carry an unnecessary item. You are never so far from a shop that this is not possible.

Packing Checklist

Backpack (35-40 litres): Your backpack should be suited to your morphology and have a rain cover.

Sleeping bag liner or super thin sleeping bag: Many hostels provide blankets so that a liner is generally sufficient.

Foot wear: (1) Light-weight hiking shoes that are water resistant, but breathable. No need to take hiking boots, which are too heavy and ill-suited for long distance walking and (2) flip flops or sandals, for the evening

Walking poles (optional)

Water bottles (at least 2 litres) or Camel-Bak (optional)

Documents: Identity Card/Passport, Insurance Card, credit cards, Pilgrim Passport/Credential, and a waterproof bag to put them in.

Miscellaneous: Safety pins (to hang clothes to dry), knife, headlamp, basic sewing kit, mobile phone and charger with international socket adapter, camera (optional), guide book.

Clothing: Invest in clothes that are specifically adapted to hiking or sport, and are breathable, lightweight and quick-dry:

- 2 quick dry T-shirts
- 1 long sleeved shirt
- 1 fleece or sweater for cool evenings
- 1-2 pairs shorts (quick-dry)
- 1 hiking pants
- 1 rain paints
- 1 ultra-light rain coat
- 3 underwear
- 3 pairs of hiking or running socks, which allow for ventilation and reduce friction
- Swim wear
- Pyjamas
- In winter add wind and rain resistant jacket, hat and gloves

Accessories and toiletries:
- Sun: hat, sunglasses, sun screen
- Toiletries: Quick-dry towel, shower gel/shampoo, toothbrush and tooth paste, moisturizer, nail clippers, comb/brush
- Earplugs (snoring protection)
- Soap/detergent for washing clothes.
- Health: First aid kit, blister prevention foot cream (applied before walking to reduce friction), blister patches
- Other medicines, as needed

To walk safely through the maze of human life, one needs the light of wisdom and the guidance of virtue.

Buddha

The Great Saint Bernard Pass
to
Saint Peter's Square, Rome
1028 Kilometres

Omnes viae Romam ducunt

All roads lead to Rome

stage 49   Col-Grand-Saint-Bernard to Aosta

Length: 30.9km

Ascent: 1963m
Descent: 3852m

Col Grand
St Bernard: 0km
Rome: 1028km

Chiesa di San Lorenzo–Saint-Rhémy-en-Bosses

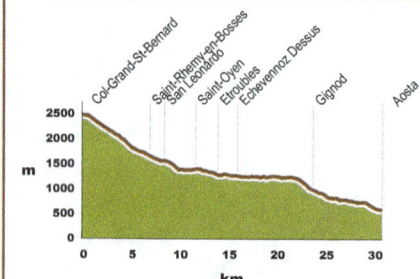

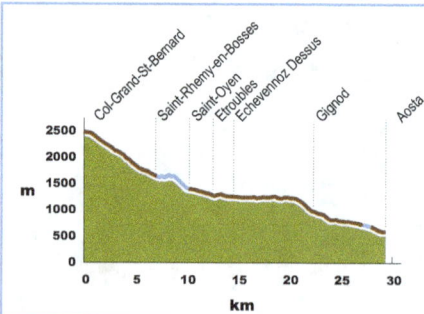

Route: on the way from Col-Grand-Saint-Bernard to Aosta, there are currently few formalities at the Swiss/Italian border, but have your papers ready just in case. The initial descent to Étroubles is gentle and progressive, largely on off-road tracks. Cyclists may wish to take advantage of the easy road descent avoiding the narrow woodland paths below Étroubles, while for walkers there are 2 short direct alternate routes.

Café/bars and food stores will be found much more frequently than in northern sections of the route and all will generally offer good value and excellent quality. You will find examples in Saint-Oyen, Étroubles, Gignod and in the outskirts of Aosta.

Below Gignod the route follows a series of very minor roads, before a section beside the SS27–Strada Statale or national road. In the outskirts of Aosta the route follows sometimes steeply descending pathways and narrow roads, before finally crossing the very busy SS26 and entering the pedestrian zone of the old town to arrive beside the cathedral.

In Italy many groups have worked at signposting their view of the best route to Rome and these views often conflict and so do not be surprised if you see via Francigena signs of many styles, some of which will diverge from our route. In the Aosta valley the route uses general footpath signs showing both distance and walking time supplemented with a pilgrim image. In addition you will find the ubiquitous yellow and white arrows.

For the Romans, Aosta's position at the confluence of two rivers and at the end of the Great and the Little St Bernard Passes, gave it considerable military importance. Its layout was that of a Roman military camp and today the ancient town walls of Augusta Praetoria Salassorum are still preserved. Towers stand at angles to the enceinte (a French term used to describe the inner ring of fortifications surrounding a town), and others are positioned at intervals, with two at each of the four gates, making twenty towers in total.

Col-Grand-Saint-Bernard to Aosta — stage 49

(0.0) With the hospice behind continue straight ahead on the road down the hill [Towards the border post]**(0.5)** At the Italian border post bear right on the path [Pass beside the hotel]**(0.6)** Go straight ahead [Beside the statue of Saint Bernard]**(0.9)** Just before the avalanche gallery cross the road to join a track at the foot of a stone slope **(1.3)** Fork left**(2.0)** Cross over the road and continue on the track **(2.5)** Cross over the road onto the grass track [Path n°13]**(3.1)** Fork right down the hill **(6.2)** Turn left onto the road, SS27**(6.5)** Turn right onto small track and then left in the direction of Saint-Rhemy**(7.0)** Enter **Saint-Rhemy-en-Bosses (XLVIII)** and continue straight ahead on the road [Frazione Cerisey] **(7.2)** At the fork at the end of the main street turn right over the bridge and then left. Note:

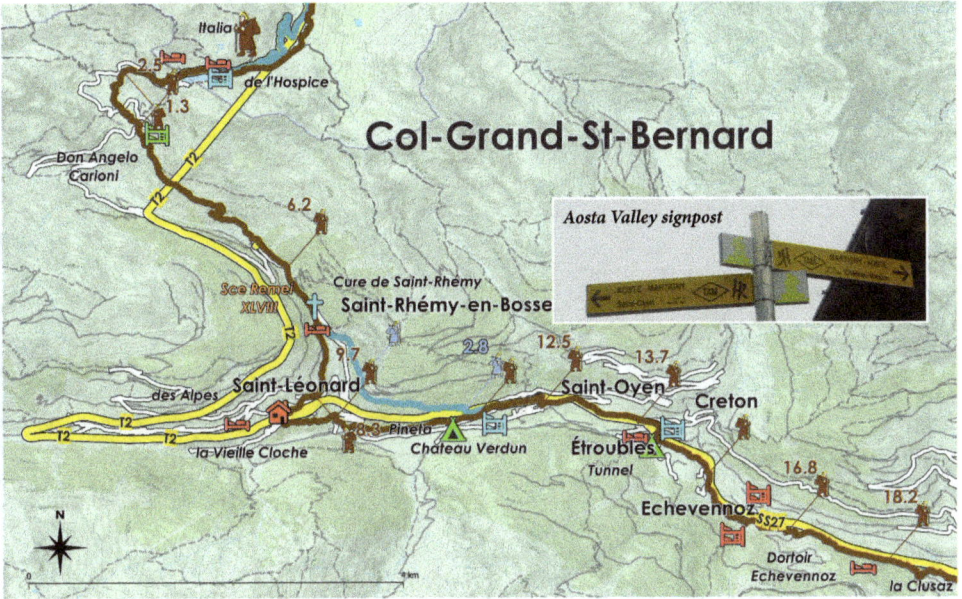

the shorter Alternate Route initially continues straight ahead on the road [River on the left after the bridge] **(8.3)** At the end of the track bear right on the road**(8.5)** On entering **San Leonardo** keep left at the first junction**(8.6)** At the crossroads go straight ahead down the hill [Frazione Predumaz Falcoz]**(8.9)** Cross the main road and continue straight ahead down the hill**(9.0)** Cross the road – Frazione Saint Leonard – and continue straight ahead [Chiesa di Saint Leonard] **(9.7)** At the T-junction with the road, turn right [Frazione Cerisey]**(9.9)** At the exit from Cerisey turn left [Before the bridge]**(10.5)** Continue straight ahead [Through fields] **(11.3)** On approaching the quiet rue de la Montée bear left uphill on the track [Towards the main road]**(11.7)** Turn right onto the SS27 via Roma into the village of **Saint-Oyen**. Note:- the Alternate Route joins from the left**(12.3)** Turn right off the main road onto via Verraz [Sign for Martigny-Aosta]**(12.4)** Turn left down the hill between houses [Sign for Martigny-Aosta] **(12.5)** At the T-junction, turn left [Strada di Flassin]**(12.8)** At the junction with the main road, cross over and take the road straight ahead [Direction Prailles]**(12.9)** Turn right and continue on the track close to the main road [Wooden statue at the junction] **(13.7)** On approaching Etroubles cross the minor road rue de Vachèry and follow the pathway towards the town centre [Shrine on the left] **(13.8)** Rejoin the main road and continue straight ahead on the pavement [Towards hairpin bend]**(13.9)** On the apex of the hairpin bend to the right, bear left to follow the minor road

stage 49 — Col-Grand-Saint-Bernard to Aosta

into Etroubles [Pedestrian zone]**(14.0)**From the crossroads in **Etroubles** pedestrian zone turn right [Rue du Mont Velan]**(14.1)**Continue straight ahead [Cross the river bridge] **(14.1)**At the end of the bridge, cross the road and bear left [Climb the steps]**(14.1)**At the T-junction with the main road, bear right and cross the road with great care into the hotel car park and bear left [Towards the Hotel Beau Sejour]**(14.2)**Bear left on rue Saint-Roch [Footpath sign for Martigny-Aosta,]**(14.3)**Turn right [Unmade road] **(15.1)**At the T-junction, turn right onto the tarmac with the main road close on your left**(15.5)**Turn right onto a grassy track**(16.0)**Join a tarmac road and then turn right at the junction in **Echevennoz Dessus** [Farm on right]**(16.1)**Beside the parking area, turn left onto the track [Martigny-Aosta sign] **(16.8)**At the T-junction with the road, turn right**(16.8)**Turn right to proceed between two houses and then bear left on the track**(16.9)**Bear left alongside the aqueduct **(18.2)**Fork left down the hill**(18.3)**Fork right back up the hill**(18.6)**Fork left on the lower track **(20.2)**Turn right onto a road and then immediately left on the track slightly up the hill**(21.1)**Take the left fork **(22.3)**Turn left on the track [Martigny-Aosta sign]**(22.5)**Remain on grass track [Ignore the dirt track on the right]**(23.0)**Cross over the road to continue down the hill on the grass track [TAM Aoste – Martigny]**(23.0)**Turn sharp left down the hill **(23.1)**Continue straight

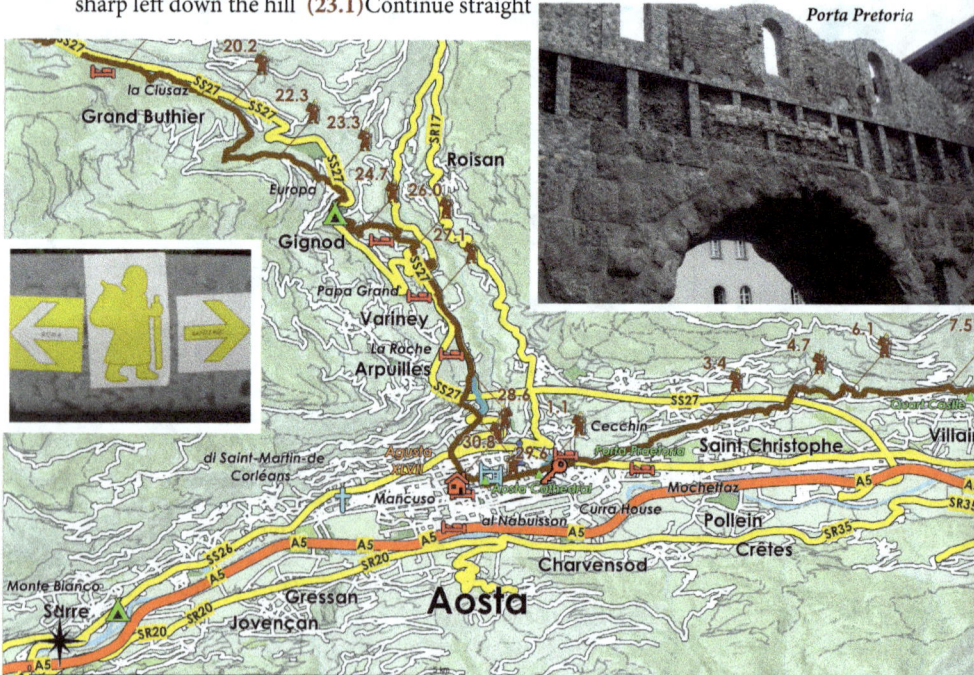

Porta Pretoria

ahead on a long flight of steps**(23.2)**Turn right onto the road and immediately turn left on the grass track **(23.3)**Turn left onto the road to proceed down the hill on Frazione Lexert**(23.4)**Turn left on a small grass track**(23.4)**Turn left onto the road and then immediately right and first left, between the houses**(23.7)**Turn right down the hill [Church on your left]**(23.7)**Turn left to go down the hill [Pass a school on your right]**(23.8)**In **Gignod**, turn right at the junction with main road [Proceed between crash barrier and stone wall]**(24.1)** Turn left, direction Aosta-Martigny [TAM sign] **(24.7)**At the end of the metal railings,

Col-Grand-Saint-Bernard to Aosta — stage 49

turn sharp left downhill on a smaller road [Direction Le Courtil]**(25.0)**Turn sharp right downhill**(25.5)**Turn left onto a tarmac road and then immediately right 🕆 **(26.0)**Turn left at the top of the hill**(26.4)**At the junction with the main road, turn right on Frazione Chez Roncoz [Pass garages on the right] 🕆 **(27.1)**At the mini-roundabout bear left down the hill on Frazione Variney [Towards the church]**(27.3)**Fork left on the lower road**(27.6)**At the T-junction with the main road, turn left and continue on a grass track on the outside of the barrier**(27.8)**Rejoin the main road and continue downhill 🕆 **(28.6)**Fork right uphill. Note:- to avoid numerous obstacles, cyclists should continue with care on the main road until re-joining the "Official Route" in 1km [Direction Grand Signayes]**(28.8)**Fork left on reaching the top of a small rise**(29.1)**Fork left onto the unmade road**(29.2)**Turn sharp left [Down-hill]**(29.3)**At the junction with the road cross over and continue straight ahead down the hill [Keep the vineyard on your right]**(29.5)**At the junction with the main road, again cross over and continue straight ahead. Cyclists rejoin from the left [Pass petrol station on your right]**(29.6)**At the T-junction bear right, downhill [Regione Saraillon] 🕆 **(29.6)**At the junction with the main road, turn left and then right on the small road [Keep house n° 71 close on your left, via Edelweiss]**(29.9)**At the junction, continue straight ahead, downhill on via Edelweissl**(30.4)**At the roundabout take the pedestrian crossing and continue into the centre of Aosta [Hospital on the right]**(30.6)**At the traffic lights, proceed straight ahead [Into pedestrian zone] 🕆 **(30.8)**In Piazza Roncas turn left and immediately right into the narrow street [Towards the Cathedral]**(30.9)**Turn right [Via Forum]**(30.9)**Arrive at **Aosta (XLVII)** centre [Piazza della Cattedrale]

Direct Route to Saint Oyen

Route: a shorter route, saving 1.5km, bypassing Saint-Léonard and following a narrow hill-side track. **(0.0)**Turn left up the hill to rejoin the SS27 [**Frazione Cerisey**]**(0.1)**At the intersection with SS27 turn left, uphill [Stone wall on the left]**(0.4)**At the apex of a hairpin bend to the left, turn right on the track [Footpath sign, direction Aosta] 🕆 **(1.1)**Fork right on the track 🕆 **(2.8)**Track intersects with **SS27**. Cross over and turn left on the track [Take steps from the lay-by]**(3.1)**Continue straight ahead beside the road, the "Official Route" via Saint Leonard joins from the right [Sign for Martigny-Aosta]

Length:	3.1km
Ascent:	265m
Descent:	485m

Accommodation and Tourist Information

Aosta

🛏 **Seminario Vescovile** ,17 Rue De Maistre Xavier, 11100 Aosta(AO), Italy; Tel:+39 0165 40115; Email:seminario@diocesia-osta.it; diocesiaosta.it; Price:D
✝ **Parrocchia di Saint-Martin-de Corléans**,Corso Saint Martin de Corleans, 201, 11100 Aosta(AO), Italy; Tel:+39 0165 553373; Email:parrocchia@saintmartina-osta.it; www.saintmartinaosta.it ; Price:D; *One bedroom*
🏠 **B&B - al Nabuisson**,Via Aubert, 50, 11100 Aosta(AO), Italy; Tel: +39 3396 090332; www.bedbreakaosta.com; Price:B; *Will do laundry for pilgrims*; **PR**

🛏 **Hotel - Mochettaz**,Corso Ivrea, 107, 11100 Aosta(AO), Italy; Tel:+39 0165 43706; +39339 7308359; Email:info@hotelmochettaz.it; www.hotelmochettaz.it; Price:B; *Special price for pilgrims may be available*
🛏 **Hotel - Cecchin**,Via Porte Romano, 27, 11100 Aosta(AO), Italy; Tel:+39 0165 45262; +39 3382 103542; Email:info@hotelcecchin.com; hotelcecchin.com; Price:A
🛏 **Hotel Ristorante - la Belle Epoque**,Via Claude d'Avise, 18, 11100 Aosta(AO), Italy; Tel:+39 0165 261196; +39 3516 365998; Email:info@hotelbellepoqueaosta.it; www.hotelbellepoqueaosta.it; Price:B

stage 49 — Col-Grand-Saint-Bernard to Aosta

📪 **Hotel - La Roche**,Località Signayes, 11100 Aosta(AO), Italy; Tel:+39 0165 262426; Email:info@laroche.it; www.laroche.it ; Price:B
📪 **Albergo - Mancuso**,Via Voison, 32, 11100 Aosta(AO), Italy; Tel:+39 0165 060333; Email:info@albergomancuso.com ; www.albergomancuso.com; Price:B
🔑 **Apartment - Curra House**,Via Vittorio Avondo, 3, 11100 Aosta(AO), Italy; Tel: +39 3470 704617; +39 3384 871355; curra-house-apartment.valle-daosta-hotels.com; Price:B
ℹ️ **Office Regional du Tourisme**,Via Frédéric Chabod, 15, 11100 Aosta(AO), Italy; Tel:+39 0165 548065; Email:office@turismo.vda.it; www.lovevda.it

Etroubles
🛏️ **Affittacamere L'Abri** ,Localita' Echevennoz, 11, 11014 Etroubles(AO), Italy; Tel:+39 0165 789646; +39 3479680595 ; Email:info@affittacamerelabri.it; www.affittacamerelabri.it; Price:C; *Single and double bedrooms also available*
🛏️ **Dortoir Ostello Echevennoz**,Localita' Echevennoz, 4, 11014 Etroubles(AO), Italy; Tel:+39 0165 78225; +39 3403 483049; Email:ruffierdidier@libero.it; Price:C; *Closed October to April*
🛏️ **Casa Alpina Sacro Cuore**,Route Nationale du Gd.Saint.Bernard, 24, 11014 Etroubles(AO), Italy; Tel:+39 0280 887811; Email:casalpina2016@gmail.com; www.exaudi.it/struttura/casa_alpina_sacro_cuore_a_etroubles; Price:C
📪 **Hotel - Beau Sejour**,Strada Statale Gran S.Bernardo, 3, 11014 Etroubles(AO), Italy; Tel:+39 0165 78210; +39 0165.789007; +39 3356 584368; Email:info@beausejour.it; beausejour.it; Price:B
⛺ **Camping Tunnel**,Rue Chevrieres, 4, 11014 Etroubles(AO), Italy; Tel:+39 0165 78292; Email:info@campingtunnel.it; www.campingtunnel.it; Price:C; *Open all year. Pods and chalets available*

Gignod
📪 **Hotel - Bellevue**,Frazione la Ressaz, 3, 11010 Gignod(AO), Italy; Tel:+39 0165 56392; +39 3494 651655; Email:hotelbellevuegignod@gmail.com ; bellevue.valle-daosta-hotels.com; Price:A

📪 **Hotel - Papa Grand**,Frazione Variney, 31, 11010 Gignod(AO), Italy; Tel:+39 0165 56076; ristorant-papagrand.valle-daosta-hotels.com; Price:B
📪 **Albergo - la Clusaz**,Frazione Clusaz, 1, 11010 Gignod(AO), Italy; Tel:+39 0165 56075; +39; Email:booking@laclusaz.it; www.laclusaz.it; Price:A
⛺ **Camping Europa**,Frazione le Plan du Chateau, 5, 11010 Gignod(AO), Italy; Tel: +39 3404 796629; Email:francapavin@hotmail.com; www.lovevda.it; Price:C; *Open all year*

Saint-Léonard
🏠 **B&B - la Vieille Cloche**,Frazione Saint Leonard, 11, 11010 Saint-Léonard(AO), Italy; Tel:+39 0165 780927; +39 3805 159554; Email:info@lavieillecloche.it; www.casevacanzavalledaosta.it; Price:B

Saint-Oyen
🛏️ **Casa Casa Per Ferie - Chateau Verdun**,Rue de Flassin, 11014 Saint-Oyen(AO), Italy; Tel:+39 9016 578247; Email:info@chateauverdun.com; www.chateauverdun.com; Price:C
⛺ **Camping Pineta**,Rue de Flassin, 19, 11014 Saint-Oyen(AO), Italy; Tel:+39 0165 78114; Email:info@campingbarpineta.it; www.campingbarpineta.it; Price:C

Saint-Rhemy-en-Bosses
⛪ **Cure de Saint-Rhémy**,Capoluogo, 5, 11010 Saint-Rhemy-en-Bosses(AO), Italy; Tel: +39 0165 363589; Email:idsc@idscaosta.it; www.idscaosta.it; Price:C
📪 **Hotel - des Alpes**,Località Cuchepache, 15, 11010 Saint-Rhemy-en-Bosses(AO), Italy; Tel:+39 0165 780818; Email:info@desalpeshotel.com; www.desalpeshotel.com; Price:A
📪 **Hotel - Suisse**,Via Roma, 26, 11010 Saint-Rhemy-en-Bosses(AO), Italy; Tel:+39 0165 780901; Email:info@suissehotel.it; suissehotel.it; Price:A

Sarre
⛺ **Camping Monte Bianco**,Frazione Saint Maurice, 15, 11010 Sarre(AO), Italy; Tel:+39 0165 258514; +39 3461 616325; Email:info@campingmontebianco.it; www.campingmontebianco.it; Price:C; *Caravan rental available*

Aosta to Châtillon   stage 50

Length:	29.1km
Ascent:	2236m
Descent:	2284m
Col Grand St Bernard:	31km
Rome:	997km

Fenis Castle

Route: the stage from Aosta to Châtillon is quite strenuous, but with the opportunity to break the journey at Nus. After quitting Aosta the route follows quiet roads, farm tracks and hillside pathways through the vineyards of the Aosta Valley, before entering the busy town of Châtillon.

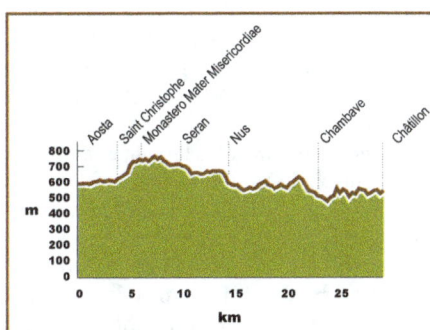

The larger villages have grocery stores and café/bars for a well earned break.

Châtillon offers a good range of facilities.

Though not directly on the route, you will see Fenis Castle dominating the south side of the valley. It first appears in a document in 1242 AD as a property of the Viscounts of Aosta, the Challant family. At that time it was probably a simple keep surrounded by walls, but from 1320 AD to 1420 AD, under the lordship of Aimone of Challant and of his son Bonifacio of Challant, the castle expanded. They gave it the distinctive pentagonal layout, external boundary wall and many of the towers. Then, in 1392, Bonifacio of Challant began a second building campaign to build the staircase and the balconies in the inner courtyard and the prison. He also commissioned Piedmontese painter Giacomo Jaqueiro to paint frescoes on the chapel and in the inner courtyard. Under Bonifacio I, the castle reached its greatest splendour, with a luxurious centre court surrounded by a vegetable plot, a vineyard and a garden where the lord and his guests could relax.

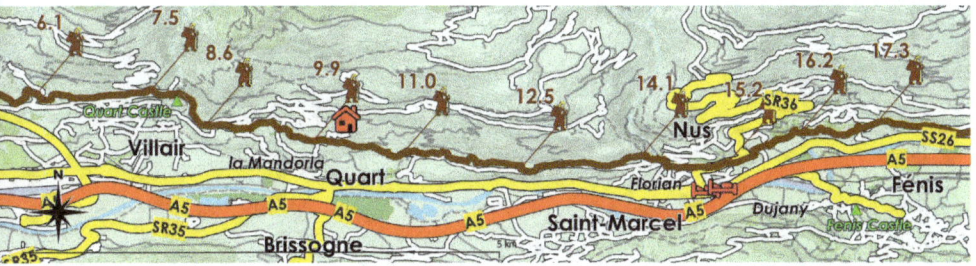

stage 50 — Aosta to Châtillon

🚶(**0.0**)Cross piazza della Cattedrale(**0.0**)Turn left [Via Monseigneur de Sales](**0.2**)Turn right [Rue de l'Hôtel des Etats](**0.3**)At the T-junction, turn left towards the Porta Pretoria [Pass Hôtel de Ville on your left](**1.0**)At the roundabout, at the end of the pedestrian zone, proceed straight ahead and cross the river bridge [Direction Torino] 🚶(**1.1**)At the traffic lights continue straight ahead. Note:- there is a flight of steps ahead – cyclists should turn left and follow via Mont-Velan, turn left on via Mont-Gelé, take the underpass under the busy ring-road and then turn right on via Scuola Militare Alpina [Follow signs for Hôpital Beauregard](**1.2**)Continue straight ahead [Via Mont-Zerbion](**1.4**)At the T-junction, turn right [Elevated road on your left](**1.5**)Turn left over the pedestrian crossing and mount the steps(**1.5**)At the top of the steps turn right on the road, via Scuola Militare Alpina [Towards garages in the wall](**1.6**)Bear right on via Luigi Vaccari [Direction St Christophe] 🚶(**3.4**)Take the left fork [Località Chaussod](**3.6**)Bear left on the track [Towards the church](**3.8**)At the junction beside the church in **Saint Christophe**, turn right and then bear left [Pass a cemetery and VF panel on your right](**3.8**)At the crossroads, continue straight ahead [Direction Bagnere] 🚶(**4.7**)At the Stop sign in Bagnere, turn left [Pass water course on your right](**4.8**)Where the road bends to the left, take the track to the right immediately before the bridge [Keep the waterway on your left](**4.9**)Bear right between the olive trees and then turn left at the road junction(**5.1**)Immediately following the turn to the right, bear left on the track [Pass the farm building on your right] 🚶(**6.1**)Cross the road and continue on the track and then keep left into the trees [Pass the monastery - **Monastero Mater Misericordiae** - on your right](**6.4**)Join the broad track and continue straight ahead(**6.6**)Turn left [Pass the village of Villair on your right] 🚶(**7.5**)At the T-junction with the road turn right on the road, downhill [Hairpin bend](**7.7**)At the next hairpin bend, bear left [Pass through the car park towards the Castello di Quart](**7.8**)Bear left [Keep the castle on your right] (**7.9**)At the junction with the broad track, turn left and then immediately right and follow the track across the hillside [Castle below on your right] 🚶(**8.6**)At the T-junction with the tarmac road, turn right, downhill [Yellow footpath sign](**8.8**)At the T-junction, turn left and then immediately right on the pedestrian ramp. Note:- cyclists should turn right and then take the first road on the left [Yellow footpath sign](**8.9**)Bear left on the No Through Road [Pass a car park on the right](**9.1**)Continue straight ahead [The road deteriorates into a path](**9.2**)After a brief climb, at a junction with a tarmac road, bear right [Chantignan](**9.5**)At the crossroads continue straight ahead on the road [Imperiau] 🚶(**9.9**)Continue straight ahead on the road [Enter **Seran**] 🚶(**11.0**)Take the left fork on the road [Towards Amerique](**11.9**)Just before the hairpin to the left, take the right fork [Pass the quarry on your right] 🚶(**12.5**)At the end of the track take the faint pathway, downhill and bearing left [Parallel to the road and motorway below](**12.8**)Cross over a water-course [Remain parallel to the road](**13.0**)Continue straight ahead [Parallel to the road](**13.3**) Continue straight ahead [Avoid the right turn] 🚶(**14.1**)At the fork take the path to the right

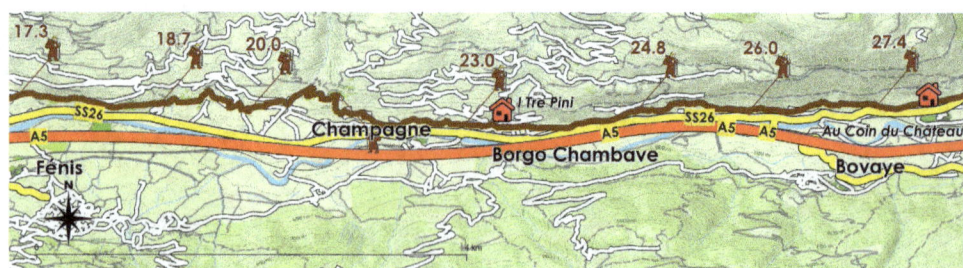

Aosta to Châtillon — stage 50

[Steeply downhill]**(14.3)** At the end of the steep path turn left on the road and cross the bridge**(14.5)** Keep left on the main road [Enter **Nus**]**(14.6)** Fork left on via Pramatton [Pass conifers in the garden on your right]**(15.0)** At the T-junction, bear left [Junction beside church] 🏠 **(15.2)** After exiting Nus and beside the monument, turn right and then immediately left on the path [Pass vines on the left]**(15.5)** At the fork bear left [Downhill]**(15.8)** At the road junction turn right and then immediately left [Frazione Plantayes, towards Rovarey] 🏠 **(16.2)** Continue straight ahead [Château on right]**(17.0)** At the T-junction, turn left to proceed up the hill into Rovarey [Large white house on the left] 🏠 **(17.3)** At the bend to the left, turn right on a small road**(17.9)** Bear right on the stony track [Downhill] 🏠 **(18.7)** At the road junction continue straight ahead [Parallel to the motorway]**(19.5)** At the Stop sign turn left [Pass parking area on the right and then turn right on the path down the hill] **(19.7)** At the junction with the road, turn left and then turn left again after the sharp right hand bend 🏠 **(20.0)** From the car park, take the track across the field towards the village**(20.2)** Bear left and right through the village of Oley and continue parallel to the main road**(20.4)** At the T-junction with the SR42, turn right and then turn left immediately after crossing the waterway 🏠 **(21.3)** In Grangeon beside an agriturismo turn right [Through vines]**(21.5)** After a steep descent take the road to the left [Beside the hamlet]**(21.7)** Join an tarmac road and bear right [Downhill]**(21.8)** Go straight ahead, avoid the turning to the left [Road bends to the right and then left]**(22.1)** At the T-junction turn left [Direction Chambave] 🏠 **(23.0)** At the T-junction, turn right direction Torino [Enter **Chambave**]**(23.3)** Turn left in front of the Café l'Arquebusier [Rue E. Chanoux]**(23.8)** At the Stop sign bear left beside the main road**(23.8)** Take the left fork on the small road towards Chandianaz [Pass wooden crucifix on your right] 🏠 **(24.8)** Continue straight ahead [Pass through the hamlet of Chandianaz]**(25.7)** Go straight ahead [Path passes through Beudegaz] 🏠 **(26.0)** Before entering the derelict hamlet take the faint path to the left [Skirt the hamlet]**(26.4)** At the T-junction with a tarmac road, turn left on the road**(26.6)** At the next bend in the road, bear right on the small road**(26.9)** Bear right on the path down the hill towards Châtillon [Beside clearing] 🏠 **(27.4)** Continue straight ahead on the tarmac road [Beside fountain and over pipeline]**(27.9)** At the T-junction, turn right**(27.9)** At the next T-junction, turn left**(28.3)** On reaching the Châtillon ring-road take the subway and continue straight ahead into the town [Via Menabreaz] 🏠 **(28.8)** In Châtillon turn left. Note:- caution travelling against the one-way system [Cross the bridge on via Emile Chanoux]**(29.0)** Turn left into piazza Abbé Prosper and climb the steps towards the church**(29.1)** Arrive at **Châtillon** centre [In front of the church of San Pietro]

21

stage 50 — Aosta to Châtillon

Accommodation and Tourist Information

Chambave
🏠 **B&B - I Tre Pini**,Rue de Cly, 15, 11023 Chambave(AO), Italy; Tel:+39 328 4480833; +39 3290 290921; Email:itrepinibnb@gmail.com; beb.it/itrepinibnb; Price:B; **PR**

Châtillon
🛏 **Convento Cappuccini**,Via Emile Chanoux, 130, 11024 Châtillon(AO), Italy; Tel:+39 0166 61471; Email:hatillon@cappucinipiemonte.com; www.parrocchia-chatillon.com/conventocappuccini; Price:D

🏠 **Casa dell'Armonia**,Via Hugonin 16, 11024 Châtillon(AO), Italy; Tel:+39 3279830219; +39 3470752616; Email:info.casadellarmonia@gmail.com; Price:C

🏠 **B&B - Clair Matin**,Via Tour de Grange, 40, 11024 Châtillon(AO), Italy; Tel: +39 3280 922916; Email:info@clairmatin.it; www.clairmatin.it; Price:A

🏠 **B&B - Au Coin du Château**,Frazione Cret de Breil, 47, 11024 Châtillon(AO), Italy; Tel: +39 3404 720974; Email:aucoinduchateau@gmail.com; au-coin-du-chateau.valle-daosta-hotels.com; Price:B; *Lower cost if you book direct*

🛏 **Hotel - Dufour**,Via Tollen, 16, 11024 Châtillon(AO), Italy; Tel:+39 0166 61467; +39 3408 262390; Email:dufourtaxi@virgilio.it; www.hoteldufourchatillon.it; Price:B

🛏 **Hotel - Rendez Vous**,Regione Soleil, 3, 11024 Châtillon(AO), Italy; Tel:+39 0166 563150; Email:info@hotel-rendezvous.com; www.hotel-rendezvous.com; Price:B

🛏 **Hotel - le Verger**,Via Tour de Grange, 53, 11024 Châtillon(AO), Italy; Tel:+39 0166 62314; +39 0166 563066; www.leverger.it; Price:B

Nus
🛏 **Hotel - Florian**,Via Risorgimento, 3, 11020 Nus(AO), Italy; Tel:+39 0165 547422 ; +39 3336333380; Email:info@hotel-florian.it; www.hotel-florian.it; Price:B

🛏 **Hotel - Dujany**,Via Risorgimento, 104, 11020 Nus(AO), Italy; Tel:+39 0165 767100; Email:info@hoteldujany.com; www.hoteldujany.com; Price:B

Quart
🏠 **B&B - la Mandorla**,Clou de Seran, 10, 11020 Quart(AO), Italy; Tel:+39 0165 762163; +39 36 6401 5709; Email:bb_la-mandorla@yahoo.it; www.lamandorla-quart.it; Price:A; *Very kind owner but no shops nearby*; **PR**

Castello di Quart

Châtillon to Verrès — stage 51

Verrès Castle Giuditta

Length:	20.2km
Ascent:	1655m
Descent:	1827m
Col Grand St Bernard:	60km
Rome:	968km

Route: another strenuous stage from Châtillon to Verrès, returning to the terraced hillsides on the north and east flanks of the Aosta valley before descending to the broadening valley floor.

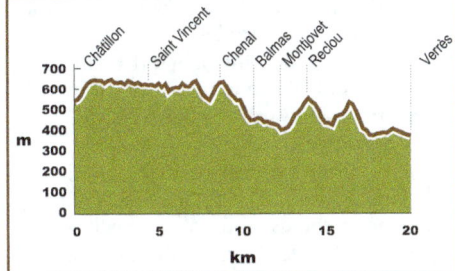

There is the opportunity to break the journey in Saint-Vincent and Montjovet.

Verrès offers a good range of facilities.

Verrès Castle, was a military fortress, built by Yblet de Challant in the 14th century. The castle stands on a rocky promontory, dominating the town access to the Val d'Ayas. From the outside it looks like an austere cube, thirty metres long on each side and practically free of decorative elements, but it is one of the most visited monuments of the Aosta Valley.

Saint-Vincent

Every element of the castle seems to have been considered to make the fortress more defensible. If you visit it, you will climb a steep mule track, which winds up the mountain until it reaches the entrance in the circuit wall, accessed by means of a drawbridge.

On the death of Yblet, in 1409, the castle and his other possessions passed to his son François de Challant. François died in 1442, without male heirs, and left his property to his daughters Marguerite and Catherine. Verrès Castle became one of the strongholds of Catherine and her husband Pierre Sarriod d'Introd.

Legend has it that, on Trinity Sunday, 1449, Catherine and Pierre left the castle and went down to the town square, where they danced with the local people. Every year, the event is celebrated in May with a four-day carnival, which involves a procession, masquerade balls, and the performance of Giuseppe Giacosa's play, *Una Partita a Scacchi* (*A Game of Chess*).

stage 51 — Châtillon to Verrès

🚶(0.0)Pass beside the church and turn left on the road up the hill [Via Gervasone](0.0) From the front of the church in Châtillon turn left [Up the hill](0.3)Take the left fork(0.5) Cross the small bridge and take the tarmac road to the left [Steeply uphill](0.6)Take the road to the left uphill [Direction Tour de Conoz](0.8)After a steep climb on the road take the path to the right [Metal hand rail](0.9)Turn right on a tarmac road [The road deteriorates into a track] 🚶(1.3)At the fork continue straight ahead(1.7)Continue straight ahead on the track(2.1)At the T-junction with a tarmac road turn right 🚶(2.4)At the Stop sign, cross straight over the road and take the gravel track(2.5)Continue straight ahead on the tarmac [Pass metal gates on your right](2.8)Continue straight ahead [Cross a water-course](3.2)At the crossroads, continue straight ahead 🚶(4.0)Continue straight ahead [Ignore the turning to the right](4.5)Enter **Saint Vincent** and continue straight ahead at the crossroads [Via Monte Bianco](4.7)Cross the road and bear left uphill(4.9)Bear right on the smaller road. Note :- to avoid a flight of steps cyclists should remain on the road and pass the entrance the Terme, then take the first road to the right – via Battaglione Aosta – and rejoin the "Official Route" as the path emerges from the trees beside house n° 32 [Metal railings] 🚶(5.1)Turn right and take the steps to the path below(5.2)Pass the funicular and the Terme building on your left(5.5)At the T-junction with the tarmac road, turn right [Downhill, yellow "F" on left](5.7)At the T-junction, turn left on via Ponte Romano and then

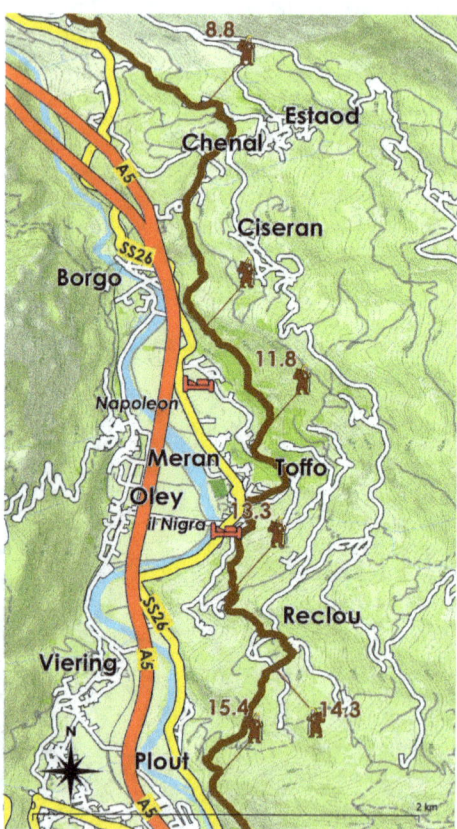

immediately turn left [Direction Emarese] 🚶(6.5)Take the right fork on the small road downhill and then turn left over the bridge [Towards the car park](6.7)Continue straight ahead [Near to the chapel] (6.7)Take the track to the left [Beside the water-fountain](6.8)Descend through the orchards and take a path to the left(6.9)After a steep climb, take the track to the left(7.2)Bear right on the path [Beside the woods](7.2)At the T-junction with the road, turn right and then bear right on the small road [Pass sign Feilley] (7.4)At the first junction bear right onto a path [Beside the stream](7.5)Cross a track and continue straight ahead on the grass track 🚶(7.6)At the T-junction with the road, turn left on the road and continue downhill(7.8)In front of the house take the track to the right [Champ de Vigne](8.1)Beside the stone house, turn to the left [Through the orchards](8.3)Near to the house bear left on the track [Into the trees](8.4)After a steep climb in the woods turn left in the clearing(8.4)After a short climb bear left on the track [Across the hillside](8.6)At the T-junction, bear right on the broad track 🚶(8.8) Continue straight ahead on the tarmac in **Chenal** [Ruined castle on the hill to the right](8.9)Take the first turning to the

Châtillon to Verrès stage 51

right and immediately right again and continue on the path after passing the small church [Metal railings on the right]**(8.9)**Bear left into the parking space and take the grass track straight ahead**(9.2)**Art the road junction, cross over and take smaller road with the wall to your left and a field on your right**(9.4)**At the junction, bear right, downhill [Pass a shrine on your right]**(9.6)**Take the right fork [After crossing bridge]**(9.7)**Bear left on the road, downhill [Direction Balmas] **(10.8)**Ignore the track to the right and continue straight ahead on the tarmac [**Balmas**]**(10.9)**Keep left [Wooden railings on your right] **(11.8)** Continue straight ahead on the tarmac [Toffo]**(12.2)**At the Stop sign, turn right on the stone track before reaching the main road**(12.4)**Beside a group of houses turn right [Towards church spire]**(12.4)**At the T-junction in **Montjovet** (XLVI), take the road to the left [Uphill]**(12.5)**At the first bend to the left take the path to the right [Downhill, towards the church]**(12.7)**At the junction immediately after passing the church, turn left and then immediately bear right on the track [Cross the hill-side in the trees] **(13.7)**Join a tarmac road and bear left, uphill [Rock face on the left]**(13.8)**Turn left on the path, steeply uphill [Yellow footpath signs]**(14.0)**The path emerges at a road junction, continue straight ahead on the road [Towards Quignonaz]**(14.0)**At the entry to **Reclou**, bear right on the track [Yellow footpath sign]**(14.1)**At the junction with the tarmac road, turn right [Pass chalet style house on your right] **(14.3)**At the crossroads, continue straight ahead on the gravel track [Water trough on the right]**(14.6)**At the crossroads in the tracks, continue straight ahead [Downhill, through the trees]**(14.8)**At the junction in the tracks, keep right [Continue downhill]**(15.0)**On the bend to the right, turn left [Downhill]**(15.1)**At the T-junction, turn left **(15.4)**Take the left fork and continue across the hill-side parallel to the river and motorway [Pass the hamlet of Viana on your right] **(16.8)**At the T-junction, turn right and continue on the road through the village [Torille]**(17.3)**Keep right on the road**(17.7)**At the T-junction with the SS26 turn left and follow the main road towards Verrès **(19.0)**As the main road makes a sharp lefthand bend, continue straight ahead on the narrow street [Direction Centro]**(19.1)**In the small piazza, bear right over the river bridge**(19.4)**Turn right on Vicolo San Rocco and then left at the end of the street and continue straight ahead towards the railway station **(20.2)**Arrive at **Verrès** beside the railway station. Note:- the hostel "Il Casello" is to the right

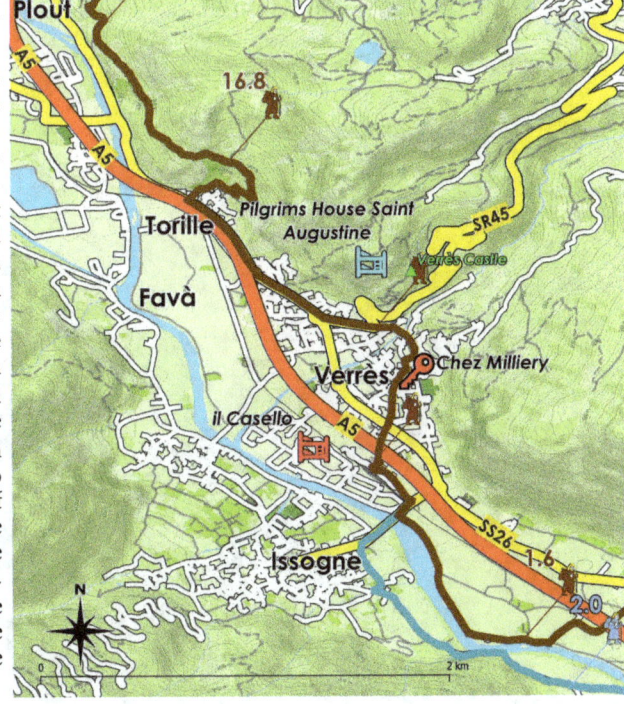

stage 51 — Châtillon to Verrès

Accommodation and Tourist Information

Montjovet

🛏 **Hotel - Napoleon**,Località Broccard, 5, 11020 Montjovet(AO), Italy; Tel:+39 0166 579111; +39 3471 542897; Email:hotelnapoleonvda@gmail.com; www.napoleonvda.it; Price:B

🛏 **Hotel - il Nigra**,Frazione.Berriaz, 13, 11020 Montjovet(AO), Italy; Tel:+39 0166 579235; Email:nigrasrl@gmail.com; web.facebook.com/NigraHotel; Price:B

Saint-Vincent

⛪ **Parrocchia San Vincenzo - "Tenda Amica"**,Piazza della Chiesa, 7, 11027 Saint-Vincent(AO), Italy; Tel: +39 0166 512350; Email:parish_stvincent@libero.it; www.parrocchiastvincent.it; Price:D; *Men only homeless shelter opens 20:15*

🏠 **B&B - le Rosier**,Frazione Crotache, 1, 11027 Saint-Vincent(AO), Italy; Tel:+39 0166 537726; +39 3391 273354; Email:omar@lerosier.it; www.lerosier.it; Price:B; *Price group A in the high season*

🏠 **B&B - Il Torchio**,Frazione Romillod Capard, 11027 Saint-Vincent(AO), Italy; Tel: +39 3355 356885; Email:info@iltorchio.info; www.iltorchio.info; Price:B

🛏 **Hotel - au Soleil**,Via Marconi, 20, 11027 Saint-Vincent(AO), Italy; Tel:+39 0166 512685; Email:info@hotelausoleil.it; www.hotelausoleil.it; Price:B; *Cheaper if you book direct*

🛏 **Hotel - Alla Posta**,Piazza 28 Aprile, 1, 11027 Saint-Vincent(AO), Italy; Tel:+39 0166 512250; Email:info@hotelpostavda.it; www.hotelpostavda.it; Price:A

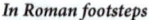 **Office Regional du Tourisme**,Via Roma, 62, 11027 Saint-Vincent(AO), Italy; Tel:+39 0166 512239; www.lovevda.it

Verrès

🛏 **Pilgrims House - Saint Augustine**,Vicolo S.Egidio, 13, 11029 Verrès(AO), Italy; Tel:+39 0125 929093; Email:francigenaverres@gmail.com; www.francigenaverres.it; Price:D; *No heating or kitchen*

🛏 **Ostello - il Casello**,Via Stazione, 79, 11029 Verrès(AO), Italy; Tel:+39 0125 921652; Email:info@ilcaselloverres.com; ilcaselloverres.com; Price:B

🏠 **Chez Milliery**,Via delle Scuole, 2, 11029 Verrès(AO), Italy; Tel:+39 3477739218; Email:millieryornella@gmail.com; Price:B; *Washing machine kitchen*

In Roman footsteps

Verrès to Pont-Saint-Martin — stage 52

Length: 15.0km

Ascent: 741m
Descent: 758m

Col Grand St Bernard: 80km
Rome: 948km

Pont Saint Martin

Route: the stage from Verrès to Pont-Saint-Martin continues on riverside tracks and small roads in the base of the valley passing the impressive fortress of Bard. The "Official Route" makes a wide loop to visit the church of Saint Martin of Tours–San Martino–in Arnad. Before crossing and recrossing the Dora Baltea. The loop may be avoided using the Alternate Route on the western side of the valley.

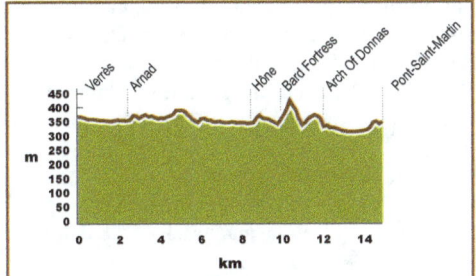

Pont-Saint-Martin is a large town with a good choice of facilities.

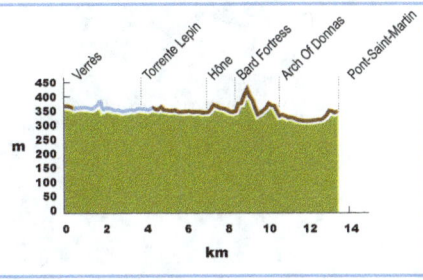

Although a pretty enough town, the main reason for lingering here is the bridge, an impressive testimony to Romanisation in Valle d'Aosta.

Its date is uncertain. Some say it was built around 120 B.C., others say 25 B.C. The wooden beam bearings dug into the rock can be seen at its base, though iron crowns were added at the end of the 19th century to strengthen the structure.

A later dated legend ascribes the construction of the bridge to the devil. The story goes that St. Martin, the Bishop of Tours, was returning to his diocese when the Lys River, overflowed and blocked the only footpath. The devil offered to resolve the problem by building a bridge, in one night, but in return he requested the soul of the first living being to cross it. The saint accepted, but the following morning he threw a piece of bread to the other side of the bridge, thus ensuring that a starving dog was the first to cross. The infuriated devil disappeared into the Lys with bolts of lightning and a sulphurous stench, leaving the bridge to the local population.

(0.0) With the railway station behind you, bear right and then turn right on rue des Alpes **(0.3)** At the T-junction, turn right and pass under the railway **(0.4)** Immediately before reaching the river bridge, turn left on the small road beside the river **(0.9)** Take the right fork

stage 52   Verrès to Pont-Saint-Martin

and then turn left over a small bridge [Towards the river] 🏠 **(1.6)** At the junction, continue straight ahead [Farm building on the left]**(1.8)** Turn left [Towards the motorway]**(1.9)** At the junction, turn right on the tarmac road and cross over the motorway**(2.5)** At the Stop sign turn right and enter **Arnad(2.6)** Turn left [Sign Clos de Barme] 🏠 **(2.7)** At the crossroads, take the road to the right**(3.0)** At the T-junction turn left [Frazione Torretta]**(3.4)** Enter Barme and continue straight ahead [Ignore the turning on the right]**(3.5)** At the Stop sign turn left [Frazione Sisan] 🏠 **(4.1)** Just after the restaurant Buon Convento, take the road to the right [Towards the clock tower]**(4.2)** At the T-junction, turn left [Parrocchiale di San Martino]**(4.3)** Cross the bridge and then bear right [Pass the school on your left]**(4.5)** Shortly after passing house n° 1 and a small shrine on your left, turn left on the road [Towards the corrugated metal barn]**(4.7)** At the crossroads, continue straight ahead on the gravel track [Vineyard on your right]**(4.8)** At the T-junction with the road, turn right and continue on the road [Cross the bridge]**(4.9)** Bear right on the small road [Direction La Kiuva] 🏠 **(5.2)** Immediately after passing the football field, turn right [Echallod cycle route]**(5.4)** Follow the track under the motorway**(5.5)** Take the right fork [Towards main road]**(5.6)** Cross straight over the main road, SS26 and continue on the track [Gully on the right]**(5.7)** Continue straight ahead [Ignore a turning to the left]**(5.8)** Continue straight ahead and cross the river bridge [Pass under the railway]**(5.9)** After crossing the river bridge and turn left. Note:- the Alternate Route joins from the right [Beside the river] 🏠 **(7.1)** Turn right onto the track just before Autostrada bridge 🏠 **(8.5)** Proceed straight ahead [Enter **Hône**] **(9.0)** Cross the road and continue straight ahead [Via Mario Collard]**(9.4)** At the crossroads in Hône, turn left [Pass under Autostrada bridge] 🏠 **(9.6)** Bear right on via E. Chanoux [Between hotel and car park]**(10.0)** After crossing the river bridge turn right on SS26 and then immediately bear left on the narrow road into the old town [**Bard Fortress** on the right] 🏠 **(10.8)** Turn right, downhill past white metal barrier [Steep tarmac track]**(11.4)** Return to

Verrès to Pont-Saint-Martin — stage 52

the old road and turn right**(11.6)**At the T-junction with the SS26, turn left and take the pavement on the left [Railway and river to the right of the road] **(12.1)**Bear away from the main road towards the centre of Donnas [Pass the **Arch of Donnas**]**(12.5)**Pass through the archway and keep right [Lower road]**(12.7)**At the T-junction at the bottom of the ramp turn left on the SS26 [Via Roma] **(14.3)**At the roundabout take the last exit [Direction Pont Saint Martin]**(15.0)**Arrive at **Pont-Saint-Martin (XLVI)** [Beside war memorial]

Direct Route Bypassing Arnad

Route: this more direct route follows minor roads and tracks on the west side of the Dora Baltea to save 2 km. **(0.0)**Continue straight ahead over the river bridge**(0.3)**Shortly after passing the chapel in Issogne, turn left[Direction Arnad]**(0.6)**Turn sharp left onto the Cycle Route, direction Arnad[Parallel to river] **(2.0)**Fork left on the track[Closer to river] **(3.1)**At the crossroads turn left on the road[Parallel to river] **(3.4)**Turn right direction Hône[Cross the bridge over **Torrente Lepin**]**(3.9)**Continue straight ahead. Note:- the "Official Route" joins from the left[River bridge on the left]

Length:	3.9km
Ascent:	114m
Descent:	113m

Accommodation and Tourist Information

Carema

B&B - Casa la Foriana,Via Roma, 40, 10010 Carema(TO), Italy; Tel: +39 3480 092102; Email:casevacanzegiusy@gmail.com; casa-la-foriana.hotelspiedmont.com; Price:B

Donnas

Parrocchia San Pietro,Via Roma, 81, 11020 Donnas(AO), Italy; Tel:+39 0125 807032; Price:D

Hône

Auberge - de la Gare,Via Stazione, 1, 11020 Hône(AO), Italy; Tel: +39 3279 856078; Email:aubergedelagarehone@gmail.com; aubergedelagarehone.com; Price:B

Ristoro Affittacamere - Saint Roch,Località Priod, 3, 11020 Hône(AO), Italy; Tel:+39 0125 803283; +39 3427 197025; Email:ristoro.saintroch@libero.it; www.ristroch.it; Price:A

Perloz

Eremo di Perloz,Località Boschi sopra, 7, 11020 Perloz(AO), Italy; Tel:+39 3477409625; Email:info@eremodiperloz.it; eremodiperloz.it; Price:D; *Maximum 4 people*; **PR**

Pont-Saint-Martin

Foresteria Saint Martin [Signora Angela],Via Schigliatta, 1, 11026 Pont-Saint-Martin(AO), Italy; Tel: +39 0125 804433; +39 0125 830619; +39 3472 232039; Email:info@comune.pontsaintmartin.ao.it; Price:C

Francigena House [Andrtea Lombardo],Via Sarus, 1, 11026 Pont-Saint-Martin(AO), Italy; Tel:+39 3757092616; Email:andrtealombardo@gmail.com; Price:C; *Kitchen and washing machine*

La Casa di Margherita [Marilena Giovanetto],Via Chanoux, 37, 11026 Pont-Saint-Martin(73032), Italy; Tel:+39 3207265693; Email:marilena.giovanetto@libero.it; Price:C; *10 beds*

B&B - al Castel [Fabio],Via Castello, 8, 11026 Pont-Saint-Martin(AO), Italy; Tel: +39 3474 767125; Email:info@alcastel.it; www.alcastel.it; Price:A; *Large newly renovated and stylish apartment*; **PR**

Hotel - Crabun,Via Nazionale Per Donnas, 3, 11026 Pont-Saint-Martin(AO), Italy; Tel:+39 0125 806069; Email:info@crabunhotel.it; www.crabunhotel.it; Price:A; *15% discount for pilgrims*

Albergo - Carla,Via Nazionale, 106, 11026 Pont-Saint-Martin(AO), Italy; Tel:+39 0125 807281; Email:info@albergocarla.it; www.albergocarla.it; Price:B

Apartment - La Grange ,Via Cascine Lys, 6, 11026 Pont-Saint-Martin(AO), Italy; Tel:+39 340 4153969; +39 0125 804253; +39 328 0870200; Email:agriturismolagrange@libero.it; agriturismolagrange.it/; Price:B

Ufficio del Turismo di Pont-Saint-Martin,Via Circonvallazione, 30, 11026 Pont-Saint-Martin(AO), Italy; Tel:+39 0125 804843; www.lovevda.it

stage 53   Pont-Saint-Martin to Ivrea

Length:	22.1km
Ascent:	862m
Descent:	946m
Col Grand St Bernard:	95km
Rome:	933km

The castle with Red Towers–Ivrea

Route: this final stage in the Aosta valley from Pont-Saint-Martin to Ivrea, continues on pathways and tracks briefly returning to the lower hillsides and passing through the old vineyards to the east of the Dora Baltea. Extra caution is necessary where the route intersects and briefly follows the busy SS62 after Carema.

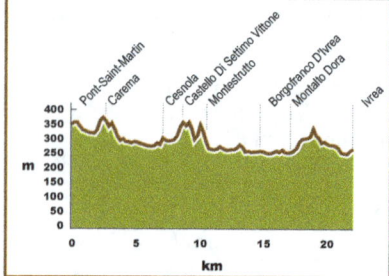

Ivrea is a large town with a wide range of accommodation choices and other facilities.

Ivrea and its surroundings have been inhabited since the Neolithic era. The Celts are believed to have had a village on the site from around the 5th century B.C.. However, the town first appears in history as a Roman cavalry station founded in 100 B.C., and set to guard one of the traditional invasion routes into northern Italy over the Alps. The Latin name of the town, Eporedia (meaning a place to change horses), has long since vanished into the mists of time, but still appears as the root of the name of the town and the residents, who are known as Porediesi. Later, Ivrea was a point of dispute between the bishops, the marquis of Monferrato and the House of Savoy. In 1356 the town was acquired by Amadeus VI of Savoy. With the exception of the brief French conquest at the end of the 16th century, Ivrea remained under Savoy until 1800.

There are two main festivals in Ivrea, both rooted in the ancient city's traditions. One is the Carnival, which takes place forty days before Easter, and ends on the night of Fat Tuesday with a solemn ceremony that involves a funeral in honour of the concluded Carnival. Though religious, the carnival is focused around the Battle of the Oranges, which involves thousands of townspeople, divided into nine teams, throwing oranges at each other, with considerable violence. The tradition is not well understood, particularly as oranges do not grow in the foothills of the Italian Alps and must be brought in, by the ton, from Sicily. The other festival is in honour of St. Savino, celebrated in the week of July 7. This involves a horse fair, carriage exhibition and horse shows.

Torre Santo Stefano - Ivrea

Pont-Saint-Martin to Ivrea   stage 53

(0.0) From beside the war memorial, continue straight ahead [Via Emile Chanoux] 🚶 **(0.2)** Cross the river bridge [Roman bridge to the left] **(0.5)** As the main road bends to the right, bear left on the small road [Via Boschetto, No Through Road] **(0.5)** Continue straight ahead, between buildings and terraces [Parking area to the right] **(0.9)** At the junction beside the main road turn left on the smaller road [Rue Sant'Erasmo, pass large fir tree on the right] 🚶 **(1.4)** At the T-junction with the main road, bear left [Tabacchi on left] **(1.5)** Take the first road on the left [Via Schigliatta] **(1.6)** Bear right on the road [Car park on the right, terraces to the left] **(1.8)** At the sharp bend in the road to the left, bear right on the steep grass path [Downhill, beside the metal railings] **(1.9)** After passing the rear of the houses take the pathway to the left [Between vines] **(2.0)** At the first turning, turn right up the hill [Signed: Sentiero dei Vigneti] **(2.2)** Continue straight ahead in the direction of Carema [Beside la Cappella di San Rocco] 🚶 **(2.7)** Continue straight ahead into the village of **Carema** and proceed downhill on via Roma [Stone pillars on your right] **(3.0)** At the T-junction, turn left on via Basiglia, uphill **(3.1)** In Piazza della Chiesa, turn right on via San Matteo [Pass the church on your left] **(3.2)** Take the right fork, downhill between the vineyards **(3.3)** At the crossroads, bear slightly right on the narrow road **(3.4)** Bear left

[Between the vines] **(3.5)** Take the right fork on the paved road **(3.6)** Take the left fork on the track 🚶 **(3.8)** At the junction with the main road turn left and proceed with care beside the busy road [SS26, stone pillars on the left] **(3.9)** Continue straight ahead behind the crash barrier in the lay-by [Road bears right] **(4.0)** Return to the main road and continue ahead towards the river [SS26] 🚶 **(4.8)** Beside the bus shelter, turn left [Direction Airale, road quickly turns to the right] **(5.0)** Continue straight ahead on via Giasso [Beside small church] **(5.3)** Continue

stage 53 — Pont-Saint-Martin to Ivrea

straight ahead on the track**(5.5)**Continue straight ahead [Cross the small bridge]**(5.6)**At the T-junction, following the bridge, bear right on a tarmac road [Low stone wall on the left] **(5.8)**Turn left on the ramp, towards the bell tower [Pass through Torre Daniele]**(5.9)**Turn right at the edge of the commune [Power lines descend the hill ahead]**(6.0)**At the T-junction turn right [Pass low stone wall on your left]**(6.1)**Before reaching the main road turn left on the part made road [Parallel to SS26]**(6.8)**Bear left on a track between the vines [Pass two concrete barns on the right] **(7.2)**Continue straight ahead [Village of **Cesnola**]**(7.3)**At the crossroads, turn right on the narrow road down the hill [Water trough on the left]**(7.4)**Take the first turning to the left into the countryside [The way quickly becomes a track]**(8.2)**At the junction turn left, uphill [Beside the ruined church in Settimo Vittone] **(8.3)**At the Stop sign, bear left and take the stony track through the break in the wall**(8.4)**Briefly join the road, before bearing left on the cobbled road [Shrines on the left]**(8.6)**Turn right [In front of the church]**(8.7)**From the car park, turn left, pass through the metal gates and proceed on the unmade road [Pass **Castello di Settimo Vittone** on the right]**(8.7)**Bear left on the path**(8.9)**Bear left uphill on the tarmac [Vines above on the right]**(9.2)**Continue straight ahead on the path [Through the vines] **(9.5)**Take the pathway to the left [Near a small tarmac road]**(9.8)**Bear left on the tarmac road [Steeply uphill]**(9.9)**Continue straight ahead on the track [Beside the hamlet of Casellino]**(10.1)**At the first turning on the track turn right downhill [View of Castello Montestrutto]**(10.3)**Bear right [Towards Montestrutto] **(10.6)**Turn left on via Vittorio Emanuele [In the centre of **Montestrutto**]**(10.9)**At the end of the stone pillars, take the track to the left around the house [Beside the electricity pylon]**(11.1)**At the crossroads, continue straight ahead on the track**(11.3)**At the crossroads, take the tarmac road to the left **(12.7)**Turn left on via San Germano [Beside the church of San Germano]**(13.1)**Bear left and then turn right on the stony track [Via del Buonumore]**(13.6)**Shortly after the road bends to the right, turn left on the track [Direction Lago Nero] **(14.3)**At the Stop sign turn right [Pass the car park on your left]**(14.4)**At the traffic lights, turn left [Pass house n° 90 on your left]**(14.8)**In piazza Ruffini in **Borgofranco d'Ivrea**, continue straight ahead on via Marini [Pass Torre Porta on your left]**(15.0)**At the Stop sign, turn left [Pass house n° 42 on your right]**(15.1)**Turn right on via Tostre [Gardens on the left and right] **(15.4)**Continue straight ahead on the track [Towards the trees]**(16.1)**At the T-junction in the tracks, turn right **(16.7)**Continue straight ahead on the tarmac road [Between industrial buildings]**(17.0)**At the mini-roundabout, bear left [Via Aldo Balla]**(17.2)**In the piazza in **Montalto Dora**, turn left [Via Casana]**(17.3)**Turn right. Note:- it seems that some signposts have been relocated to route around Lago Pistono adding 2 km to the stage. If you wish follow the route around the picturesque lake

Pont-Saint-Martin to Ivrea stage 53

then turn left and follow the road keeping the lake to your right until you reach the restaurant Monella. Then take the wooded path until you return to the "Official Route: beside the chapel of Santa Croce [Via Cappella]**(17.4)**At the T-junction turn left and then right and then keep left beside the garden wall [Pass house n° 27 on your left]**(17.5)**Take the left fork, up the hill [Pass silos on your right] **(17.9)**At the junction bear right on the larger road [The road quickly makes a double bend]**(18.2)**Turn right. Note: the circuit of Lago Pistono joins from the left [Beside the chapel of Santa Croce]**(18.4)**At the end of the tarmac, continue straight ahead on the track**(18.6)**Turn left on a track [Direction Cappella di San Pietro] **(19.0)**At the top of the hill continue straight ahead on the track**(19.2)**Beside Cappella di San Pietro, continue straight ahead on the tarmac road**(19.4)**At the T-junction, beside the restaurant take the track to the left [Into the woods]**(19.6)**Continue straight ahead on the tarmac road [Car Park on the left]**(19.7)**At the Stop sign, bear left on the road [Lake below on the left]**(19.9)**Turn right on the small road just before the T-junction [Via Sant'Ulderico] **(20.3)**Continue straight ahead on the unmade road [Field on the right, woods on the left]**(20.6)**At the bottom of the hill continue on the tarmac**(20.9)**Continue straight ahead on the pavement on the left of the road **(21.4)**Turn left [Car park on your left]**(21.5)**At the T-junction turn right on the busy road [Beside the old city walls of Ivrea]**(21.7)**Cross the road and continue straight ahead [Torre del Castello to the left]**(21.8)**At the traffic lights, turn left [Via Amedeo di Castellamonte, No Entry]**(21.8)**Turn left, under the arch and bear right under the second arch [Castello – Duomo]**(21.9)**Bear right on the narrow street [Via Quattro Martiri]**(22.0)**At the T-junction, turn left on via Arduino**(22.1)**Arrive at **Ivrea (XLV)** centre [Piazza Ferruccio Nazionale]

Accommodation and Tourist Information

Borgofranco-d'Ivrea

Ostello San Germano,Piazza Pertini, 3, 10013 Borgofranco-d'Ivrea(TO), Italy; Tel: +39 3486 705143; +39 3474 278351; Email:ferrandopatrizia64@gmail.com; ostellosangermano.it; Price:C; *Price group b in private room*

B&B - Verde Musica,Via Camillo Benso Conte di Cavour, 10, 10013 Borgofranco-d'Ivrea(TO), Italy; Tel: +39 3490 835837; Email:bbverdemusica@gmail.com; bbverdemusica.com; Price:B; *Pilgrim discount please book a few days in advance*

Ivrea

Ostello - Ivrea Canoa Club,Via Dora Baltea 1d, 10015 Ivrea(TO), Italy; Tel: +39 3715780055; Email:info@ostelloivrea.it; www.ostelloivrea.it; Price:C

Albergo - Aquila Nera,Corso Costantino Nigra, 56, 10015 Ivrea(TO), Italy; Tel:+39 0125 641416; Email:aquilanera.ditony@gmail.com; booking.com; Price:B

Albergo - Luca,Corso Garibaldi, 58, 10015 Ivrea(TO), Italy; Tel:+39 0125 48697; albergo-luca-ivrea.hotelmix.it; Price:B

Affittacamera - Sei Da Noi,Via Francesco Ruffini, 17, 10015 Ivrea(TO), Italy; Tel: +39 3403 739587; Email:seidanoi@yahoo.com; web.facebook.com/seida.noi; Price:B

Ufficio del Turismo,Piazza Ottinetti, 10015 Ivrea(TO), Italy; Tel:+39 0125 618131; Email:info.ivrea@turismotorino.org; www.turismotorino.org

Settimo Vittone

Fuori Tempo [Federica Quaccia],Via Casellino 49, 10010 Settimo Vittone(TO), Italy; Tel:+39 3453957267; Email:fquaccia@gmail.com; *9 beds*

B&B - L'Ospitalità del Castello,Piazza Conte Rinaldo, 7, 10010 Settimo Vittone(TO), Italy; Tel: +39 3484 527017; Email:moreno.nico@gmail.com; web.facebook.com/lospitalitadelcastello; Price:B

Camping Mombarone,Frazione Torredaniele, 54, 10010 Settimo Vittone(TO), Italy; Tel:+39 0125 757907; +39 349 5591346; Email:info@campingmombarone.it; www.campingmombarone.it; Price:C; *Caravan available for pilgrims*

stage 54 — Ivrea to Santhià

Length:	36.9km
Ascent:	891m
Descent:	969m
Col Grand St Bernard:	117km
Rome:	911km

Lake Viverone

Route: this long stage from Ivrea to Santhià follows minor country roads and tracks over generally level ground at the foot of the mountains. The "Official Route" follows a route chosen by pilgrims in the 12th and 13th centuries and although it is longer than the more traditional Alternate Route it offers more intermediate accommodation in the area close to lake Viverone.

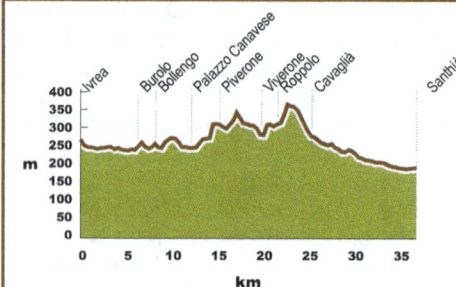

On the approach to Santhià the route will enter the low lying rice fields that will be the dominant terrain for several days ahead. If you are travelling in the summer months then this is the time to buy your mosquito repellent.

Lake Viverone is named after the nearby town. Wildlife, particularly mallard, coots, grebes and gulls thrive here. The lake is also an important archaeological site, with finds dating back to the Bronze Age. Leaving Viverone and the landscape dominated by the Alps, the route now crosses the Padana Plain and takes you through small forests that are home to pheasant and roe deer.

Santhià has been inhabited since the Roman period and is thought to have taken its name from Saint Agatha, a Christian martyr.

🛌 **(0.0)** Piazza Ferruccio Nazionale, continue eastwards on via Palestro **(0.4)** In piazza Balla, go straight ahead on via d'Azeglio [Keep trees and large parking area to the right] **(0.8)** Bear left towards Biella. Note:- The more traditional Alternate Route to the south of lake Piverone bears right [Via Cascinette] 🛌 **(1.1)** At the crossroads, continue straight ahead [Traffic island to the left] **(1.5)** At the roundabout bear left [Via Cascinette, shrine straight ahead] **(1.9)** Shortly after passing the tyre store on the left, bear left onto a smaller road [Via Mon-

Ivrea to Santhià   stage 54

te della Guardia] (2.3)At the T-junction turn right [Via Tinasse di Sopra](2.4)Take the small road to the left [Into open country](2.7)Turn left [Towards lake, woods on the left](3.0)As the gravel road turns right, continue straight ahead through the barrier [Keep Lago Campagna on the left](3.3)At the end of the path keep straight ahead [Across the parking area](3.4)Take the tarmac road to the left [Via Lago Campagna](3.6)At the T-junction with the main road turn left [Pass house n° 62 on your right](3.7)On the crown of the bend to the left, turn right [Via Gorrere](3.7)At the first junction, turn left on the track [Into the woods](4.0)At the next junction turn right (5.0)On leaving the woods take the track to the left [Via Lavatoio, leading back towards the woods](5.5)At the Stop sign, turn right on the tarmac (6.1)At the T-junction with the main road (SP76), cross over, turn left and continue on the right-hand side of the road [Towards the village of Burolo](6.3)Shortly before the road turns left in **Burolo**, turn right [Via Vivier](6.5)At the fork keep left [Remain on via Vivier](6.8)At the junction with the main road, bear right downhill [Castello Basso to the left at the junction](7.0)Take the minor road to the left, opposite the bus stop [Via Bollengo] (7.4)After the bend to the right, turn left [Via Bollengo](8.0)In Bollengo at the junction beside the rear of the chapel of San Rocco, bear left, uphill(8.3)In the centre of **Bollengo**, turn right on via P. Cossavella [Direction Biella] (8.5)At the fork, keep left towards Biella [Via Scuole](8.6)At the next fork, keep right [School on your right](8.7)At the major crossroads, continue straight ahead [Strada Palazzo, direction Piverone](9.2)On the crown of the bend to the right turn left into the parking area and take the path [Towards the trees](9.3)At the T-junction beside the church of San Pietro e Paolo, turn right on the tarmac road [Strada Piane Inferiore] (11.0)At the crossroads at the bottom of the hill, turn left on the main road [Direction Piverone](12.0)Turn right into the village of Palazzo Canavese [Via Garibaldi] (12.2)In piazza Adriano Olivetti in **Palazzo Canavese**, bear right on via Vittorio Emanuele II(12.4)Turn left between the church and the clock tower. Then turn right on via del Castello and left down the steps(12.5)At the junction with via Parrochia, turn right and the left at the crossroads, turn left [Pass car park on your right] (12.7)At the junction, continue straight ahead [Via Asilo](12.8)At the T-junction, turn right [Via Piverone](13.2)At the Stop sign, turn right [Via Piverone] (15.3)Continue straight ahead through the archway in the **Piverone** tower(15.4)Cross the piazza and bear left and right on via Castellazzo [Pass the church close on your left](15.8)Bear left on the small road [Downhill](16.2)Beside a farm entrance take the track to the left [Uphill]

stage 54 — Ivrea to Santhià

(17.0)At the junction, beside the small ruined church of Gesiun, turn left and immediately right [Towards the farm](17.8)At the T-junction turn right [Views of lake Viverone] (17.9)At the T-junction with the tarmac, road turn left [Towards the towers on the horizon] (19.0)Take the right fork [Via Cascine di Ponente](19.9)At the Stop sign in **Viverone**, bear left on via Umberto I [Towards the centre of Viverone] (20.8)At the roundabout, continue straight ahead in the direction of Roppolo [Pass Chiesa di Santa Maria on your left](21.7)At the crossroads continue straight ahead into **Roppolo** [Via G. Massa, direction Poste](21.8)In the piazza beside the bell tower, turn left [Towards the castle, via al Castello] (22.4)At the junction, continue straight ahead on the road [Avoid the turning towards Pigglio](22.6)At the junction beside the well, turn sharp right on the road, towards Salomone [Large VF pilgrim mural to your right](23.4)Pass the cemetery and after a brief climb ignore the first track to the right and a little after take the unmade road on the right across the hillside (24.4)After descending on the track through the fields and woods, turn left and then immediately right on the tarmac(24.5)Take the right fork onto the gravel track, between the fields(24.8)At the T-junction turn left [Beside house n° 11](25.0)At the junction, keep left on the tarmac [Direction Santhià, via Moriando](25.4) At the Stop sign turn right [Town of **Cavaglià**] (25.4)Turn left, towards the town centre [No Entry](25.7)At the end of the road, turn left(25.7)At the mini-roundabout, turn right [Direction Santhià](25.8)Bear right on strada Vicinale della Crocetta and then bear left around the industrial building(26.1)Continue straight ahead on the gravel road [Via Don Albera Virgilio](26.4)At the T-junction, turn right [Church of Nostra Signora di Babilone on your left] (26.7)At the T-junction turn left [Pass beside large white building](27.4)At the T-junction turn left [Farm buildings ahead at the junction](27.6)Bear right on the road and continue straight ahead(27.6)At the junction, keep right on the road [Open fields to the left] (28.0)Cross the main road (SS143) and take the tarmac road slightly to the right [Direction Agriturismo il Molino] (29.4)At the T-junction beside the farm buildings, turn right on the tarmac [Trees on the right of the road](29.9)At the junction in the woods, keep right (30.5)Continue straight ahead [Cross the canal bridge] (30.7)At the junction, after the bend to the right, continue straight ahead [Trees on the right](31.1)At the crossroads, continue straight ahead [Farm to the right] (31.9)

Ivrea to Santhià stage 54

At the next crossroads turn left [Towards the motorway bridge]**(32.1)**Bear left over the Autostrada**(32.6)**Immediately after descending from the bridge turn sharp right. Note:- pedestrians maybe able to eliminate the loop ahead by turning sharp left along the edge of the field and then turning right on the track under the railway [Towards Autostrada] **(32.8)**At the T-junction turn right [Under bridge, with Autostrada to the left] **(33.0)** Turn sharp right on the track**(33.2)**Bear left on the track [Pass under railway]**(33.8)**At the crossroads continue straight ahead [Cross the canal] **(34.2)**Take the right fork [Towards the electricity pylon]**(34.7)**At the junction after passing a farm on your right, keep left on the track [Beside line of trees] **(35.9)**At the T-junction, turn left [Farm buildings on your left]**(36.1)**At the junction with the main road turn right [Shrine on left at junction] **(36.3)**At the roundabout, continue straight ahead [Pass a sports ground on the left]**(36.8)** At the traffic lights go straight ahead [Via Svizzera]**(36.8)**Turn left [Via Edmondo de Amicis] **(36.9)**Turn right [Via Jacapo Durando]**(36.9)**Arrive at **Santhià (XLIV)** centre in piazza Roma [Beside chiesa Sant'Agata]

Direct Historic Route to the South of Lake Viverone

Route: this route cobines country roads and broad tracks and offers great views of Lake Viverone. Unfortunately the final stages require using busier roads to bypass a major motorway intersection. **(0.0)**Take the right fork on Corso Vercelli [Direction Santhià]**(0.6)**At the roundabout, continue straight ahead [Between the petrol stations]**(0.9)**At the next roundabout,

Length:	31.0km
Ascent:	594m
Descent:	650m

take the first exit [Via Casale] **(1.1)**Beside the bus stop, turn left [Direction Strada Cascine Forneris]**(1.6)**Fork right along Strada Vicinale della Fornace [Direction Strada Cascine Forneris] **(2.9)**Take the right fork between the trees [Via della Fornace] **(3.9)**Beside house n° 1 take the right fork on the small road [Keep hedge on your right] **(5.0)**Take the right fork [Pass STT bus stop on your left]**(5.1)**At the Stop sign, continue straight ahead beside the main road [Pass chapel and large farmhouse on your right]**(5.9)**Immediately after passing house n° 38 on your left, turn left on the gravel track [Pass white metal fencing on your left] **(6.2)**At the Stop sign, turn left beside the road [Open field on your left, trees to the right] **(8.0)**At the road junction, continue straight ahead through the village of **Pobbia** [Towards the church] **(10.6)**At the crossroads with the main road, at the top of the hill, continue straight ahead in the small road [Uphill skirting the village of **Azeglio**] **(11.0)**At the Stop sign in the centre of the village, turn left. Note:- to the right is the village square with a bar [Via Roma]**(11.2)**At the crossroads, continue straight ahead [Direction Santuario di S. Antonio Abbate]**(11.4)**Take the right fork [Direction Santuario S. Antonio] **(11.5)**With the play area directly ahead, take the left fork [Direction Santuario di S. Antonio] **(11.6)**With the red brick shrine on your right, take the left fork [Direction Santuario di S. Antonio] **(13.0)**Continue straight ahead [Pass **Santuario di S. Antonio** on your right] **(17.5)**At the T-junction at the top of the hill, turn right on the road [Keep the field on your left and the trees on your right]**(17.8)**Take the right fork [Towards the main road]**(17.9)**At the junction with the main road, turn right and remain beside the road to the town of Alice Castello [Towards fruit trees on trhe brow of the hill] **(21.4)**At the crossroads in **Alice Castello**, turn left [Direction Torino]**(21.6)**At the Stop sign with the chapel on your left, turn left on via Cavaglià [Direction Biella]**(21.9)**At the junction with the main road, continue straight ahead [Towards the petrol station]**(22.2)**Immediately before the exit from Alice Castello, turn right on the gravel road [Direction Agriturismo il Ciliegio] **(24.3)**At the T-junction with the road, turn left [Silos on your right at the junction]**(24.7)**At the T-junction, turn right on strada della Benna and keep left after crossing the small bridge [Direction Cascina Ciorlucca]**(25.1)**Take the right fork on the lower road [Avoid the road towards the autostrada bridge]**(25.3)**Beside Cascina Ciorlucca,

stage 54 — Ivrea to Santhià

continue straight ahead [Autostrada close on your left] 🏠 (26.2)On the crown of the third bend to the right, take the underpass under the autostrada [Shortly after passing a farmhouse on your right](26.3)At the T-junction with the railway track directly ahead, turn left [Keep embankment on your right](27.0)With the railway viaduct on your right, turn left [Take the underpass under the autostrada slip road] 🏠 (27.3)After emerging from a further underpass take the next turning to the right through the hamlet of **la Mandriotta** [Pass between red brick pillars] 🏠 (28.4)At the junction with the main road, turn left and follow the road to the centre of Santhià [Towards distant commercial buildings] 🏠 (30.7)At the crossroads, after passing a park on your right, continue straight ahead [Enter the pedestrian zone](30.9)At the crossroads with via Ospedale, continue straight ahead and then take the first road to the left [Towards the piazza](31.0)Arrive in **Santhià (XLIV)** at the end of the section [Piazza Roma, beside chiesa Sant'Agata]

Accommodation and Tourist Information

Azeglio

🏠 **B&B - Il Giardino dei Semplici**,Via Roma, 78, 10010 Azeglio(TO), Italy; Tel:+39 0125 687549; +39 3398 837233; +39 3407 746520; Email:info@giardinodeisemplici.com; www.giardinodeisemplici.com; Price:B

Cavaglià

🛏️Ostello Per Pellegrini,Via Generale Pietro Giovanni Salino, 13881 Cavaglià(BI), Italy; Tel:+39 0161 96038; Email:biblio.cavaglia@ptb.provincia.biella.it; Price:D; *Very basic 4 beds*; **PR**

Magnano

🛏️**Monastero di Bose**,Via Bose 1, 13887 Magnano(BI), Italy; Tel:+39 0156 79185; Email:ospiti@monasterodibose.it; www.monasterodibose.it; Price:D

Roppolo

🛏️**Casa del Movimento Lento**,Via al Castello, 8, 13883 Roppolo(BI), Italy; Tel:+39 0161 987866; +39 3792370405; Email:casa@movimentolento.it; casa.movimentolento.it; Price:B; *Discount with credentials*; **PR**

🏠 **B&B - le Lune**,Via Cavaglià, 2, 13883 Roppolo(BI), Italy; Tel:+39 0161 980938; +39 3462 109706; Email:bblelune@libero.it; www.bblelune.eu/bb; Price:A; **PR**

Santhià

🛏️**Ostello Degli Amici della via Francigena**,Vicolo Madonnetta, 4, 13048 Santhià(VC), Italy; Tel: +39 3886 333865; +39 36 6440 4253; www.santhiasullaviafrancigena.it; Price:D; *Keys at Caffé della Piazza(closed Mondays) Immobilcasa - Massimiliano Corradini or call the local police on 0161936220.*

🏠 **B&B - il Giardino dei Cedri**,Via Giacomo Puccini, 6, 13048 Santhià(VC), Italy; Tel:+39 0161 939912; +39 3333 483466; +39 3517 033600; Email:ilgiardinodeicedri@gmail.com; www.ilgiardinodeicedri.com; Price:B

🏠 **B&B - la Sosta**,Strada Vecchia di Biella, 6, 13048 Santhià(VC), Italy; Tel: +39 3355 481452; Email:gabry.corti@gmail.com; www.eng.lasosta.eu; Price:B; *Can arrange baggage transport from Ivrea to Vercelli*

🛏️ **Hotel Restaurant - Piccadilly**,Corso XXV Aprile, 51, 13048 Santhià(VC), Italy; Tel:+39 0161 921196; Email:info@ristorantepiccadillysanthia.it; www.ristorantepiccadillysanthia.it; Price:B

🛏️ **Albergo - San Massimo**,Corso XXV Aprile, 18, 13048 Santhià(VC), Italy; Tel:+39 0161 94617; Email:sanmassimo.ss143@tele2.it; migliorhotel.top/hotel-ristorante-san-massimo; Price:B

ℹ️ **Santhià Turismo**,Piazza Roma, 16, 13048 Santhià(VC), Italy; Tel: +39 0161 936111; Email:infosanthia@santhiaturismo.it; www.santhiaturismo.it

Viverone

⛺ **Camping la Rocca**,Viale Lungo Lago, 35, 13886 Viverone(BI), Italy; Tel: +39 3477 107146; Email:laroccaviverone@hotmail.com; la-rocca.org; Price:C; *Caravan available to pilgrims in price group C also reduced price tent pitches for pilgrims*

⛺ **Camping Internazionale del Sole**,Via del Lago, 45, 13886 Viverone(BI), Italy; Tel:+39 0161 98169; +393392218047; Email:info@campeggiodelsole.com; www.campeggiodelsole.com; Price:C

Santhià to Vercelli

stage 55

Length:	29.1km
Ascent:	111m
Descent:	160m
Col Grand St Bernard:	154km
Rome:	874km

The basilica of Sant'Andrea-Vercelli - watercolour by Jannina Veit Teuten

Route: The "Official Route" from Santhià to Vercelli, meanders on farm tracks between the rice fields occasionally crossing the busy main road SS143/SP11. The via Francigena sign posts are often casualties of the intensive farming in the area and so be sure to keep track of your position in the guide.

There is the opportunity to break your journey at San Germano where you can find a café and shops. You will also pass close by a large commercial centre on the outskirts of Vercelli

As you approach Vercelli the prior route has been blocked and diversions put in place adding some distance, which may be recovered by taking an unmarked Alternate Route.

Vercelli is one of the oldest urban sites in northern Italy, founded, according to most historians, around the year 600 B.C.. When Sigeric stopped off here, the area was covered by vast forests with some clearings, fields and marshes, but today it is the rice capital of Europe.

The world's first university funded by public money was established in Vercelli in 1228, but was closed in 1372. Today it has a university of literature and philosophy, as part of the Università del Piedmont Orientale, and a satellite campus of the Politecnico di Torino.

There is so much to see, and just wandering the streets is an experience in itself, but if you want to stop off and investigate its treasures in more detail, there are some options of particular interest: The Cathedral of Vercelli, was built centuries ago and remodelled several times. Ornately designed, the structure houses several very beautiful paintings by local artists. There is also a library in the cathedral, which holds a number of important ancient manuscripts.

The basilica of Sant'Andrea was built in 1219 by Cardinal Guala Bicchierie, along with an old monastery. Built in the Romanesque style of architecture, the monument is known to be one of the most well preserved and beautiful basilicas in Italy.

stage 55 — Santhià to Vercelli

🚶(0.0)Leave piazza Roma keeping the church to the left [Via Roma, towards the bank] (0.1)At the T-junction, turn left [Pedestrian zone – corso Nuova Italia](0.6)At the crossroads, continue straight ahead. Note:- to avoid the footbridge ahead, turn left and then right at the traffic island and rejoin the "Official Route" at the turning to Cascine Nuova Bella Vittoria [No Through road, railway station to the right](0.7)On reaching the railway track, bear left and then right and cross the railway on the foot-bridge(0.9)After crossing the bridge, continue straight ahead [Corso Vercelli, large irrigation channel on the right] 🚶 (1.4)Just before the chapel, cross to the right side of the road and go straight ahead beside the busy SS143 [Keep water to the right](1.7)Turn left, carefully cross the main road and take via Pragilardo over the small bridge [Towards railway line](2.2)After crossing the railway bridge bear right on the unmade road [Towards farm] 🚶(3.9)After passing cascina Pragilardo turn right [Beside electricity sub-station](4.6)At the T-junction turn left 🚶 (5.1) At the crossroads, continue straight ahead towards the farm buildings(5.7)After crossing the canal bridge, turn right 🚶 (7.0)Turn right on the track(7.4)At the T-junction with the road, turn left and immediately sharp right [Direction Cascina Castellano](8.0)Turn right and take the subway under the railway [Bike ramp] 🚶 (8.2)After leaving the subway, go straight ahead [**San Germano Vercallese** station behind you](8.4)Turn left on via Cavour [Pass arches on your right](8.6)Continue straight ahead across piazza Giuseppe Mazzini

[Beside the church](8.7)Beside Palazzo del Commune, in piazza Garibaldi turn right [Towards the main road](8.8)Cross the main road and turn left [Keep the café on your right] (8.9)At the end of the small park and turn right [Cross the bridge over the canal](8.9)After the bridge, immediately turn left on via Franzoi [Returning towards the main road](9.1)At the junction with the main road turn hard right on the smaller road [Towards Salasco] 🚶 (9.6)On the crown of the bend to the right, turn sharp left on the track(10.0)At the T-junction, turn left [Towards the main road](10.0)Carefully cross the main road and turn left on the pavement [Canal on the right of the pavement](10.1)Turn right through the break in the crash barriers, cross over the bridge and bear right on the track 🚶 (11.2)At the crossroads continue straight ahead [Obliquely towards the railway on your left] 🚶 (12.5) Pass under the road bridge and continue straight ahead at the junction [Railway on your left](13.1)The track bears right beside the irrigation channel [Channel on your right] 🚶 (14.5)At Cascina Castellone turn right [Keep the farm buildings on the left](14.6)At the entrance to the farm buildings, turn right. Note: the route ahead has been blocked on the established path and 2 diversions marked from Cascine Strà and Montonero both require that you cross to the south of the busy SP11 before returning to the north side. It is possible to avoid the road crossings and save a minimum of 2 km by taking the unmarked alternate direct route(15.0)Carefully cross the main road and turn left on the track [Close beside the

Santhià to Vercelli — stage 55

main road]**(15.1)**Follow the track to the right**(15.3)**Continue straight ahead passing the barrier **(15.6)**At the next crossroads turn left [Parallel to main road]**(16.5)**At the T-junction turn left and then right [Remain parallel to the main road] **(17.0)**At the T-junction with the tarmac road, turn left on the road [Towards the main road]**(17.2)**Just before reaching the main road turn right on the track, pass behind the small church and continue close to the main road [Blue highway sign ahead]**(17.9)**At the T-junction with the tarmac road, turn right on the road. Note:- the route ahead previously followed a direct path to Vercelli. Sadly this has been blocked and the route now make a loop via the small village of Montonero before returning to the north side of the SP11. The Amici della Via Francigena di Vercelli have marked a more direct route bypassing Montonero which may be joined by turning left. [**Cascine Strà** to the left at the junction] **(18.5)**Turn left over a small bridge onto a track between fields and skirt the field on your right**(19.3)**Bear left on the track**(19.4)**Take the right fork over the bridge, towards the farm [Keep the waterway on the right] **(19.6)**At the T-junction with the road, turn left. Note:- the via Domitia route, connecting Arles and Santiago de Compostela to the via Francigena, join from the right [Towards Montonero]**(19.8)**Continue straight ahead on the tarmac road [Pass through Montonero, church on the left]**(20.1)**As you leave Montonero turn left on the road [Caution, former route, now blocked, continued ahead on the gravel road] **(21.3)**On reaching the main road, turn right and keep right on the broad grass verge**(21.5)**Carefully turn left, cross the road and follow the tarmac road over the canal bridge **(22.0)**Turn right and continue on the road to cross the railway bridge. Note:- the alternate route joins from the track ahead **(23.1)**Shortly after crossing the railway and the road turning to the right, turn left and then right to cross the canal and follow the farm track parallel to the railway [Pass a farm on the right] **(24.7)**Shortly before reaching an overhead power line, turn right, re-cross the railway and follow the track as it turn left **(25.8)**At the T-junction turn left on the broad track**(26.0)**Shortly before reaching the main road, turn left and follow the canal-side path [Canal on your right]**(26.5)**As you approach the roundabout, turn left. Note:- it is possible to save 500 m by taking the second exit and following the main road, Corso Torino [Garage compound on your left]**(26.7)**At the first road crossing, turn right [Towards commercial complex] **(27.1)**As the track turns right join the path beside the road and continue towards the main road [Decathlon on your left]**(27.2)**At the roundabout, turn left and follow the cycle track to the centre of Vercelli **(28.9)**At the roundabout, continue straight ahead, direction centro [Petrol station ahead at the roundabout]**(29.1)** Arrive at **Vercelli (XLIII)** centre [Piazza Paietta]

stage 55 — Santhià to Vercelli

Direct Route From Cascina Castellone

Route: this unmarked route follows farm tracks, avoids crossing the busy main road and saves a minimum of 2 km. **(0.0)** Turn left and immediately right to skirt the farm buildings [Building close on your right] **(0.1)** As the track around the buildings again turns right, take the grass track beside the irrigation channel [Parallel to the main road] **(0.5)** At the end of large field on your right, take the small bridge over the irrigation channel and bear slightly left on the broader track [Towards the farm buildings] **(1.8)** At the entrance to the farm building the route marked by the VF amici joins from the right and continues straight ahead [Parallel to the railway track].

Length:	1.8km
Ascent:	5m
Descent:	10m

Amici Direct Route Avoiding the Montonero Loop

Route: this slightly more direct route will save approximately 1 km by bypassing the B&B in Montonero. The route recrosses the main road and continues on farm tracks intersecting first with the unmarked route from Casina Castelllone before rejoining the "Official Route". **(0.0)** Turn left and immediately right and pass between the buildings **(0.2)** Cross the main road with care and take the bridge over the water course **(0.3)** Immediately turn left [Water course on your left] **(0.6)** Take the first turning to the right **(1.5)** At the T-junction with the farm buildings directly ahead, turn right. Note: the direct unmarked route joins from the left **(2.5)** At the T-junction beside the railway tracks, turn right and cross the water course **(2.9)** At the 3 way junction, turn left and rejoin the "Official Route".

Length:	2.9km
Ascent:	11m
Descent:	14m

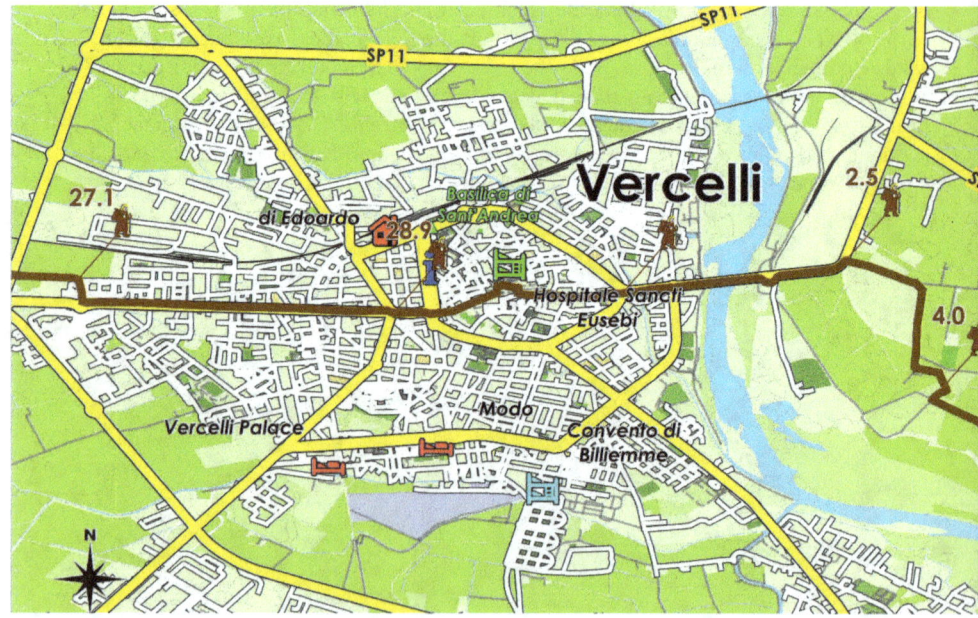

Santhià to Vercelli — stage 55

Accommodation and Tourist Information

San-Germano-Vercellese

Ostello Pellegrini Lungo la via Francigena, Corso Giacomo Matteotti, 60, 13047 San-Germano-Vercellese(VC), Italy; Tel: +39 3771 136597; Email: viafrancigenasangermanovc@gmail.com; www.ostellosangermano.it; Price:C

Albergo - delle Miniere, Corso Giacomo Matteotti, 91, 13047 San-Germano-Vercellese(VC), Italy; Tel:+39 0161 933111; Email:albergoleminiere@live.it; www.italia-italy.org/ana36079-hotel-san-germano-vercellese/hotel-delle-miniere-san-germano-vercellese; Price:B

Vercelli

Hospitale Sancti Eusebi [Olivetta Edoardo],Vicolo Degli Alciati, 4, 13100 Vercelli(VC), Italy; Tel: +39 3342 386911; +39 3386 177070; Email:info@amicidellaviafrancigena.vercelli.it; www.amicidellaviafrancigena.vercelli.it; Price:D

Convento di Billiemme,Corso Alessandro Salamano, 139, 13100 Vercelli(VC), Italy; Tel:+39 0161 250167; Price:C

B&B - la Casa di Edoardo,Via Brighinzio, 7, 13100 Vercelli(VC), Italy; Tel: +39 36 6282 9677; booking.com; Price:B

B&B - Montonero ,Frazione Montonero, 17 , 13100 Vercelli(VC), Italy; Tel: +39 3462339585; +39 3299807455 ; Email:mritabalossino@hotmail.com ; Price:C; *Reduced price with credentials*

Hotel -Modo,Piazza Medaglie d'Oro, 21, 13100 Vercelli(VC), Italy; Tel:+39 0161 217300; +39 34779089302; Email:modohotel@virgilio.it; www.modohotel.com; Price:B; *Book directly for lower rates*

Hotel - Vercelli Palace,Via Tavallini, 29 , 13100 Vercelli(VC), Italy; Tel:+39 0161 300900; Email:reservation@vercellipalacehotel.it ; www.vercellipalacehotel.it; Price:B; *Book directly for lower rates*

Tourist Office,Corso Giuseppe Garibaldi, 90, 13100 Vercelli(VC), Italy; Tel:+39 0161 58002; Email:infovercelli@atlvalsesiavercelli.it; www.atlvalsesiavercelli.it

Sant'Eusebio di Vercelli

stage 56 — Vercelli to Mortara

Length:	33.4km
Ascent:	184m
Descent:	215m
Col Grand St Bernard:	183km
Rome:	845km

In woodland–leaving Vercelli

Route: from Vercelli to Mortara the route initially follows the *argine* (embankment) beside the river Sesia to Palestro. At the time of writing, a wooden bridge on this section had been damaged and the provincial authorities advise taking the train from Vercelli to Palestro. The Vercelli tourist office should be able to advise the current status.

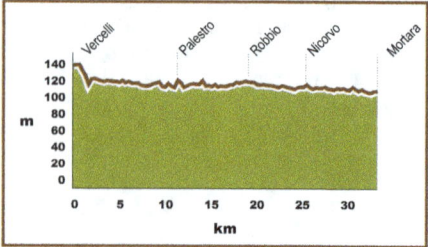

Between Palestro and Mortara the route continues on farms tracks and minor roads over flat ground, but intensive farming may once again have affected some of the tracks and signs.

There is a café and grocery store in Palestro.

Robbio is a small town but still offers the possibility of splitting the stage with an adequate choice of accommodation and eating places, while Mortara has a wider choice.

The area of Robbio has been settled since Neolithic times. As a Roman centre it was named Redobium and mentioned by Pliny the Elder. Later, the settlement was ceded to the Lombards and became a possession of the Catholic diocese of Vercelli. Around the 11th century, it was acquired by the De Robbio family, who ruled it and the neighbouring area until the 13th century, when it was contended between Vercelli and Pavia. In 1220 the latter definitively acquired Robbio through a diploma issued by Emperor Frederick II. Then part of the Duchy of Milan, it was entrusted to several feudal families. In 1748 it was acquired by the Kingdom of Sardinia and, in the 19th century, Robbio finally became part of the province of Pavia, under the newly formed Kingdom of Italy.

Of particular interest is the Romanesque church of St. Peter, housing 16th century frescoes attributed to Tommasino da Mortara and the 15th century church of San Michele, with a late Gothic-style façade.

Originally named Pulchra Silva by the Romans, the settlement became Mortara after the bloody battle during which Charlemagne defeated the Longobard King Desiderius in 773.

During the Middle Ages, San Albino was a compulsory halting-place for Via Francigena pilgrims and still is today. Just outside Mortara, San Albino is one of the Christian mother-churches of the 5th century Lomellina and was re-used by Charlemagne as a burial ground for soldiers falling in the battle between the Longobard and Frank armies.

Vercelli to Mortara stage 56

🚶(**0.0**)From piazza Paietta continue straight ahead [Corso Libertà](**0.4**)After passing the kiosk, turn left on via Camillo Benso Cavour [Towards the arches](**0.4**)Turn right into piazza Cavour and go straight ahead keeping to the right side of the piazza [Statue in the centre of the piazza](**0.5**)Bear right on via Francesco Crispi [Paved road](**0.5**)In the small piazza, turn right, towards the tower [Remain on via Crispi](**0.6**)At the end of the road turn left in piazza San Paolo [Corso Libertà] 🚶(**1.0**)At the mini-roundabout at the end of Corso Libertà continue straight ahead [Piazza Modesto Cugnolio](**1.2**)At the roundabout continue straight ahead, direction Pavia [Cross bridge over waterway](**1.5**)At the next roundabout go straight ahead, direction Pavia (SS11) [Cross over the Sesia river bridge] 🚶(**2.5**)After the bend to the left on the main road, turn right on the small road Strada del Boarone(**2.9**)At the fork, bear right towards the river(**3.5**)At the fork, keep right, and then bear left [Pass the farm house on your right] 🚶(**4.0**)Cross the bridge and turn left on the embankment [Pass a house on the left](**4.6**)At the crossroads in the track, continue straight ahead 🚶(**5.4**)Continue straight ahead [Under the Autostrada bridge](**5.8**)At the crossroads in the track, continue straight ahead on the embankment 🚶(**6.5**)At the crossroads in the

track, continue straight ahead(**6.9**)Continue straight ahead [Avoid the turning towards the farm on the left] 🚶(**8.1**)At the crossroads in the track, continue straight ahead [Fields to the left woods on the right](**8.4**)Continue straight ahead and right on the embankment [Ignore the track on the left and right](**8.8**)At the crossroads in the track, continue straight ahead 🚶(**9.5**)At the junction in the tracks, bear left(**10.2**)Turn left [Wooden bridge](**10.4**)At the T-junction in the tracks, turn right 🚶(**10.8**)At the T-junction, turn left, towards the village of Palestro(**11.4**)At the Stop sign in **Palestro**, turn right on the SP56 - via Garibaldi(**11.7**)Cross the bridge and proceed straight ahead at the next Stop sign 🚶(**11.8**)Turn right direction Rosasco on via Rosasco(**11.9**)Immediately before crossing the irrigation channel, turn left on the broad track [Trees on your right](**12.7**)Turn right [Cross the irrigation channel] 🚶(**12.9**)Follow the sign to the left(**13.0**)Turn right on the track [Beside the trees](**13.7**)Bear right [Trees to the right] 🚶(**14.0**)At the end of the path beside the trees turn right on the track(**14.2**)Follow the sign to the left and immediately turn right [Track zigzags around fields] 🚶(**15.5**)Turn right towards the farm(**15.7**)At the farm turn left(**15.9**)At the crossroads continue straight ahead 🚶(**16.5**)At the T-junction with the tarmac road turn left on the road(**17.0**)At the road junction, continue straight ahead [Direction Robbio] 🚶(**18.1**)At

stage 56 — Vercelli to Mortara

the crossroads with the SS596 proceed straight ahead [Towards Robbio centre]**(18.4)** At the crossroads, after passing the building material yard, turn right [Via Rosasco]**(18.9)** At the crossroads, proceed straight ahead [Direction Mortara]**(19.1)** At the traffic lights beside the park in **Robbio**, Giardini San Pietro, bear right, direction Mortara [Via Mortara, pass the

church of San Pietro on the left] ⛪ **(19.4)** Turn left onto via Roggetta**(19.8)** At the crossroads with a major road, continue straight ahead beside the sports ground [Tarmac road becomes a gravel track] ⛪ **(20.8)** Bear left after crossing a small bridge**(21.4)** Fork right passing a large concrete barn on the right ⛪ **(22.5)** Fork right ⛪ **(23.7)** At the junction with road bear left [Irrigation ditch on the right]**(24.0)** Take the left fork over the small bridge**(24.2)** At the T-junction, turn right, direction Nicorvo, SP6 [Towards mobile-phone mast] ⛪ **(25.4)** At the T-junction in **Nicorvo**, turn left [Direction Cilavegna]**(25.7)** In the centre of Nicorvo with the bell tower on the left, turn right, direction Mortara [Via Albonese] ⛪ **(26.9)** Turn right onto the part grassed track between rice fields**(27.2)** At the T-junction, turn left**(27.7)** Cross the gravel track and continue on the grass track [Large red farm building on the right] ⛪ **(28.4)** Turn right to cross over concrete bridge**(28.9)** At the crossroads in the track, continue straight ahead ⛪ **(29.3)** Bear right at the T-junction in track**(30.3)** Bear right at T-junction in track ⛪ **(30.5)** Proceed straight ahead and pass through the village of Madonna del

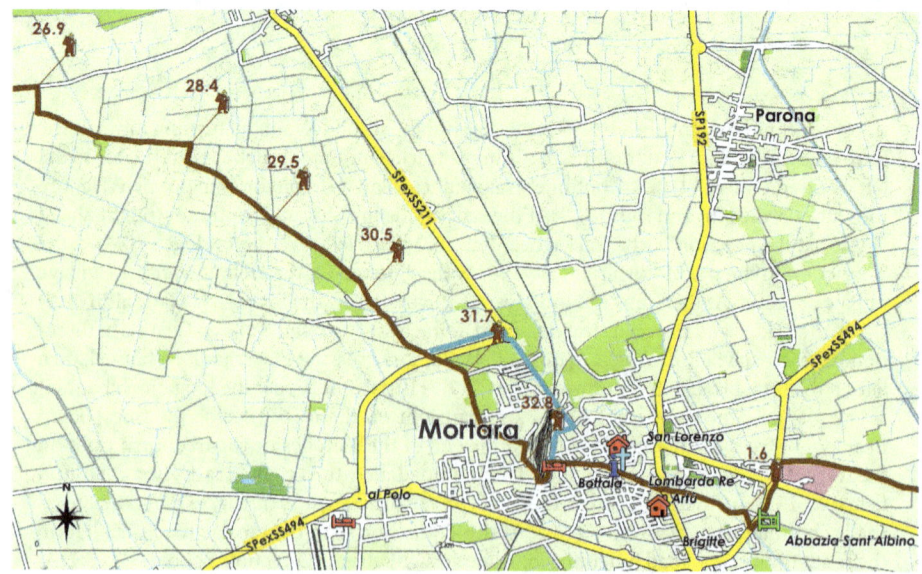

Vercelli to Mortara — stage 56

Campo [Walled gardens on both sides of the road]**(31.3)**Continue straight ahead across the railway tracks [Towards apartment buildings on the horizon] 🚶 **(31.7)**At the junction, continue straight ahead [Concrete barn on the left]**(32.3)**At the junction bear left towards the railway and the prominent apartment block [Via de Cantiano]**(32.7)**At the rear of the railway sidings turn right [Railway on the left] 🚶 **(32.8)**In the square beside a water-tower continue straight ahead into the No Through Road [Railway close on the left]**(33.1)**Take the pedestrian subway under the railway and continue straight ahead on the far side**(33.4)** Arrive at **Mortara** centre in front of the railway station [Beside fountain]

Accommodation and Tourist Information

Mortara

🛏**Abbazia Sant'Albino**,Sant'Albino, 782, 27036 Mortara(PV), Italy; Tel:+39 0384 298609; +39 3484 283203; Email:abbazia.santalbino@gmail.com; Price:C; *Wonderful host*; **PR**

✝ **Parrocchia San Lorenzo - Casa Parrocchiale**,Contrada San Dionigi, 1, 27036 Mortara(PV), Italy; Tel:+39 0384 99772; Price:C

🏠 **B&B Brigitte** [Brigitte Hoffmann],Via Gaetano Marzotto, 1, 27036 Mortara(64774), Italy; Tel:+39 366 47 45 310; Email:ibis27036@gmail.com; Price:C; *Credentials required for price group C*

🏠 **B&B - Foresteria Lombarda Re Artù**,Contrada della Torre, 11, 27036 Mortara(PV), Italy; Tel: +39 3356 003750; Email:foresteriareartu@libero.it; Price:B; *Pilgrim friendly*

🛌 **Albergo - Bottala**,Via Giuseppe Garibaldi, 1, 27036 Mortara(PV), Italy; Tel:+39 0384 99106; Email:davide@ilcuuc.191.it; www.ilcuuc.it; Price:B; *Above the restaurant Il Cuuc*

🛌 **Hotel - al Polo** [Deborah],Via Xi Settembre, 27036 Mortara(PV), Italy; Tel:+39 0384 298470; +39 3285 867779; Email:info@alpolo.it; alpolo.it; Price:B

ℹ **Ufficio Cultura**,Piazza Martiri della Libertà, 21, 27036 Mortara(PV), Italy; Tel:+39 0384 256411; Email:cultura@comune.mortara.pv.it; www.comune.mortara.pv.it

Nicorvo

🛏**Ospitale San Giacomo e della Madonnina**,Piazza Libertà, 2, 27020 Nicorvo(PV), Italy; Tel:+39 371 5174578; Email:ospitale.nicorvo.francigena@gmail.com; Price:D; *Credentials necessary*

Palestro

🏠 **B&B - Ospitaliere la Torre Merlata**,Via Vodano, 5, 27030 Palestro(PV), Italy; Tel: +39 3497 909044; Email:castellaniambra@gmail.com; www.latorremerlata.it; Price:B; *Can arrange baggage transport it is also possible to camp in the garden Open April to October*; **PR**

Robbio

🛏**Ostello Comunale - Robbio**,Piazza della Libertà, 2, 27038 Robbio(PV), Italy; Tel: +39 3485 538337; +39 3391 265426; Price:D; *Basic but close to shops. For access ask at the Bar Tre Archi*

🛏**Agriturismo Pescarolo** [Paola Lazzarin],Cascina Molino Miradolo, 27038 Robbio(PV), Italy; Tel:+39 3939222566; +39 3355852955; Email:fulvio@fulviopescarolo.it; www.agriturismopescarolo.it; Price:A; *Meals available. Pension for horses and donkeys possible*

✝ **Parrocchia di Santo Stefano**,Via Santo Stefano, 2, 27038 Robbio(PV), Italy; Tel:+39 0384 670436; +39 3401 539929; Email:protocollo@comune.robbio.pv.it; Price:D

ℹ **Municipio**,Piazza della Libertà, 2, 27038 Robbio(PV), Italy; Tel:+39 0384 6751; Email:info@comune.robbio.pv.it; www.comune.robbio.pv.it

stage 57 — Mortara to Garlasco

Length:	20.7km
Ascent:	125m
Descent:	137m
Col Grand St Bernard:	217km
Rome:	811km

Beside Sant'Albino

Route: from Mortara to Garlasco the route continues to meander through the rice fields and passes through small villages and the pleasant pilgrim conscious town of Tromello.

An Alternate Route visits the Santuario Madonna della Bozzola, where you can also find accommodation or break your journey at the sanctuary café/bar.

Garlasco is a small town straddling the busy SS596, but offers a good choice of facilities.

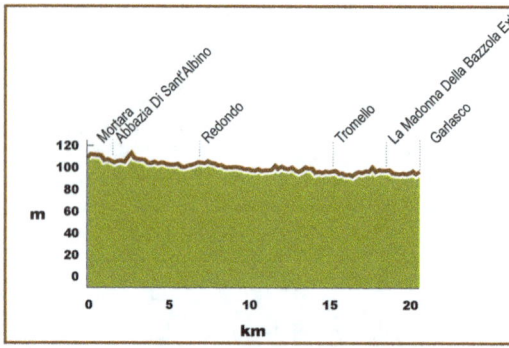

Our Lady of Bozzola,

The alternate route will take you beside the sanctuary of la Madonna delle Bozzola, built around the Shrine of Our Lady of Bozzola, which dates back to a miraculous event in 1465. A thirteen-year-old deaf-mute girl, Mary of Garlasco, was grazing her animals when suddenly a thunderstorm broke. Mary sought shelter in a small chapel where there was a fresco of the Blessed Virgin Mary, painted by Augustine of Pavia, after being saved from drowning in the river Ticino. Suddenly a ball of light appeared and the Blessed Virgin Mary spoke, entrusting the girl with a mission: "Here at Garlasco I want a sanctuary to protect the whole Lomellina. Many are the graces that I pour into this place and my children will experience the treasures of my mercy." Maria returned to Garlasco and neighbours, hearing the child speak for the first time, believed her story. The sanctuary was indeed built, Mary was renamed Maria Benedett, and she subsequently withdrew to a convent nearby.

Mortara to Garlasco   stage 57

(0.0) From the railway station in Mortara, go straight ahead on Corso Garibaldi [Railway station directly behind] **(0.4)** Take the right fork [Corso Cavour] **(0.9)** At the roundabout, bear left and keep right on via Sant'Albino Alcuino [Towards the water tower] **(1.6)** After crossing the second small bridge turn right and take the subway under the main road, turn left at the exit from the subway and continue beside the busy main road [Pass **Abbazia di Sant'Albino** on your right] **(2.3)** Continue straight ahead at the roundabout and then take the first turning to the right **(5.4)** At the crossroads, continue straight ahead **(6.6)** At the T-junction with the road, turn right [Cemetery ahead at the junction] **(7.0)** At the crossroads, in the centre of **Redondo**, turn left [Direction Gambolò, bar on the left] **(7.0)** At the crossroads, turn right on via Arturo Ferrarin [Church on the right, war memorial on the left] **(7.3)** At the junction continue straight ahead [Via Arturo Ferrarin] **(7.8)** Take the left fork [Pass apartments on your left] **(8.1)** Take the right fork [Water channel directly on the right] **(8.4)** Continue straight ahead across the railway and the main road **(8.8)** Take the left fork [Towards the radio masts] **(10.6)** Pass through the farm and then turn right and follow the track as it turns right [Keep the buildings close on your right. Note:- the Al-

ternate Route joins from the left] **(11.7)** Pass through a clump of trees and at the T-junction turn left **(11.9)** At the junction turn sharp right [Parallel to the main road] **(12.3)** Continue straight ahead [Cross the Langosco canal] **(12.6)** At the crossroads proceed straight ahead [Towards cascina San Vincenzo] **(13.3)** At the T-junction turn left and then immediately right on the tarmac **(14.0)** At the T-junction, turn left and then carefully cross the main road and continue straight ahead [Direction Tromello] **(14.9)** At the T-junction, turn right on via Cavour **(15.3)** In piazza Campegi, in the centre of **Tromello (XLII)**, continue straight ahead and bear left into via Montello [Pass the clock tower on your right] **(15.5)** Shortly before the end of the street, turn left and then right **(15.5)** At the T-junction turn right [Pass a bar] **(15.7)** After crossing the bridge turn left [Towards Borgo S. Siro] **(15.9)** After crossing the railway, take the right fork [Via Cascinino] **(16.3)** Take the right fork on the track [Valve on the left at the junction] **(16.8)** At the crossroads, continue straight ahead [Towards the power line] **(17.4)** At the junction continue straight ahead **(17.7)** At the canal crossing, turn right [Keep canale Cavour on your left] **(18.0)** At the junction, keep left [Remain beside the canal] **(18.6)** At the next junction turn right. Note:- to visit the sanctuary of **la Madonna della Bazzola exit** left and follow the Alternate Route [Bridge on your left] **(18.9)** At the junction, continue straight ahead **(19.6)** Continue straight ahead on the tarmac road [Cross the railway] **(20.0)** At the T-junction with the main road, turn left and continue straight ahead at the roundabout [Direction Centro] **(20.7)** Arrive at **Garlasco** centre [Beside piazza Repubblica]

stage 57 — Mortara to Garlasco

Sanctuary of la Madonna della Bozzola

Route: this short diversion on farm and canal-side tracks will lead you to the Sanctuary of la Madonna della Bozzola, but will bypass Garlasco rejoining the "Official Route" in the next stage. **(0.0)** Bear left and then right over the canal [Continue with the canal on your right] **(0.7)** Cross over road and bear left on the track with the canal on the left **(1.0)** Fork right away from the canal [Trees on your left] **(1.3)** Take the second turning on the right [Into the trees] **(1.7)** Turn left and then right [Trees on the left] **(2.5)** At the junction in front of the sanctuary, turn left and immediately right [Pass the Sanctuary on your right] **(2.7)** Immediately after crossing over the bridge, turn right beside the canal [Canal on your right] **(3.9)** Continue straight ahead with a bridge on the right [Canal on the right] **(4.2)** Cross the road and continue on the track beside the canal [Bridge on right] **(4.7)** Turn right, cross over bridge, then turn immediately left to skirt the large building on the right [Canal on the left] **(5.1)** Beside bridge, continue straight ahead with water on left and rejoin the "Official Route"

Length:	5.1km
Ascent:	36m
Descent:	40m

Accommodation and Tourist Information

Garlasco

Casa del Pellegrino, Via Santissima Trinità 6 , 27026 Garlasco(PV), Italy; Tel:+39 0382 801009; +39 3343435810; Email:bibliogarlasco@yahoo.it; Price:D

Casa del Pellegrino Exodus - Cascina di Toledina, Via Toledina, 3, 27026 Garlasco(PV), Italy; Tel:+39 0382 820002; +39 3494 051840; Email:garlasco@exodus.it; www.exodus.it; Price:C

Santuario Madonna della Bozzola, Piazzale Santuario, 1, 27026 Garlasco(PV), Italy; Tel:+39 0382 822117; Email:madonna.bozzola@gmail.com; www.madonnadellabozzola.org; Price:D

Albergo - il Pino, Corso Cavour, 1, 27026 Garlasco(PV), Italy; Tel:+39 0382 822265; Email:ilpinogarlasco@tin.it; hotelperiviaggi.top/hotel-il-pino; Price:B; *Nice people*; **PR**

Tromello

Parrocchia San Martino Vescovo [Giancarlo Bindolini],Via Branca, 1, 27020 Tromello(PV), Italy; Tel:+39 0382 86020; +39 3493 325080; Email:viefrancigene.com/parrocchia-san-martino-tromello; Always a warm welcome from Giancarlo; Price:D; **PR**

Hotel - Duca di Tromello,Via Cesare Battisti, 4, 27020 Tromello(PV), Italy; Tel:+39 0382 868089; Email:hotelducaditromello@gmail.com; www.hotelducaditromello.it; Price:B

Garlasco to Pavia

stage 58

Length:	24.6km
Ascent:	262m
Descent:	274m
Col Grand St Bernard:	237km
Rome:	791km

Ponte Coperto–Pavia

Route: the stage from Garlasco to Pavia will initially follow canal-side paths and pass through the small town of Gropello Cairoli before finally leaving the rice fields and entering the city of Pavia beside the banks of the river Ticino.

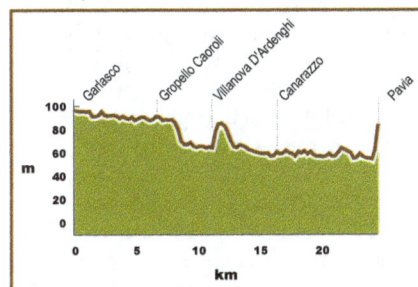

Pavia stretches along the right bank of the Ticino River, and is dominated by medieval towers which testify to the artistic and architectural treasures waiting to be discovered.

A vibrant and multi-faceted town with a great love of art and culture, there will be art exhibitions and other cultural events for you to enjoy, if you want to take a day off.

The monuments, cobbled streets and house facades in the heart of Pavia's historical centre are strong reminders of its glorious past. Dating back to pre-Roman times, the town of Pavia (then known as Ticinum), was a municipality and an important military site under the Roman Empire. Later the city became known as Papia (probably as a reference to the Pope), which evolved to the Italian name Pavia.

During Pavia's golden age, the city was the Lombard's capital and later witnessed coronations of Charlemagne and Frederick Barbarossa. Even after it lost its status to Milan in 1359, Pavia remained an important city and great Romanesque churches, tall towers and other monuments still reflect this.

(0.0) From piazza Repubblica, continue on Corso Camillo Cavour [Church of San Rocco on your right] **(0.7)** At the second mini-roundabout, turn left [Via Dante Alighieri] **(1.0)** At the crossroads, turn right [Via Toldeo] **(2.1)** Immediately before the bridge over the canal, turn right. Note:- the Alternate Route joins from the left **(3.1)** At the T-junction, turn left towards the canal bridge and then right to continue with the canal on your left **(4.1)** At the crossroads with the SP206 cross the road and continue on the track beside the canal [Canal on the left] **(4.5)** At the crossroads, continue straight ahead [Canal on the left] **(4.7)** Fork right, away from the canale Cavour on the lower track direction Gropello Cairoli **(5.7)** Continue straight ahead at the junction [After passing behind the cemetery] **(5.8)** Fork left on the track [Avoid the tarmac road ahead] **(6.2)** Cross the canal and continue straight

stage 58 — Garlasco to Pavia

ahead**(6.3)**Take the first road on the right [Between apartment buildings]**(6.4)**At the end of the road, turn left [Via Verdi]**(6.6)**At the end of the road, turn right and then immediately left [Via C. Battisti] **(6.7)**At the T-junction, turn right [Park entrance on your left] **(6.8)**At the T-junction with the main road, turn left [Towards the centre of **Gropello Caoroli**]**(7.4)**Pass the church of San Rocco (in centre of main road) and immediately bear left on viale C.B. Zanotti [Sign for Centro Ippico Sant'Andrea] **(7.9)**On leaving the town

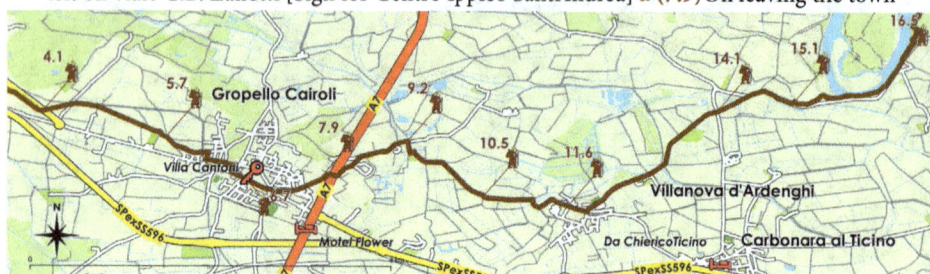

continue straight ahead on the bridge over the motorway [Pass telephone mast on the right]**(8.2)**After crossing the bridge bear left on strada del Morgarolo [Factory on the right]**(8.6)**Continue straight ahead [Pass beside Centro Ippico Sant'Andrea] **(9.2)**At the junction before the canal bridge, turn right [Direction cascina Morgarolo]**(9.4)**At the entrance to the farm turn left, cross over the canal and then immediately turn right between the buildings [Proceed with canal close on the right]**(9.6)**Take the left fork [Between broad and narrow channels]**(9.8)**At the fork bear right [Channel close on the right] **(10.5)**After crossing a bridge bear left [Ditch close on the left]**(11.1)**At the T-junction, turn right, away from the main irrigation channel [Bridge on the left at the junction]**(11.2)**At the fork, bear left into **Villanova d'Ardenghi** on the tarmac road [Uphill between trees] **(11.6)**Continue straight ahead through the town [Via Pollini]**(11.9)**At the crossroads turn left on via Roma [Direction Zerbolo] **(14.1)**At the crossroads, continue straight ahead**(14.5)**At the junction, continue straight ahead on the raised road [Cascina Gaviola on the left]**(14.8)** Shortly after the bend to the right, descend from the embankment and take the grass track on the left. Note:- to avoid potentially wet ground, cyclists may wish to remain on the road for the 8.8km to the Ponte Coperto in Pavia **(15.1)**Turn right to follow the watercourse**(15.7)**Continue straight ahead on the path [River Ticino on the left]**(16.0)**Continue straight ahead on the riverside path **(16.5)**Take the right fork, climb the embankment and continue straight ahead on the road [Village of **Canarazzo** on the right]**(16.7)**Bear left to leave the embankment and return to the riverside path**(17.0)**Cross a car park and at the T-junction turn left and then bear right [Path branches away from the road]**(17.2)**Take the left fork [Right fork leads to farm buildings] **(17.8)**Continue straight ahead [Avoid the turning to the beach on the left]**(18.2)**At the T-junction bear left [Towards the river]**(18.4)** At the T-junction, turn right on the broad straight track**(18.7)**Bear left on the track **(19.0)**Continue straight ahead [Ignore the turning towards the river]**(19.5)**Continue straight ahead on the riverside path**(19.7)**Continue straight ahead [Pass beside a restaurant] **(20.9)**At the T-junction in the woods turn right [Pass a lake on the left]**(21.4)**Take the right fork**(21.6)**Continue straight ahead on the tarmac road [Towards the elevated highway]**(21.7)**Pass under the highway and continue straight ahead [The road ahead is closed to traffic] **(22.4)**Continue straight ahead on the unmade road [Parallel to the river]**(22.8)**Continue on the riverside track [Pass under the railway]**(23.0)**Continue straight ahead on the riverside path [Ignore the turning to the right] **(23.7)**Continue straight

Garlasco to Pavia — stage 58

ahead on the riverside path [Pass under the road bridge]**(23.9)**Pedestrians continue on the riverside path. Cyclists should turn right and take the road to the entrance to the Ponte Coperto [Borgo Ticino to the right and the Ponte Coperto directly ahead]**(24.2)**Climb the steps and cross the covered bridge [No Entry sign on the bridge]**(24.4)**At the traffic lights cross the piazzale Ponte Ticino and take the road ahead [Corso Strada Nuova]**(24.6)**Arrive at **Pavia (XLI)** centre. [Crossroads with Corso Garibaldi]

Accommodation and Tourist Information

Carbonara-al-Ticino
Hotel - Da Chierico - Ticino,Via Roma, 14, 27020 Carbonara-al-Ticino(PV), Italy; Tel:+39 0382 400477; Email:ticinoalbergo@gmail.com; www.ticinodachierico.it; Price:B

Gropello-Cairoli
Hotel - Motel Flower,Via Lecco, 14, 27027 Gropello-Cairoli(PV), Italy; Tel:+39 0382 815154; Email:info@hotelmotelflower.it; www.hotelmotelflower.it; Price:B

Affittacamera - Villa Cantoni,Via Libertà, 110, 27027 Gropello-Cairoli(PV), Italy; Tel: +39 340 6044509 ; Email:cantonivilla@gmail.com; villacantoni.it; Price:A; **PR**

Pavia
Pavia Ostello,Via Brenta, 3, 27100 Pavia(PV), Italy; Tel:+39 0382 528865; Email:info@paviaostello.it; www.paviaostello.it; Price:C

Saint Maria In Betlem,Via Pasino Degli Eustachi, 7, 27100 Pavia(PV), Italy; Tel: +39 3313 046459; Email:info@ostellosantamariainbetlem.com; www.ostellosantamariainbetlem.com; Price:B; *Discount for pilgrims with credentials*

Casa della Carità,Via Giuseppe Pedotti, 14, 27100 Pavia(PV), Italy; Tel:+39 0382 23138; Email:casadellacarita@hotmail.it; www.casadellacaritapavia.it; Price:C

Parrocchia della Sacra Famiglia,Viale Ludovico il Moro, 1, 27100 Pavia(PV), Italy; Tel:+39 0382 575381; +39 3383 555168; www.sacrafamigliapv.it; Price:D

Hotel - Aurora,Viale Vittorio Emanuele II, 25, 27100 Pavia(PV), Italy; Tel:+39 0382 23664; Email:info@hotel-aurora.eu; www.hotel-aurora.eu; Price:A

Pavia Affittacamere,Via Giovanni Rasori, 1, 27100 Pavia(PV), Italy; Tel:+39 0382 526783; +39 337 1104958; Email:iinfo@paviaaffittacamere.it; paviaaffittacamere.it; Price:B

Camping Ticino,Via Mascherpa, 16, 27100 Pavia(PV), Italy; Tel:+39 3401358854; +39 3391 166674; +39 3401 358854; Email:camping.ticino@libero.it; www.campingticino.it; Price:C; *Open late May to mid-October. Mobile homes avauilable*

Tourist Office,Piazza Italia, 2, 27100 Pavia(PV), Italy; Tel:+39 0382 5971; Email:visitpavia@provincia.pv.it; www.visitpavia.com

stage 59 — Pavia to Santa Cristina

Length:	28.0km
Ascent:	254m
Descent:	266m
Col Grand St Bernard:	262km
Rome:	766km

San Giacomo

Route: after exiting the centre the stage from Pavia to Santa Cristina follows suburban roads before negotiating the crossing of the busy ring road. From there the route follows a mix of quiet country roads and gravel tracks making for easy going for all groups.

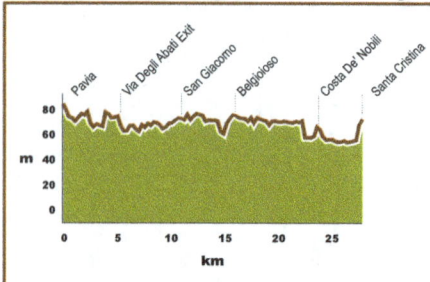

You also have the choice of following the via Francigena di Montagna or via degli Abati (the Bishops' Way) which links Pavia with Pontremoli, passing beside the burial place of Saint Colombanus in Bobbio and experiencing more of the dramatic Apennine landscapes and perhaps saving a day on your journey to Rome. The route branches south from the official Francigena route 5 km to the west of Pavia. The route is described in detail at the end of this guide.

Belgioioso offers a broader range of facilities than Santa Cristina.

If you plan to use the Pò ferry from Corte Sant'Andrea, we recommend that you call well in advance, preferably between 20.00 and 22.00 in the evening and be flexible in the timing of your crossing. In case of difficulties with the ferry we suggest that you plan to stay in Orio Litta or Corte Sant'Andrea to avoid the risk of having to substantially extend your journey to the next stopping place in the event of ferry problems. You will find details in the introduction to stage 61.

The history of Sante Cristine is linked to the old Benedictine abbey of the same name. Founded by Liuthprand, the King of the Lombards, the monastery was dedicated to St. Christine in the 9th century. In 1513 the Vallumbrosan monks replaced the Benedictine order in the monastery until its closure in 1654. As a point of interest Conradin, Duke of Swabia was given hospitality there in 1267, on his way across Lombardy to move against Charles I of Anjou.

🕯 **(0.0)**From the crossroads turn right [Corso Garibaldi] 🕯 **(1.0)**At the traffic lights go straight ahead direction Piacenza [Cross the waterway on viale dei Partigiani] 🕯 **(2.2)**At San Pietro in Verzolo continue straight ahead [Pass church on the right]**(2.6)**Turn right on via Francana [Kiosk on the corner] 🕯 **(3.2)**Continue straight ahead [Ignore the turning to the left on via Scarenzio]**(3.4)**At the end of the road continue straight ahead on the tarmac

Pavia to Santa Cristina — stage 59

which quickly becomes an unmade track and winds from left to right and then turns back towards the main toad **(3.7)** At the crossroads at the end of the track take the tarmac road straight ahead [Uphill] **(3.8)** At the T-junction turn right on the broader road [Via Montebolone] **(4.0)** At the roundabout, continue straight ahead [Church on the right] **(4.1)** At the T-junction, turn right [Pedestrian and cycle path] **(4.7)** At the T-junction turn left on strada Scagliona [Factory buildings directly ahead at the junction] **(5.1)** Bear right [Direction Broni] **(5.4)** For the **via degli Abati exit** by the right fork on the more minor road [Pass close by the farm buildings on your right] **(5.9)** At the roundabout, proceed with care to take the second exit [Direction San Leonardo] **(10.7)** At the sharp bend to the left, after passing through Ospedaletto, bear right on the tarmac and then turn right on the unmade road [Direction S. Giacomo] **(11.1)** At the first crossroads turn left and follow the road

through **San Giacomo** and Santa Margherita **(15.1)** Remain on the road into Belgioioso [Factory to the right] **(16.1)** In **Belgioioso** turn right on via P. Nenni [Direction carabinieri] **(16.6)** At the T-junction, turn right on the SP9 towards Torre de' Negri [Exit Belgioioso] **(18.6)** Pass through Torre de' Negri and on the crown of the right-hand bend continue on the road [Ignore the track to the left] **(19.4)** On the crown of a further bend to the right, bear left on the gravel road [Direction Cascina Campobello, pass silos on the right] **(20.1)** At the crossroads with the SP199 continue straight ahead [Towards the quarry] **(20.3)** Besides the quarry buildings, turn left on the gravel track [Skirt the quarry on your right] **(21.1)** Bear right following the fence **(21.9)** At the T-junction turn left **(22.3)**

stage 59 — Pavia to Santa Cristina

At the next junction, at the end of the field, continue straight ahead [Slightly downhill] **(22.6)** Cross the bridge and continue straight ahead on the broad track beside the canal [Woodland to the right and canal close on the left] **(23.6)** Turn left over the next bridge [Via Aldo Moro] **(23.8)** At the T-junction turn right on the main road into the village of **Costa de' Nobili** [Via Roma] **(23.9)** Turn left towards Cascina Padulino [Shortly after turning the tarmac gives way to an unmade road] **(24.5)** By the farm entrance continue straight ahead [Farm on the left] **(25.5)** At the T-junction turn left **(27.6)** Continue straight ahead into Santa Cristina [Conifers on the right] **(27.8)** At the T-junction turn left **(27.8)** Take the next turning to the right [Via Gibelli] **(28.0)** Arrive at **Santa Cristina (XL)** centre [Beside the church]

Accommodation and Tourist Information

Belgioioso

Associazione Saman, Via Cantone, 42, 27011 Belgioioso(PV), Italy; Tel:+39 0382 960268; Email:samanbelgioioso@saman.it; www.saman.it/dove_siamo/sedi_di_pavia; *Rehabilitation centre*

Hotel Ristorante - Cavaliere, Via Cavallotti, 50, 27011 Belgioioso(PV), Italy; Tel:+39 0382 971128; Email:hotelcavaliere@outlook.it; www.hotelristorantecavaliere.it; Price:B

Locanda - della Pesa Ristorante Albergo, Via 20 Settembre, 111, 27011 Belgioioso(PV), Italy; Tel:+39 0382 969073; +39 3351 859556; Email:info@lalocandadellapesa.it; www.lalocandadellapesa.it/albergo-pensione-completa-pavia; Price:B

Municipality of Belgioioso, Via Garibaldi, 64, 27011 Belgioioso(PV), Italy; Tel:+39 0382 978420; Email:info@comune.belgioioso.pv.it; www.comune.belgioioso.pv.it

Miradolo-Terme

Parrocchia San Michele Arcangelo [Don Maurizio], Via Garibaldi, 34, 27010 Miradolo-Terme(PV), Italy; Tel:+39 0382 77116; +39 339 2792 925; Email:parrocchia.miradolo@gmail.com; Price:D; *2 double beds and small kitchen*

Santa-Cristina

Parrocchia di Santa Cristina e Bissone [Don Antonio Pedrazzini], Via Vittorio Veneto, 118, 31055 Santa-Cristina(TV), Italy; Tel:+39 0382 70106; +39 3333 429685; Email:scristinaparrocchia@gmail.com; www.parrocchiasantacristinaebissone.it; Price:D; *Credentials required Open April to end September. Closed Sundays and for 3 weeks mid August*

Market day in Santa Cristina

Santa Cristina to Orio Litta   stage 60

Length:	16.3km
Ascent:	116m
Descent:	124m
Col Grand St Bernard:	290km
Rome:	738km

Villa Litta Carini in the morning mist

Route: for the stage from Santa Cristina to Orio Litta we again use farm tracks and minor roads over generally level ground on this short section as we approach the Po crossing.

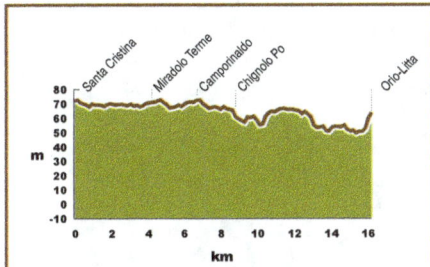

Orio Litta, Miradolo Terme, Cignolo Po and San Colombano al Lambro offer a range of facilities, while a little further at the hamlet of Corte Sant'Andrea is the convenient Ostello ad Padum.

Described elsewhere in this guide is a via Francigena variant passing beside the resting place of the Irish Saint Columbanus (*San Colombano*) in Bobbio. A network of paths is being developed that trace his journey from Ireland to his final resting place. An Alternate Route to Orio Litta will allow you to pass through San Colombano al Lambro and travel a small section of this network.

In Orio-Litta you will pass the impressive Villa Litta Carini, an ancient noble villa dating back to the second half of the 17th century and built by Count Antonio Cavazzi of Somaglia who entrusted the work to architect Giovanni Ruggeri. Today the villa is used for events, but it does host a permanent antiques exhibition on two floors of the central part of the building.

There is always a warm welcome

stage 60 — Santa Cristina to Orio Litta

🚶(0.0) Facing the church in Santa Cristina turn right and proceed along the main street [Via Vittorio Veneto](0.2) Turn left on viale Rimembranze [Direction Stazione](0.5) Cross the main road (SS234) and continue straight ahead [Pedestrian traffic lights](0.6) Cross the railway line and immediately turn right on the path beside the railway [Open fields to the left and railway to the right] 🚶(1.2) Turn right and then immediately left [Between the railway and the irrigation channel](1.7) Bear left over the irrigation channel [Continue between the open fields] 🚶(3.8) Cross the main road and continue straight ahead on the road towards Miradolo Terme [Pass the cemetery on your left](4.3) In piazza del Comune in **Miradolo Terme**, bear right towards Piacenza!. Note:- for the alternate route to follow the **Cammino di San Colombano exit** to the left [Via Garibaldi](4.6) At the junction beside the archway, bear right(4.6) Bear right [Via Garibaldi](4.7) Take the first turning to the left and follow the road into open country [via San Marco](4.7) Take the first turning to the left and follow the road into open country [Via San Marco] 🚶(5.4) Take the left fork on the road [Pass between the trees] 🚶(6.8) At the crossroads beside the mini-market in the centre of **Camporinaldo** turn right [Via C. Vignali] 🚶(7.8) Turn right and then immediately left [Cross the small canal bridge] 🚶(8.9) At the road junction, continue straight ahead [Towards the **Chignolo Po** castle tower] 🚶(11.3) Continue straight ahead on the cycle track [Pass a cemetery on the right] 🚶(13.0) At the T-junction with the main road, turn right and continue beside the road using the guard rail for protection from the traffic

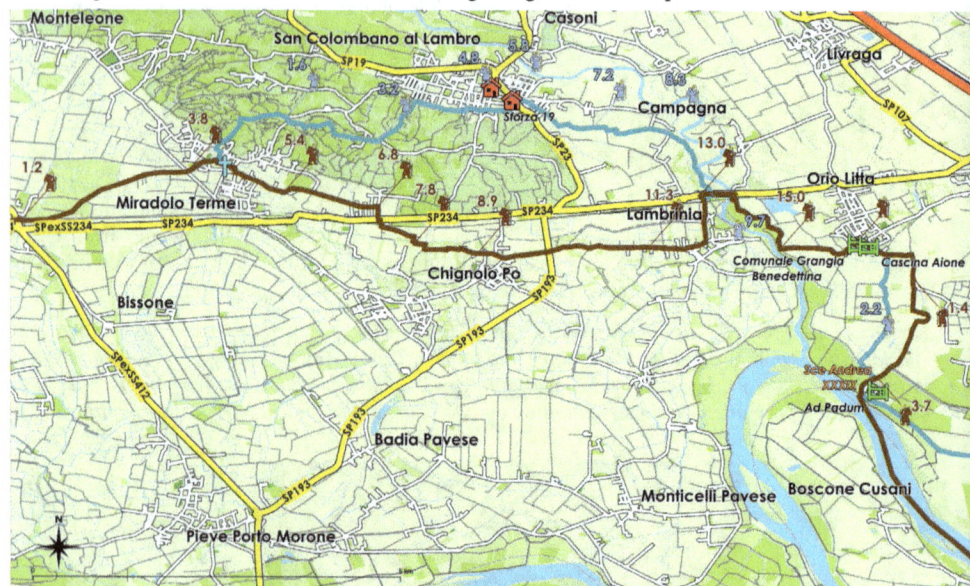

[SS234, cross over river bridge](13.5) Immediately after crossing the river bridge, turn right onto the unmade road [Towards the railway] 🚶(15.0) Leave the embankment on the second track to the left. If you wish to bypass Orio Litta and save 1km, continue on the argine to Corte Sant'Andrea [Towards Orio Litta and between fields](15.9) Beside the first houses in Orio Litta turn left on the tarmac road [Via Roma] 🚶(16.1) Bear left into via Valle and then turn right and right again to enter piazza Benedettini(16.3) Arrive at **Orio Litta** centre, piazza dei Benedettini [Beside pilgrim hostel]

Santa Cristina to Orio Litta
stage 60
Cammino di San Colombano

Route: this diversion on minor roads and farm and riverside tracks will allow you visit San Colombano al Lambro and sample the emerging network dedicated to the saint. The route breaks away from the Po plain and climbs through hillside vineyards to the town of named for the saint that passed this way 300 years before Sigeric. **(0.0)** At the roundabout, bear left [Pass the Municipio on your left] **(0.2)** At the T-junction beside the church, turn left **(0.3)** At the junction, keep right as you climb the hill [Direction Madonnina del Latte] **(1.0)** Beside the shrine or **Madonnina del Latte** bear right on the gravel road [Pass vines on your left] **(1.6)** At the T-junction with the tarmac road turn right **(1.7)** As the road turns right, turn left on the track and immediately left again [Towards the radio tower] **(2.0)** Turn left up the hill **(2.2)** Beside the entrance to the farmhouse turn left **(3.2)** At the junction withe the tarmac road, after passing the church of **Madonna del Monte**, bear right and then immediately left on the small road [Fresco of Madonna and child] **(4.2)** At the foot of the hill beside **Madonna del Latte**, bear right on the tarmac [Houses on your left and hillside to your right] **(4.8)** As the principal road turns left, continue straight ahead on the narrow road [No Entry] **(4.9)** At end of the road turn left [Cobbled street] **(4.9)** After passing the Caribinieri office, take the next right **(5.1)** In Piazza Gnocchi, pass between the church and the castello and bear left [Via Gallotta and then via Valsasno] **(5.5)** Turn left on via Don Bosco. Then turn left and immediately right [Pass oratorio don Giovanni Bosco on your right] **(5.8)** At the T-junction turn right and carefully continue straight ahead at the traffic lights [Join **Cammino di San Colombano**] **(6.0)** Fork right [Via Colombana] **(7.2)** At the junction continue straight ahead **(7.4)** Beside the chapel, bear left **(8.1)** Continue straight ahead with care on the tarmac road **(8.3)** Bear left on the gravel track **(9.7)** Pass under the road bridge and then take the first turn to the right **(9.9)** At the crossroads, turn right to rejoin the via Francigena

Length:	9.9km
Ascent:	182m
Descent:	192m

Accommodation and Tourist Information

Orio Litta
🏠 **Cascina Aione**, Piazza Aldo Moro, 2, 26863 Orio Litta(LO), Italy; Tel:+39 334 6176963; Email:cfcap@libero.it; Price:C
🏠 **Ostello Comunale Grangia Benedettina** [Romina Pastori], Piazza dei Benedettini, 26863 Orio Litta(LO), Italy; Tel:+39 339 1720018; +39 0377 944436; +39 345 0487706; Email:oriolittacomune@gmail.com; www.comune.oriolitta.lo.it; Price:D; *Well equipped open March to October*; **PR**

San Colombano Al Lambro
🏠 **B&B - Amici del Colle**, Via Valsasino, 72, 20078 San Colombano Al Lambro(MI), Italy; Tel:+39 328 8061850; Email:info@amicidelcolle.eu; www.amicidelcolle.eu; Price:A
🏠 **B&B - Sforza 19** [Marco and Marina], Via Pasino Sforza, 19, 20078 San Colombano Al Lambro(MI), Italy; Tel:+39 338 345 1601; +39 3391635673 ; Email:marco.gallotta@tiscali.it; sforza19.com; Price:B

Senna-Lodigiana
🏠 **Ostello Ad Padum**, Localita Corte Sant'Andrea, 26856 Senna-Lodigiana(LO), Italy; Tel:+39 0377 802155; +39 339 7707 118; +39 3391 268946; Email:favarigiovanni@gmail.com; www.compagniadisigericolaudense.it; Price:D; *Fully equipped close to the guado*

Castello di San Colombano al Lambro

stage 61 — Orio Litta to Piacenza

Length:	24.0km
Ascent:	155m
Descent:	153m
Col Grand St Bernard:	306km
Rome:	722km

Pillar marking the Pò ferry (Guado) boat dock

Route: the route from Orio Litta to Piacenza reaches the Guado di Sigerico (Pò ferry crossing) using a minor road and the argine. From the ferry dock to the outskirts of Piacenza

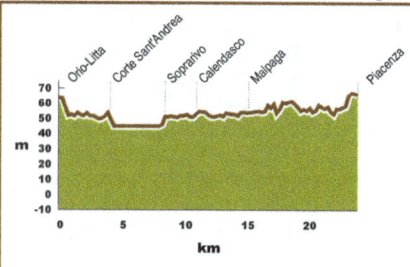

the route continues on pleasant country roads, but the long final entry into Piacenza requires a choice between the very busy via Emilia Pavese SP10 and a longer route crossing and recrossing the autostrada. Alternate Routes are described to help shorten your path to the ferry and the approach to Piacenza. For those not able to take the ferry a route is described along the argine. The ferry crosses only on request and should be booked at least 24 hours in advance: Danilo Parisi Tel:+39 0523 771607 Mobile:+39 331 8768456

In Piacenza there is a vast range of facilities. However, the popular Ostello San Pietro is close to the route but 5 km beyond the stage end, though usefully shortening the next long stage.

In Piacenza you will pass Palazzo Farnese, commissioned by Ottavio's wife, Margaret of Austria, and built over a former fortress built by the Visconti in 1352, part of which can still be seen. In 1558, the architect Giacomo Barozzi da Vignola, produced drawings for a vast palace on a scale with the Vatican Palace, but the actual construction included less than half of his original project and lacked many of the planned architectural features. After the death of the last Farnese duke in 1731, the palace fell into disrepair and restoration only began in the early 20th century.

Today, the Palazzo houses an important series of museums and exhibitions.and is the home of the European Association of the Via Francigena.

Palazzo Farnese

Orio Litta to Piacenza — stage 61

(0.0) From the hostel entrance in piazza dei Benedettini bear right through the entrance and then immediately turn right[Via Bassano Rubbiati] **(0.2)** At the T-junction, turn left on via Montemalo **(0.4)** At the T-junction beside Villa Litta bear right, down the hill **(0.5)** At the bottom of the hill continue straight ahead and follow the tarmac road. Note:- approximately 600m may be saved by turn right and following the direct route to Corte Sant'Andrea[Cross bridge] **(0.9)** Turn right and remain on the tarmac **(1.4)** Take the right fork[Direction Corte S. Andrea] **(3.7)** Approaching Corte Sant'Andrea bear right onto the argine. Note:- direct route joins from the right[Ciclovia del Po] **(4.1)** Arrive beside the Pò river ferry (Guado di Sigerico). Note:- the ferry is only suitable for pedestrians or a small number of bikes. Those not wishing to take the ferry will need to continue straight ahead on the Alternate Route[**Corte Sant'Andrea (XXXIX)** to the left] **(8.4)** After climbing from the ferry landing stage at **Soprarivo**, proceed to the left on the gravel track[Pò on the left] **(9.2)** At the fork in the track, continue straight ahead. Note:- 500m may be saved by taking the grass track to the right and then turning right at the T-junction **(9.8)** At the crossroads on the embankment, turn right on the stony track[Towards the farm buildings, the track will become a tarmac road] **(11.0)** At the crossroads, turn left directly in front of a large building - Commune di **Calendasco**[Via Mazzini] **(13.2)** On the crown of the bend to the right, in the hamlet of Incrociata, turn left[Direction Cotrebbia Nuova] **(15.2)** At the fork in **Malpaga**, bear right and take the tarmac path to the left of the road[Direction Piacenza] **(16.9)** After passing under the railway and the road bridges turn immediately right and climb the ramp **(17.2)** At the junction with the main road, turn

right to cross the bridge and continue on the long straight via Emilia Pavese. Note:- caution on the narrow pavement/sidewalk[Direction Piacenza] **(18.8)** Immediately after passing a row of shops and a cafe on your left, turn left on the narrow road and pass under the railway[Via Bertucci] **(19.1)** As the tarmac road turns left, continue straight ahead on the path[Trees continue on your left] **(19.3)** As the end of the path, turn left and keep right on the road[Pass the service areas on both sides of the autostrada] **(20.6)** Shortly after reaching a small park on your left, turn right and recross the autostrada[Strada Campo Santo Vecchio] **(21.0)** At the end of the road, turn left[Via Trebbia] **(21.9)** At the next

stage 61 — Orio Litta to Piacenza

roundabout turn left and keep left[s](22.1)At the roundabout take the first exit[Pass under the railway] (23.3)In piazza del Borgo go straight ahead[Via Garibaldi](23.7)At the crossroads with corso Vittorio Emanuele II, go straight ahead. The Alternate Route joins from the left[Strada Sant'Antonino](24.0)Arrive at **Piacenza (XXXVIII)** centre[Beside the church of Sant'Antonino]

From Corte Sant'Andrea to Piacenza by the Argine

Route: avoiding the Pò ferry, the route follows the argine and farm tracks before approaching Piacenza on the pedestrian and cycle path over the new Pò river bridge. (0.0)Continue straight ahead[Remain on the argine] (2.4)Again continue straight ahead on the embankment[Ciclovia del Po] (4.2)Continue straight ahead on the embankment[Village of **Guzzafame** on the left](4.6)Bear right and remain on the argine[Ciclovia del Po] (6.8)Bear right and pass through the barrier[Ciclovia del Po] (7.6)At the crossroads, continue straight ahead on the embankment[Somaglia to the left, landing stage and restaurant on the right] (9.5) Bear right and continue on the argine[Cascina Minuta on the left] (10.6)Bear right on the embankment[Parallel to the road below](11.2)Beside the village of **Valloria**, turn sharp left to leave the embankment and then turn right and pass through the centre of the village[Via Dante Alighieri] (12.6)At the junction with the embankment, turn left[Follow the embankment] (14.3)At the crossroads, continue straight ahead[Remain on the embankment] (15.7)Shortly before the T-junction with the main road, turn right on the gravel track and continue on the cycle track until after the subway under the main road[Pass an industrial zone on your left] (19.4)After emerging from the subway turn right and right again and join the pedestrian path beside the main road[Cross the **Pò bridge**] (21.0)At the roundabout, continue straight ahead and cross to the right side of the road[Memorial on roundabout](21.4)Continue straight ahead beside Pallazo Farnese. Note:- the headquarters for the European Association of the Via Francigena (**AEVF**) are located in this building(21.7)Continue straight ahead on via Cavour[Pass Piazza Cavalli on the right](21.9)At the crossroads, turn left and rejoin the "Official Route"[Via Sant'Antonio]

Length:	21.9km
Ascent:	174m
Descent:	160m

Direct Route to Corte Sant'Andrea

Route: this short alternate route follows on off-road track and the former "Official Route" avoiding the road and saving 10 minutes for those hurrying for the ferry. (0.0)After turning right follow the unmade road[Irrigation channel on your left] (0.6)Take the left fork beside the gas sub-station[Remain beside the water course] (2.2)At the T-junction turn left on the embankment - argine[River in the distance on your right](2.5)Turn right remaining on the argine and rejoin the "Official Route"[River in the distance on your right]

Length:	2.6km
Ascent:	12m
Descent:	16m

Direct Route to Piazenca Centre

Route: this alternative route will save 1.3 km at the expense of remaining beside the via Emilia Pavese. (0.0)At the next roundabout continue straight beside via Emilia Parvese[Autostrada entrance to your left](0.7)At the roundabout in piazzale Torino turn left on via XXI Aprile[Fountain in roundabout] (2.1)Continue straight ahead beside the main road[Via Emilia Pavese](2.4)At the next roundabout, go straight ahead on via Campagna. Note:- direct route rejoins from the right[Pass park and citadel walls on the left]

Length:	2.4km
Ascent:	14m
Descent:	20m

Orio Litta to Piacenza — stage 61

Accommodation and Tourist Information

Calendasco

Ostello le Tre Corone, Via Mazzini Nuova, 59, 29010 Calendasco(PC), Italy; Tel:+39 3406 322837; Email:info@trecorone.it; www.trecorone.it; Price:C; *Private rooms available at additional cost*

Agriturismo - Il Tramonto Sul Po, Località Masero, 2, 29010 Calendasco(PC), Italy; Tel:+39 335 6001065; Email:ilemerline@yahoo.it; visitpiacenza.it/en/accomodation/agriturismo-il-tramonto-sul-po; Price:B

Piacenza

Ostello San Pietro [Don Pietro Bulla], Via Emilia Parmense, 73, 29100 Piacenza(PC), Italy; Tel:+39 0523 614256; +39 3331 493595; Email:sanlazzaro@libero.it; www.parrocchiasanlazzaropiacenza.com/ostello-sulla-via-francigena; Price:C; *The key is obtained at this address but the accommodation is a further 2km at N° 189 on the old via Emilia*

Ostello del Teatro, Via Trento, 29c, 29122 Piacenza(PC), Italy; Tel:+39 0523 469599; +39 3298 521350; Email:info@ostellodelteatro.it; www.ostellodelteatro.it; Price:B

Ostello Papa Giovanni XXIII, Cantone San Nazzaro, 2a, 29100 Piacenza(PC), Italy; Tel:+39 0523 490104; Email:info@ostellodipiacenza.it; www.ostellodipiacenza.it; Price:B

Santuario Santa Maria di Campagna, Piazzale delle Crociate, 5, 29121 Piacenza(PC), Italy; Tel:+39 523490729; Email:santamariadicampagna@gmail.com; santamariadicampagna.com; Price:D

B&B - Angela, Via Giuseppe Mazzini, 88, 29100 Piacenza(PC), Italy; Tel:+39 3396408589; Email:angela.aime48@gmail.com; Price:A

Hotel - VIP, Via Vittorio Cipelli, 41, 29100 Piacenza(PC), Italy; Tel:+39 0523 715139; +39 3381 730718; Email:info@viphotel.it; www.viphotel.it; Price:B

Associazione Europea delle Vie Francigene, Palazzo Farnese - piazza Cittadella 29, 29121 Piacenza(PC), Italy; Tel:+39 0523 492792; +39 0523 492793; Email:segreteria@viefrancigene.org; www.viefrancigene.org

Informazione Turistica, Piazza Cavalli, 7, 29121 Piacenza(PC), Italy; Tel:+39 0523 492001; Email:iat@comune.piacenza.it; visitpiacenza.it

stage 62 — Piacenza to Fiorenzuola-d'Arda

Length:	31.5km
Ascent:	243m
Descent:	224m
Col Grand St Bernard:	330km
Rome:	698km

Castello di Paderna

Route: a long stage from Piacenza to Fiorenzuola-d'Arda meandering through isolated farmland on minor roads and tracks, but occasionally passing grand fortified buildings that hint at its history.

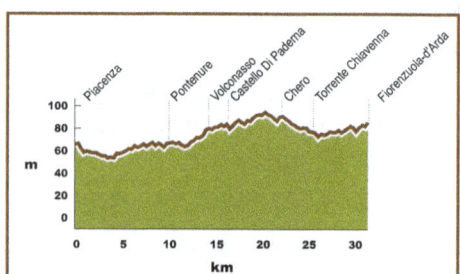

The "Official Route" exit from Piacenza initially follows or parallels the very busy via Emilia including a dangerous section without pavements.

There is an opportunity to take a break in Pontenure, Volcanasso or Chero.

Fiorenzuola-d'Arda has a good choice of accommodation and other facilities.

Fiorenzuola-d'Arda is an attractive stopping place, this little town's name is derived from Florentia, meaning prosperous and d'Arda, which refers to the river Arda flowing from the Apennine Mountains into the valley, where Fiorenzuola is situated. It is also claimed the name could have been chosen in honour of Fiorenzo of Tours, who was said to have performed a miracle there while on his way to Rome in the 6th century.

Fiorenzuola-d'Arda was the most important stopping place for pilgrims, after Piacenza. Towards the end of the 11th century, King of Denmark, Henry I Svendsson, established a hospital there. Records also note the presence of a monastic institution entrusted to Tommaso, bishop of Piacenza.

🛏 **(0.0)** From the church of Sant'Antonino continue straight ahead on via Sant'Antonino and via Scalabrini [Church to the right] **(0.5)** In piazzale Roma continue straight ahead on the right side of the long, straight via Emilia Parmense [Pass a sculpture of Romulus and Remus] 🛏 **(2.2)** Shortly after passing the roundabout for Carpaneto, turn left on Via G. Modonesi [Pass the Conad supermarket on your left] **(2.4)** Turn left vand then right on Via Carlo Barbieri [Railway parallel on your left] **(2.9)** At the end of the road, take the cycle track and then bear right across the car park beside the cemetery [Via G. Maggi] 🛏 **(3.3)** At the roundabout, take the pedestrian crossing on the left and continue straight ahead on the cycle track on the left side of via Martelli 🛏 **(5.3)** Bear right, away from the railway tracks

Piacenza to Fiorenzuola-d'Arda stage 62

and then turn left on via Modena [Pass play area on your right] (**6.6**)At the roundabout at the end of the industrial zone, turn left and carefully follow the via Emilia Parmese [Direction Pontenure] (**8.3**)Immediately before the roundabout, turn left on the short track and then follow the minor road [Strada Privata] (**10.1**)At the Stop sign in **Pontenure**, turn left and then right on via Guglielmo Marconi(**10.7**)At the end of the road, turn right(**11.0**)At the roundabout bear left [Direction Volconasso] (**14.7**)At the T-junction in **Volconasso**, turn left and then right [Pass a factory on your right] (**15.4**)Continue straight ahead remain on the road as it bends to the left (**16.4**)At the crossroads, shortly after passing **Castello di Paderna**, turn right(**17.2**)At the T-junction,turn left [Towards Montanaro] (**17.6**)Turn left on via Napoli(**18.2**)Bear right on the elevated track in front of Chiesa San Michele Arcangelo and keep right as you return to the road (**19.0**)At the T-junction with the main road, turn right and then take the first road on the left [Direction

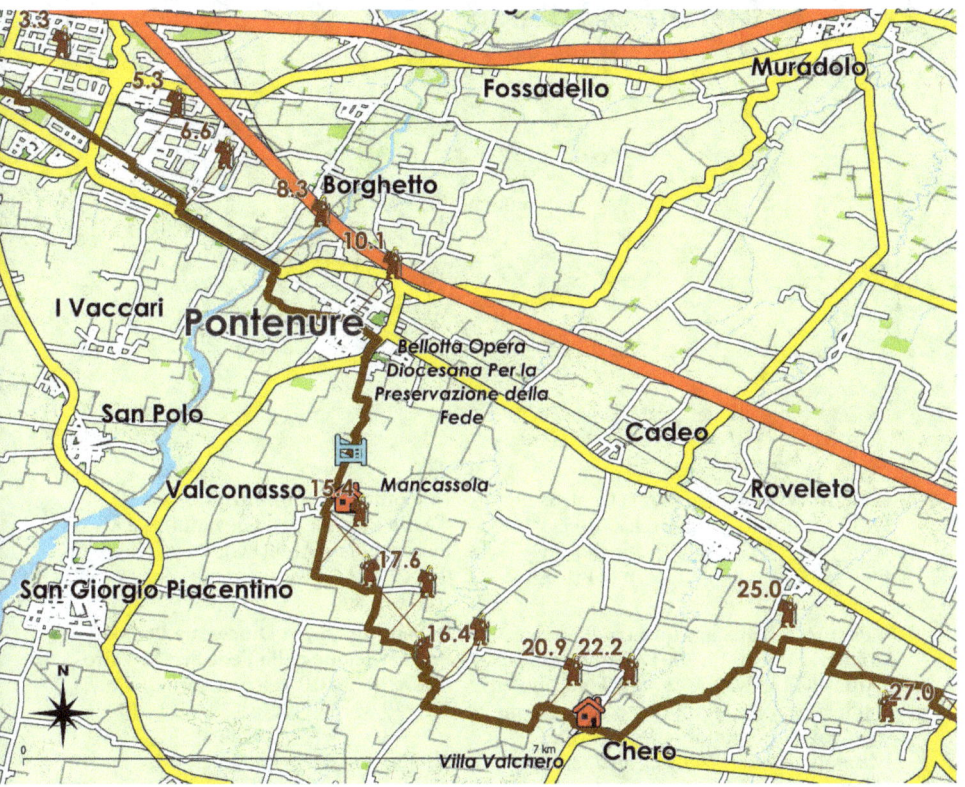

Cerreto Landi] (**20.9**)At the end of the long straight road, turn left(**21.5**)Turn right [Pass the cemetery on your left](**21.8**)Bear right towards the village of Chero [Keep the church on your left] (**22.2**)At the crossroads in the centre of **Chero**, continue straight ahead [Pizzeria on your right](**22.4**)At the T-junction, turn right and join the main road(**22.8**)Immediately bedore the water treatment plant, turn left (**25.0**)At the junction, bear left [Via Emilia 2km](**25.6**)Take the next turning to the right and take the stepping stones over **torrente Chiavenna**(**25.9**)Shortly after crossing the stream turn left and then right and

stage 62 — Piacenza to Fiorenzuola-d'Arda

pass between 2 farms 🏠 **(27.0)**At the T-junction with the tarmac road, turn right**(27.4)**Immediately after passing farm buildings, close on the left side of the road, turn left on the unmade road [Strada Vicinale della Felina] 🏠 **(29.0)**Turn right on the tarmac road**(29.3)** Bear left and remain on the tarmac [Towards the highway]**(29.8)**At the road junction after the underpass continue straight ahead 🏠 **(30.7)**Follow the main road to the left [Enter Fiorenzuola-d'Arda]**(31.0)**Turn right on the cycle track [Cross the bridge over the river Arda]**(31.1)**Bear left towards the main road**(31.2)**Take the pedestrian crossing over the main road and turn right and follow Corso Giuseppe Garibaldi towards the centre of the town [Keep the water tower on your left]**(31.3)**Continue straight ahead on the main street [Corso Giuseppe Garibaldi]**(31.5)**Arrive at **Fiorenzuola-d'Arda (XXXVII)** centre [Crossroads with via della Liberazione]

Accommodation and Tourist Information

Chero
🏠 **B&B - Villa Valchero**,Via Centro, 28, 29013 Chero(PC), Italy; Tel:+39 0523 852376; +39 3473 200502; Email:info@villavalchero.it; villavalchero.it; Price:A

Fiorenzuola-d'Arda
⛪**Parrocchia di San Fiorenzo**,Piazza Molinari Fratelli, 15, 29017 Fiorenzuola-d'Arda(PC), Italy; Tel:+39 0523 982247; Email:ufficiparrocchiasanfiorenzo@gmail.com; www.parrocchiasanfiorenzo.it; Price:C; *Warm welcome centrally located rooms redecorated* ; **PR**

🛏 **Hotel - Mathis**,Viale Giacomo Matteotti, 68, 29017 Fiorenzuola-d'Arda(PC), Italy; Tel:+39 0523 943800; Email:info@mathis.it; mathis.it; Price:A

🛏 **Hotel - Bastimento**,Via 20 Settembre, 54, 29017 Fiorenzuola-d'Arda(PC), Italy; Tel:+39 0523 982827; Email:info@hotelbastimento.com; www.hotelbastimento.com; Price:B; *Choice of B&B or hostel accommodation*

ℹ **Comune di Fiorenzuola d'Arda**,Piazzale San Giovanni, 2, 29017 Fiorenzuola-d'Arda(PC), Italy; Tel:+39 0523 9891; www.comune.fiorenzuola.pc.it

Valconasso
⛪**Bellotta Opera Diocesana Per la Preservazione della Fede**,Strada Valconasso, 10, 29010 Valconasso(PC), Italy; Tel:+39 0523 517110; +39 0523 510896; +39 3703 406124; Email:labellotta@virgilio.it; www.bellotta.net; Price:B; *Advance booking necessary*

🏠 **Agriturismo Mancassola**,Via Milano, 48, 29010 Valconasso(PC), Italy; Tel:+39 0523 519875; +39 3356 621198; +39 3333 265938; Email:info@agriturismomancassola.it; www.agriturismomancassola.it; Price:A

Fiorenzuola-d'Arda to Fidenza

stage 63

Length:	22.3km
Ascent:	159m
Descent:	162m
Col Grand St Bernard:	362km
Rome:	666km

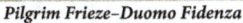

Pilgrim Frieze–Duomo Fidenza

Route: a gentle stage Fiorenzuola-d'Arda to Fidenza on level ground generally using country roads and passing beside the Abbey of Chiaravalle de Colomba.

There is a café beside the abbey but few other opportunities for refreshment before the large and thriving town of Fidenza.

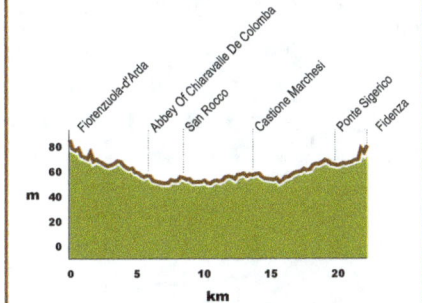

For a considerable number of years, Fidenza was known as Borgo San Donninore (in honour of Saint Domninus), but it was renamed Fidenza in 1927, recalling its Roman name of Fidentia. In Roman times, the town was an important staging point on the via Emilia, but during the Middle Ages it was almost completely abandoned, until the remains of St Donnino were rediscovered in a grave on the eastern bank of the river Stirone. This was followed by a series of other miracles–the healing of a sick man, the location of a stolen horse, and the preservation of a number of believers when the bridge collapsed. The town has suffered destruction at the hands of the troops of Parma and most recently the Allies during the Second World War, but has been carefully restored and developed.

The Fidenza Cathedral/Duomo, constructed in the 12th century, was dedicated to Saint Domninus. The saint's relics were brought to Fidenza in 1207, and are believed to be contained in an urn in the crypt. The cathedral is an example of the Lombard-Romanesque style. The upper part of the façade is incomplete, but the lower, with its three portals and sculptures, is a fine example of Romanesque architecture, including two statues by Benedetto Antelami and bas-reliefs depicting the Histories of St. Domninus. The interior is simple and well-proportioned, and has not been spoilt by restoration. The statue of the apostle Simon Peter, at the front of the cathedral, is famous for its pointing in the direction of Rome.

(0.0) From the centre of Fiorenzuola, near n° 55 Corso Garibaldi, turn left onto the narrow street [Via della Liberazione]**(0.1)** At the crossroads, continue straight ahead on the tree lined road [Direction Busseto]**(0.3)** Pass under the railway and bear right on the road [Viale dei Tigli]**(0.9)** Just after passing the cemetery turn right [Towards agriturismo Battibue] **(3.1)** At the T-junction at the end of the road turn right [Towards the farm on the

stage 63 — Fiorenzuola-d'Arda to Fidenza

left of the road]**(3.6)**Turn left on the road [Towards Chiaravalle] (**5.8**)Continue straight ahead [Towards the Abbey courtyard]**(5.9)**In front of the **Abbey of Chiaravalle de Colomba** bear left to follow the road [Towards Busseto]**(6.6)**Continue straight ahead [Cross the Autostrada bridge] **(8.2)**Bear left on the road and ignore the junction to the right [Beside Cascina Ongina]**(8.5)**Continue straight ahead on strada Borre [Beside the entrance to the village of **San Rocco**]**(8.8)**Turn right [Before reaching church] **(9.4)**At the T-junction at the end of the road turn left [Industrial area ahead at junction]**(9.6)**Take the next turning to the right [Strada Orsi]**(9.9)**Bear right on the tarmac [Pass a barn on the right]**(10.1)**Bear left on the unmade road [Entrance to farm on the right] **(10.7)**At the crossroads, turn right [Bridge ahead]**(11.6)**Continue straight ahead on strada Fossa Superiore [Ignore the turning on the tarmac road to the left] **(12.0)**At the T-junction with a tarmac road turn left [Strada Portone] **(13.4)**At the T-junction, turn left [Direction Fidenza]**(13.5)**At the traffic lights, turn right [Direction Fidenza]**(13.8)**After rounding the first bend in **Castione Marchesi**, turn left [Towards Bastelli] **(13.9)**At the T-junction turn right [Towards Bastelli] **(14.8)**Continue straight ahead on the long straight road [Cross the railway] **(16.0)**At the T-junction turn right [Towards Bastelli] **(17.0)**In hamlet of Bastelli with silos on the right, turn left [Towards Soragna] **(17.1)**Turn right on the road and cross the railway and Autostrada [Towards Fidenza] **(19.0)**Shortly before reaching the power lines,

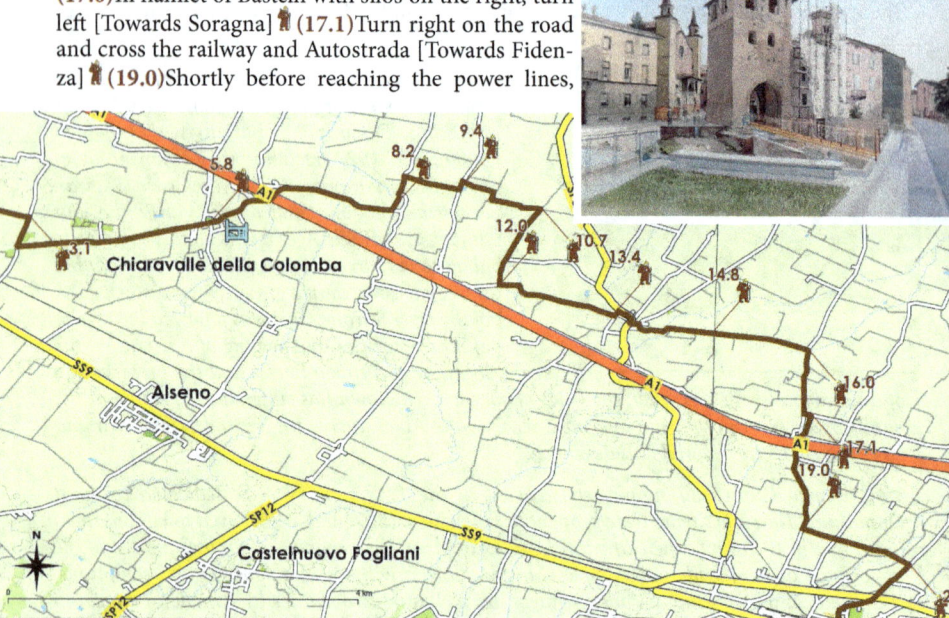
Piazza Grandi - Fidenza

turn left [Towards Fidenza]**(19.4)**At the mini-roundabout, continue straight ahead [Direction Fidenza]**(19.8)**Continue straight ahead [Cross **Ponte Sigerico**] **(20.3)**Keep right on the main road**(21.0)**Continue straight ahead [Pass under highway] **(21.6)**At the traffic lights turn right under the railway [Car park on the left at the junction]**(21.8)**After emerging from under the railway, turn right direction Duomo [Pass Hotel Astoria on the left] **(22.1)**Continue straight ahead at the roundabout and then quickly bear left towards the old city gate [Piazza Grandi]**(22.3)**Arrive at **Fidenza (XXXVI)** centre [Piazza Cremoni, beside the Duomo]

Fiorenzuola-d'Arda to Fidenza — stage 63

Accommodation and Tourist Information

Chiaravalle
Abbazia Chiaravalle della Colomba, Via San Bernardo, 29010 Chiaravalle(PC), Italy; Tel:+3932702894051; +39 0523 940132; Email:abbazia.chiaravalle@gmail.com; www.chiaravalledellacolomba.it; Price:D; *4 beds*

Fidenza
Albergo - Ugolini, Via Cornini Malpeli, 90, 43036 Fidenza(PR), Italy; Tel:+39 0524 522422; +39 0524 83264; Email:albergo.ugolini@gmail.com; www.albergougolinifidenza.it; Price:B

Hotel - Astoria, Via Gandolfi, 5, 43036 Fidenza(PR), Italy; Tel:+39 0524 524314; Email:Info@hotelastoriafidenza.it; www.hotelastoriafidenza.it ; Price:A

Hotel - Fidenza, Via Galileo Ferraris, 2, 43036 Fidenza(PR), Italy; Tel:+39 0524 82718; +39 3297346430; +39 3286634310; Email:info@www.hotelfidenza.it; www.hotelfidenza.it; Price:B

Albergo - San Donnino, Via Agostino Berenini, 134, 43036 Fidenza(PR), Italy; Tel:+39 0524-071438; +393889214014; Email:hotelsandonnino@gmail.com; web.facebook.com/SanDonnino134; Price:B; *Basic 2 star hotel*

Affittacamere - al Duomo, Via Arnaldo Da Brescia, 2, 43036 Fidenza(PR), Italy; Tel: +39 3475 819065; Email:affittacamerealduomo@hotmail.com; www.affittacamerealduomo.it; Price:C; *Pilgrim discount*

Informazione e Accoglienza Turistica, Casa Cremonini - piazza Duomo, 16, 43036 Fidenza(PR), Italy; Tel:+39 0524 83377; Email:iat.fidenza@terrediverdi.it; www.terrediverdi.it

Duomo Fidenza

stage 64 — Fidenza to Fornovo-di-Taro

Siccomonte–La Chiesa di San Giovanni Decollato

Length:	34.0km
Ascent:	901m
Descent:	838m
Col Grand St Bernard:	384km
Rome:	644km

Route: the well marked route from Fidenza to Fornovo-di-Taro begins to climb into the beautiful, rolling foothills of the Apennines. The long stage is largely conducted on small country roads and tracks and can be challenging in hot weather and so be sure to carry enough water.

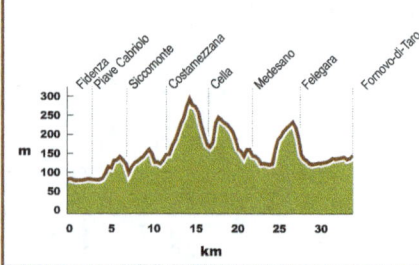

For the next few days you will be travelling in the province of Parma that has provided some excellent support for the via Francigena. Costamezzana is a very small and isolated village but offers a warm welcome to pilgrims.

There are additional opportunities for a break in Cella, Medesano or as you approach the Taro valley. Accommodation choices in Fornovo can be limited, but the tourist office is always helpful.

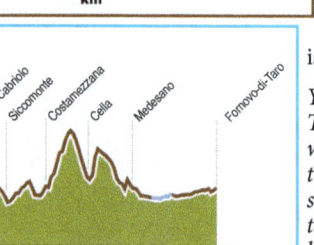

You will pass beside the church dedicated to Thomas Becket. Born around 1120, he was well educated and quickly became an agent to Theobald, Archbishop of Canterbury, who sent him on several missions to Rome. Becket's talents were noticed by Henry II, who made him his chancellor and the two became close friends. When Theobald died in 1161, Henry made Becket archbishop, after which he transformed himself from a pleasure-loving courtier into a serious, simply-dressed cleric. The friendship was put under strain when it became clear that Becket would stand up for the church in its disagreements with the king. In 1164, realising the extent of Henry's displeasure, Becket fled to France, and remained in exile for several years. He returned in 1170. On the 29 December 1170, four knights, believing the king wanted Becket out of the way, confronted and murdered him in Canterbury Cathedral. Becket was made a saint in 1173.

In Roman times, Fornovo di Taro was an important roadway settlement on the Parma-Lucca road, a market town known as Forum Novum and perhaps also a place of worship on the east bank of the Taro River. The church of Santa Maria Assunta incorporates the statue of a pilgrim in its façade, indicating the direction of the route as a permanent sign

Fidenza to Fornovo-di-Taro — stage 64

🚶(0.0)From piazza Cremoni beside the Duomo pass in front of the church and turn left to skirt the church [Church on the left](0.1)At the rear of the church turn right [Pedestrian zone, via Micheli](0.2)Continue straight ahead across the small square and take via Antini(0.3)Continue straight ahead in piazza del Palazzo, pass under the porch and turn right [Via Amendola](0.4)At the end of the road, bear left across the small park [Keep the playground on your left](0.5)At the roundabout turn right into the tree lined street [Via Gramsci](0.8)At the roundabout, cross the main road – via 24 Maggio – and bear a little to the left towards the trees [Via Caduti di Cefalonia] 🚶(1.7)At the roundabout continue straight ahead on the cycle track [Sports ground to the right before the roundabout](2.0)Continue straight ahead on the pedestrian and cycle track on the right side of the road [Open field on your left](2.2)Continue straight ahead [Footpath sign and small wooden bridge on the left](2.4)Shortly after passing a large house on the left, bear left on the tree lined track 🚶(2.8)Bear right into the trees [Towards the buildings](2.9)Turn left on the tarmac driveway Note:- to your right is **Piave Cabriolo** (dedicated to Thomas Becket) [Bell tower on your right at the junction](3.0)At the T-junction with the main road, turn left(3.2)Take the first turning to the right [Towards the trees](3.5)Continue straight ahead on the gravel road [Ignore the turning to the right] 🚶(4.4)Turn right towards the hilltop [Via Cabriolo](5.1)At the junction with a tarmac road – on a sharp bend – turn left [Uphill, towards the top of the ridge] 🚶(6.2)At the junction, turn left [Towards Siccomonte](7.0)In front of the Chiesa di **Siccomonte** turn right then left on the grassy path, downhill [Keep church to the left](7.2)Leave the grass and turn left on the gravel track 🚶(7.6)At the T-junction at the top of the hill, turn right on the tarmac road [Direction Tabiano] 🚶(9.8)Take the left fork [Towards Pieve Cusignano](10.2)At the T-junction, at the bottom of the hill, turn right, towards Costamezzana [Osteria on your left at the junction](10.3)Turn left [Towards Costamezzana](10.7)Keep left [Towards Costamezzana] 🚶(11.7)From the junction at the entrance to **Costamezzana**, turn towards the Castello(11.9)At the crossroads, just before reaching the farm, turn left [Via Costa Canali](12.0)Take the narrow road to the left [Towards the Hostaria Castello] 🚶(13.1)Beside the Castello di Costamezzana bear left and remain on the broad track [Keep the trees close on your right] 🚶(14.3)At the T-junction, turn left on the tarmac road [Towards the houses on the skyline](14.4)At the T-junction with the road turn right [Leaving via Costa Canali](15.0)On the crown of the bend to the right, take the track downhill to the left [Towards a small wood] 🚶(15.4)Turn left [Pass large barns below on the right](15.7)Continue straight ahead [Pass a farm on your left](16.0)Bear right towards the road below(16.2)At the T-junction turn left on the grass track [Road below on the right](16.3)At the junction with the tarmac road, continue straight ahead, then bear right downhill 🚶(16.5)At the T-junction with the main road, turn left and follow the pavement on the left [Car parks on the right and left at junction](16.7)In the centre of **Cella**, cross the road and continue straight ahead with care on the other side [Restaurant on the left](16.8)Just after a slight bend to the right in the road, turn right on

Thomas Becket church

stage 64 — Fidenza to Fornovo-di-Taro

the track [House on the right]**(17.0)**Cross the river ford and continue straight ahead [Between fields and steeply uphill] **(17.8)**At the T-junction, after a steep climb, turn left on a tarmac road [Large house on the hilltop to the right] **(19.1)**At a bend in the road to the left, continue straight ahead on an unmade road [Pass between farm buildings] **(20.1)**At the T-junction, turn left on the track and follow the gravel track close to the hay barn **(21.4)**At the crossroads, at the top of the hill, in the hamlet of Arduini, continue straight ahead [Via Giuseppe Verdi]**(22.0)**At the roundabout, at the entry to **Medesano (XXXV)**, continue straight ahead [Towards the spire] **(22.6)**Before reaching the main road turn right into the church grounds. Pass the church - Parrocchia San Pantaleone - entrance on your right and descend the steps to the main road and turn right**(23.3)**Take the pedestrian crossing and continue on the left side of the road **(24.3)**Shortly after entering Carnevala, turn right on via G. la Pira. Note:- 2km may be saved and an additional climb avoided if you continue straight ahead on the cycle track, bear left at the next roundabout and continue on the minor road - no pavements - to the roundabout in Felegara where the "Official Route" joins from the right**(24.5)**Just after crossing the small bridge, bear left and then immediately right on the road [Pass conifers on your left]**(24.9)**Follow the road as it turns right [Metal gate ahead at the turning]**(25.2)**Turn left on the road [Uphill towards the houses]**(25.3)**Beside the farm bear right on the grassy track **(25.4)**Bear left on the track [Straight track along the ridge] **(26.0)**Continue straight ahead on the gravel road [Driveway to a house on the right]

The Taro river on the approach to Fornovo di Taro

Fidenza to Fornovo-di-Taro

stage 64

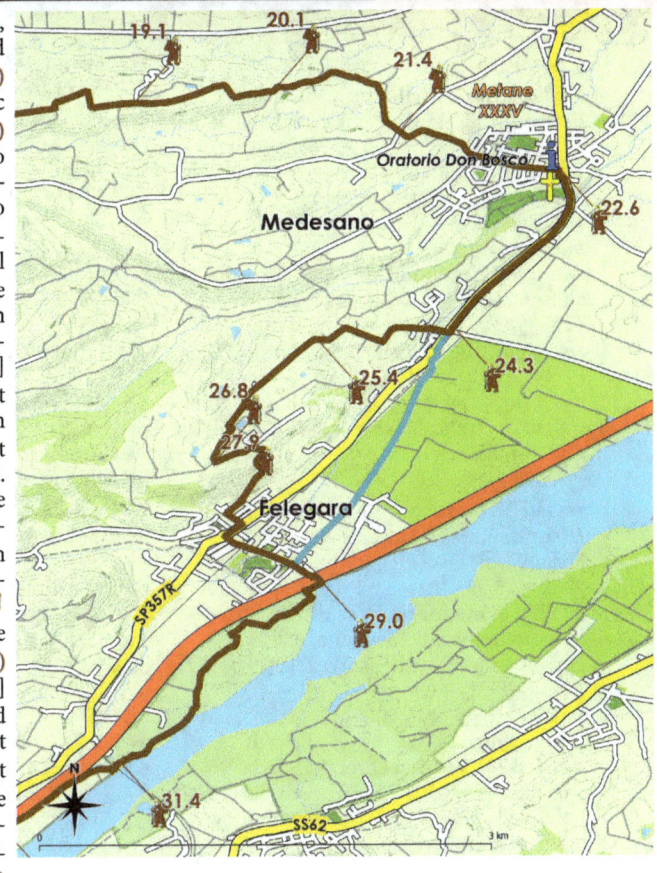

(26.8) At the T-junction, turn left on the tarmac road [Shrine on the left] **(27.1)** Turn right on the tarmac road [Steep descent] **(27.7)** On the crown of a bend to the left, on the entry **Felegara**, turn right [Via Damiano Chiesa] **(27.9)** At the T-junction, turn left, downhill [Via Campioni] **(28.0)** At the T-junction with the main road, turn right [Via Repubblica towards the pharmacy] **(28.2)** At the roundabout with a fountain, turn left **(28.7)** At the roundabout continue straight ahead. Note:- the Alternate Route joins from the left [Via Pattigna] **(28.8)** Bear right on the track under the Autostrada [Chain barrier] **(29.0)** At the exit from the underpass, turn right **(29.1)** Turn left [Towards the river] **(29.3)** Ford the stream and continue straight ahead **(29.6)** Take the right fork **(29.7)** Turn left on the footpath [Parallel to the Autostrada] **(29.9)** At the T-junction, turn left **(31.4)**.

Santa Maria Assunta - facade

Cross the stream, pass under the railway bridge and bear right [Keeping the quarry on the left] **(32.5)** Take the left fork away from the motorway and close beside the quarry [Beside Fornace Grigolin and further barrier] **(32.8)** On reaching the football field, turn right [Keep football field to the left] **(32.9)** Turn left in the parking area [Keep football field on the left] **(33.1)** At the T-junction with the main road, turn left and cross the bridge over the river Taro [Bar ahead at the junction] **(33.7)** At the end of the pedestrian path, turn right and descend the steps into the car park and then turn left to follow via Pietro Zuffardi. Note:- cyclists should continue on the bridge and take the next left turn and turn left again to reach the car park **(33.9)** At the end of the road turn right and immediately left in the small piazza **(33.9)** Bear right across piazza Giacomo Matteotti [Direction Duomo, via 20 Settembre] **(34.0)** Arrive at **Fornovo-di-Taro (XXXIV)** centre [Piazza IV Novembre in front of the Duomo]

stage 64 — Fidenza to Fornovo-di-Taro

Accommodation and Tourist Information

Costamezzana
Famiglie del Pellegrino,Via Costa Pavesi, 47, 43015 Costamezzana(PR), Italy; Tel: +39 324 6073800; +39 3356 398600; Email:info@famigliadelpellegrino.it ; www.famigliadelpellegrino.it; Price:C; *Newly renovated house with 6 beds and washing machine*; **PR**
Ostello Comunale di Costamezzana,Via all'Isola, 1, 43015 Costamezzana(PR), Italy; Tel:+39 0521 622137; +39 0521629149; www.parmawelcome.it/it/scheda/organizza-il-tuo-viaggio/dove-dormire/ostelli/ostello-di-costamezzana; Price:C; *Helpful staff at the trattoria where pilgrim menus are also available* ; **PR**

Fornovo-di-Taro
Ostello Parrochia Santa Maria Assunta,Piazza 4 Novembre, 43045 Fornovo-di-Taro(PR), Italy; Tel:+39 0525 2218; +39 3332194636; Price:D
Villa Santa Maria Casa di Esercizi Spirituali,Località Magnana, 43045 Fornovo-di-Taro(PR), Italy; Tel:+39 0525 2347; +39 327 6786108; Email:accoglienza@villasantamariafornovo.it; villasantamariafornovo.it; Price:B
B&B - la Vecchia Quercia,Strada Spagnano, 29, 43045 Fornovo-di-Taro(PR), Italy; Tel: +39 3343 545492; Email:info@beblavecchiaquercia.it; www.beblavecchiaquercia.it; Price:A; **PR**

Locanda - Al Ponte,Via Solferino, 2, 43045 Fornovo-di-Taro(PR), Italy; Tel: +39 328 441 2091; Email:faver29@libero.it; web.facebook.com/profile.php?id=100054244550292; Price:B
IAT Fornovo Tourist Office,Via XXIV Maggio, 2, 43045 Fornovo-di-Taro(PR), Italy; Tel:+39 0525 2599; Email:iatfornovo@gmail.com; web.facebook.com/iatfornovo.ufficioturistico

Medesano
Oratorio Don Bosco,Via Conciliazione, 2, 43014 Medesano(PR), Italy; Tel:+39 0525 420447; Email:fra.pon@virgilio.it; www.parrocchiadimedesano.com; Price:D
Comune di Medesano,Piazza Guglielmo Marconi, 6, 43014 Medesano(PR), Italy; Tel:+39 0525 422711; www.comune.medesano.pr.it

Noceto
Fraternità Francescana di Betania,San Pio Da Pietralcina, 43015 Noceto(PR), Italy; Tel:+39 0521 624052; +39 0521 624582; +39 3488 860440; Email:cella.noceto@ffbetania.net; www.ffbetania.net; Price:D
B&B - Civico 75,Via Gabbiano, 75, 43015 Noceto(PR), Italy; Tel: +39 3293 353532; Email:bbcivico75@gmail.com; www.bbcivico75.it; Price:B; *Eco friendly accommodation 2km from the route*

Fornovo-di-Taro to Cassio

stage 65

Length:	21.5km
Ascent:	1554m
Descent:	906m
Col Grand St Bernard:	418km
Rome:	610km

Towards Terenzo

Route: from Fornovo-di-Taro to Cassio this first stage of the climb to the summit of the Cisa Pass begins on minor roads and the SP39 before taking to forest and mountain tracks.

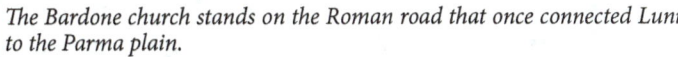
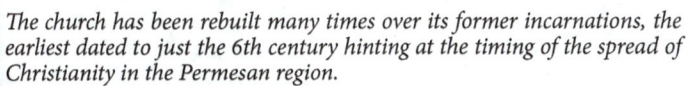

If you are travelling in spring, autumn or winter then there is the risk of snow near the summit (1200m). Some of the tracks are narrow, steep and over broken ground. The route includes a number of short stretches on the SS62, which is a favourite with high-speed motorcycle groups particularly on Sundays and holidays.

There is an opportunity to take a break a Sivizzano, but there are no other possibilities for refreshments until you reach the village of Cassio.

The Bardone church stands on the Roman road that once connected Luni to the Parma plain.

The church has been rebuilt many times over its former incarnations, the earliest dated to just the 6th century hinting at the timing of the spread of Christianity in the Permesan region.

(0.0)From the Duomo in Fornovo di Taro, take via XXIV Maggio [Pass the Duomo on the left](0.1)Cross piazza Tarasconi and continue straight ahead [Kiosk on the right, pedestrian zone](0.2)Cross the main road (SS62) and continue straight ahead on via Guglielmo Marconi [Pass bank on the right](0.4)At the end of the pavement bear left on the road uphill [Via Guglielmo Marconi](0.5)Follow the road as it turns right and winds up the hill [Via Guglielmo Marconi](0.7)Bear left on the road (1.1)Continue to follow the road to the left as it climbs the hill [Avoid road to right](1.5)Continue straight ahead [Direction Caselle] (2.5)At the fork in **Caselle**, bear right, downhill [Narrow road, shrine on the left](3.1)Bear right and downhill on the tarmac road [House on the hill to your left] (3.5)Take the right fork downhill [Towards the main road](3.6)At the T-junction at the bottom of the hill turn left on the main road, SP39 [Metal fence on

stage 65 — Fornovo-di-Taro to Cassio

embankment on your left] 🚶(**5.3**)Continue straight ahead on strada Val Sporzona [Ignore the turning to San Vitale] 🚶(**7.8**)Continue straight ahead on the SP39 [Village of **Sivizzano** to the right](**8.1**)The "Official Route" continues straight ahead on the road. Note:- if you need some relief from the tarmac the Alternate Route follows a marked path through the woods on the left 🚶(**9.3**)Continue straight ahead on the road. Note:- the Alternate Route rejoins from the left [Pass modern bungalow on your right](**9.9**)Fork right on the road

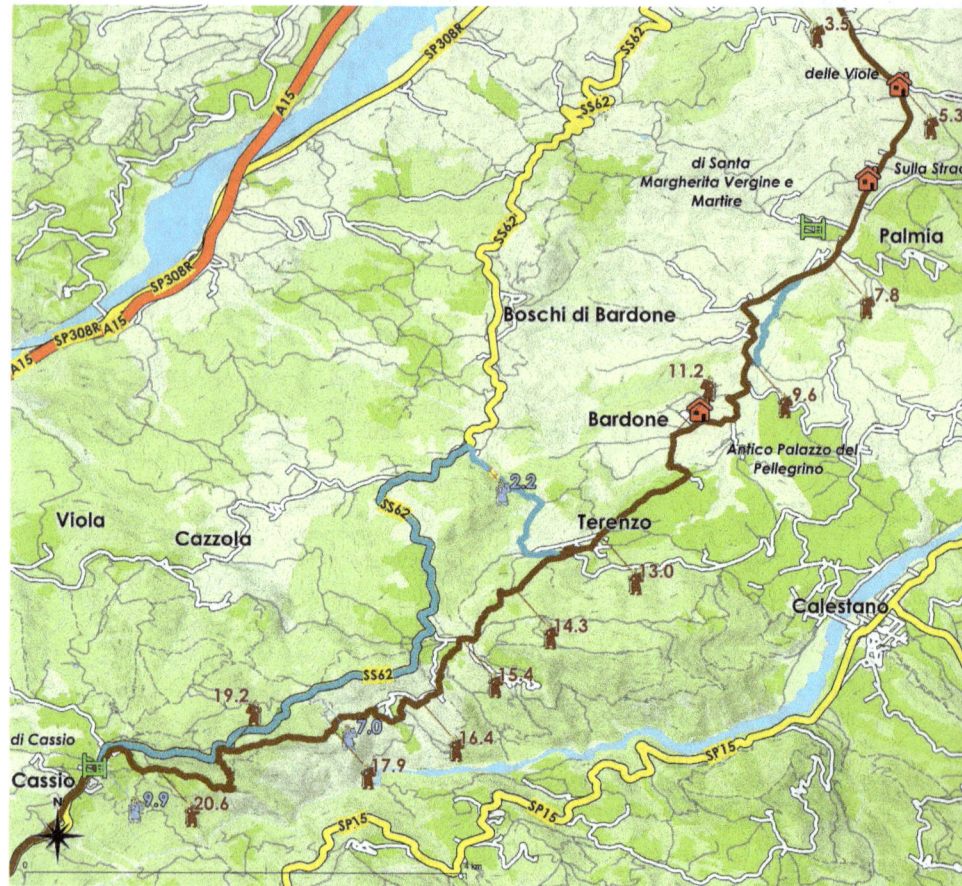

[Direction Bardone] 🚶(**11.2**)After passing through **Bardone** bear left [Strada Ca'di Bardone to the right](**11.8**)Bear right up the hill [Ca'di Fucinello to the left] 🚶(**13.0**)Fork left into **Terenzo** [Strada della Posta](**13.1**)At the T-junction, in front of the Piave di Terenzo turn right [Strada della Posta](**13.2**)Fork left up a small paved passageway(**13.4**)At the T-junction, turn left uphill [Via Capoluogo](**13.5**)Turn left at the top of the hill. Note:- the route ahead is off-road and strenuous with steep climbs over broken ground. Cyclists are advised to turn right on the Alternate Route joining the SS62(**13.6**)Turn right onto an unmade road 🚶(**14.3**)Continue straight ahead on the track [Fence on your right](**14.8**)Con-

Fornovo-di-Taro to Cassio   stage 65

tinue straight ahead towards the top of the hill **(15.2)** Bear right on the widening track **(15.3)** At the T-junction, turn right onto a minor road [Towards the large pylon] 🚶 **(15.4)** Just after passing the house on the left, turn left on the grassy path [Towards the church tower] **(15.9)** Continue straight ahead on the track [Citi di Bardone route] **(16.1)** In **Castello di Casola** cross the tarmac road and continue straight ahead [Downhill] 🚶 **(16.4)** Cross the track and continue straight ahead on the faint path [Between the trees] **(16.7)** Fork right [Towards the houses] **(16.8)** Turn right between the houses in Villa di Casola [Strada Vici Villa] **(16.9)** Continue straight ahead on the tarmac and then bear right [Wooden fence on the left] **(16.9)** Take the left fork [Strada Cà Chioldi] **(17.0)** Continue straight ahead at the crossroads [Strada della Fontana] **(17.1)** Proceed straight ahead onto a small track [Garden on the right] **(17.2)** At the T-junction turn left **(17.3)** Turn left onto the grassy track 🚶  **(17.9)** Cross the unmade road and continue straight ahead on the footpath **(18.6)** At the junction following a bend in the track, continue straight ahead [Signpost to Cassio] **(18.8)** Take the left fork. Note:- cyclists and walkers in wet conditions may find the route ahead difficult. If in doubt, continue straight ahead to the road junction and turn left for the final kilometre to Cassio 🚶 **(19.2)** At the junction in the tracks, turn left. Note:- the track to the right again leads to the road **(19.5)** At the junction keep right on the broad track **(19.7)** Turn right on the footpath 🚶 **(20.6)** Join a track and continue straight ahead [Uphill] **(20.6)** Continue straight ahead [Ignore turnings on both sides] **(20.7)** Join a broadening track and turn to the right **(21.1)** Take the right fork [Enter Cassio] **(21.1)** Turn left along the main street through Cassio [Pieve di Cassio ahead] **(21.4)** At the end of the street turn right and then left on the main road – SS62 [Towards the old hostel] **(21.5)** Arrive at **Cassio** [Beside Ostello di Cassio]

Ostello di Cassio

stage 65 — Fornovo-di-Taro to Cassio

A Short Diversion from the SP39

Route: for some relief from the SP39 this short diversion follows woodland paths parallel to the SP39. The track includes a number of river crossings which may be difficult for cyclists or walkers in wet conditions. (0.0) Bear left on the track [Direction Campo Sportivo] (0.1) After crossing the river and passing a group of buildings on your left, turn right on the faint track on the edge of the field [Trees close on your right] (0.4) At the T-junction with broader track, turn right [Towards the river] (0.4) Cross the river and continue straight ahead (0.4) At the T-junction, turn left (0.6) Bear right [River close on the left] (0.7) Take the right fork, then bear left [House on the hill to the right] (0.8) Take the left fork, cross the river and continue straight ahead [Uphill] (1.0) Bear right on the faint track [Field on your left, trees on right] (1.3) Turn right [Over footbridge] (1.4) At the T-junction with the road, turn left and rejoin the "Official Route" [Bungalows ahead at the junction]

Length:	1.4km
Ascent:	39m
Descent:	7m

Cyclist's Diversion

Route: for cyclists and those not wishing to deal with the steepest climbs over broken ground in the woods. (0.0) Turn right on the road [Strada Terenzo-Calestano] (2.2) At T-junction turn left on the main road [SS62 direction Cassio and Berceto] (7.0) Continue straight ahead on the main road (9.9) Arrive in Cassio and rejoin the "Official Route".

Length:	9.9km
Ascent:	784m
Descent:	570m

Accommodation and Tourist Information

Bardone

🏠 **B&B - Antico Palazzo del Pellegrino** [Alessandra Giuffredi],Str. Terenzo - Bardone, 42, 43040 Bardone(60237), Italy; Tel:+39 388 804 8307; Email:anticopalazzodelpellegrino@gmail.com; Price:A

Cavazzola

🏠 **Biutiful** [Federico and Rossana],Località Cavazzola, 70, 43042 Berceto(PR), Italy; Tel:+39 3358 262768; +39 3335287812; Email:against_the_winds@hotmail.com; Price:D; *Reservation recommended*

🏠 **B&B - Le Spine Pub**,Localita Cavazzola, 73, 43042 Berceto(PR), Italy; Tel: +39 3519 956678; Email:lespine.info@gmail.com; lespineberceto.it; Price:B

Fornovo Di Taro

🏠 **Agriturismo Casa delle Viole**,Strada Val Sporzana, 90, 43045 Fornovo Di Taro(PR), Italy; Tel:+39 0525 56344; Email:agriturismocasaviole@alice.it; web.facebook.com/profile.php?id=100054602792387; Price:B; *Pilgrim discount available*

Sivizzano

✉️ **Parrocchia di Santa Margherita Vergine e Martire** [Pietro Adorni],Località Sivizzano Centro, 18, 43045 Fornovo-di-Taro(PR), Italy; Tel:+39 0525 56258; Email:iatfornovo@gmail.com; Price:D; *In the village centre quaint bar close-by;* **PR**

🏠 **B&B - Sulla Strada**,Strada Val Sporzana, 135 - Sivizzano, 43045 Fornovo-di-Taro(PR), Italy; Tel: +39 345 214 2774; Email:bbsullastrada@gmail.com; web.facebook.com/bbsullastrada; Price:B; **PR**

Terenzo

✉️ **Ostello di Cassio**,Loc.Cassio via Nazionale, 43040 Terenzo(PR), Italy; Tel:+39 0525700885; +393516111362; +393479069545; Email:ostello@asp-terenzo.org; web.facebook.com/Ostello-di-Cassio-110641828346368; Price:C; *Open March to October*

Cassio to the Cisa Pass Summit

stage 66

Length: 20.1km

Ascent: 1288m
Descent: 1049m

Col Grand
St Bernard: 440km
Rome: 588km

San Moderanno–Berceto

Route: the "Official Route" from Cassio to the Cisa Pass Summit initially follows the SS62 before making diversions onto forest and farm tracks and descending into the centre of the town of Berceto.

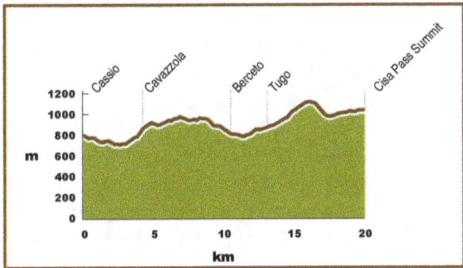

Berceto is the largest town on the road over the pass and offers a good choice of accommodation, restaurants and shops.

Cyclists should plan to remain on the SS62 to avoid the steepest off-road climbs.

The Ostello-della-Cisa is an isolated building that is not permanently staffed. Be sure to telephone in advance to reserve a place. Reaching the large and well equipped Ostello requires leaving the forest path and returning to the SS62. Remaining on the forest path will lead you initially to Monte Valoria (1231m) and then return to the SS62 at the summit of the pass close to the small Capanna Twin refuge.

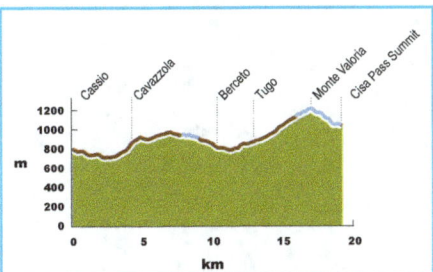

The Cisa Pass runs along the border between the Duchy of Parma and the grand Duchy of Tuscany, while also offering stunning views. Dominated by the chapel of Nostra Signora della Guardia, built in 1921, the pass is part of the via Francigena, but also one of the favourite itineraries in the province of Parma followed by motorbike lovers.

At the top of the pass, in San Giorgio di Filattiera, a memorial tablet records the existence of a hospital for pilgrims dedicated to the Virgin Mary. Such was the importance of the pass that Parma's town council decreed that whoever went to live near the church should be tax exempt, the idea being to encourage the population of the pass and thereby make it safer. "If no one goes there of their accord," the decree continues, "it will rest with the men of Berceto, Valbona, Corchia and Bergotto to send groups of men in shifts throughout the month of May to secure the pass."

stage 66   Cassio to the Cisa Pass Summit

🚶(0.0)Continue straight ahead on the SS62 [Ostello on your right](0.5)On a bend in the road to the left take the footpath to the right [Second track on right after strada Perdella]🚶(1.0)Rejoin the main road and continue straight ahead on the right side of the road [Km 75, SS62]🚶(3.4)On the crown of the bend to the right take the small tarmac road to the left. Note:- cyclists with heavily packed bikes may prefer avoid the steep tracks ahead and remain on the road [Sign Cavazzola di Sopra 700m](3.8)After a stretch on a level track, turn right [Steep forest track uphill](4.3)In **Cavazzola** bear left on the track🚶(4.5)At the fork in the tracks, keep right [Downhill](4.6)Take the left fork(4.8)Join a track and bear left [Under the electricity lines](4.9)Turn right into the main street [Castellonchio](5.0)Bear left, downhill [Church to the right](5.5)Take the last turning to the left before reaching the main road🚶(5.7)Continue straight ahead on the unmade road [Wooden fence on your left](5.9)Take the right fork [On the footpath](5.9)At the junction with the main road turn right, cross over and continue on the left side of the road [SS62](6.1)On the crown of the next bend, turn left on the track [Into the woods](6.3)In the woods take the left fork(6.5)Bear right [Ignore the turning to the left](6.6)Shortly before reaching the main road turn right on the track [Towards the edge of the woods](6.7)Continue straight ahead [Keep close to the woods on your right]🚶(6.9)Bear left [Avoid the turning to the right](7.0)Bear right [Trees on your right, field on your left](7.1)At the T-junction with the road, turn

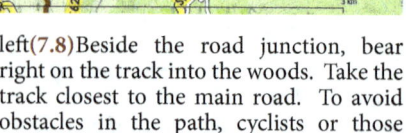

left(7.8)Beside the road junction, bear right on the track into the woods. Take the track closest to the main road. To avoid obstacles in the path, cyclists or those wishing to save a short distance should remain on the road [Pilgrim milestone at the entry to the woods]🚶(7.9)Continue straight ahead over the stile on the path through the woods [Main road close on the left](8.1)Continue straight ahead [Path joins a track](8.1)Continue straight ahead [Track broadens into a road](8.4)Bear left towards the radio mast

80

Cassio to the Cisa Pass Summit — stage 66

[Beside disused stile]**(8.7)**After a short paved section turn right on the footpath**(8.9)**Bear right on the track **(9.1)**Pass through the cattle gate and continue on the path [Towards the main road]**(9.2)**Bear right on the main road remaining on the right side [SS62 (IV) marker on the left]**(9.5)**As the road bears left, bear right on the footpath [Towards Berceto below]**(10.0)**Take the right fork [Downhill, towards Berceto] **(10.2)**Continue straight ahead on the tarmac [Via Ripasanta]**(10.4)**Continue straight ahead [Castle to the left]**(10.5)**In Largo Castello continue towards the centre of the town on the paved road [Via Rossi]**(10.6)**At the crossroads of via Martiri Libertà and via P.M. Rossi in the centre of **Berceto (XXXIII)**, take via Romea [Pass in front of the Duomo]**(10.6)**Continue on via Romea [Information Office to the left]**(10.7)**At the end of the small cobbled street in piazzale le Baruti, turn right and then immediately left [Via al Seminario]**(10.8)**Proceed straight ahead onto via E. Colli **(11.3)**At T-junction with main road turn right and almost immediately left onto a gravel track**(12.1)**At the fork, bear right**(12.5)**Fork right at the top of the rise **(13.1)**In the parking area in the hamlet of **Tugo** follow the tarmac to the junction with the main road**(13.3)**Cross the main road and continue straight ahead towards Monte Valoria. Note:- to avoid climbing on further forest tracks which include stiles follow the SS62 to the right to the end of the section beside the Ostello-della-Cisa **(14.2)**Take the right fork [Farm Felgara to the left]**(14.5)**On the crown of a bend to the left bear right on the track [Uphill]**(14.9)**Continue straight ahead [Altitude 1000m] **(15.4)**Take the right fork**(16.0)**Turn right. Note: for the more direct route to the summit of the pass and Monte Valoria take the left fork on the broad track and follow the Monte Valoria Alternate Route**(16.1)**Take the left fork **(16.6)**Keep left**(17.0)**Turn sharp right**(17.1)**Bear left**(17.4)**At the T-junction with the main road, turn right. Note:- if you wish to bypass the Ostello-della-Cisa, turn left and follow the road to the summit of the pass **(17.5)**At the Ostello-della-Cisa retrace your steps up the hill and continue to follow the road[Hostel on the left] **(17.8)**After recrossing the river remain on the road to the summit of the pass **(19.9)**Continue stright ahead on the road. Note:- the "Twin" refuge shared with the Via Francigena and the Sentiero Italia CAI is to the left. The CAI path to the left leads in 2km to the summit of Monte Valoria with panoramic views over northern Tuscany**(20.1)**Arrive at the **Cisa Pass Summit**

stage 66 — Cassio to the Cisa Pass Summit

Direct Route to Monte Valloria and the Cisa Pass Summit

Route: the route bypasses the Ostello-della-Cisa, remaining on woodland paths to pass Monte Valoria before arriving at the pass summit. (0.0)Take the left fork(0.5)Take the right fork, remain on the broad track continuing uphill (1.2)At the summit of **Monte Valoria** (1231m) with your first views of Tuscany ahead, turn right and proceed with the woods on your right (3.0)Pass beside the Capanna Twin Refuge and continue ahead to join the "Official Route" on the SS62

Length:	3.0km
Ascent:	271m
Descent:	87m

Accommodation and Tourist Information

Berceto

Capanna Twin - Refuge,Passo della Cisa - SS62, 43042 Berceto(PR), Italy; Tel:+39 3479069545; +39 3348 696728; Email:turismoberceto@gmail.com; www.twin.polimi.it; Price:C; *Small shelter at the summit of the pass open August and September*

Casa della Gioventù Parrocchiale,Via Martino Iasoni, 43042 Berceto(PR), Italy; Tel: +39 3472 451918; Email:casagioventuberceto@libero.it; web.facebook.com/profile.php?id=100068311627590; Price:D

Ostello della Cisa - Tugo,Passo della Cisa - SS62, 43042 Berceto(PR), Italy; Tel: +39 3282114870; +390525264153; Email:turismoberceto@gmail.com; Price:C; *This is a large but isolated hostel and is not always manned be sure to telephone before arrival* ; **PR**

Ostello Seminario,Via Seminario, 43042 Berceto(PR), Italy; Tel:+39 0521 282951; +39 3471 423340; Email:amministrazione@seminariovescovile.parma.it; www.chiesadi-parma.it/curia/seminario-vescovile/seminario-di-berceto-pr.html; Price:C

B&B - Gioli,Via Ripasanta, 5, 43042 Berceto(PR), Italy; Tel:+39 0525 64251; +39 3315 421268; Email:bebgioli@gmail.com ; sites.google.com/site/bebgioli; Price:B

B&B - La Casa dei Nonni,Via Pier Maria Rossi, 8, 43042 Berceto(PR), Italy; Tel:+39 0525 629103; +39 3332 942210; Email:info@lacasadeinonniberceto.it ; lacasadeinonniberceto.it; Price:B; *Exceptionally helpful host*; **PR**

Albergo Ristorante - Vittoria Da Rino,Via Guglielmo Marconi, 5, 43042 Berceto(PR), Italy; Tel:+39 0525 64306; Email:info@darino.it; www.darino.it; Price:B; *Price group A in high season*

Ufficio Turistico,Piazza Don .Giovanni Bosco, 2 , 43042 Berceto(PR), Italy; Tel:+39 0525 1939109; Email:turismoberceto@gmail.com; www.parmawelcome.it

Ostello della Cisa

Cisa Pass Summit to Pontremoli

stage 67

Length: 20.0km

Ascent: 1133m
Descent: 1923m

Col Grand
St Bernard: 460km
Rome: 568km

Museo delle Statue Stele Lunigianesi–Castello del Piagnaro–Pontremoli

Route: the short but strenuous stage from the Cisa Pass Summit to Pontremoli has few intermediate options for refreshments but does provide options to break the journey if required. The "Official Route" remains largely off-road, but after a pleasant descent from the summit of the Cisa Pass the route again climbs to the 700m Crocetta Pass. A less strenuous Alternate Route descends gently from the summit on minor roads to the outskirts of Pontremoli and avoids the Crocetta Pass. Cyclists may prefer this route or cruise along the rarely busy SS62. For the most direct hiking route, join the Alternate Route in Groppoli.

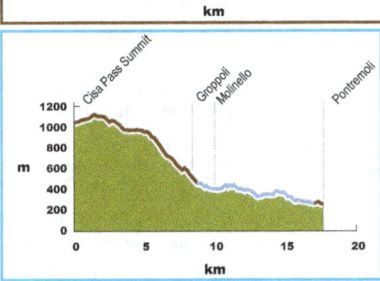

Pontremoli offers a full range of facilities and good rail connections to both the north and south. While there is the opportunity to spend the night in the medieval Piagnoro castle.

Contested since its origin, the little town of Pontremoli has been split between the regions of Parma, Liguria and Tuscany so many times that it has acquired a quite unique personality, dialect and charm. Set on a strip of land between the two converging waterways, the river Magra and Verde, this little town has been burned to the ground, destroyed and conquered, only to rise time and time again. The focus for all this combative activity was the settlement's singular position, which opened roads not only east-west but also north-south, with a continuous parade of pilgrims searching for the Holy Land and Rome, attested by the number of hospitals built within the town or nearby – including Ospedale dei Santi Giacomo e Leonardo and the church of San Pietro run by the monks of Altopascio.

Pontremoli is believed to have been settled around a thousand years before Christ and was called Apua by the Romans. Medieval in plan, the town is dominated by the imposing mass of the Piagnoro castle, high above the rest of the town spreading along the banks of the Magra. Literally translated, Pontremoli means Trembling Bridge (from the Italian tremare–to tremble), named after a prominent bridge across the Magra, which, one presumes, trembled. If you happen to be in Pontremoli in January, you could experience one of the more exciting traditions of the town, where the two competing rioni (districts) stage a bonfire in honour of San Geminiano, under the arches of the Ponte della Cesa. The winner is the rioni that presents not only the highest flames, but also the most beautiful fire.

stage 67 Cisa Pass Summit to Pontremoli

(0.0) From the summit of the Cisa Pass, cross the main road and bear right on the footpath. Note:- the Alternate Route offers a pleasant descent to Pontremoli on generally quiet roads and may be preferred by cyclists. The "Official Route" includes sometimes difficult water crossings as well as steep descents and steps and a further climb over the Crocetta Pass. There are many intersecting CAI routes also using red and white signs and so be sure to check for the pilgrim on the signs [Parallel to the steps to the church]**(0.8)**At an intersection between 3 tracks, take the left track **(1.4)**Continue straight ahead across the stream [Cairn ahead]**(1.6)**Take the left fork [Downhill]**(1.7)**Bear right and cross the stream [Continue on the small track]**(1.8)**Bear left, cross the stream and a small grassy area and bear right [Re-enter woods]**(1.9)**Turn right on the forest road**(1.9)**Turn left on another forest road [Cross another stream]**(2.4)**At a T-junction of forest-tracks, turn right **(2.5)**Ignore a turning to the right and continue straight ahead [Downhill]**(2.5)**Turn right on the path [Gentle descent, parallel to the main road below]**(3.4)**The path enters a track, bear right down the hill [Parallel and closer to the main road] **(3.6)**Cross the main road and bear right on the path**(3.9)**Bear left on the unmade road. Note:- to visit Montelungo (XXXII) follow the main road with care. The main road continues to Pontremoli [Pass the electricity substation on your right]**(4.5)**Pass a radio mast and continue straight ahead **(5.1)**Keep left and pass the metal hut on your right**(5.0)**At the T-junction with a broader track, turn right [Downhill]**(5.7)**At the fork in the tracks, bear right [Follow the larger track]**(5.8)**At a T-junction in the tracks, bear left [Downhill]**(5.9)**Continue straight ahead [Ignore turning to the right] **(6.2)**Continue straight ahead [Ignore the turning to the left and to the right] **(6.3)**Beside the road junction, bear right on the track into the woods. Take the track closest to the main road. To avoid obstacles in the path, cyclists should remain on the road [Ignore the turning to the right]**(6.5)**At a turn in the track continue straight ahead on the path [Into the woods] **(6.9)**Continue straight ahead [Ignore the turning to the right] **(7.2)**At a fork in the tracks, take the right fork**(7.6)**At a T-junction with a grassy track, turn left [Church ahead]**(7.9)**At the fork in the tracks, take the right fork [Downhill] **(8.4)** Continue straight ahead on the tarmac road [Enter **Groppoli**]**(8.5)**At the intersection with the tarmac road continue straight ahead on the cobbled road [Pass between houses]**(8.6)**Continue straight ahead [Narrow cobbled path]**(8.7)**At the exit from Gropolli take the left fork**(8.7)**At the junction with the main road turn right and immediately left on

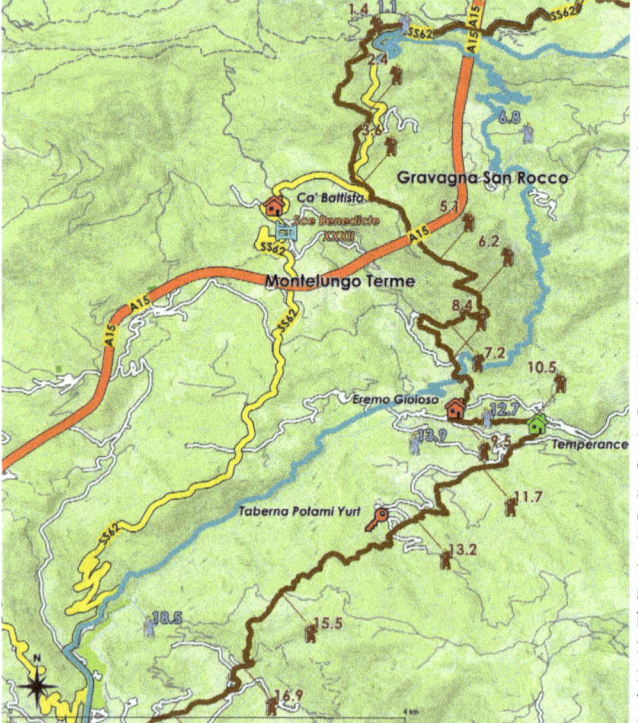

Cisa Pass Summit to Pontremoli — stage 67

the track. Note:- to reduce total distance by 2.5km and avoid further off-road tracks and the climb over the Crocetta Pass continue to the right on the road and join the Alternate Route [Vines and wooden fence on the right]**(9.1)**Continue straight ahead and take the bridge across the Civasola torrente [Continue uphill] **(9.5)**At the intersection with the tarmac road, turn right and immediately left onto a footpath [Steep descent into Previdè] **(9.6)**On reaching **Previdè** turn left onto the tarmac and then immediately left again [Towards the village centre]**(9.7)**At the exit from the village take the left fork, uphill on the grass track [Shrine on the left]**(9.9)**Take care to locate an indistinct junction and bear right over a dry wall [Between the olive trees]**(10.2)**After an uphill section take a footpath to the right [Across the hillside] **(10.5)**Continue straight ahead [Enter Groppodalosio]**(10.6)**In the centre of the village turn right [Down a flight of steps]**(10.8)**Continue straight ahead [Over the old stone river Magra bridge]**(11.1)**Join a tarmac road and turn right [Towards the village of Casalina]**(11.2)**Bear left away from the road on a footpath**(11.3)**At the first junction in **Casalina** continue straight ahead [On the paved road]**(11.5)**Continue straight ahead [Pass an old mill] **(11.7)**Continue straight ahead on the road [Between the stone walls]**(11.9)**Bear left on the well signed path, uphill [Into the woods]**(12.3)**Join the track and bear left**(12.4)**At a bend to the left in the track, continue straight ahead on the path**(12.7)**Cross a stream and turn sharply to the right **(13.2)**After a steep climb turn right on the track [Towards the village]**(13.3)**At the junction with the tarmac road turn left on the road and skirt the village of **Toplecca di Sopra** [Towards the garages]**(13.3)**Bear left on the stony footpath**(13.4)**At the T-junction turn left**(13.5)**Cross the tarmac road and continue straight ahead on the old stone mule track [Shrine on your left]**(13.7)**Continue straight ahead [Over the bridge] **(15.5)**At the summit of the **Crocetta Pass**, continue straight ahead on the track [Pass beside the chapel]**(15.5)**Take the grass track to the left and downhill [Towards the village of Arzengio] **(16.9)**At the first houses in Arzengio, take the tarmac road to the left**(17.1)**Take the first turning to the left [**Arzengio** village centre on the hilltop to the right]**(17.2)**On the far side of the village take the small path to the left [Between the olive trees]**(17.3)**At the next junction turn right on the path [Across the hillside]**(17.4)**Cross the tarmac road and take right fork on the small road beside the house [Initially parallel to the tarmac road on the left]**(17.5)**Continue straight ahead [The road becomes a track] **(18.1)**Continue straight ahead [Ignore the turning to the right]**(18.3)**Continue straight ahead [Tarmac road] **(19.2)**At the T-junction with the road, turn right [Conifers in the garden on your right]**(19.3)**Continue straight ahead over the old bridge over the Magra [Towards the hospital]**(19.4)**Pass through the archway and at the junction with the main road turn left [SS62]**(19.4)**At the fork in the road, bear right. Note:- to avoid a pedestrian subway bear left on the main road and then turn right to the centre of Pontremoli [Via di Porta Parma]**(19.6)**Bear right and cross the stone bridge over the railway**(19.7)**Go under the archway – Porta Parma – and into the narrow street ahead [Via Garibaldi]**(20.0)**Arrive at **Pontremoli (XXXI)** centre [Piazza della Repubblica]

stage 67 — Cisa Pass Summit to Pontremoli

Direct Descent to Pontremoli Avoiding the Crocetta Pass

Route: a less challenging descent to Pontremoli. After a short stretch on the main road, the route follows quiet country roads for much of its length before rejoining the SS62 for the final 2km to Pontremoli. For the shortest route, walkers may join this route in Groppoli. (0.0)Continue straight ahead on the main road [Church on the right] (1.1)Turn left away from the SS62. Note:- to visit Montelungo (XXXII) follow the main road with care. The main road continues to Pontremoli [Direction Gravagna] (6.8)At the bottom of the hill continue straight ahead into the village of **Gravagna San Rocco**(7.1)At the bottom of the hill continue straight ahead(7.5)Fork right before entering **Gravagna Montale** [Large house directly in front] (12.7)Continue straight ahead on the road [The "Official Route" crosses from the right] (13.9)In **Molinello**, at the T-junction turn right [Towards Pontremoli] (18.5)At the T-junction, turn left and proceed with caution on the potentially busy road [SS62, downhill, towards Pontremoli] (21.0)Rejoin the "Official Route" and continue straight ahead on the road [Towards the centre of Pontremoli]

Length:	21.0km
Ascent:	1772m
Descent:	2550m

Accommodation and Tourist Information

Montelungo
Casa Alpina San Benedetto [Signora Rita], 54020 Montelungo(MS), Italy; Tel: +39 3391 741919; www.regione.toscana.it/-/ospitalita-ecclesiastica; Price:C

Pontremoli
Castello del Piagnaro,Via dei Voltoni, 54027 Pontremoli(MS), Italy; Tel:+39 0187 831439; Email:info@statuestele.org; www.statuestele.org; Price:C; *Do not miss the museum* ; PR

Convento Cappuccini - Ospitale San Lorenzo,Via dei Cappuccini, 2, 54027 Pontremoli(MS), Italy; Tel:+39 0187 830395; +39 3391 956770; Email:info@cappuccini-pontremoli.it; www.cappuccinipontremoli.it; Price:D; *Large well run place credentials required* ; PR

Seminario de Pontremoli,Piazza San Francesco, 10, 54027 Pontremoli(MS), Italy; Tel:+39 0187 830045; +39 3333 321782; +39 3386 231144; Email:foresteriaseminario.pontremoli@gmail.com; www.seminariopontremoli.it; Price:D

Temperance [Greta and Marco],Località Groppodalosio Inferiore, 54027 Pontremoli(MS), Italy; Tel: +39 3471 720027; Email:temperance1617@gmail.com; Price:D

Agriturismo - Lucchetti Ferrari,Via Costa San Nicolò, 2, 54027 Pontremoli(MS), Italy; Tel:+39 0187 1676538; +39 3401 447903; +39 3356 702547; Email:lucchettiferrari@gmail.com; www.lucchettiferrari.it; Price:A

B&B - Ca' Battista,Località Montelungo Superiore, 63, 54027 Pontremoli(MS), Italy; Tel: +39 3278 387687; Email:bbcabattista@libero.it; booking.com; Price:B

B&B - Eremo Gioioso [Marzia and Marco],Località Previdé, 54027 Pontremoli(MS), Italy; Tel:+39 0187 915598; +39 3283142916; Email:info@eremogioioso.it ; eremogioioso.it; Price:B; *Can arrange to collect at the Cisa Pass but reported to be considering retirement*; PR

B&B - Ai Chiosi,Via Chiosi, 15, 54027 Pontremoli(MS), Italy; Tel: +39 3402 357583; Email:aichiosibb@gmail.com ; www.aichiosi.it; Price:A; *Pilgrim discount*

Taberna Potami - Yurt,Localita Toplecca di Soprai, 54027 Pontremoli(MS), Italy; Tel: +39 3427 064227; Email:alessandro.bocchi@mac.com; web.facebook.com/TabernaPotamiVegToplec-caDiSopra; Price:C

Turismo In Lunigiana,Via Pietro Bologna, 4, 54027 Pontremoli(MS), Italy; Tel:+39 0187 830056; +39 3283120525; Email:info@turismoinlunigiana.it; turismoinlunigiana.it

Pontremoli to Aulla

stage 68

Length:	32.4km
Ascent:	817m
Descent:	1004m
Col Grand St Bernard:	480km
Rome:	548km

Filetto Centre

Route: the "Official Route" from Pontremoli to Aulla involves mixed conditions varying from short stretches on busy and potentially dangerous roads near Pontremoli to isolated tracks through hilly woodland. A cycle route is available on more level ground on the western side of the river Magra.

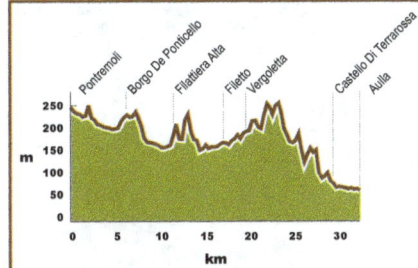

Filetto is a small but pretty village adjacent to the larger Villafranca in Lunigiana where it is possible to break the stage. There is also the opportunity for a refreshment stop at Filattiera and a Terrarosa.

The small town of Filetto dates back to the 6th and 7th centuries, a period of time when Byzantine populations required fortresses for defence against the Longobards. The original town layout is a square defended by four cylindrical towers, one of which still stands today. The first town centre was later transformed into a fortified residence that underwent numerous renovations until the 17th century. The interior part of town, accessed by two monumental city gates houses a church dedicated to the saints Filippo and Giacomo.

The name Aulla probably comes from the Latin words lacus or lacuna, meaning lake. Traces of Roman and Etruscan civilizations found in the church of Saint Caprisio indicate that there were settlements in Aulla long before the 8th century, when Adalberto of Tuscany founded a village and castle to accommodate pilgrims travelling the via Francigena. The church, dedicated to Santa Maria Assunta, has since undergone profound changes, but the primitive 10th century structure remains, along with the semi-circular apse and a fragment of stone carved with vegetal motifs.

🚶 **(0.0)** Cross piazza della Repubblica into the narrow street ahead [Via Armani] **(0.2)** At the crossroads continue straight ahead. Note:- to use the Cycle Route turn right and continue over the bridge on the Alternate Route [Via Cavour] **(0.3)** Turn left and cross the river bridge [Ponte Cesare Battisti] **(0.4)** Pass through the archway and turn right [Via Mazzini] **(0.9)** At the crossroads continue straight ahead to join the main road, remain on the right-hand side [Direction Aulla] 🚶 **(1.6)** Continue straight ahead [Pass beside the church of San Lazzaro] **(1.7)** Cross the road and bear left on the narrow paved street. Note:- where possible the route will try and avoid this busy road. However, in light traffic conditions cyclists

stage 68 — Pontremoli to Aulla

may prefer to stay on the road [Via Santissima Annunziata]**(1.8)**With house n° 32 immediately on your right, turn left and then right at the end of the short street**(1.9)**Join the track between the trees and the church and continue uphill [Pass the stone walled terraces on your left]**(2.0)**Bear right around the brick building and turn right on the small road**(2.2)** Continue straight ahead on the elevated road [Main road on your right]**(2.3)**At the hairpin, continue straight ahead [No Through Road]**(2.6)**Bear left on the track [Towards the railway] **(2.7)**Cross the stream and turn right onto the small road [Return under the railway bridge]**(2.9)**At the T-junction with the main road, turn left and follow the road with great care**(3.2)**Immediately after the marble yard, turn right on the track and continue ahead on the road beside the industrial buildings**(3.6)**At the end of the road take the path over the grass to return to the main road on the left **(4.3)**Turn left and leave the main road [Pass shop on your right]**(4.4)**Take the right fork onto the gravel track [Large drainage ditch to your right]**(4.9)**At the junction with a minor road turn sharp left on the road [Towards railway]**(5.0)**Take the right fork [Direction Ponticello] **(5.3)**At the junc-

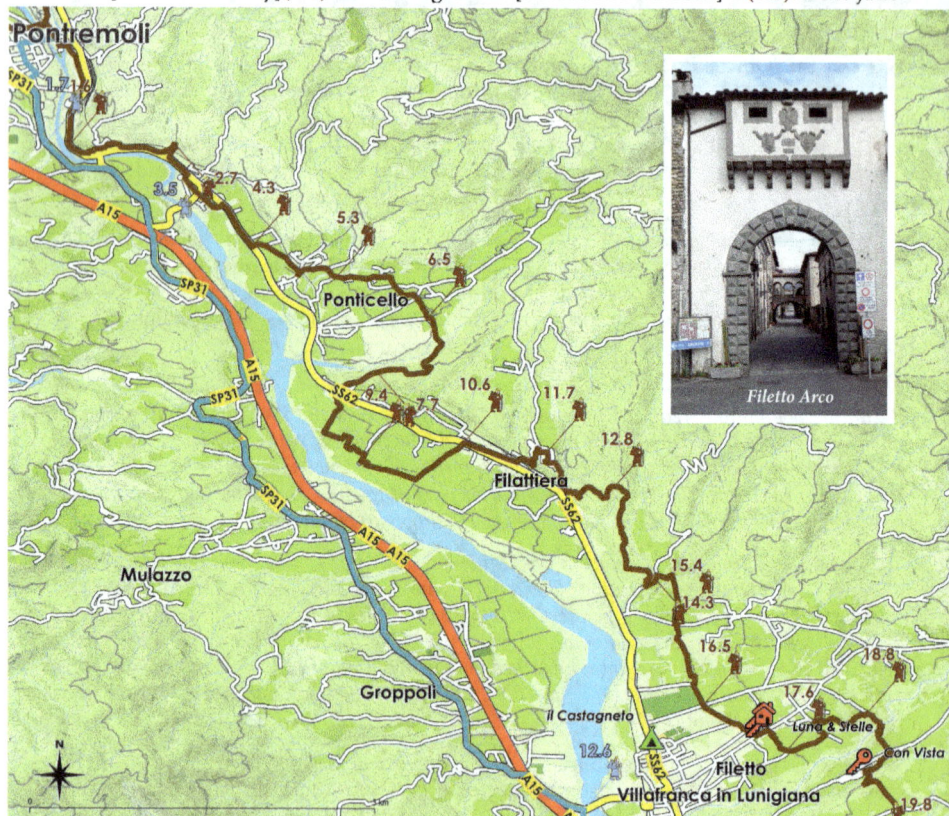

Filetto Arco

tion, continue straight ahead [Up the hill]**(5.6)**Fork left on the road [Direction Canale] **(5.8)**At the end of the parking area, continue to the right on the road**(5.9)**At the crossroads, continue straight ahead on the gravel track**(6.1)**At the T-junction with a minor road, turn left**(6.2)**At the road junction, cross over and pass the church on your right [**Bor-**

Pontremoli to Aulla   stage 68

go de Ponticello](**6.2**)Pass under an archway and turn right [Volta a Crociera](**6.3**)Bear left [Pass under a second arch] (**6.5**)At the crossroads take the second turning on the left [The track crosses a river and climbs the ridge](**7.2**)Turn sharp right(**7.4**)Take the right fork onto the grassy track (**7.7**)Take the left fork [Line of trees and fence on the left](**8.1**) At the T-junction, turn right [Pass under the railway](**8.1**)Bear left and then turn right in a narrow passageway(**8.2**)Cross straight over the main road and continue straight ahead(**8.2**) Turn left between houses(**8.4**)At the fork in the track, bear right [Towards the barns] (**9.4**)At the T-junction with the tarmac road turn right and then take the next left beside the metal gates(**10.0**)At the T-junction, turn left between the trees [Farm on your left] (**10.6**) At the T-junction with the main road, turn right [Towards the church – Pieve di Sorano] (**10.7**)Take the left fork and leave the SS62 [Direction Biglio](**11.1**)Turn left under the railway bridge and turn right at the T-junction(**11.4**)Turn right up a flight of steps. Note:- cyclists should remain on the road and then bear right into the centre of the village [**Filattiera Alta**](**11.6**)Continue straight ahead [Pass through the car park](**11.6**)At the road junction turn sharp right [Towards the square in the centre of Filattiera] (**11.7**)Turn right to leave the square [Pass a café on your left] (**11.8**)At the end of the road bear right and then turn left at the junction(**12.3**) At the T-junction, turn left and then right over a bridge and climb the hill on a stony track [Railway bridge on the right at the junction](**12.5**)Bear left towards the chapel on the brow of the hill(**12.6**)Take the right fork (**12.8**) Take the left fork [Into the trees](**13.2**) Turn right towards the pylon (**14.3**) Turn right beside the river(**14.5**)At the road junction, turn left(**14.7**)Turn right on the broad gravel track (**15.4**)At the junction with the road turn left and then immediately right on the stony track [Electricity station on the left](**16.2**) Bear left onto the road [Golf course on the right] (**16.5**)At the crossroads with the SP29, continue straight ahead into Filetto [Via San Genesio](**17.1**) Turn left and proceed north-east through **Filetto** old town [The facilities of the larger Villafranca-in-Lunigiana are to the right](**17.2**)Immediately after leaving the old town, turn right [Via del Canale] (**17.6**)At the T-junction, turn left [Parallel to the river and wooded ridge](**18.0**)At the end of the road, turn left [Direction Bagnone](**18.2**)Turn right on the footpath [Signpost - Bagnone](**18.4**)Bear right [Between stone walls] (**18.8**)At the junction with the gravel road, turn right and cross the bridge and continue uphill(**19.2**)At the

stage 68 — Pontremoli to Aulla

top of the hill, continue straight ahead on the track**(19.4)**Cross the road and continue uphill between houses and then turn right at the T-junction**(19.5)**At the junction below the medieval village of **Vergoletta**, turn left and continue beneath the village walls **(19.8)**Turn left on the road [Pass the water source on the left]**(19.9)**Bear left continuing up the hill [Via delle Fontane]**(20.4)**At the crossroads, continue straight ahead towards the cemetery**(20.6)**As the road becomes a track, continue straight ahead with the football pitch on the left **(20.8)**Fork left downhill onto a narrow grassy track [Garden on the right]**(20.8)**Continue straight ahead [Ignore turning to the right]**(21.1)**Fork left across the stream and continue on the narrow track**(21.1)**After crossing the stream take the right fork**(21.3)**Take the right fork up the hill**(21.7)**At the T-junction with the small road, at the top of the hill, turn left [Wooden balustrade on left]**(21.7)**Fork left [Avoid stony track on the right] **(22.1)**Turn sharp right [Between the embankments] **(23.4)**At the fork bear right**(24.3)**Continue straight ahead [Roman road] **(24.8)**Bear left **(26.0)**At the T-junction with the minor road, bear left direction La Valle del Sole**(26.0)**Turn right to go between two buildings, then immediately turn left**(26.4)**After a steep ascent and a rough flight of steps, bear left with an old building immediately on the left and a wall on right**(26.5)**Turn left onto the road [Up the hill]**(26.5)**Turn left up the steep narrow track**(26.7)**Bear right on track**(26.9)**Turn left at the T-junction [Private property on the right] **(27.0)**Take the right fork**(27.4)**Take the left fork**(27.8)**Bear right [In the clearing]**(27.8)**Bear right on the broader track [White house directly on the left] **(28.6)**Take the right fork**(28.9)**Track emerges onto a minor tarmac road – via dei Pini, immediately turn left on the track [Cemetery on right at the junction]**(29.1)**Bear right on the tarmac road [Pass apartment buildings on the left]**(29.3)**At the T-junction with the SS62, bear left and briefly follow the main road [Childrens playground on the right at the junction]**(29.4)**At the crossroads turn left on the narrow road [Pass the **Castello di Terrarossa** on your right]**(29.5)**Just before the archway, turn right and then left [Pass over the river bridge]**(29.6)**After crossing the bridge turn right on the road [Continue under the power lines] **(29.8)**Bear left on the road [Pass building materials store on your left]**(30.0)**At the T-junction, turn right [Shopping street]**(30.2)**At the T-junction continue straight ahead through the gap in the trees and then turn left on the old railway **(31.5)**At the road junction, turn right [Towards the church]**(31.6)**At the T-junction, continue straight ahead, climb the short flight of steps and descend into the piazza and turn left at the crossroads**(32.4)**Arrive at **Aulla** **(XXX)** centre beside Abbazia di San Caprasio [Bridge over the river Magra to your right]

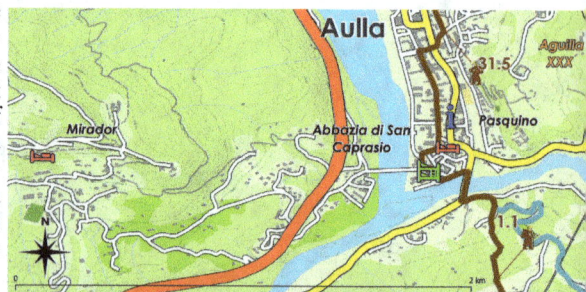

Magra Valley Cyclist's Route

Route: the cycle route takes you to Terrarossa on the outskirts of Aulla. This tarmac route remains in the valley on the western side of the river Magra. The section to Ponte Magra (near Villafranca) is generally flat, before a stiff climb to Lusuolo.

Length:	22.0km
Ascent:	845m
Descent:	1011m

(0.0) At the crossroads turn right and cross the river bridge [Via Pietro Bologna]**(0.2)**At the next crossroads, continue straight ahead [Via Roma]**(0.3)**At the crossroads, turn left [Via Pirandello]**(0.7)**At the T-junction

Pontremoli to Aulla — stage 68

turn right [Strada di Maggio Galante] (0.9)At the crossroads, turn left onto via Europa and via Groppomontone [Factory building straight ahead](1.0)Bear right on via Groppomontone [Keep river and bridge to the left] (1.7)Continue straight ahead, cross the bridge over the Magra tributary [Via Antonino Siligato](2.1)Take the left fork – remain beside the river [Direction La Spezia](2.4)Bear right on SP31 [Between the hill and the river plain] (3.5)Continue straight ahead, direction Villafranca [**Motorway** entrance on the left] (12.6)In **Ponte Magra**, turn right onto via Pontemagra. Note:- to rejoin the "Official Route", turn left and cross the bridge into the centre of Villafranca [Direction Lusuolo] (14.6)Continue straight ahead on the road [Avoid the turning to the right] (16.4)At the junction beside the hairpin bend, bear left [Enter **Lusuolo**] (18.8)At the junction, bear left remaining on the road [VF cycle route sign](19.6)Bear right into Barbarasco [Via Chiesa](19.7)At the T-junction in Barbarasco, turn left [SP23, via Roma] (21.2)After crossing the river, continue straight ahead [Via Barbarasco](21.5)At the T-junction, turn right [Via Nazionale, direction Aulla](22.0)At the Stop sign rejoin the "Official Route" and continue straight ahead across the main road [Pass the castle on your right]

Accommodation and Tourist Information

Aulla

🛏 **Abbazia di San Caprasio** [Don Giovanni Perini],Piazza Abbazia, 54011 Aulla(MS), Italy; Tel:+39 0187 1780776; +39 36 6977 8206; +39 0187420148; Email:sancapraisio@gmail.com; www.sancapraisio.it; Price:D

🏠 **B&B - Bed and Bike** [Elisabetta and Paolo],via Cheri, 71-73, 54011 Aulla(MS), Italy; Tel:+39 3358159015; +39 3357795484; +39 0187 408020; Email:info@bedebike.it; bedebike.it; Price:A; *Bike rental available*

🛏 **Albergo Ristorante - Pasquino**,Piazza Giuseppe Mazzini, 22, 54011 Aulla(MS), Italy; Tel:+39 0187 420509; www.albergopasquino.it; Price:B

ℹ **Ufficio Informazioni Turistiche**,Piazza Antonio Gramsci, 24, 54011 Aulla(MS), Italy; Tel:+39 0187 4001; Email:infoturisticheaulla@gmail.com; comune.aulla.ms.it

Filetto

🏠 **B&B - Luna & Stelle** [Lucia Barbiere],Piazza Immacolata, 13, 54028 Filetto(MS), Italy; Tel: +39 3396 222592; www.bedandbreakfast.eu; Price:A

🔑 **Apartment - La Casa dei Quadri** [Federico],Via Ariberti, 54028 Filetto(MS), Italy; Tel:+39 3471368265; Price:D

🔑 **Guest House - Gredo Antica Dimora**,Via Borgo Ariberti, 19, 54038 Filetto(MS), Italy; Tel:+39 3494275289; +39 3498 487416; Email:massydonati@libero.it; www.terredilunigiana.com/villafranca/appartamentigredo.php; Price:B

Podenzana

🛏 **Hotel - Mirador**,Via del Gaggio, 22, 54010 Podenzana(MS), Italy; Tel:+39 0187 410064; Email:info@albergoristorantemirador.com; www.albergoristorantemirador.com; Price:B

Villafranca-In-Lunigiana

🛏 **Albergo - Manganelli**,Piazza San Nicolò, 5, 54028 Villafranca-In-Lunigiana(MS), Italy; Tel:+39 0187 493062; Email:albergomanganelli@lunigiana.net; web.facebook.com/people/Albergo-Ristorante-Manganelli/100067067419854; Price:B; *Pilgrim discount*

⛺ **Camping il Castagneto**,Via Nazionale, 54028 Villafranca-In-Lunigiana(MS), Italy; Tel:+39 0187 493492; +39 3395 252154; Email:info@campingilcastagneto.it; www.campingilcastagneto.it; Price:C; *Bungalows also available*

Virgoletta

🔑 **Camera - Con Vista**,Via dei Calzolari, 66, 54028 Virgoletta(MS), Italy; Tel: +39 3337 003712; web.facebook.com/CameraconvistaVirgoletta; Price:B

stage 69 — Aulla to Sarzanna

Length:	18.2km
Ascent:	1305m
Descent:	1336m
Col Grand St Bernard:	512km
Rome:	516km

Fortezza Firmafede–Sarzana

Route: the route from Aulla to Sarzanna is another rugged and largely forested stage over the final ridge before the coastal plain.

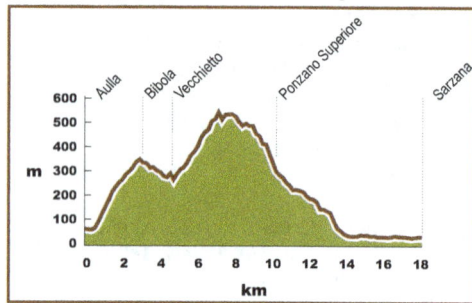

The Alternate Routes offer options for all groups to bypass the most challenging forest tracks and also to visit Santo Stefano di Magra (XXIX). Sadly there are no cafes or grocery stores between outskirts of Aulla and Sarzana directly on the "Official Route". However, the excellent *la Volpara* restaurant can be accessed on the "Ponzano Superiore Cyclist's Descent". Sarzana offers a full range of facilities with a frequent train service to La Spezia and the Cinque Terre.

The first mention of Sarzana is found in 983, but owing to its militarily strategic position, it changed masters more than once, belonging first to Pisa, then to Florence, then to the Banco di San Giorgio of Genoa and from 1572 to Genoa itself. The town is based around the via Francigena that passes between the city gates of Parma and Romana, but is also known as a centre for trade in antiques.

The Firmafede Fortress was built in the second half of the 15th century on the ashes of the former 13th century Pisan fortification. It represents an important example of Florentine military architecture of the end of the 15th century. With the annexation of the republic to the kingdom of Savoy, and the radical changes of defensive strategies, the fortress was first used as a police station and later as a prison until the 1970s. Between 1985 and 2003, a series of restorations have made the Fortress usable once again, and it is now used for many cultural activities, which make visits to the interior difficult. Nevertheless, seen from the outside it is an impressive, almost overwhelming presence.

Club Alpino Italiano - CAI signpost

Aulla to Sarzanna   stage 69

🚶 **(0.0)** With the bridge over the river Magra behind you and Abbazia di San Caprasio to your left, bear right [Piazza Abazzia, direction La Spezia] **(0.1)** At the T-junction, turn right, pass under the arch and then turn left [Towards the riverside] **(0.1)** At the riverside, turn left, direction Massa and La Spezia [Piazza L. Corbani] **(0.3)** At the T-junction, turn right and cross the river bridge [SS62, direction La Spezia] **(0.4)** At the end of the bridge, turn left across a disused railway line and then bear left [Direction Bibola] **(0.7)** Bear right, uphill and away from the larger road. Note:– the Alternate Route to the left offers a longer but easier option for all groups and is recommended for cyclists [Via Prascara] **(0.7)** Bear left on the footpath [Beside the wall] 🚶 **(1.1)** Cross the track and continue ahead up the hill [Beside the vineyard] **(1.2)** At the junction with the road turn right and immediately left on the steep footpath [Into the woods] **(1.8)** At the T-junction with the gravel road, turn right [The road makes a sharp left turn] 🚶 **(2.4)** At the crossroads in the clearing, keep left on the gravel road- the Alternate Route crosses the "Official Route" and continues to the right [Uphill towards Bibola] **(2.9)** Approaching the top of the hill take the footpath to the right [Steps and shrine on the corner] **(3.1)** Rejoin the broad track and turn right downhill [**Bibola** is on the hilltop to the left] **(3.2)** Take the next turning to the right and then immediately right again on the gravel road [Pass the bus stop on your left] 🚶 **(3.7)** At the junction, bear right on the tarmac [Towards Vecchietto] **(4.7)** Take the right fork into the village of **Vecchietto** [Towards bell tower] 🚶 **(4.8)** Turn right under the archway [Via Fontana] **(5.0)** On the edge of the village, bear right on the track, beside the olive grove [Climbing into the forest] 🚶 **(6.0)** Take the steep footpath to

The last ridge before the Mediterranean, seen from Bibola

stage 69 Aulla to Sarzanna

the right [In the clearing] 🍴(7.7)At the crossroads continue straight ahead on the forest track – the Alternate Route joins from the right [At the top of the hill](8.2)Continue straight ahead. Note:- the turning to the left leads to a viewpoint overlooking La Spezia and the coast(8.5) Continue straight ahead on the narrow track - the descent on the "Official Route" is over broken ground and is difficult for cyclists. The Alternate Route leaves to the right and descends on a broader easier track🍴(9.0) Continue straight ahead down a narrow track [Direction Sarzana](9.2)Fork left(9.9)At the junction, continue straight ahead [Between olive groves towards the village]🍴(10.2)Turn right onto a small tarmac road [Downhill](10.3)Turn left [Enter **Ponzano Superiore**] (10.4)Turn left in piazza Aia di Croce direction Sarzana - the pathway ahead has narrow sections over rough ground with steep descents and bypasses Santo Stefano di Magra (XXIX). Cyclists and those wishing to visit Santo Stefano should bear right on the Alternate Route

Cathedral of Santa Maria Assunta

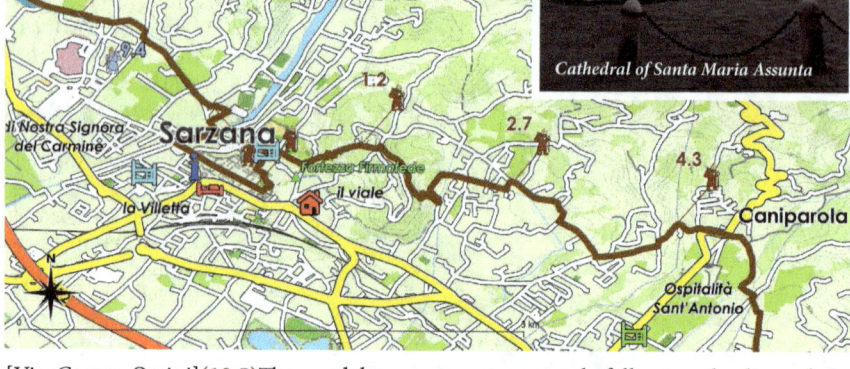

[Via Cesare Orsini](10.5)The road becomes a grassy track following the line of the ridge(10.7)Turn right onto a minor road and proceed downhill on via Cattarello 🍴(12.1) Fork right [Up the hill](12.4)Bear right at the top of the hill [Archaeological dig site](12.4) After passing the archaeological site, bear right [Down the hill] 🍴(13.4)Take the lower track to the left(13.6)Turn left onto the small tarmac road(13.6)Turn right at the T-junction [Continue on via Lago](14.2)On the crown of the sharp turn to the right, turn left into the trees 🍴(14.5)At the junction, continue straight ahead, cross the bridge over the canal, bear left and recross the canal and then turn right on the canal-side cycle path [Continue with the canal on your right](14.8)Bear left and right, recross the canal [Continue with the canal on your left] 🍴(15.8)Turn left and cross the small bridge, then turn right to recross the waterway and then left to continue on the path beside the water. Alternate Route rejoins from the right(16.2)At the end of the cycle track, turn right on via Turi and then turn left at the T-junction(16.5)Rejoin the canal-side cycle track🍴(17.0)Turn left over the bridge and then right beside the canal. On reaching the carpark, turn right between the apartment buildings(17.2)At the T-junction, turn left, cross the river bridge and then im-

Aulla to Sarzanna   stage 69

mediately turn right**(17.6)** At the crossroads beside the next river bridge, turn left and pass through the archway [Porta Parma] **(18.2)** Arrive at **Sarzana** centre [Beside the church of Santa Maria]

Monte Grosso Cyclist's Route

Route: a more progressive route suitable for cyclists and for those on foot wishing to avoid the most rugged climbs. The route takes a quiet road to Bibola and then broad gravel tracks over the Monte Grosso ridge. **(0.0)** Bear left on the road over a small bridge [Direction Bibola] **(1.1)** Fork right up the hill [Woodland to the right]**(1.9)** Remain on the road to Bibola **(3.2)** Fork right on the road [Direction Bibola]**(3.5)** Turn right at the top of the hill in the direction of Bibola centre**(3.6)** At T-junction turn left [Away from the hill-top centre of Bibola]**(3.7)** Bear right onto the gravel track **(4.5)** At the junction take the first track on the left **(5.7)** Turn left onto a minor road and proceed uphill [Towards the quarry]**(6.3)** Bear right on the gravel track [**Quarry** entrance on your left]**(6.4)** At fork bear right [Away from quarry]**(6.6)** At T-junction turn right **(10.9)** At the crossroads in the tracks, rejoin the "Official Route" and turn right.

Length:	10.9km
Ascent:	1396m
Descent:	943m

Bike repairs - Sarzana

Ponzano Superiore Cyclist's Descent

Route: an easier descent for cyclists avoiding more of the stony track.**(0.0)** Turn right**(0.1)** At the junction, bear right **(2.2)** Take the left fork [Pass **la Volpara** restaurant - provides excellent regional food] **(3.6)** At the junction, rejoin the "Official Route" and turn right [Into the village of Ponzano Superiore]

Length:	3.6km
Ascent:	216m
Descent:	391m

stage 69 — Aulla to Sarzanna

Santo Stefano di Magra (XXIX)

Route: for cyclists and those wishing to visit Santo Stefano di Magra (XXIX). The route includes approximately 3 km on the busy SP62, which can be avoided by taking one of the frequent buses. (0.0) In piazza Aia di Croce bear right on the road [Proceed down the hill on via Antonio Gramsci] (2.1) 400 metres after third right-hand hairpin turn sharp right leaving the road. [Via Brigate Alpine] (3.5) At the T-junction at the entry to **Santo Stefano di Magra (XXIX)**, turn left [Via Roma] (3.8) At the T-junction, turn left [SP62, via Cisa Sud] (4.9) At the roundabout, continue straight ahead [SP62, via Cisa Sud] (6.1) At broad junction in Ponzano Magra bear right on the smaller road [Via Cisa Vecchio] (6.4) After passing under the railway, join via Seconda Piano Vezzano and proceed straight ahead [Keep railway to the left] (8.0) At the mini-roundabout, turn left, cross the railway and immediately turn right at the roundabout [Rejoin SS62] (8.2) With a bridge over the road ahead, bear left to leave the main road [Uphill] (8.6) At the T-junction with the SS62, turn left [Enter Sarzana] (8.9) At the fork, bear left on the small road [Via San Gottardo] (9.4) Bear left over the small bridge and rejoin the "Official Route".

Length:	9.4km
Ascent:	140m
Descent:	397m

Accommodation and Tourist Information

Caniparola

Ospitalità Sant'Antonio [Don Giovanni], Via Borghetto, 111, 54035 Caniparola(MS), Italy; Tel:+39 0187 673530; +39 3396380331; Email:perignon@alice.it; ospitalita-sant-antonio.webnode.it; Price:C; *Please call in advance*

Santo-Stefano-di-Magra

B&B - la Costa, Via Mario Baria, 11, 19037 Santo-Stefano-di-Magra(SP), Italy; Tel: +39 3339 999870; Email: miria.giannoni@libero.it; www.bbplanet.com; Price:B

Albergo Ristorante - la Trigola, Via Antonio Gramsci, 63, 19037 Santo-Stefano-di-Magra(SP), Italy; Tel:+39 0187 696872; +39 0187 695201; Email:info@hotellatrigola.it; hotellatrigola.it; Price:A

Sarzana

Parrocchia di Nostra Signora del Carmine, Via Paganino Da Sarzana, 80, 19038 Sarzana(SP), Italy; Tel:+39 0187 620260; +39 36 8729 4423; Price:D

Convento San Francesco D'Assisi [Don Renzo Cortese], Via Agostino Paci, 8, 19038 Sarzana(SP), Italy; Tel:+39 0187 620356; +39 0187916823; Email:info@sanfrancescosarzana.it; www.sanfrancescosarzana.it; Price:D

B&B - il viale, Viale Giuseppe Mazzini, 75, 19038 Sarzana(SP), Italy; Tel:+39 0187 610866; +39 3337 705145; Email:info@ilvialedivaleria.it; www.ilvialedivaleria.it; Price:B

Albergo - la Villetta, Via Sobborgo Emiliano, 24a, 19038 Sarzana(SP), Italy; Tel:+ 39 0187 300998; +39 328 262 6440; Email:info@albergolavilletta.net; www.albergolavilletta.net; Price:B

IAT Tourist Office - Sarzana, Piazza San Giorgio, 19038 Sarzana(SP), Italy; Tel:+39 0187 305551; Email:iatsarzana@gmail.com; web.facebook.com/iatsarzana-turismo

Sarzana to Massa

stage 70

Length:	29.1km
Ascent:	1107m
Descent:	1064m
Col Grand St Bernard:	530km
Rome:	498km

Marble Quarries above Carrara

Route: the stage from Sarzana to Massa is largely undertaken on suburban roads and canal-side tracks before climbing onto hillside tracks and narrow roads through the vineyards overlooking the coastal plain. The Alternate Route from Luni to Pietrasanta provides an opportunity to stroll beside the Mediterranean beaches, avoids some further climbing in the foothills and reduces the total distance to Pietrasanta.

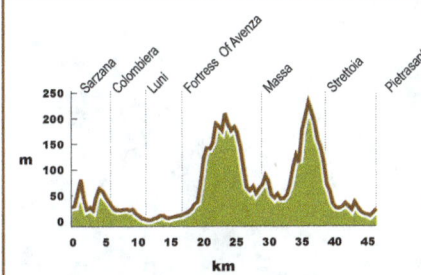

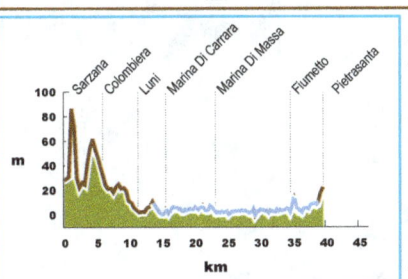

The Roman city of Luna was established in 177 B.C., as a military stronghold for the campaigns against the Ligures. There are different theories regarding the origins of the town's name. Some believe it was named after the ancient goddess Lunae, while others claim the name was inspired by the shape of its territory and harbour, which resembled a crescent moon (luna). Luni derived its importance from its harbour, which was on a gulf of the Tyrrhenian Sea, now known as the Gulf of La Spezia. The site was used as a base for carrying marble from the quarries of modern-day Carrara, after which it was shipped directly to Rome.

The spreading of malaria in the area and the silting up of the port contributed to the settlement's steep decline, and in 1058 the whole population moved to Sarzana, while other refugees went on to found Ortonovo and Nicola.

Luni was excavated in the 1970s and the artefacts are now housed in the adjacent museum. Archaeological evidence suggests that the Roman forum had been abandoned as a public space by the end of the 6th century, its buildings fell to ruin or were demolished and decorative marbles removed. Today's via Francigena route offers a short cut directly through Luni, and so a wonderful opportunity to visit the archaeological site.

Female in marble - Luni

stage 70 — Sarzana to Massa

(**0.0**)Continue along via Giuseppe Mazzini [Cathedral of Santa Maria on the left](**0.1**)Turn left on piazza Firmafede. Bear left with the citadel on your right and then right on via Nicolo Mascardi(**0.3**)At the Stop sign turn right(**0.5**)At the end of the road, turn right [Via San Francesco](**0.7**)As the road turns right, turn left on the small road towards the hillside [Pass a small shrine in the wall on your left](**0.8**)Bear right on the track [Towards the fortress on the hilltop] (**1.2**)Bear right [Keep the fortress of Sarzanello immediately on the left](**1.3**)Turn left on the cobbled road and quickly turn right on the small lower road [Via Luperello](**1.6**)Bear right on the grass track(**1.9**)Turn left down the hill(**2.0**)Cross the bridge and turn sharp left to follow the canal path (**2.6**)Beside the third bridge,turn left and then turn right at the T-junction(**3.3**)Bear left and remain on via Canalburo(**3.7**)At the T-junction, turn left [Bus stop (Fermata) on the left] (**4.3**)Bear right over the bridge(**4.4**)At the complex junction continue straight ahead on via Caniparola [Pass small parking area on your left](**4.6**)On the apex of a bend to the left continue straight ahead on the small road [Pass an archway on your right](**5.2**)At the T-junction, turn right and then immediately left on via Montecchio and enter Colombiera [Olive grove on the left at the junction] (**6.0**)At the crossroads in **Colombiera** continue straight ahead [Towards the pizzeria] (**6.1**)Take the left fork [Direction Campo Sportivo](**6.4**)Just before entering the village of Canale,turn left on the path beside the canal (**7.2**)Bear left across the road and continue beside the canal(**7.3**)Cross the road and continue with the canal on the left(**7.9**)Cross the bridge and continue with the

Fortress of Avenza

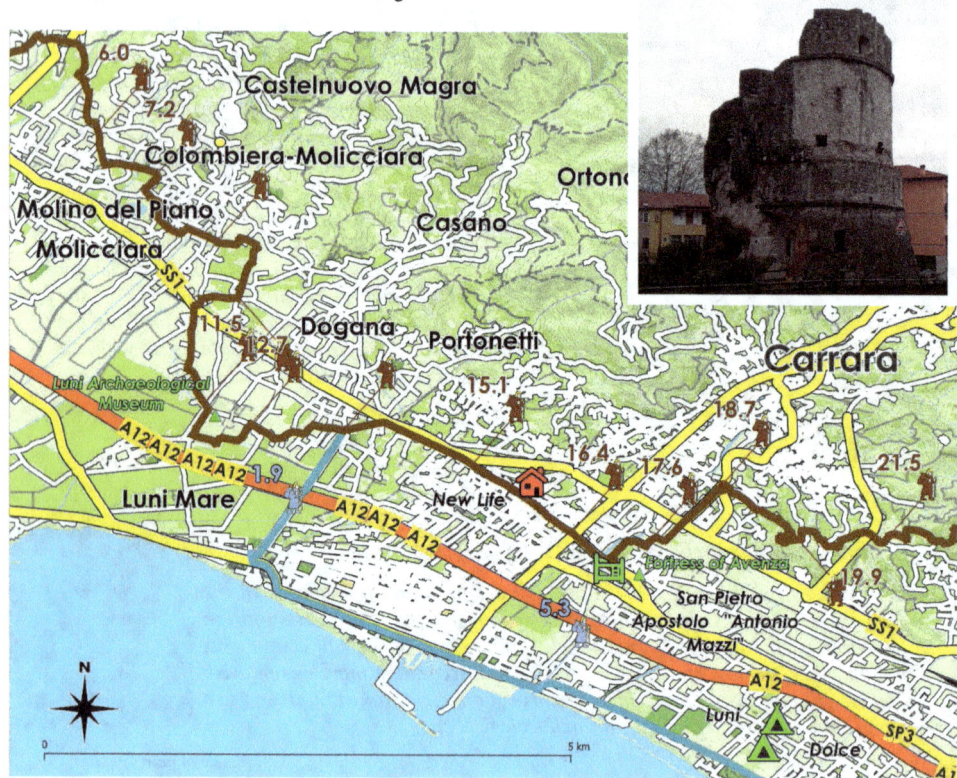

Sarzana to Massa — stage 70

canal on the right**(8.0)**Turn left on the road and then turn right after passing the shops [Direction Palvotrisia] **(8.5)**Turn right and then left to continue beside the canal **(9.7)** At the road junction, turn right [Enter Palvotrisia]**(10.0)**At the Stop sign, turn left**(10.2)**At the T-junction with the very busy via Aurelia, cross the pedestrian crossing and turn left. Continue with care on the right hand side of the road [Towards traffic lights] **(11.5)**At the crossroads with the main road continue straight ahead [Towards the archaeological site of **Luni (XXVIII)**]**(11.6)**At the entrance to the site, turn right [Continue beside ditch]**(11.9)** Turn left on track**(12.4)**Turn left, [Small bridge to the right] **(12.7)**Turn right on the tarmac road [Via Appia]**(12.9)**Continue straight ahead [Luni amphitheatre on the left]**(13.2)** Take the right fork [Via Appia]**(13.4)**Turn right on via Marina **(13.7)**At the T-junction, cross the road and take the footbridge. Then bear left on the road on via del Parmignola [Beside the waterway and then the railway track. Note:- the beach-side route leaves to the right at the junction] **(15.1)**At the crossroads continue straight ahead [Railway bridge on the left] **(16.1)**At the roundabout, continue straight ahead [Via Giovan-Pietro, pass bar on the right]**(17.0)**After passing the **Fortress of Avenza** on your left, immediately turn left [Pass through the arch]**(17.1)**At the T-junction, turn left**(17.1)**At the end of the road, turn right on Via Colombera [No Entry sign] **(17.6)**At the T-junction, turn left [Over the level crossing]**(17.8)**At the crossroads, turn right [Marble yard on the right]**(18.2)**At the traffic lights, continue straight ahead [Tyre store on the left] **(18.7)**At the roundabout, cross the via Provinciale Nazzano and continue straight ahead [Direction Bonascola]**(18.9)** Turn right uphill [Via Forma Bassa]**(19.6)**After sharp left and right turns, continue straight ahead on the track **(19.9)**Turn right [Into the woods]**(20.0)**Turn left [Towards the farm] **(20.0)**Turn left beside the farm and then left again uphill [Towards the electricity pylon and between the vines]**(20.5)**At the top of the ridge turn right on the road, via Forma Alta [Vines on the right]**(20.7)**At the road junction, continue straight ahead [Metal fence and

vines to the right]**(20.8)**At top of the hill, turn left on the narrow road [Along the ridge] **(21.5)**Bear left [Quarry on the right]**(22.0)**Bear right on the white road, via dell'Uva [Be-

stage 70 — Sarzana to Massa

Piazza Mercurio - Massa

tween the vines] 🚶 **(23.2)** Beside the restaurant, turn sharp left, uphill [Via dell'Uva] 🚶 **(24.7)** Take the right fork [The lower road] 🚶 **(26.7)** At the end of the road, turn sharp right **(26.8)** Cross the main road and take the smaller road opposite [Via Ponte del Vescovo, No Entry] **(27.0)** At the T-junction, turn left into piazza della Libertà and then immediately right [Via San Vitale] **(27.6)** At the T-junction with the main road, turn right [Via Foce, Mirteto sign on the left] 🚶 **(27.7)** Turn left [Direction Lavacchio, via Frangola] **(27.8)** Take the first turning to the right [Via Ortola] **(28.0)** Turn left and then right [Take the bridge over the stream] **(28.1)** Bear right down the steps **(28.2)** At the T-junction turn left [Keep the river on the right] **(28.2)** Turn right over the bridge [Continue on via Ponte Vecchio] **(28.5)** Bear right and immediately take the left fork [Via Palestro towards the centre of Massa] 🚶 **(29.0)** At the mini roundabout bear right on via Cavour [No Entry sign, Seminary on the left] **(29.0)** Turn left [Towards the Duomo] **(29.1)** Arrive at **Massa** centre [Beside the Duomo]

Direct Beach-side Route to Pietrasanta

Route: the shorter route to Pietrasanta, provides relief from further climbs and descents by following the broad promenade beside the Mediterranean before turning inland on the cycle track to find the centre of Pietrasanta. It is easy going for cyclists. There are numerous camp sites, hotels, bars and restaurants beside the route.

Length:	25.2km
Ascent:	220m
Descent:	219m

(0.0) At the T-junction, turn right on via del Parmignola [Towards Autostrada] 🚶 **(1.9)** At the crossroads, turn left towards the sea [Via della Repubblica] **(2.0)** At the T-junction with the main road, turn left on the road [Cross the waterways on the SP432 and enter **Marina di Carrara**] 🚶 **(5.3)** After passing through Marina di Carrara, bear left to turn inland and remain on the main road [Viale delle Pinete, coast road dead ends at a boat marina] 🚶 **(9.3)** At the roundabout, turn right towards the sea [Via Casola, direction Viareggio] **(9.5)** Turn left, continue with sea on right [Pass through **Marina di Massa**] 🚶 **(11.0)** At the roundabout continue straight ahead. Note:- to regain the "Official Route" in Massa centre turn left and follow viale Roma [Direction Forte dei Marmi] 🚶 **(20.9)** Shortly after crossing the waterway and before the traffic lights in **Fiumetto**, turn left on the path across the grassed area [Hotel Coluccini on the left] **(21.0)** Cross the road and continue straight ahead into the car park **(21.1)** Continue straight ahead on the broad track [Keep kiosks on your right] 🚶 **(22.7)** Beside the roundabout with a slender stone sculpture in the centre, continue straight ahead at the pedestrian crossing and follow the cycle track [Direction Pietrasanta] 🚶 **(24.0)** At the traffic lights, take the pedestrian crossing and continue straight ahead on the cycle track [Tree lined road towards the hills] **(24.7)** At the T-junction turn left on the cycle track [Direction Seravezza, pass commercial centre on the left] **(25.0)** At the roundabout take the cycle track beside the first exit and pass under the railway [Via Vincenzo Santini, direction Pietrasanta centre] 🚶 **(25.2)** At the T-junction turn right to join the "Official Route" [Via Marconi]

Sarzana to Massa stage 70

Accommodation and Tourist Information

Carrara
Parrocchia San Pietro Apostolo - Ostello "Antonio Mazzi",Piazza Finelli, 11, 54033 Carrara(MS), Italy; Tel:+39 0585 857203; +39 3388 333413; Email:alpi500@interfree.it; Price:D; *A lovely basement level hostel*; **PR**
B&B - New Life [Emanuela and Elisa],Via Provinciale Avenza Sarzana, 48, 54033 Carrara(MS), Italy; Tel: +39 3737 482862; Email:newlifecarrara@gmail.com; Price:C; *Special price fpor pilgrims*

Forte-dei-Marmi
Ufficio Turistico,Via G.Carducci, 6, 55042 Forte-dei-Marmi(LU), Italy; Tel:+39 0584 280292; www.visitforte.com

Marina-di-Massa
Hotel - Caprice,Via delle Pinete, 3, 54100 Marina-di-Massa(MS), Italy; Tel:+39 0585 082514; +39 3394 526286; Email:info@hotelcaprice.net; www.hotelcaprice.net; Price:B; *Price group A at weekends in the high season*
Camping Luni,Via Luni, 16, 54100 Marina-di-Massa(MS), Italy; Tel:+39 0585 869278; +39 3388 330266; Email:info@campingluni.com; www.campingluni.com; Price:C; *Cabins and caravans available*

Massa
Ostello Palazzo Nizza,Piazza Mercurio, 13, 54100 Massa(MS), Italy; Tel:+39 0585 1886345; Email:ostellopalazzonizza@gmail.com; ostellopalazzonizza.it; Price:B; *Excellent modern facilities perfect location advanced booking recommended* ; **PR**
Convento Cappuccini,Piazza San Francesco, 3, 54100 Massa(MS), Italy; Tel:+39 9058 542181; www.cappuccinitoscani.it; Price:D
Pieve di San Vitale Martire e San Giovanni Battista,Via San Vitale, 38, 54100 Massa(MS), Italy; Tel: Email:anspimirteto@libero.it ; Price:D
B&B - Abbaino,Via Castagnola di Sopra, 99, 54100 Massa(MS), Italy; Tel: +39 3384 137475; Email:info@abbainomassa.it; abbainomassa.it; Price:A
Hotel - Annunziata,Via Villafranca, 4, 54100 Massa(MS), Italy; Tel:+39 0585 41023; +39 0585 810205; Email:info@hotelannunziata.com; www.hotelannunziata.com; Price:B; *Price group A in the high season*

Camping Dolce,Via Degli Unni, 13, 54100 Massa(MS), Italy; Tel:+39 0585 869409; campingdolcesole.it; Price:C; *Pods available in price group B*
Campeggio Citta' di Massa,Via delle Pinete, 384, 54100 Massa(MS), Italy; Tel:+39 0585 869361; Email:camping@cittadimassa.it; www.cittadimassa.it; Price:C; *Mobile homes and bungalows also available*
Comune di Massa,Via Porta Fabbrica, 1, 54100 Massa(MS), Italy; Tel:+39 0585 4901; Email:comune.massa@postacert.toscana.it; www.comune.massa.ms.it
Agenzia Per il Turismo,Lungomare Vespucci, 24, 54100 Massa(MS), Italy; Tel:+39 0585 240063; Email:infoturismo@comune.massa.ms.it; www.aptmassacarrara.it

Strettoia
B&B - Podere Gabrielli,via Albatreta, 42, 55045 Strettoia(LU), Italy; Tel:+39 3387192727; Email:elisainchains@yahoo.it; Price:C; *Washing machine and kitchen good value*

Leaving Massa by Porta Quaranta

stage 71 — Massa to Camaiore

Length:	25.9km
Ascent:	1002m
Descent:	1043m
Col Grand St Bernard:	559km
Rome:	469km

Piazza Duomo–Pietrasanta

Route: the route from Massa to Camaiore begins on the busy via Aurelia, before crossing the ridge above the vineyards and olive groves on a narrow hillside road and then descending through an industrial zone for the entry to the attractive and artistic town of Pietrasanta. Leaving Pietrasanta there is another short stretch of busy main road before crossing the Monteggiori ridge to the canal-side track which leads to the pretty and bustling town of Camaiore. Strettoia and Pietrasanta offer the possibility of a meal or drink break.

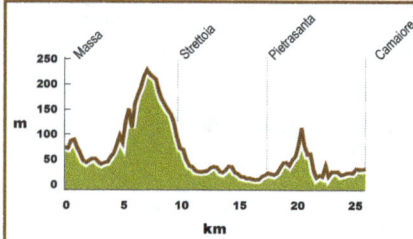

Pietrasanta has Roman origins. Part of the Roman wall still exists. The medieval town was founded in 1255 and built on the pre-existing Rocca di Sala fortress of the Lombards. At its height, Pietrasanta was a part of the Genova city state (1316 -1328). Then, in 1494, Charles VIII of France took control of the town, and it remained so, until Pope Leo X gave Pietrasanta back to the Medici family. It grew in importance during the 15th century, mainly due to its connection with marble. Michelangelo was the first sculptor to recognize the beauty of the local stone. Camaiore also owes its origins to the Romans, who, after establishing Lucca, set up outposts on the slopes of Monte Prana. Among these was Camaiore, whose name comes from the ancient toponym Campus Major, the large plain that linked Lucca to the port in Luni.

🚶 **(0.0)** With the Duomo behind go straight ahead on via Dante Alighieri [Towards piazza Aranci] **(0.1)** At the entrance to piazza Aranci, turn left [Trees and obelisk on the right] **(0.2)** At the exit from the piazza, bear left and immediately right [Keep the palazzo immediately on you right] **(0.3)** Keep to the left side of piazza Mercurio and turn left to climb the steps. Note:- to avoid the steps continue straight ahead on via Mario Bigini and via Prado [Via Bigini on the right] **(0.3)** At the T-junction with the road, turn right [Via Piastronata] **(0.5)** Beside Chiesa della Madonna del Carmine, bear right on via Santa Chiara [Keep Castello Malaspina high on your left] 🚶 **(1.0)** At the T-junction, turn left on the small road [Via Grondini] **(1.0)** At the T-junction with the larger road, turn right [Via del Bargello] **(1.2)** At the crossroads turn left and proceed with caution on the pavement beside the main road [Pizzeria on the left] **(1.4)** Take the left fork [Remain beside the main road] 🚶 **(2.9)** After passing the hospital on the left, bear left away from the via Aurelia [Via Carlo Sforza, No Entry] **(3.7)** At the end of the road, turn left [Concrete wall ahead, No Entry sign] 🚶 **(4.2)**

Massa to Camaiore — stage 71

Turn right across the road and then left [Car park on the left, river immediately to your right]**(4.4)**Cross the footbridge and turn left. Note:- cyclists should take the road bridge 150m ahead [Via Bottaccio]**(4.5)**At the end of the road turn right up the hill on via Patatina [Pass Fortezza Aghinolfi on the hilltop] **(7.2)**Keep right on the road [Avoid the left fork] **(9.8)**In **Strettoia** continue straight ahead on the road [Pass the hotel on your left]**(9.9)**Just before the road bends to the left, turn right on the small road [Via Riccio]**(10.0)**At the junction at the end of the road, turn right [Bar beside the junction]**(10.1)**Just before reaching the bridge, turn left [Via della Chiesa]**(10.4)**Keep right [Pass the church on your left]**(10.4)**After passing the church grounds, turn left on the small road [Via SS Ippolito e Cassiano] **(10.8)**At the T-junction, turn right [Via Risciolo]**(11.3)**At the T-junction, turn left on via Romana [Pass a small shrine on your right] **(11.9)**Keep right on via Romana [Avoid via del Pergolene on the left]**(12.5)**At the Stop sign, turn right and then immediately left at the traffic lights [Direction Seravezza]**(12.7)**At the crossroads, turn right [Via della Pace]**(12.8)**At the next crossroads, turn left [Towards the church - Sant'Antonio Abate] **(13.0)**At the crossroads beside the church, turn right [Via G. Alessandrini]**(13.2)**At the traffic lights bear left with great care on the walled road [Keep river on your left]**(13.3)**Cross the river bridge and then turn right on the riverside track**(13.8)**At the T-junction with the road, turn left and then take the next right [Direction Solaio] **(14.0)**At the crossroads turn right [Narrow bridge]**(14.1)**Facing the water fountain, turn right [Via Pozzone]**(14.4)**Take the right fork [Via Pozzone]**(14.7)**Cross the SP8 and take the grass track beside the river [River on the right] **(15.5)**Go down the steps onto the road and continue ahead. Then turn left on via Torraccia [Pass a wood yard on the right]**(16.0)**At the junction, continue straight ahead [Via Torracia]**(16.5)**Bear left beside the road [Away from railway] **(16.6)**At the major junction, continue straight ahead on the cycle track beside the road. The coastal Alternate Route joins from the right [Via Marconi]**(17.0)**In piazza Matteotti bear slightly right towards the centre of Pietrasanta [Pass gladiator sculpture on your left]**(17.1)**Continue straight ahead [Car park on your left]**(17.1)**Continue straight ahead into the pedestrian zone [Pass mirrored sculpture, via Mazzini]**(17.4)**In piazza Duomo in **Pietrasanta** take via Giuseppe Garibaldi [Beside the Duomo] **(17.8)**At the junction, proceed straight ahead with care on the main road [SP439, direction Lucca]**(18.4)**Beside the cemetery turn left, on via Valdicastello Carducci [Signpost chiesa and VF map] **(19.7)**Turn right on via Regnalla [Road bends to the left in 200m]**(20.0)**Take the second right after the bend [Uphill]**(20.1)**Take the right fork [Keep industrial building on your left]**(20.3)**Pass beside the factory and a quarry and take the footpath to the right through

stage 71 — Massa to Camaiore

the woods [Towards the brow of the hill]**(20.6)**Bear right on the footpath at the end of the woods and proceed directly downhill 🛈 **(20.7)**Turn left towards the electricity substation**(20.7)**At the T-junction with the road, turn left and immediately right on the road [Pass the high stone wall on your left]**(21.0)**At the T-junction, turn left [Conifers on your left]**(21.1)**At the junction with the main road turn left and immediately right [Strada di Monteggiori]**(21.2)**Bear left onto a small footpath**(21.6)**Bear right on the broad track**(21.6)** Join the road and continue straight ahead**(21.7)**At the T-junction, turn left 🛈 **(21.8)**Fork left [Junction beside large ornamental gates]**(22.1)**At the crossroads with via Selvaiana continue straight ahead [Map on your right at the junction]**(22.4)**Bear right down the hill**(22.7)**Bear left [Via Dietro Monte] 🛈 **(22.9)**Turn left on via del Pezzigno**(23.7)**Turn right, towards the main road**(23.8)**Just before the T-junction with the main road, turn left and follow the path parallel to the busy road [Line of trees on your right] 🛈 **(24.0)**Beside the playground, turn right, carefully cross the road and take the bridge over the canal. Then turn left [Keep the canal close on your left] 🛈 **(25.1)**Continue straight ahead on the road beside the canal, via Virgilio Boschi [Pass football ground on the left]**(25.7)**Take the bridge to the left, cross the main road and continue straight ahead [Direction Centro, via Carignoni]**(25.8)**At the T-junction, turn left [Direction Centro]**(25.9)**Before reaching the petrol station turn right [Piazza 29 Maggio]**(25.9)**Arrive at **Camaiore (XXVII)** [Via IV Novembre]

Accommodation and Tourist Information

Camaiore

Ostello del Pellegrino di Camaiore,Via Madonna della Pietà, 1, 55041 Camaiore(LU), Italy; Tel:+ 39 0584 986224; +39 3451 168661; Email:info@ostellodicamaiore.it; ostellodicamaiore.it; Price:C; *Discount with credentials*

La Nuova Selvaiana,Via la Stretta, 228, 55041 Camaiore(LU), Italy; Tel: +39 3894 308212; Email:biomela81@gmail.com; Price:C; *Accommodation in a yurt*

B&B - Casa Nostra,Via Fonda, 93, 55041 Camaiore(LU), Italy; Tel: www.bedandbreakfast.eu; Price:B

Locanda - le Monache,Piazza 29 Maggio, 36, 55041 Camaiore(LU), Italy; Tel:+39 0584 989158; +39 3391 976535; Email:info@lemonache.com; lemonache.com; Price:A

Guest House - la Stagione Dell'Arte [Luca],Via Vittorio Emanuele, 185, 55041 Camaiore(LU), Italy; Tel: Email:la.stagione.arte@gmail.com; lastagionedellarte.jimdo.com; Price:B

Comune di Camaiore,Piazza San Bernardino, 1, 55041 Camaiore(LU), Italy; Tel: +39 0584 9861; Email:comune.camaiore@cert.legalmail.it; www.comune.camaiore.lu.it

Nocchi

Apartment - La Casa di Ciaccia [Maria Grazia],Via XX Settembre, 114, 55041 Nocchi(LU), Italy; Tel: +39 3285751851; Price:B

Pietrasanta

Casa Diocesana "la Rocca",Via della Rocca, 55045 Pietrasanta(LU), Italy; Tel:+39 0584 793093; +39 0584 793094; Email:casarocca@tiscali.it; Price:C

Ostello San Francesco,Via San Francesco 72 , 55045 Pietrasanta(LU), Italy; Tel:+39 353 4302467; +39 3895297667; +39 3486001527; +30 3395668841; Email:sanfrancescopietrasanta@gmail.com; ospitalitareligiosa.it; *Open April to Octpober*

B&B - la Bugneta,Via Degli Olmi, 55, 55045 Pietrasanta(LU), Italy; Tel: +39 3885 611873; Email:info@labugneta.com; www.labugneta.com; Price:B; *Price group A in the high season*

B&B - Da Pio,Via Traversagna, 54, 55045 Pietrasanta(LU), Italy; Tel: +39 3482 517448; Email:info@dapio.it; www.dapio.it; Price:A

Art Hotel,Via Provinciale Vallecchia, 50, 55045 Pietrasanta(LU), Italy; Tel:+39 0584 742470; Email:info@arthotelpietrasanta.it; arthotelpietrasanta.it; Price:A

Comune di Pietrasanta,Piazza Matteotti, 29, 55045 Pietrasanta(LU), Italy; Tel:+39 0584 7951; www.comune.pietrasanta.lu.it

Camaiore to Lucca

stage 72

Length:	26.7km
Ascent:	1083m
Descent:	1089m
Col Grand St Bernard:	585km
Rome:	443km

Lucca

Route: the stage from Camaiore to Lucca uses minor roads, farm and forest tracks before a long stretch of a sometimes busy road. The route finally approaches Lucca along a riverside track and suburban roads before entering the historic centre of the walled city through Porta San Donata.

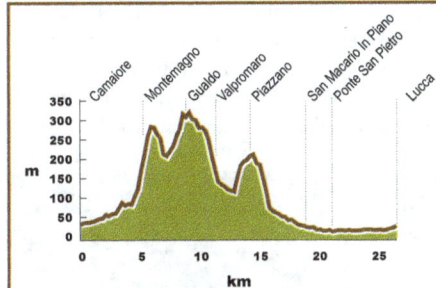

The village of Valpromaro has a welcoming cafe/bar and an excellent hostel.

Approaching Lucca, a short diversion, immediately before crossing Ponte San Pietro, will take you to Pasticceria Dianda, a café selling delicious pastries.

Lucca is one of the highlights of the journey and so if you are needing a rest day then this is an ideal place.

Lucca's origins are the object of historical research and disagreement. Some scholars claim that the Ligurians first set up in the area and that the name, Lucca, might therefore come from the Celtic-Ligurian word Luk, meaning marsh. Other researchers attribute the birth of the city to the Etruscans, according to recent archaeological finds. However, it is agreed by all that Lucca was colonised and developed by the Romans in 180 BC. The city still maintains the Roman orthogonal planning, which divided the space within the walls into regular blocks. In later years, Lucca became an independent republic as part of feudal Italy, but was conquered by Napoleon and finally became part of Unified Italy in 1860.

Lucca is a fascinating city, packed full of monuments representing all the various historical epochs it has lived through, beginning with a Roman amphitheatre – today piazza dell'Anfiteatro – a circular space that has retained its original shape and sense of communal venue, thanks to its architect, Lorenzo Nottolini. Following this, there is the Medieval era, and perhaps what one could say are Lucca's true treasures. Its nickname, the city of one hundred churches, is not a random choice, because it does have a remarkable and vastly varied collection.

Labyrinth - Cattedrale di San Martino, Lucca

stage 72 — Camaiore to Lucca

⛪ **(0.0)** With the church directly ahead, take the first turn to the right [Via IV Novembre] **(0.5)** After passing the church on your right, turn left and then take the next turning to the right [Contrada la Rocca leading to via Vittorio Emanuele] **(0.6)** At the roundabout in piazza Carlo Romboni, continue straight ahead [Via Roma] ⛪ **(1.8)** At the junction with the SP1, cross over the main road and take the minor road over the bridge [Towards the sports ground "Tori"] **(2.1)** Continue straight ahead on the footpath [Sports ground to the left] **(2.3)** At the T-junction with the tarmac road turn left [Frazione Marignana] **(2.6)** Just before reaching the canal, turn right on the road [Keep canal to the left] ⛪ **(3.0)** As the road enters a farm turn right on the track [Towards the woods] **(3.1)** Turn left on the footpath [Between the woods and a field] **(3.3)** Beside the farm buildings, cross the tarmac driveway and bear right on the track [Beside the woods] ⛪ **(4.0)** Turn left on the track [Towards the church] **(4.1)** At the T-junction with the road, turn left and immediately right [Pass the church on the right] **(4.7)** After passing a large country house, bear left onto the track [Keep house on right] **(4.7)** Turn right onto the SP1 [Uphill] **(4.8)** On the apex of the bend to the left, turn right up the stony track ⛪ **(5.1)** Continue straight on, up the narrow pathway [Beside electricity substation] **(5.2)** At the top of the steps turn right and right again [Via del Leccio] **(5.3)** Turn right onto the main road – SP1 and enter **Montemagno** [Bar and restaurant on left and right] **(5.4)** At the junction continue straight ahead [Hedgerow on your right, houses to your left] **(6.0)** At the T-junction at the top of the hill, turn right and immediately left on the path into the trees [Hamlet of Licetro to your left] ⛪ **(6.5)** Bear left on the gravel road **(7.1)** At the T-junction at the end of the road, turn right beside the main road [Cross a small bridge] **(7.3)** Turn sharp left to take the road into Gualdo ⛪ **(7.6)** As the road turns sharply left, cross the bridge and then turn sharp right on the track beside the river - Rio della Presa **(8.0)** Cross the stream and continue straight ahead, up the hill **(8.2)** Cross the stream and climb the winding track ahead **(8.6)** At the T-junction in Quaivra, turn left on the tarmac road ⛪ **(8.9)** As you enter the village of **Gualdo** keep right until after passing through the archway you arrive beside a small chapel **(9.0)** Continue on via della Chiesa dei Santi Nicolao e Giusto [Pass the church on your right] **(9.1)** At the T-junction at the foot of the hill turn right and then fork left on the gravel track ⛪ **(11.4)** Turn left on the narrow street and then right at the T-junction [Enter the village of

Camaiore to Lucca — stage 72

Valpromaro](**11.5**)Continue straight along the main street [Pass beside the hostel "Casa del Pellegrino"](**11.9**)Continue along the main street of the village [Pass the church on your right](**11.9**)After passing through the village, turn right onto track between houses (**12.9**) At the T-junction, turn right onto the minor road [Direction Piazzano](**13.1**)Just before the road turns to the left, turn right onto a gravel track. Note:- the off-road section can be slippery and difficult for cyclists. If necessary they should remain on the road to Piazzano(**13.2**) Turn left over the bridge(**13.7**)At the T-junction with a minor road turn left [Via delle Gavine](**13.8**)Take the right fork into Piazzano [Via della Chiesa XII] (**14.3**)At the crossroads in centre of **Piazzano** turn right(**14.7**)On leaving the village, continue straight ahead on the road [Pass the church on the left](**15.1**)Bear right on the track . Note:- cyclists continue straight ahead on the road to the T-junction [Pass cemetery on your right](**15.1**) Bear left at the fork (**15.9**)At the T-junction with the road, turn left [Across the stream] (**16.2**)Continue straight ahead on via delle Gavine. Cyclists rejoin from the road on the left [Stream on the right] (**19.1**)At the Stop sign in **San Macario In Piano**, bear right and remain on the major road [Sign to Piazzano on your left at the junction](**19.7**)Bear left on the narrow street, in the direction of the church tower [Via della chiesa Ventitreesima] (**20.1**) Bear right on the road [Embankment on your left](**20.8**)At the crossroads, continue straight ahead onto a small road skirting the village [Towards church](**21.2**)At the crossroads, turn left over the river bridge **Ponte San Pietro**(**21.4**)Immediately after crossing the bridge, turn left onto a small tarmac riverside road [Keep river close on your left] (**24.5**)Pass under the footbridge and fork right onto the tarmac road(**25.1**)At the crossroads turn left onto via Cavalletti (**25.9**)At the traffic lights, cross the road and pass under the arch into walled medieval centre of Lucca(**26.2**)At the T-junction, turn right on piazza Giuseppe Verdi [Pass the ancient Porta San Donata on your right](**26.3**)Take the first left turn [Towards Ostello S. Frediano, No Entry](**26.7**)Arrive at **Lucca (XXVI)** centre in piazza San Michele [Church to the left]

Accommodation and Tourist Information

Camaiore
Casa del Pellegrino,Valpromaro, 55041 Camaiore(LU), Italy; Tel:+39 0584 956028; +39 0584 956159; +39 3276 948204; Email:valpromaro@gmail.com; web.facebook.com/CasaDelPellegrinoValpromaro; Price:D; *Welcoming with a strong pilgrim spirit* ; **PR**

Lucca
San Davino Pilgrim's Village,Via San Leonardo, 12, 55100 Lucca(LU), Italy; Tel:+39 0583 53576; +39 36 6106 2641; Email:sandavino@luccatranoi.it ; www.luccatranoi.it; Price:D

stage 72 — Camaiore to Lucca

Canonici Regolari Lateranensi, Via San Nicolao, 76, 55100 Lucca(LU), Italy; Tel: +39 3311 311522; Email: francigenalucca2017@gmail.com; Price:D

Ostello San Frediano, Via della Cavallerizza, 12, 55100 Lucca(LU), Italy; Tel: +39 0583 442817; Email: info@luccaitinera.it ; ostello-san-frediano.business.site; Price:B

Convento dei Frati Cappuccini, Via della Chiesa - Monte San Quirico, 87, 55100 Lucca(LU), Italy; Tel: +39 0583 341426; +39 0583 341424; Email: lucca@fraticappuccini.it; www.fraticappuccini.it; Price:D; Approximately 2km from the city centre

Lorenzo Frassa, Via del Tiro a Segno, 44, 55100 Lucca(LU), Italy; Tel: +39 3392967826; Email: lorenzo.frassa@gmail.com; Price:C

B&B - Al Cardinale , Corte Dell'Angelo, 13, 55100 Lucca(LU), Italy; Tel: +39 3397 786914; Email: alcardinalelucca@gmail.com; alcardinalelucca.it; Price:B; **PR**

B&B - Il Seminario, Via del Seminario, 5, 55100 Lucca(LU), Italy; Tel:+39 0583 954488; +39 328 326 4280; Email:info@bebseminario.com; luccabedandbreakfast.com; Price:A; *Expensive but efficient and convenient for the railway station*; **PR**

B&B - La Gemma di Elena, Via della Zecca, 33, 55100 Lucca(LU), Italy; Tel:+39 0583 496665; +39 3202 346331; Email:lagemma@interfree.it; www.lagemmadielena.it; Price:B

Affitacameret - il Ponte, Via Sarzanese, 11, 55056 Lucca(LU), Italy; Tel:+39 0583 329815; +39 3496 128128; Email: receptionilpontelucca@gmail.com; www.affittacamereilponte.com; Price:B

Affittacamere - la Camelia, Piazza San Francesco, 35, 55100 Lucca(LU), Italy; Tel:+39 340 4792471; Email:info@affittacamerelacamelia.com; www.affittacamerelacamelia.com; Price:B

Azienda di Promozione Turistica, Piazzale Giuseppe Verdi, 55100 Lucca(LU), Italy; Tel:+39 0583 583150; Email:info@turismo.lucca.it; www.turismo.lucca.it

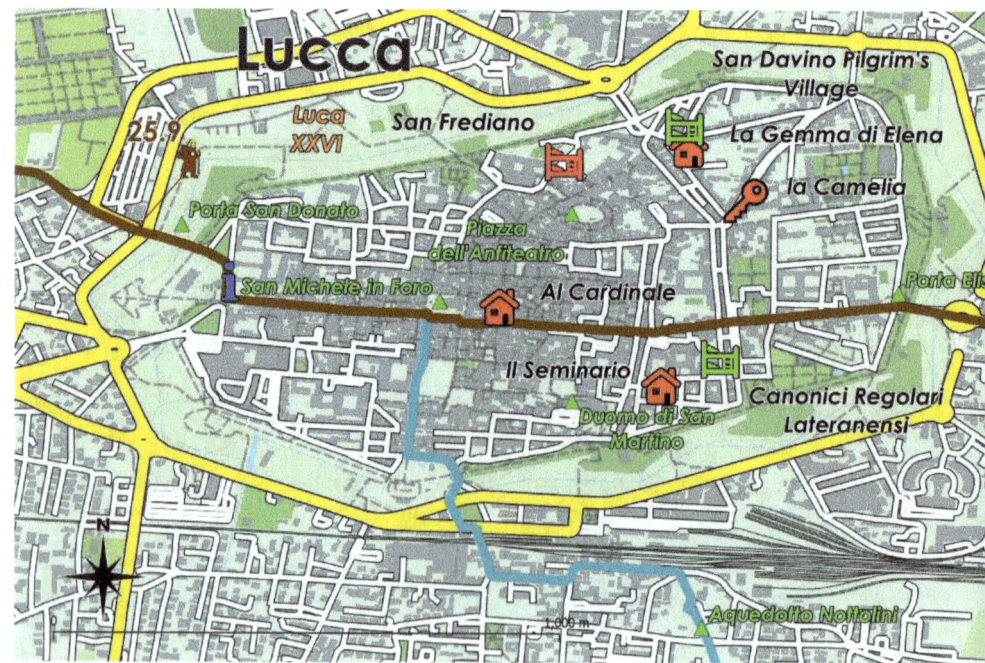

Lucca to Altopascio

stage 73

Length:	18.5km
Ascent:	137m
Descent:	147m
Col Grand St Bernard:	612km
Rome:	416km

Labirinto del Pellegrino–Capannori

Route: the route from Lucca to Altopascio is substantially undertaken on the tarmac weaving a course on minor roads to the south and north of the busy SP6.

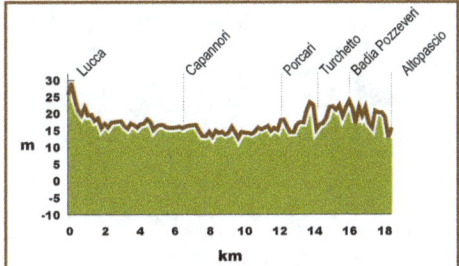

For those preferring a more rural experience a longer Alternate Route is described initially following the 19th century Acquedotto del Nottolini before traversing wooded hills to the south of Lucca. Capannori and Porcari have cafés and shops. Close to the museum, hostel and tourist centre in Capannori, you will also find a modern day labyrinth.

Altopascio has been known as a stopover for pilgrims on the via Francigena for centuries, but it is also called the "city of bread" because of the long-standing traditions passed down through generations in a region known for its abundance of grain.

In the historic centre, the church of San Jacopo, built in 1100, during the great reign of the Order of Hospitallers is worth stopping for. The façade is decorated with smooth stone at the base and with horizontal stripes of white and green marble at the top. There is also a notable marble lunette above the doorway with two stone lions standing guard. The impressive bell tower was built in 1280 and its medieval turrets can still be seen intact.

The piazza dei Ospitalieri, the most significant square in the historic centre, has an interesting octagonal well at its centre. Altopascio's hospital does not appear on Sigeric's itinerary, because it was founded (1084) after his pilgrimage. Nevertheless, it was an important institution because of its position on a particularly difficult section of road that passed between the marshes of Fucecchio and Bientina, an ideal place for brigands to attack the unprotected pilgrims. This formed the basis of the later Order of Saint James of Altopascio founded by Matilda of Canossa between 1070 and 1080.

Chiesa di San Jacopo

stage 73 — Lucca to Altopascio

🚶(0.0) From piazza San Michele, take via Roma and then via San Croce [Keep church to the left](0.6) Go through archway, Porta San Gervasio and across the canal onto via Elisa(1.0) After passing through the triple arched Porta Elisa, continue straight ahead across the main road onto viale Luigi Cadoma [Direction Pontedera] 🚶(1.3) At the T-junction, turn left onto via di Tiglio [Towards the domed Santuario di S. Gemma](1.5) Turn right onto via Romana [Towards the hotels] 🚶(3.0) Turn right onto the small road, via dei Paladini [Distinctive tiny chapel on the corner] 🚶(4.5) At the Stop sign, continue straight ahead on via Vecchia Romana [Pass the church of San Michele on the left](4.9) At the crossroads with the main road, continue straight ahead on the small road [Pass house n° 1241 on your left](5.1) At the next crossroads, continue straight ahead on the small road. Note:- at the time of writing maintenance work was being undertaken in the area - it is possible that a more direct route is now available to the centre of Capannori [Enter Capannori] 🚶(5.5) At the junction, after passing the cemetery on the right, continue straight ahead [Pass a shrine on your right](5.8) Keep right at the junction [House n°21 on your right](6.2) At the crossroads, turn left [Crucifix at the junction](6.3) At the T-junction, turn left. Note:- your credentials can be stamped in the museum [Pass labyrinth and museum on your left] 🚶(6.6)

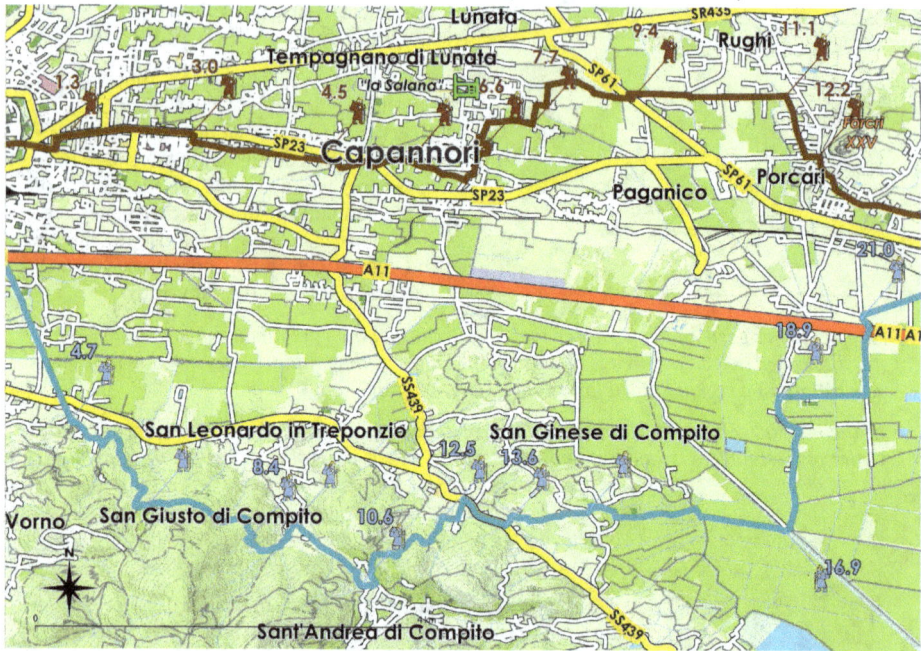

At the crossroads beside the church of San Quirico in the centre of **Capannori** turn right and then take the first road to the left [Into the parking area](6.8) At the end of the parking area, bear left, pass through a second parking area [Towards the shops](6.9) At the junction with the road, turn right [Cycle track on the right of the road](7.0) At the next junction turn right and then immediately left [Continue to follow the cycle track](7.3) At the crossroads, turn right [Via dei Colombini] 🚶(7.5) Turn left on the small road, via del Fontana [Pass the sports ground on the left](8.1) Turn left [Keep the drainage ditch on your left] (8.4) At the T-junction, turn right [Pass house n° 46 on your right] 🚶(9.4) At the junction

Lucca to Altopascio — stage 73

with the main road, SP61, turn left and immediately right [Over the bridge, towards the industrial zone]**(10.1)**At the roundabout, turn right and then left on the road [Via Ciarpi, enter Porcari] **(11.1)**Just after crossing the stream turn right [Via Pacconi]**(12.0)**At the T-junction, turn left on via Capannori [Towards the post office] **(12.2)**In the centre of **Porcari (XXV)** turn right at the traffic lights [Pass church on the hill to the left] **(14.3)** Immediately after entering **Turchetto**, bear right on the small road [Towards industrial area]**(14.6)**At the junction with a major road, cross straight over onto via Pistoresi-Tappo-Turchetto [Pass supermarket on your left]**(15.0)**Turn right onto the track towards trees [Commercial building on left at junction]**(15.5)**Turn left at the end of the cemetery wall, pass the church on your right and follow the access road **(15.5)**Follow the road keeping the church to your left [Via Chiesa]**(16.1)**At the crossroads, proceed straight ahead into **Badia Pozzeveri** on via Catalani [Small shrine to the right] **(18.0)**At the T-junction with the SP3, turn right to go under the road bridge [Towards the bell-tower]**(18.5)**In Piazza Vittorio Emanuele with the chiesa di San Jacopo to your right, cross the piazzas and pass through the arches, then turn right on via San Rocco**(18.5)**Arrive at **Altopascio** [Beside Chiesa di San Jacopo]

Rural Route to Altopascio

Route: this longer but more rural and isolated route begins by following the Acquedotto del Nottolini before climbing 250 m then descending into the Compito valley, where Sant'Andrea lies on another section of the *via di San Colombano***(0.0)**

Length:	23.6km
Ascent:	768m
Descent:	772m

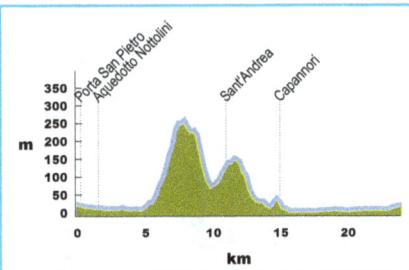

From piazza San Michele, head south on via Veneto**(0.4)**At the end of the road turn left and exit the old town by **Porta San Pietro(0.5)** After passing through Porta San Pietro, continue straight ahead and take the pedestrian bridge over the railway tracks**(0.8)**After crossing the bridge take the first turning to the left [Via Lorenzo Nottolini] **(1.2)**Turn right on via del Tempietto and begin to follow the aqueduct - **Aquedotto Nottolini** [Towards the tower]**(2.1)**Take the pedestrian bridge over the highway and continue beside the aqueduct **(4.7)**At the tower at the end of the elevated aqueduct, bear left [Former water course to your left]**(5.1)**At the T-junction beside the stone tower, turn right and immediately bear left into the woods **(6.9)**Close to the top of the hill, turn left on the track **(8.4)**Join the broader track and skirt the olive grove on your right **(9.4)**At the T-junction between the walls in San Giusto, turn right**(10.4)**As the road turns to the left and crosses a small bridge, continue straight ahead [Between the woods and the olive groves] **(10.6)**At the T-junction in **Sant'Andrea**, turn left [Towards the bell tower]**(10.8)**At the T-junction, turn left and then fork right [Direction San Leonardo] **(11.2)**On leaving the hamlet, turn right [Skirt the summit of the hill on your right] **(12.5)** At the crossroads at the foot of the hill, turn right**(13.0)**At the T-junction with a major road, turn right **(13.6)**Turn left [Direction San Ginese] **(14.6)**At the crossroads in **Capannori**, continue straight ahead and then take the next right on via Colombaia [Via Centoni]**(15.0)**Turn left and pass between the fields [Via Francigena Variante] **(16.9)** Cross the waterway and bear left **(18.9)**With a small bridge to your left, turn right and then left at the T-junction [Via Boccaione] **(21.0)**At the junction following the highway bridge, turn right [Direction Altopascio] **(23.4)**After crossing the railway bridge bear right and rejoin the "Official Route" [Direction Altopascio]

stage 73 — Lucca to Altopascio

Accommodation and Tourist Information

Altopascio

Ostello Per Pellegrini - Magione Cavalieri del Tau, Piazza Ospitalieri, 6, 55011 Altopascio(LU), Italy; Tel: +39 338 4957991; Email:turismo@comune.altopascio.lu.it; www.altopasciocultura.it; Price:D *Stefano and Nicoletta at the Magione Cavalieri del Tau restaurant in Piazza Ricasoli will provide food information and a stamp*

Hospitale San Pietro, Via della Chiesa - Badia Pozzeveri, 55011 Altopascio(LU), Italy; Tel: +39 338 4957991; Email:accoglienzesdfodv@gmail.com; web.facebook.com/sentieriumani; Price:D

B&B - La Porta di San Rocco, Vicolo Dell'Ortaccio, 3, 55011 Altopascio(LU), Italy; Tel:+390583 1795055; +39 3883 669468; Email:altopasciobb@gmail.com; www.bbaltopascio.com; Price:B

B&B - Mansarda Sulla Francigena, Località Carbonata, 22, 55011 Altopascio(LU), Italy; Tel: +39 3703 125766; Email:valcastel2001@yahoo.it; booking.com;

Price:B

Hotel - Da Paola, Via Francesca Romea, 24, 55011 Altopascio(LU), Italy; Tel:+39 0583 276453; +39 36 8765 0227; Email:info@hotelpaolalucca.it; www.hotelpaolalucca.it; Price:B

Albergo - Cavalieri del Tau, Via Gavinana, 56, 55011 Altopascio(LU), Italy; Tel:+39 0583 25131; +39 339 6145608; Email:info@cavalierideltau.it; www.cavalierideltau.it; Price:A

Comune di Altopascio, Piazza Vittorio Emanuele, 24, 55011 Altopascio(LU), Italy; Tel:+39 0583 216455; Email:informa@comune.altopascio.lu.it ; www.comune.altopascio.lu.it

Capannori

Ostello "la Salana", Via del Popolo, 182, 55012 Capannori(LU), Italy; Tel: +39 3397 237912; Email:info@ostellolasalana.it; www.ostellolasalana.it; Price:C

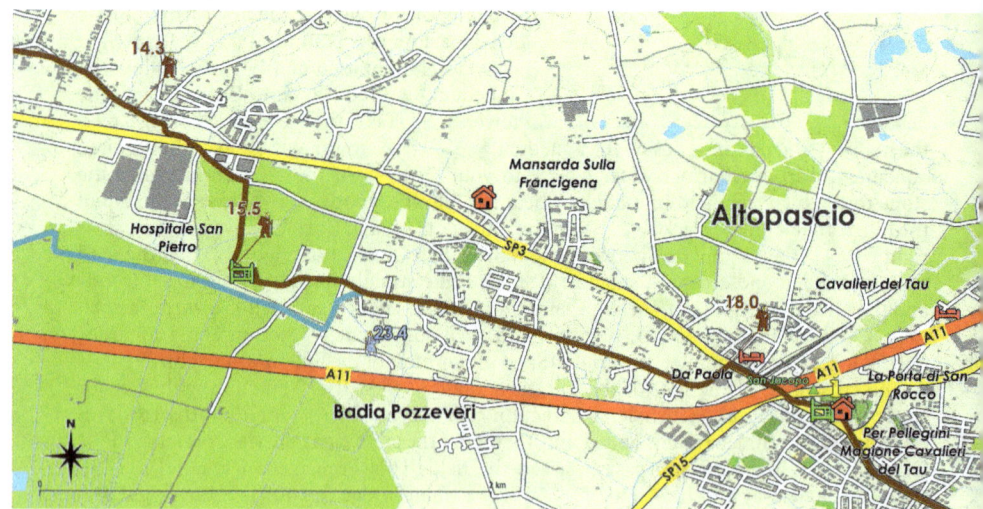

Altopascio to San-Miniato-Alto stage 74

Length:	29.3km
Ascent:	590m
Descent:	480m
Col Grand St Bernard:	630km
Rome:	398km

Ponte a Cappiano - watercolour by Jannina Veit Teuten

Route: the route from Altopascio to San-Miniato-Alto follows the highways to Galleno before discovering an ancient stretch of the via Francigena leading to the hilltop paths of the Cerbaie.

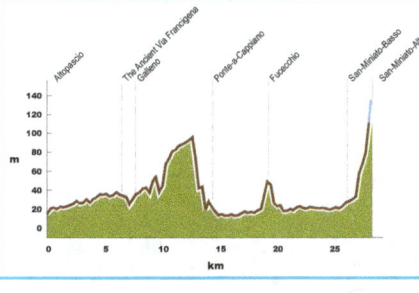

From Ponte a Cappiano the route follows the canal to Fucecchio before crossing the valley of the river Arno and climbing to the historic hilltop town of San Miniato. There are ample stopping places en route.

It does not seem that Sigeric passed through San Miniato, but rather stayed by the waterside at Borgo Santo Genesio.

Leaving Altopascio and beyond Galleno, the road runs downhill towards Padule di Fucecchio, and passes the site where the monastery and parish church of Cappiano once stood. Here, it reaches the bridge of the same name built in its current form in the 16th century by order of Cosimo de Medici to regulate the waters and increase the numbers of fish. The construction is huge and more accurately described as an elongated building suspended over the waters of what used to be the greatest inland marsh in Italy.

The bridge was first put in place when the area was little more than a system of waterways. It is therefore likely that Sigeric disembarked here after travelling by boat from Borgo Santo Genesio. The bridge was destroyed in 1325 during the war between Lucca and Florence and rebuilt again by the monks of the Badia a Settino. Given the strategic importance of its position, the bridge was fortified with a tower and three draw bridges in the late 14th century. In the drawing by Leonardo da Vinci, the structure was equipped with a lock, used both for eel fishing and controlling the flow of water from the swamp.

Today, pilgrims can sleep in the hostel built into the Medici bridge.

stage 74   Altopascio to San-Miniato-Alto

🚶(0.0)Turn left across the car park in the direction of the arches(0.2)At the junction with the main road, bear right on via Cavour, direction Fucecchio [Small building with arched portico to the left](0.4)At the roundabout continue straight ahead [Direction Fucecchio] 🚶 (1.5)At the roundabout turn right on the tarmac track beside the new road [Houses on the right of the track](1.9)As road bears right, remain on the track gently bearing left(2.4)At the T-junction, turn left [Open field on your right] 🚶 (2.6)Approaching the end of the woods, turn left and then turn right(3.3)At the junction with the tarmac road, bear left [Pass the parking area on your left](3.4)At the T-junction, turn right [Towards the Tabacchi](3.4)At the Stop sign, turn left [Direction Orentano] 🚶 (3.7)At the end of the road, turn left and then right on the gravel track(4.2)At the junction, bear right and then left on the long straight track [Beside the copse] 🚶 (4.7)Continue straight ahead, briefly on the tarmac and then following the track ahead(5.3)At the junction in the woods, turn left(5.6)Cross the bridge and continue straight ahead 🚶 (6.0)Turn right following the gravel road [Entrance gates on your left](6.3)At the T-junction with the main road, turn right [Leave the region of Lucca](6.4)Fork right onto the unmade road [**The ancient via Francigena**] 🚶 (7.2)Continue straight ahead [Cross the small bridge](7.7)Arrive in **Galleno** and continue straight ahead on the main road [Via Romana Lucchese, direction Fucecchio] 🚶 (8.7)Bear right at the major road junction [Direction Fucecchio](8.8)Shortly after crossing a bridge, turn right on the track [Pass a house on your left](8.9)Take the left fork [Towards the woods](9.4)Cross over the driveway and continue straight ahead [Equestrian centre on the

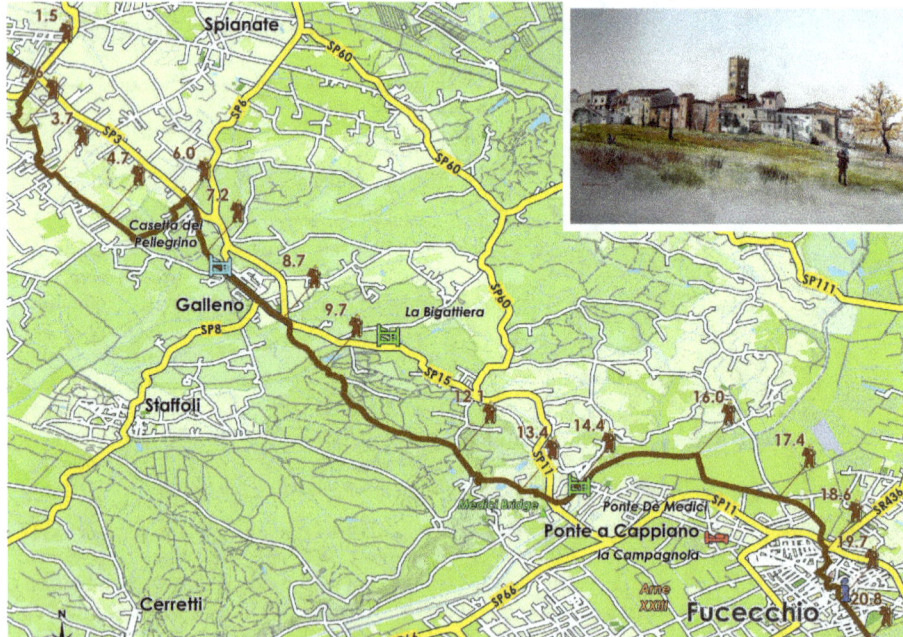

right](9.4)Keep left on the track into the woods [Downhill](9.6)At the T-junction with the road, turn right 🚶 (9.7)Shortly after passing the buildings on the left, join a white road and continue straight ahead(10.0)Brear right, uphill [Pond on the left](10.3)At the first junction after a short climb, continue straight ahead(10.3)At the next junction bear left(10.5)

Altopascio to San-Miniato-Alto — stage 74

Join a broader track and bear slightly left ☗ **(12.1)** At the T-junction with a busy tarmac road, bear right on the SP 61 **(12.5)** Take the left fork on the narrow, busy road, via di Poggio Adorno [Direction Santa Croce] **(12.7)** After the first bend to the left, turn sharp left on the track downhill into the woods ☗ **(13.4)** Bear left on the road [Via De Medici] **(13.8)** Cross the SP11 and continue straight ahead **(13.9)** Bear left [Brick garden wall on your left] ☗ **(14.4)** At **Ponte a Cappiano (XXIV)**, in piazza A. Donnini, turn right [Towards the covered bridge] **(14.4)** Cross the bridge and turn left into the car park and continue along the banks of the canal [Canal immediately to the left] ☗ **(16.0)** Shortly after the canal begins to bend to the left, turn right away from the canal-side onto another embankment [Right angle to canal] **(16.5)** Cross the waterway and turn left - cyclists can continue on the left bank to the next Waypoint where they can cross on a more substantial bridge [Waterway on the left] **(17.0)** Cross the road and continue straight ahead on the embankment [Keep waterway on your left] ☗ **(17.4)** Cross another road and continue straight ahead on the embankment [Pass an industrial complex on the right] **(18.4)** Cross the SP11 and continue on the small road opposite, via Ponte del Rio [Pass a roundabout on the left] ☗ **(18.6)** Cross

viale Napoleone Bonaparte and continue straight ahead [Via Sotto la Valle] **(18.8)** Take the next turning to the right up a long flight of steps [Via Sant'Antonio] **(19.0)** At the T-junction, turn left towards the centre of Fucecchio [Pass house n° 69 on your right] **(19.2)** After passing piazza S Lavagnini on the left, take the next turning to the right [Via G. di San Giorgio] **(19.3)** In the centre of **Fucecchio (XXIII)**, cross piazza Garibaldi and take the small road straight ahead. Note:- cyclists bear left into piazza Veneto to avoid a flight of steps [Parking area on your left] **(19.4)** Turn left [Church on the left] **(19.4)** Go down the steps and cross piazza Vittorio Veneto and bear right down the hill [Via del Cassero] **(19.5)** In piazza Niccolini, turn right [Via Donateschi] ☗ **(19.7)** Continue straight ahead across piazza G. Montanelli and take via N. Sauro [Statue to your right] **(19.8)** At the crossroads, continue straight ahead on the road [Direction San Miniato] **(20.6)** Continue straight ahead. Note:- caution narrow pavements on the bridge [River Arno bridge] ☗ **(20.8)** At the

stage 74 — Altopascio to San-Miniato-Alto

end of the bridge, turn sharp left and then right through the industrial area [Trees and river on the left]**(21.2)**Continue straight ahead on the footpath [On the embankment beside the river]**(21.6)**Bear right on the track and then turn left under the highway and then immediately right [Parallel to the main road] **(22.4)**Continue straight ahead between the embankment and the busy road [Main road on your right]**(22.6)**Turn left on the track into the fields [Garden allotments on the right]**(23.1)**At the T-junction with a road, turn left [Road quickly bends to the right] **(23.6)**Pass through the hamlet of Ontraino and then turn right on the small road immediately after crossing the irrigation channel [Via Candiano]**(24.1)**Take the first turning to the right, gravel track [Between vines] **(24.6)**Bear left on the track [Towards the hilltop town of San Miniato] **(25.9)**At the roundabout, cross the grass and continue straight ahead [Direction San Miniato, tree lined road]**(26.2)**At the traffic lights, in **San Miniato Basso**, turn left [Pass Tabacchi on the left]**(26.3)**Turn right on the small road. Note:- to visit the Sigeric location – Borgo Santo Genesio (XXII) - continue straight ahead on the Alternate Route on the main road. For the Misacordia accommodation, take the second right on the main road [Pass the church on your left]**(26.4)**Bear left on the embankment**(26.8)**Turn left down the steps [Pass between the houses]**(26.8)**At the junction with the road, turn right on via Pozzo [House n° 52 on your right] **(27.2)**At the end of via Pozzo continue straight ahead on the footpath [Pass house n° 89 on your left]**(27.5)**At the junction with the main road, turn right uphill [Enter San Miniato]**(28.1)**Take the right fork. Note:- the "Official Route" makes a loop around the hill following the main road before arriving in the old town. Some relief from the traffic can be found by following the paths in the parks on either side of the road. The Alternate Route to the left follows a more direct but narrow road [Direction San Miniato Centre] **(28.3)**Continue straight ahead, uphill following the road [Pass park on your left]**(28.4)**On the crown of bend to the left, bear right up the steps and continue on the path beside the road**(28.4)**Take the right fork, remaining on the main road [Park on the right]**(28.8)**In piazzetta del Fondo, turn sharp left [Towards the archway]**(29.2)**Take the right fork [Direction "ospedale"]**(29.3)**Arrive at **San-Miniato-Alto** at the stage end [Piazza Bonaparte].

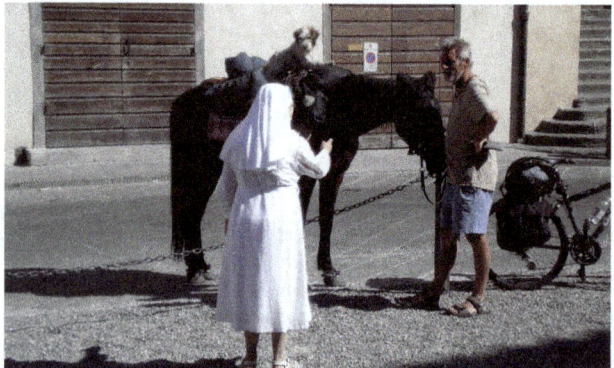

No room at the inn San Miniato

Diversion to Borgo Santo Genesio (XXII)

Route: the diversion bypasses the historic centre of San Miniato to allow a visit to the location of Borgo Santo Genesio (XXII). The route initially follows the busy road from San Miniato Basso towards Ponte a Elsa before climbing to rejoin the "Official Route" near Calenzano on a quiet country road.

Length:	6.2km
Ascent:	171m
Descent:	51m

Altopascio to San-Miniato-Alto — stage 74

(0.0)Continue straight ahead on the SP40 [Direction Ponte a Elsa] (3.7)At the entry to **Ponte a Elsa** bear right on via Nazionale. Note:- the chapel of San Genesio (XXII) and an archaeological dig is to the left [Towards bus stops](3.9)Bear right uphill on the small road [Via Poggio a Pino](4.1)Continue uphill on the small road(4.2)At the Stop sign, continue straight ahead [Church on the right](4.4)Fork right [Uphill](4.6)At the Stop sign, turn left [SS67, direction Calenzano] (6.2)In **Calenzano** bear left on the main road to rejoin the "Official Route" [Downhill]

Direct Route to San-Miniato-Alto

Route: a more direct route to the centre of the high town. (0.0) Fork left onto viale Giacomo Matteotti [Enter the historic centre] (0.2)Bear left onto via San Francesco [Chiesa di San Francesco on your right at the junction](0.2)Take the left fork(0.3)Arrive in San-Miniato-Alto at the section end [Piazza Bonaparte]

Length:	0.3km
Ascent:	29m
Descent:	18m

Accommodation and Tourist Information

Fucecchio

Ostello Ponte Dè Medici,Via Cristoforo Colombo, 237, 50054 Fucecchio(FI), Italy; Tel:+39 0571 297831; Email:ostellopontedeimedici@gmail.com; www.comune.fucecchio.fi.it/node/22000; Price:C

Hotel - la Campagnola,Viale Cristoforo Colombo, 144, 50054 Fucecchio(FI), Italy; Tel:+39 0571 260786; +39 0571 261925; Email:Info@Lacampagnolahotel.com ; www.lacampagnolahotel.com; Price:A

Comune di Fucecchio,Via la Marmora, 34, 50054 Fucecchio(FI), Italy; Tel:+39 0571 2681; Email:comune.fucecchio@postacert.toscana.it; www.comune.fucecchio.fi.it

Galleno

La Bigattiera,Via della Bigattiera, 4, 50054 Galleno(FI), Italy; Tel: +39 3383 906736; Email:eb1960@libero.it; Price:A; *3 bedroom house*

Casetta del Pellegrino,Via della Chiesa, 20, 50054 Galleno(FI), Italy; Tel:+39 0571 299931; Email:sanpietrogalleno@gmail.com; www.parrocchiedellecerbaie.it; Price:D; *small kitchen*

San-Miniato-Alto

L'Hospitale del Pellegrino,Via Gargozzi, 34, 56028 San-Miniato-Alto(PI), Italy; Tel: +39 3499 5126; +39 2958 8422; Email:lhospitaledelpellegrino@gmail.com; Price:D; *Open mid-April to November. Private rooms with bath for 2 or 3 people available.*

Ostello San Miniato,Piazza Giuseppe Mazzini, 1, 56028 San-Miniato-Alto(PI), Italy; Tel: +39 3387 997004; Email:ostellosanminiato@gmail.com; www.ostellosanminiato.com; Price:C; *Pilgrim discount*

Le Finestre del Seminario ,Piazza della Repubblica 7, 56028 San-Miniato-Alto(PI), Italy; Tel: +39 342 0738008; Email:lefinestredelseminario@gmail.com; lefinestredelseminario.it; Price:B; *Historic building*; **PR**

Convento San Francesco,Piazza San Francesco, 1, 56028 San-Miniato-Alto(PI), Italy; Tel:+39 0571 43051; +39 0571 43398; Price:B

Affittacamere - San Miniato,Via Carducci, 2, 56028 San-Miniato-Alto(PI), Italy; Tel: +39 3533 890839; Email:affittacameresanminiato@gmail.com; web.facebook.com/CamereSanminiato; Price:B

Associazione Turistica Pro Loco,Piazza del Popolo, 31, 56028 San-Miniato-Alto(PI), Italy; Tel:+39 0571 42745; Email:ufficio.turismo@sanminiatopromozione.it; www.sanminiatopromozione.it

San-Miniato-Basso

Misericordia San Miniato Basso,Piazza Vincenzo Cuoco, 9, 56028 San-Miniato-Basso(PI), Italy; Tel:+39 0571 419455; Email:misericordiasmb@libero.it ; www.misericordiasanminiatobasso.org/Via-Francigena.htm; Price:D; **PR**

stage 75 — San-Miniato-Alto to Gambassi-Terme

Length:	23.8km
Ascent:	941m
Descent:	745m
Col Grand St Bernard:	660km
Rome:	368km

Piazza del Castello–Gambassi-Terme

Route: as you enter picture book Tuscany, the route from San-Miniato-Alto to Gambassi-Terme follows a mix of country roads and broad tracks (the white roads–*strade bianche*) over the rolling Tuscan hills. The section can be challenging in the summer heat with a stiff final climb and few opportunities for water stops. There is an absence of cafés and shops on the route before the outskirts of Gambassi-Terme, but it is possible to divert to Castelfiorentino.

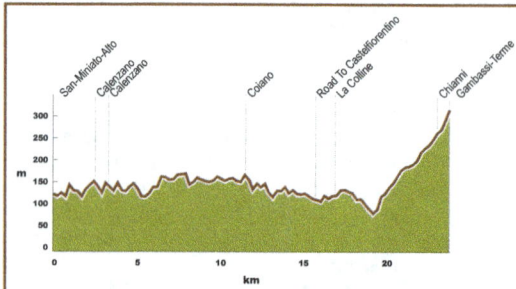

The recommended Ostello Sigerico at Chianni (XX) is on the left shortly before reaching Gambassi-Terme.

The territory around Gambassi-Terme was densely populated from the 7th century B.C., until the Late-Roman age in the 3rd century A.D.. Its history is heavily influenced by its position and featured as a transit route for the Etruscans and later the Romans on the via Clodia, which linked Lucca with Rome. The town was also used as a stopping place for pilgrims on the via Francigena, The establishment of a hospice was recorded in the 13th century. Between the 12th and 13th centuries the inhabitants of Gambassi-Terme enjoyed relative autonomy and prosperity, but this ended when the town was absorbed into the district of San Gimignano. A harsh conflict took place as a result, with considerable loss of life and property. Eventually, the castle of Gambassi was annexed to the territories under the powerful jurisdiction of Florence. From the Middle Ages to the modern era, the area around Gambassi became known for its glass production, and since 1977, Gambassi-Terme has become recognised as a spa resort. The waters are proven to be therapeutic and curative for many ailments.

Church of Santa Maria - Chianni (XX)

San-Miniato-Alto to Gambassi-Terme — stage 75

🚶 **(0.0)** Bear left in piazza Bonaparte and follow via Paolo Maioli [Statue of Leopold II on your right] **(0.4)** Turn right on via Vicolo Borghizzi and almost immediately turn left through an archway. Note:- the pathway ahead involves a flight of steps – cyclists are advised to remain on the road towards Calenzano **(0.5)** Turn right down a small brick passage separated by metal balustrades [Flight of steps] **(0.6)** At the T-junction with the road, turn right - cyclists rejoin from the left [Direction Calenzano] **(0.8)** Bear right up the steps 🚶 **(1.1)** Just before the left bend be, turn left on the path 🚶 **(2.5)** Fork left, in **Calenzano** [Church on right] **(3.3)** Fork right downhill [Direction Castelfiorentino] **(3.3)** At the junction, turn right - Alternate Route rejoins from the left 🚶 **(5.1)** Following a sharp bend to the left, turn right and right again onto a gravel track 🚶 **(6.2)** Fork right **(6.3)** Fork left up the hill towards trees **(6.6)** At the T-junction, turn left 🚶 **(7.5)** Turn sharp left up the hill 🚶 **(8.4)** Turn left with a house directly on the right. Then bear right on via di Meleto 🚶 **(9.6)** Turn onto the furthest left of the tracks via della Poggiarella. Then take the left fork 🚶 **(11.6)** At the crossroads in **Coiano (XXI)** continue straight ahead on the gravel road, via Coianese **(11.9)** Continue straight ahead on the gravel track 🚶 **(12.8)** Fork right down the hill **(13.0)** Fork left

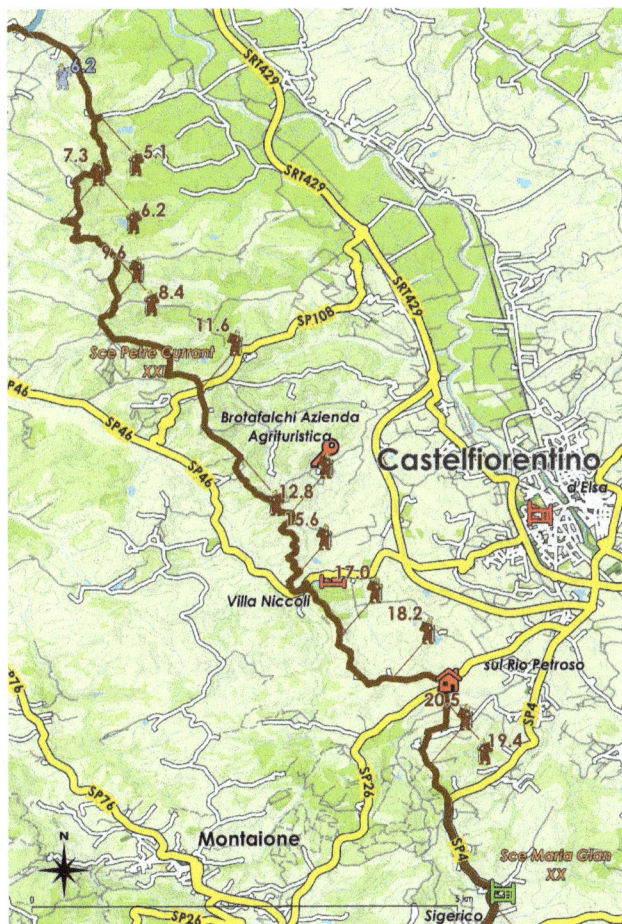

up the hill **(13.4)** Keep left into the trees, avoid the turning to the right 🚶 **(14.1)** Fork right towards the conifers on the ridge 🚶 **(15.6)** At the T-junction, turn left between two houses **(15.8)** At the T-junction with the SP46, turn left on the path beside the road [**Road to Castelfiorentino**] **(16.0)** Turn sharp right onto the track 🚶 **(17.0)** After passing the hamlet of **La Colline** continue straight ahead on the grass track **(17.8)** At the T-junction turn left 🚶 **(18.2)** Keep right on the gravel road along the ridge **(18.9)** Turn right at an elevated T-junction, descend the ramp and join the main road **(19.1)** Turn left over the pedestrian crossing and continue straight ahead on an unmade road 🚶 **(19.4)** Bear right and then left, continue between the vines **(19.7)** At the T-junction, turn right with house on left **(19.9)** Fork left up the hill 🚶 **(20.5)** Keep left, uphill on the gravel road [Hedged garden on your

stage 75 — San-Miniato-Alto to Gambassi-Terme

right]**(21.2)**At the T-junction, turn right onto the SP4 [Shrine just before the junction] 🛏 **(23.1)**Santa Maria a **Chianni (XX)** is to the left. To follow the route to Gambassi-Terme, continue uphill on the main road**(23.6)** At the traffic lights, fork left direction Gambassi**(23.8)** Arrive at **Gambassi-Terme** [Beside the church of Cristo Re in Santi Jacopo e Stefano]

Accommodation and Tourist Information

Castelfiorentino
🛏**Locanda d'Elsa**,Viale Franklin Delano Roosevelt, 26, 50051 Castelfiorentino(FI), Italy; Tel:+39 0571 165 6348; locanda-delsa.business.site; Price:C; *Large modern youth hostel*

🛏 **Hotel - Villa Niccoli** ,Via dei Praticelli, 70, 50051 Castelfiorentino(FI), Italy; Tel: +39 340 645 3039; booking.com; Price:B

🗝 **Brotafalchi Azienda Agrituristica**,Via Don Lorenzo Milani, 12, 50051 Castelfiorentino(FI), Italy; Tel: +39 3490536849 ; Email:info@brotafalchi.it; brotafalchi.it; Price:D; *Farmstay 12 minutes from the trail look for the sign after 12 km*

Certaldo
⛺ **Agricamping - Poggio Ai Pini**,SP 50 di S Donnino, 50052 Certaldo(FI), Italy; Tel:+39 3899564156; +39 3384 783260; Email:info@poggioaipini.it; poggioaipini.it; Price:C

Gambassi-Terme
🛏**Ostello Sigerico** [Anna Giubbolini],Chiani, 50050 Gambassi-Terme(FI), Italy; Tel:+39 0571 639044; +39 3247 968837; Email:ostello.sigerico@yahoo.com; www.ostellosigerico.it; Price:C; **PR**

🏠 **B&B - Casa il Castello**,Via delle Campane, 46, 50050 Gambassi-Terme(FI), Italy; Tel:+39 333 834 4351; Email:crirenie@gmail.com; hotelescon.com.es/casa-il-castello; Price:B; *Central yet with panoramic views. Baggage transport can be arranged*

🏠 **B&B - Hospitalera di Gambassi**,Via Dell' Ecce Homo, 16, 50050 Gambassi-Terme(FI), Italy; Tel: +39 3342 391002; Email:direzione@3beautyfirenze.it; www.3beautyfirenze.it/en/hospitalera-di-gambassi-bb; Price:B

🏠 **B&B - Casa sul Rio Petroso** [Teresa and Andrea],Via San Michelino in piano, 63, 50050 Gambassi-Terme(FI), Italy; Tel: +39 347 2108595; +39 349 5291804; Email:casariopetroso@yahoo.com; www.casariopetroso.com; Price:B

🗝 **Apartment - Casa Giulia sulla Francigena** [Franco Giangrossi],Vicolo del Giglio, 1a, 50050 Gambassi-Terme(FI), Italy; Tel:+39 3297323818; Email:fgiangrossi6@gmail.com; casa-giulia-sulla-francigena.business.site; Price:C; *Kitchen and washing machine available*

ℹ **Comune di Gambassi Terme**,Via Giuseppe Garibaldi, 7, 50050 Gambassi-Terme(FI), Italy; Tel: +39 0571 639154; +39 571 1655111; Email:comune.gambassi@postacert.toscana.it; www.comune.gambassi-terme.fi.it

Gambassi-Terme to San-Gimignano

stage 76

Length:	14.0km
Ascent:	606m
Descent:	595m
Col Grand St Bernard:	683km
Rome:	344km

Piazza Duomo–San Gimignano

Route: this short stage from Gambassi-Terme to San-Gimignano is undertaken substantially on remote tracks winding over the Tuscan hills.

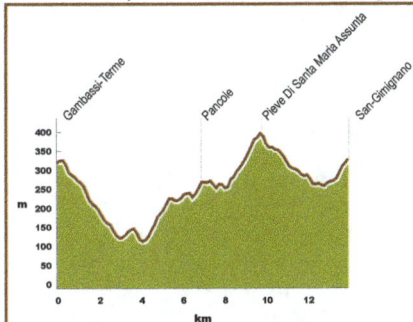

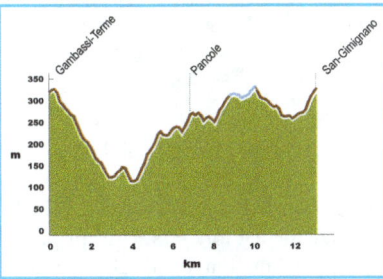

Although beautiful, the section can again be very tiring in the heat of summer. Once more ensure that you have adequate water.

There are neither shops nor cafés between Gambassi-Terme and San-Gimignano.

The foundation of San Gimignano dates back to ancient times. According to legend, in 63 B.C. two brothers, Muzio and Silvio, two young patricians escaping from Rome after their implication in the conspiracy of Catiline, sheltered in Valdelsa and built two castles: the Castle of Mucchio and the Castle of Silvia, which would develop into the future San Gimignano.

The first historical document mentioning the name of the town is dated 30th August 929, when Ugo di Provenza donated to the Bishop of Volterra the so-called Mount of the Tower prope Sancto Geminiano adiacente (next to San Gimignano). The name of San Gimignano probably comes from the bishop of Modena. According to legend, during the barbaric invasions the saint appeared miraculously on the city walls, and saved the town from Totila's threat.

San Gimignano, is famous for its fascinating medieval architecture and seventy-two towers rising above of all the other buildings (today only thirteen towers remain).In medieval times the tower was a symbol of power, mainly because the building process was neither simple nor cheap. Materials needed to be dug and transferred to town, and the building site arranged. Only the richest families of merchants and moneylenders could afford them. The house only occupied part of the tower, the ground floor consisting of workshops, the first floor of bedrooms, and the higher level the kitchen. From the end of the 12th century, towers built according to the same model were also attached to other buildings of lower height.

stage 76   Gambassi-Terme to San-Gimignano

(0.0)From the church of Cristo Re in Santi Jacopo e Stefano, the signed route makes a tour of Gambassi before joining the road opposite the church, via Icilio Franchi, 300m ahead. To tour the town, continue up the hill and the main road and bear right [Pass the car park on your right](0.1)Take the left fork [Center Storico sign](0.2)In the piazza Roma, after passing the Albergo, turn sharp left on via Gonnelli(0.3)At the end of piazza del Cas-

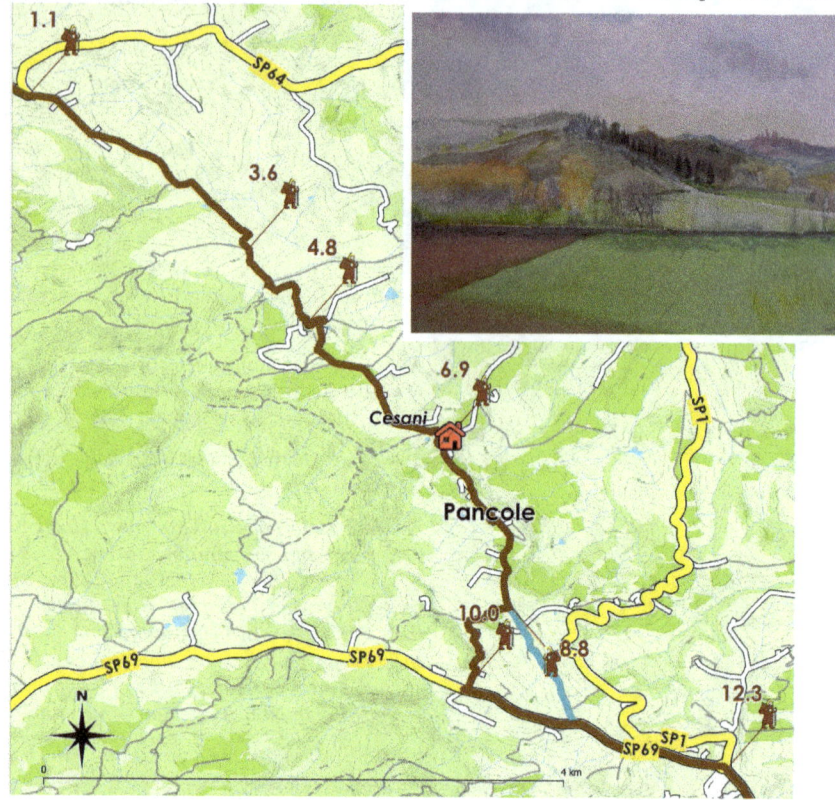

tello, turn left and immediately right through the arch(0.4)Cross piazza Arfaioli and take via delle Monache [No Entry sign](0.6)At the T-junction, turn right. Note:- the shorter route joins from the left (1.1)On the apex of the bend to the left, bear right onto a small road [Direction Luiano](1.7)Beside the small chapel, take the left fork (3.6)At the junction, keep left down the hill(4.1)Cross the bridge and the T-junction, turn right then immediately left(4.3)In the opposite corner of the field, bear right through the trees and continue on the track, uphill [Trees on your left] (4.8)Directly in front of a farmhouse, turn left onto a gravel track [Continuing up the hill](4.9)At the T-junction in the track, turn right up the hill(5.2)Fork left [Via San Piero] (6.9)At the T-junction with a tarmac road, turn right up the hill [Pass through **Pancole**] (8.8)Turn right on the gravel track. Note:- the Official Route makes a loop towards the woods and extends the distance to be covered on the busy SP69. 1km may be saved my remaining on this road and rejoining the "Official Route" at the T-junction ahead(9.1)Take the left fork(9.3)Continue straight ahead [Pass through the archway](9.8)Bear right across the car park [**Pieve di Santa Maria Assunta** on

Gambassi-Terme to San-Gimignano — stage 76

your left] 🚶 **(10.0)** At the T-junction with the SP69, turn left and follow the main road **(11.0)** Continue straight ahead, down the hill [Direction San Gimignano] 🚶 **(12.3)** At the roundabout, bear right, direction San Gimignano centre [Via Martiri di Citerna] 🚶 **(13.4)** Fork right up the hill on via Niccolo Cannicci [Pass crucifix on your left] **(13.6)** At the junction, continue straight ahead [Uphill] **(13.6)** At the intersection with the main road, take the underpass to enter San-Gimignano [Pass through the arch, porta San Matteo] **(13.7)** Continue straight ahead on the paved road [Via San Matteo] **(14.0)** Arrive at **San-Gimignano (XIX)** in piazza Duomo [Tourist offices to the right]

Accommodation and Tourist Information

San-Gimignano

🏠 **Convento Sant'Agostino e Giacomo**, Piazza Sant'Agostino, 2, 53037 San-Gimignano(SI), Italy; Tel:+39 3890271946; +39 0577907012; Email:segreteria@fraternitaospitalieri.it; www.confraternitadisanjacopo.it; Price:D; *4 cells open Easter to early October*

🏠 **Agriturismo Cesani**, Località Pancole 82a, 53037 San-Gimignano(SI), Italy; Tel:+39 0577 955084; Email: info@cesani.it; www.cesani.it; Price:B

🏠 **B&B - Locanda Il Pino**, Via Cellolese, 4, 53037 San-Gimignano(SI), Italy; Tel:+39 347 707 2469; + 39 0577 907003; Email:locandailpino.it; locandailpino.it; Price:B; *10% discount for pilgrims*

🏠 **Hotel - Palazzo Buonaccorsi**, Via S.Matteo, 95, 53037 San-Gimignano(SI), Italy; Tel:+39 0577 940908; +39 3498 079349; Email: info@palazzobuonaccorsi.it; palazzobuonaccorsi.it; Price:B

🏠 **Hotel - Donna Nobile**, Via delle Romite, 15, 53037 San-Gimignano(SI), Italy; Tel: +39 3477 856352; +39 36 6345 5414; Email: info@donnanobile.it; donnanobile.it; Price:A

🔑 **Apartment - Casa dei Potenti**, Piazza delle Erbe, 10, 53037 San-Gimignano(SI), Italy; Tel: +39 3271 833950; Email: maurizio3333@virgilio.it; casadeipotenti.com; Price:B

⛺ **Camping Boschetto di Piemma**, Località Santa Lucia, 53037 San-Gimignano(SI), Italy; Tel:+39 0577 907134; Email:info@boschettodipiemma.it; www.boschettodipiemma.it; Price:C; *Mobile homes also available pilgrim aware - camp ground is also known as Villaggio del Pellegrino*

ℹ️ **Pro Loco San Gimignano**, Piazza Duomo, 1, 53037 San-Gimignano(SI), Italy; Tel: +39 0577 940008; Email: info@sangimignano.com; www.sangimignano.com

stage 77 — San-Gimignano to Abbadia-a-Isola

Length:	27.2km
Ascent:	744m
Descent:	877m
Col Grand St Bernard:	697km
Rome:	330km

Abbadia-a-Isola

Route: the section from San-Gimignano to Abbadia-a-Isola offers a choice of following the current "Official Route" passing through the busy town of Colle-di-Valle-d'Elsa or following the longer former official and more historic rural route passing through Quartaia.

Depending on your choice, there are opportunities to break the journey at Colle-di-Valle-d'Elsa, Quartaia, Gracciano and Strove. The shorter profile to the left incorporates a more direct route from Gracciano.

While there are 2 excellent hostels in Abbadia-a-Isola, those pilgrims with an excess of energy may wish to add a further 4 km to the striking hilltop town of Monteriggioni.

Abbadia a Isola is a small, medieval village, built around the Cistercian Abbey of San Salvatore e Cirino, which was founded there in the 10th century, by Countess Ava di Staggia, as a stopping place for pilgrims along the via Francigena. The name originates from its position in the middle of a huge marshy basin.

The complex still retains its medieval charm with the 11th century church in the Lombard style, best known for the early 16th century fresco by Vincenzo Tamagni, and a 15th century marble baptismal font. The interior of the church has three naves, but only the remains of the bell tower are visible to the right of the sacristy. On the facade of the current church the remains of a twin portal, typical of the pilgrimage churches, can be seen.

The fortified garrison of Monteriggioni was established by the Sienese in the 13th century to prevent the Florentines from attacking Siena along what was and still is the main road linking the 2 cities. Following the final defeat of Siena in the 1550's the castle lost its importance. However, it remains one of the most spectacular historic sites in the whole of Tuscany.

San-Gimignano to Abbadia-a-Isola — stage 77

🛉(0.0)From piazza Duomo, continue straight ahead [Duomo and steps to the right](0.1) In piazza Cisterna, continue straight ahead down a narrow passage way, via San Giovanni [Pass through arch](0.1)Bear left on via San Giovanni(0.4)After passing underneath the last archway, porta San Giovanni, continue straight ahead [Keep small park to your right] (0.4)Turn left and go down the steps. Note:- cyclists remain on the road and take the first left turn [Towards the stopping place for buses](0.6)Turn right on via Baccanella(0.7)At the roundabout, take the exit direction Montauto(0.8)Turn left direction Santa Lucia🛉 (2.7)Turn right [Near to a shed](3.0)At the junction take the central track [Downhill]🛉 (4.0)Approaching the house, take the small path to the left, cross the stream in the valley bottom and then climb the hill(4.1)Take the right fork(4.2)Bear right around the field [Trees on your right](4.5)Turn left on the track [Keep olive trees on your right](4.7)At the junction in the tracks, bear right on the tree lined track [Agriturismo on your left](4.9)At the junction at the top of the ridge turn left(4.9)Take the track to the right [Downhill]🛉 (5.3)At the bottom of the hill, continue straight ahead [Cross the stream](5.7)Turn right and then left to skirt the house [Villa della Torraccia di Chiusi](6.0)At the intersection with the entrance to the house, turn right on the downhill track [Beside the wooden fence]🛉 (6.4)Just before the hamlet of **Aiano (XVIII)** turn right [Pass between the buildings](6.6) Just after passing La Casa delle Spezie turn right at the T-junction and then take the left fork on the track(6.9)Cross the stream and then take the left fork(7.4)Turn left. Note: the Alternate Route via Quartaia leaves to the right🛉(7.4)Emerge from the woods and continue straight ahead [Between the fields](7.7)Re-enter the woods and continue uphill(8.1)Turn sharp right and continue uphill [On the broad track]🛉(8.7)Keep left and pass between the buildings [Cascina Prodeggia](8.8)Continue straight ahead on the tarmac road [Pass water tap on the building on the left](8.9)At the junction, continue straight ahead [Large metal gates on your right]🛉(10.6)Keep right [Cemetery on your right](11.0)At the Stop sign, turn right and then turn left beside the main road [Enter **Colle di Val D'Elsa**]🛉(12.3)At the junction beside the turreted town gate, bear left [Porta Nova](12.4)At the crossroads, turn right [Via Porta Vecchia](12.5)Pass to the left of the brick turret and take the small road overlooking the valley on the left [Via Dietro le Mura](12.8)Bear right into piazza

stage 77 — San-Gimignano to Abbadia-a-Isola

Santa Caterina and then bear left [Via F. Campana] ⛪ **(13.4)** At the end of the street turn right and take the ramp to leave the old town **(13.6)** Turn right and right again on the street at the foot of the hill [Via Meoni] **(13.7)** Turn left on the narrow street [Continue through the archway] **(13.8)** Turn left **(14.0)** At the end of the street turn left and immediately right to cross piazza Arnolfo di Cambio [Keep the monument and fountain to your left] **(14.1)** On reaching the main road, turn sharp right on the footpath [Pass behind the bus shelter and under the arch] **(14.3)** At the road junction turn left and immediately right [Towards Cartiera la Buca] **(14.3)** Turn left and follow the footpath/cycle track as it weaves through the apartments ⛪ **(14.5)** Cross the parking area and bear left to take the footbridge. Then, bear right on the swimming pool service road. [Pool on your left] **(14.7)** At the end of the service road, turn left [Pass in front of **Ostello Cartiera la Buca**] **(14.8)** Turn left on the footpath and then sharp right to begin to follow the riverside path ⛪ **(17.6)** On approaching the road bridge, bear right to leave the park and then turn left and cross the bridge [Enter the village of Gracciano] **(17.7)** At the roundabout, bear right. Note:- for the more direct route and to more quickly escape the traffic turn left towards the sports field [Pass a parade of shops on your left] ⛪ **(18.7)** Take the right fork on the narrow road between the trees. Note:- the Alternate Route via Quartaia joins from the right **(19.1)** At the crossroads, turn left on the stony track and bear left at the next junction **(19.2)** Take the pedestrian crossing over the road and continue straight ahead on the gravel road [Towards the hotel Il Pietreto] **(19.6)** Take the left fork [Pass the hotel on your right] ⛪ **(19.9)** After passing the hotel and the trees

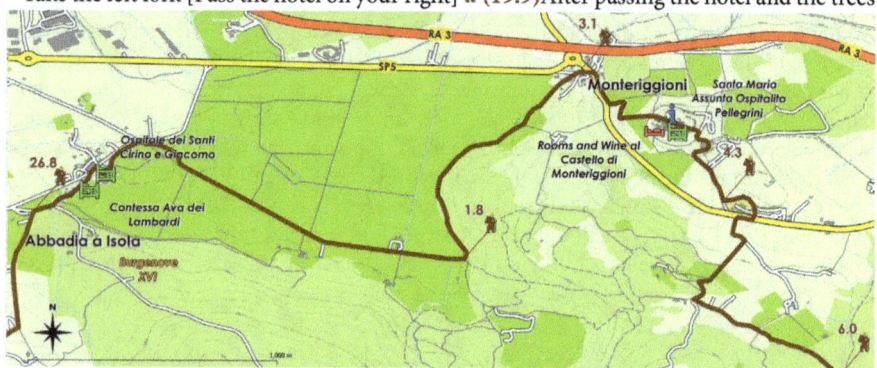

on your right, turn left on the track **(20.3)** At the T-junction, turn left and then right [Follow the line of trees] **(20.8)** At the crossroads in the tracks, continue straight ahead [Line of trees on the right] ⛪ **(21.1)** Turn right [Keep the open field on your left] **(21.6)** At the T-junction with the white road turn left **(21.9)** Keep left on the white road ⛪ **(22.5)** At the junction, continue straight ahead on the gravel road. Note:- the direct Alternate Route from Gracciano rejoins from the left [Strada della Cerreta] **(22.6)** Turn right, direction Strove [Strada di Acquaviva] **(23.3)** Bear right on the tarmac [Stone wall on the right] ⛪ **(24.1)** The "Official Route" makes a short tour of **Strove**, passing close to a cafe, fork right. Fork left if you wish to shorten the section [Beside brick electricity tower] **(24.2)** At the T-junction, turn left **(24.3)** Turn left on via Orlando Gazzezi [Cafe ahead] **(24.3)** At the T-junction, turn left down the hill **(24.5)** At the T-junction with the main road, turn left [Gravel path beside main road] **(24.7)** Take the pedestrian crossing and turn right [Towards Castel Pietraia] **(24.8)** On the apex of the bend to right, turn left on the track **(25.1)** At the junction, after passing between the houses, go straight ahead into the woods ⛪ **(25.4)** Turn right on the path into the woods and then quickly fork to the left [Ignore road on the left leading into

San-Gimignano to Abbadia-a-Isola — stage 77

an industrial site]**(25.5)**In the woods, take the right fork and then a left fork**(26.2)**At the T-junction, turn left on the white road, strada di Certino [Between stone walls] **(26.8)**At the T-junction, turn right**(26.9)**Take the left fork [Downhill, between houses]**(27.1)**Rejoin the main road and turn right and turn right again to enter the courtyard of the old abbey**(27.2)** Arrive at **Abbadia-a-Isola (XVI)** [Ancient church on the right]

Historic Route via Quartaia to Gracciano

Route: this marked route largely follows exposed *strade bianche* which continue to wind through the Tuscan hills and make a number of normally shallow water crossings. **(0.0)**Take the right fork for the route via Quartaia **(1.4)**At the junction, continue straight ahead**(2.0)**Turn right, beside the road, take the pedestrian crossing and then turn left on the track [Trees on your left]**(2.3)**At the T-junction, turn right [Pass a church high on the hill to your right] **(3.0)**Bear left beside the trees**(3.2)**After a section of an old paved road bear right**(3.3)**At the T-junction, turn right**(3.5)**At the top of the hill, turn right on the road [**Abbey of S. Maria Assunta** to the left of the road]**(3.8)**At the foot of the hill, turn left [Direction Il Timignano] **(4.6)**Turn left on the stony track. At the top of the hill, turn left and then right remaining in the edge of the woods**(4.9)**At the junction continue straight ahead**(5.0)**Take the right fork**(5.4)**At

Length:	11.9km
Ascent:	402m
Descent:	372m

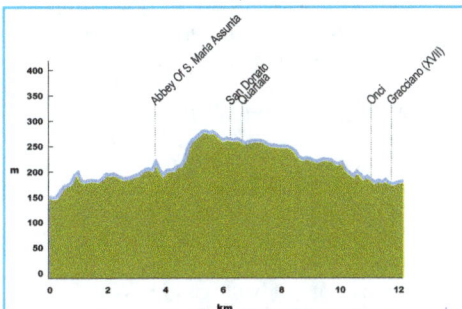

the T-junction, turn left on the unmade road**(5.6)**At the junction, continue straight ahead **(6.1)**At the T-junction, turn left towards the village [**San Donato**]**(6.4)**Take the left fork on the tarmac [Towards the main road]**(6.5)**In **Quartaia**, at the T-junction with the main road (SP27), take the pedestrian crossing and turn right on the pavement [Gantry overhead]**(6.7)**Turn left into Quartaia, on via degli Aragonesi [Pass Tabacchi on the right]**(6.8)**Turn right [Via della Concordia]**(7.0)**At the T-junction, turn left on the unmade road [Exit the village] **(8.0)**Pass through the farm and continue on the unmade road [Road bears right]**(8.5)**At the T-junction at the foot of the hill, turn left and continue straight ahead [Beside the woods]**(9.0)**Turn left on the track [Just before reaching the bridge] **(9.1)**Take the right fork**(9.5)**Take the right fork**(9.8)** Bear right on the white road [Towards Molino le Vene] **(10.8)**Join a tarmac road and bear right [Village of **Onci** to the left]**(10.9)**Turn left on the road [Beside the canal]**(11.5)**After crossing the waterway in **Gracciano (XVII)**, bear right and right again [Via Voltumo] **(11.9)**At the junction with the main road, turn right to rejoin the "Official Route"

Direct Route from Gracciano Towards Strove

Route: this brief short cut follows quiet roads avoiding an unnecessary loop through the outskirts of Gracciano and saving 1.5km. **(0.0)**At the roundabout, after crossing the river Elsa, turn left and pass Parrocchia San Marziale on your left. Note:- the church offers accommodation [Continue beside the sports field]

Length:	3.1km
Ascent:	113m
Descent:	64m

(0.4) Pass under the road bridge and bear right at the junction [Climb the hill to the hamlet of Ponelle] **(1.5)**Take the left fork on the broad track **(2.6)**In the centre of the village of **Scarna**, take the right fork, downhill**(3.1)**At the T-junction, turn left and rejoin the "Official Route".

stage 77 — San-Gimignano to Abbadia-a-Isola

Accommodation and Tourist Information

Castellina-Scalo-Abate

✝ **Parrocchia di Cristo Re e Santa Maria Nascente**,Piazza Cristo Re, 1, 53035 Castellina-Scalo-Abate(SI), Italy; Tel:+39 0577 304214; +39 371 471 7079; Email:casaferiesma@yahoo.it; Price:C; *Email reservations preferred*

Colle-di-Val-d'Elsa

🛏 **Ostello Cartiera la Buca** [Irene],Via XXV Aprile, 104, 53034 Colle-di-Val-d'Elsa(SI), Italy; Tel: +39 3760622460; Email:info@ostelliframcigena.it, ostellifrancigena.it; Price:C

🛏 **Convento di San Francesco**,Via San Francesco, 4, 53034 Colle-di-Val-d'Elsa(SI), Italy; Tel:+39 0577 920040; +39 3276 799124; Email:tabor@arcidiocesi.siena.it; www.visitcolledivaldelsa.com/convento-san-francesco; Price:D

🛏 **Hotel - la Vecchia Cartiera**,Via Oberdan, 5, 53034 Colle-di-Val-d'Elsa(SI), Italy; Tel:+39 0577 921057; Email:info@lavec-chiacartiera.it | lavecchiacartiera.it; Price:A

🛏 **Hotel - il Pietreto**,Località Pietreto, 73, 53034 Colle-di-Val-d'Elsa(SI), Italy; Tel:+39 0577 928838; +39 3331 492102; Email:info@hotelpietreto.it; www.hotelpietreto.it; Price:A; *On the route*

🛏 **Hotel - Relais della Rovere**,Via Piemonte, 10, 53034 Colle-di-Val-d'Elsa(SI), Italy; Tel:+39 0577 1700305; Email:info@relaisdellarovere.it; www.relaisdellarovere.it; Price:A

ℹ **Ufficio Turistico**,Via del Castello, 33, 53034 Colle-di-Val-d'Elsa(SI), Italy; Tel:+39 0577 922791; +39 0577 922621; Email:turisticocolle@tiscali.it; www.prolococollevaldelsa.it

Gracciano-di-Colle-Val-d'Elsa

✝ **Parrocchia S.Marziale**,Via San Marziale, 1, 53034 Gracciano-di-Colle-Val-d'Elsa(SI), Italy; Tel:+39 3297 465518; +39 0577 928677; Email:feaesi@gmail.com; Price:C; *Credentials required* ; **PR**

Monteriggioni

🛏 **Ospitale dei Santi Cirino e Giacomo**,Località Abbadia d'Isola, 53035 Monteriggioni(SI), Italy; Tel:+39 0577 304214; +39 371 471 7079; Email:casaferiesma@yahoo.it; Price:C; *Open Easter to October Email reservations preferred*

🛏 **Ostello Contessa Ava dei Lambardi**,Località Abbadia d'Isola, 53035 Monteriggioni(SI), Italy; Tel:+3905771794759; Email:info.contes-saava@gmail.comt; www.hotelsitalic.com/ostello-contessa-ava-dei-lambardi; Price:C; *Located inside the old abbey a choice of single or double rooms discount if you book directly and have credentials no shops or restaurant close by*

🛏 **Casa Per Ferie Santa Maria Assunta Ospitalita Pellegrini**,Piazza Roma, 23, 53035 Monteriggioni(SI), Italy; Tel:+39 0577 304214; +39 371 471 7079; Email:casaferiesma@yahoo.it; www.monteriggionviafrancigena.it; Price:C; *Email reservations preferred*

🛏 **Rooms and Wine al Castello di Monteriggioni**,Via Dante Alighieri, 1, 53035 Monteriggioni(SI), Italy; Tel:+39 347 7200713; Email:stefano@roomsandwine.com; roomsandwine.com; Price:A

ℹ **Ufficio Turistico**,Piazza Dante Alighieri, 23, 53035 Monteriggioni(SI), Italy; Tel:+39 0577 304834; Email:info@monteriggioniturismo.it; www.monteriggioniturismo.it

Quartaia

⛺ **Campo Piro e More** [Monica Rodani],Località San Donato, 53034 Quartaia(SI), Italy; Tel:+39 3453918301; Email:campopiroemore@gmail.com; *Free basic camping*

Strove

🏠 **B&B - Relais Castelbigozzi**,Strada di Bigozzi, 13, 53035 Strove(SI), Italy; Tel:+39 0577 300000; Email:info@castellobigozzi.it; www.castellobigozzi.it; Price:A

🛏 **Albergo - Casalta**,Via Giacomo Matteotti, 22, 53035 Strove(SI), Italy; Tel:+39 0577 301002; +39 392 7356343; Email:info@casaltahotel.com; www.casaltahotel.com; Price:A

Abbadia-a-Isola to Siena

stage 78

Length:	24.5km
Ascent:	758m
Descent:	621m
Col Grand St Bernard:	725km
Rome:	303km

Siena rooftops from the Pinacoteca Nazionale

Route: the route from Abbadia-a-Isola to Siena largely follows tracks and small roads to the edge of Siena adding a little distance to Sigeric's route by visiting Monteriggioni and making a large loop to the west of the via Cassia.

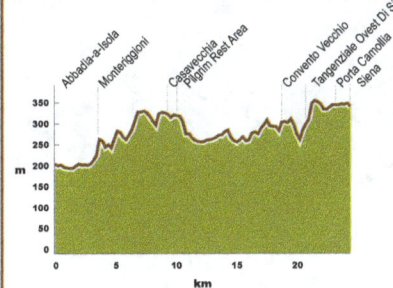

There is a *donativo* pilgrim rest and water stop (*Punto Sosta*) at La Villa (km 10.1) but there are no commercial facilities between Monteriggioni and the outskirts of Siena. An alternative more direct route will reduce the journey by 5.5 km.

The Hospital of Santa Maria della Scala refers to its position in front of Siena Cathedral. From the earliest documentation, the hospital was used as a shelter for foreigners, for the most part pilgrims, and travellers following the Francigena. Later, it specialized in supporting and caring for abandoned children in the so-called Casa delle Balie. Meticulous records were kept of the details relating to each child. At age eight, they were taught a trade and any profits they made were kept for them. When eighteen, the children had the option of leaving with all their saved earnings, plus one hundred soldi, a set of clothing, and furnishings for a house. Girls were given an additional fifty as a dowry. In addition, meals were served to the poor three times a week and the sick were given free treatment.

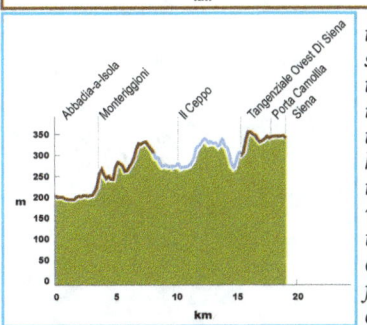

The Hospital's treatment of the sick was unusual for the time. Their policy was to have one bed for each sick patient, and the sheets were kept clean. Also, in what has been suggested as "one of the earliest examples of such a therapeutic objective," patients were treated in order to be cured. The Hospital employed one doctor and one surgeon. In the 16th century, it added an additional surgeon. As the Hospital became a training ground for doctors, there was, for the 17th and 18th centuries, a unique emphasis on using a more hands-on learning approach. Pilgrims were also included in their programme, receiving free room and board in the pilgrimage halls, and when they left, vouchers for food and drink in the Sienese territory, as they continued their travels.

stage 78 — Abbadia-a-Isola to Siena

(0.0) Facing the church take the steps to the left. At the foot of the steps, turn left then right and follow the track beside the main road [Monteriggioni on hill-top to the right] (0.3) At the crossroads, turn right and then bear left on the track [Strada di Valmaggiore] (1.8) At the end of the road, turn left. Note:- the turning to the right reduces the distance, but bypasses Monteriggioni and involves a steep climb [Woods close on the right] (3.1) At the T-junction with the SP5, turn right and cross the via Cassia, then follow the track on the left side of the road (3.3) Turn left on the unmade road [Steeply uphill, towards the entrance to the walled town] (3.6) Pass through the arched Porta Fiorentina into **Monteriggioni** and continue straight ahead [Via Primo Maggio] (3.9) On leaving the town, turn right and then left on the tarmac road. On the right-hand bend descend the steps into the car park and keep right before returning to the road [Porta Senese] (4.3) Turn left on the track and then bear right as the track skirts the school (4.6) At the junction with the main road, take the pedestrian crossing, turn right on the track and then take the first turning to the left [Towards Gallinalo] (4.8) Take the right fork [Uphill] (5.1) Take the next turning to the left [White road, between trees] (5.2) At the crossroads, turn left on the track (6.0) At the junction, take the sec-

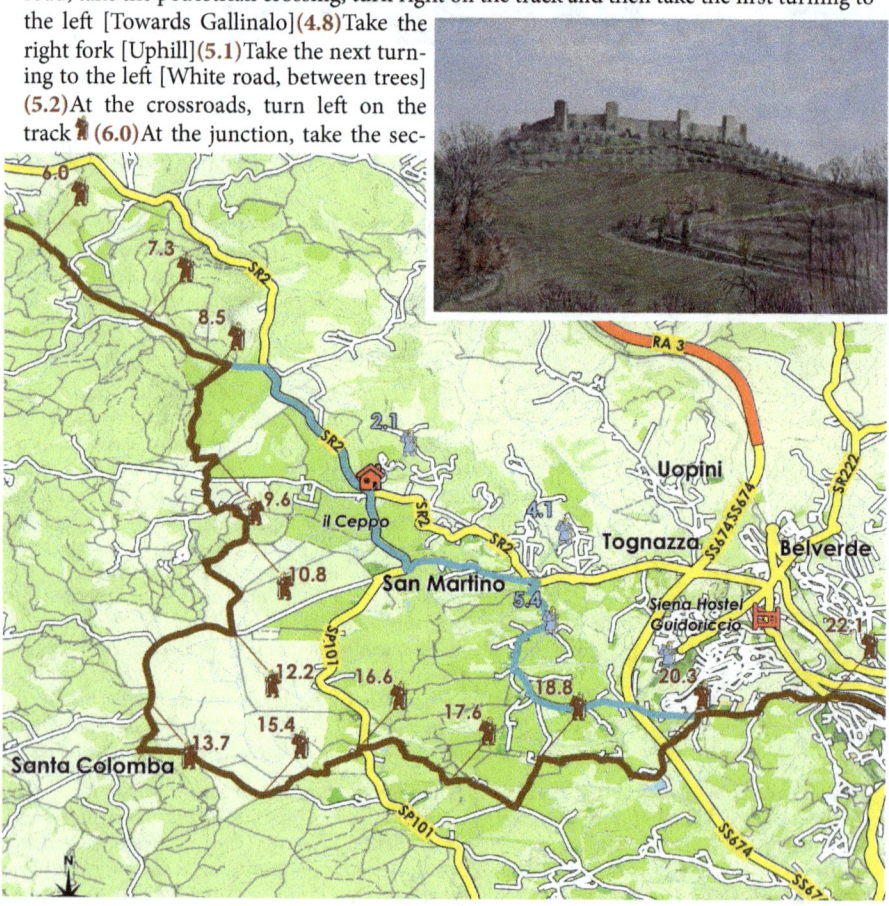

ond track from the left (6.2) Bear right (6.5) At the crossroads in the tracks, continue straight ahead on the gravel road [Stone wall on the right of the road] (7.3) At the T-junction, turn left [Large farmhouse on left] (8.2) Turn right on the track. Note:- to avoid broken ground

Abbadia-a-Isola to Siena — stage 78

and reduce distance by 5.5 km continue ahead on the Alternate Route [Across the fields towards woods] ☂ **(8.5)** On the crossroads take the pathway to the left [Field to the left, woods to the right]**(9.4)** Turn left on the access road to the farm [**Casavecchia**] ☂ **(9.6)** At the T-junction, turn right [Towards the church]**(9.8)** Cross the tarmac road and take the unmade road straight ahead [Castello della Chiocciola on the hill to the right]**(10.1)** Turn left on the track**(10.2)** At the junction with the tarmac road, turn left on the road and then right at the next junction [Pass **pilgrim rest area** on your right]**(10.3)** Take the right fork [Towards the La Villa castello]**(10.4)** Bear right on the track [Pass circular building on the left] ☂ **(10.8)** Take the right fork on the broader track [Downhill and with fields on the left] **(11.3)** Turn left on the track between fields [Line of trees on the left of the track]**(11.8)** Turn right on the track [Continue with a stream on your left] ☂ **(12.2)** At the T-junction with the tarmac road, SP101, turn right [Small bridge on the left at the junction] ☂ **(13.7)** Keep left at the junction [Direction Scorgiano]**(14.2)** At the junction in the woods, turn left on the gravel road [Via dell'Osteriaccia, direction S. Leonardo al Lago] ☂ **(15.4)** Bear left on the road and quickly take the pathway to the left [Beside house on the edge of the woods]**(15.9)** Bear left across the field**(16.0)** Beside the monument, bear right and then keep left on the track**(16.4)** At the junction bear left on the broad track ☂ **(16.6)** At the T-junction beside the house, turn right, take the pedestrian crossing and continue straight ahead on the track**(16.9)** Take the track to the right uphill [Into the woods]**(17.0)** At the crossroads, turn left and then right**(17.3)** Turn right on the track**(17.4)** Keep right on the track and left at the next junction ☂ **(17.6)** At the T-junction, turn left**(17.7)** Emerge from the woods and turn right [Equestrian centre on your left]**(18.2)** At the junction with the tarmac road, turn left [Cemetery on your left] ☂ **(18.8)** At the top of the hill, beside **Convento Vecchio** turn right [Strada delle Coste]**(19.2)** Take the right fork on the tarmac road ☂ **(20.3)** Continue straight ahead [Under the highway and then up the hill]**(20.8)** At the crossroads, turn right. Note:- the Alternate Route rejoins from the left [Via Gaetano Milanesi]**(21.3)** At the T-junction, turn left on strada di Marciano [Between stone walls] ☂ **(22.1)** At the roundabout, turn right direction Centro [Viale Camillo Benso Conte di Cavour]**(22.9)** Go straight ahead under the archway - antiporto di Camollia [Direction centro] ☂ **(23.3)** Cross the piazza and take via Camollia straight ahead [Pass bike shop on the left]**(23.3)** At the traffic lights, continue straight ahead [Pass through **porta Camollia**]**(23.7)** At the crossroads, continue straight ahead on via Camollia [Direction Porta Romana] ☂ **(24.4)** At the junction, continue straight ahead down the steps [Vicolo S. Pietro]**(24.5)** Arrive at **Siena (XV)** centre in piazza del Campo [Beside Torre di Mangia]

Direct Route

Route: a shorter route, strongly recommended for cyclists to bypass difficult ground in the woodland. The route follows the via Cassia (SR2) for 2 km before continuing on quieter country roads and reduces the length of the section by 5.5 km. **(0.0)** Continue straight ahead [Towards the main road]**(0.3)** At the crossroads,

Length:	7.2km
Ascent:	206m
Descent:	211m

turn right down the hill towards Siena on the SR2. Walkers keep to the grass verge [Brown signpost ahead for Poggiolo] ☂ **(2.1)** Turn right on strada del Pecorile direction Sovicille [**Il Ceppo** restaurant and B&B on the right at the junction]**(3.0)** Turn left and then left again on strada del Pian del Lago [Direction Siena] ☂ **(4.1)** At the T-junction, turn right direction Siena, SR2**(4.3)** Turn right direction Montalbuccio [Strada del Petriccio e Belriguardo] ☂ **(5.4)** Bear left at the fork in road [Strada del Petriccio e Belriguardo]**(5.8)** Take the left fork [Towards Petriccio] ☂ **(7.2)** At the crossroads, continue straight ahead and rejoin the "Official Route" [Via G. Milanese]

stage 78 — Abbadia-a-Isola to Siena

Accommodation and Tourist Information

Monteriggioni
🏠 **B&B - - il Ceppo**, Via Cassia Nord, 3, 53035 Monteriggioni(SI), Italy; Tel:+39 0577 593387; Email:info@bedandbreakfastilceppo.it; ilceppo-bedandbreakfastmonteriggioni.com; Price:A

Siena
🛏️ **Accoglienza Santa Luisa** [Suor Ginetta],Via Delli Servi, 4, 53100 Siena(SI), Italy; Tel:+39 0577 284377; +39 0577 21271; +39 3408 721787; Email:casaprovinciale@yahoo.it; Price:D; **PR**
🛏️ **Foresteria San Clemente Ai Servi** [Dario],Piazza Alessandro Manzoni, 5, 53100 Siena(SI), Italy; Tel:+39 3892983135; +39 0577 222633; Email:weabis1233@gmail.com; viafrancigena.visittuscany.com/site/en/hospitality/foresteria-san-clemente-ai-servi-siena; Price:D
🛏️ **Siena Hostel Guidoriccio**,Via Fiorentina, 89, 53100 Siena(71276), Italy; Tel:+39 0577 169 8177; Email:info@sienahostel.it; Price:B; *3.5 km from the historic centre*
🛏️ **Caritas**,Via della Diana, 4, 53100 Siena(SI), Italy; Tel:+39 0577 280643; Email:segreteria@caritas-siena.it; www.caritas-siena.it; Price:D; *Homeless shelter men only*

🏠 **B&B - Casa di Antonella**,Via delle Terme, 72, 53100 Siena(SI), Italy; Tel: +39 3393 004883; Email:r_e_d@libero.it; www.labella-toscana.it/la-casa-di-antonella/; Price:B
🏠 **B&B - Casa di Osio**,Via dei Montanini, 66, 53100 Siena(SI), Italy; Tel: +39 3425 989555; Email:info@casadiosio.com; casadiosio.com; Price:B; *On the route in the city centre*
🛏️ **Hotel - Tre Donzelle**,Via delle Donzelle, 5, 53100 Siena(SI), Italy; Tel:+39 0577 270390; +39 3387 615052; Email:info@tredonzelle.com; tredonzelle.com; Price:B
⛺ **Camping Siena Colleverde**,Via Scaccapensieri, 47, 53100 Siena(SI), Italy; Tel:+39 0577 334080; +39 0577 332545; Email:info@sienacamping.com; www.sienacamping.com; Price:C; *Mobile homes available*
ℹ️ **Siena Tourist Information Office**,Palazzo Berlinghieri - Il Campo, 7, 53100 Siena(SI), Italy; Tel:+39 0577 292222; Email:siena.iat@terredisiena.it; terredisiena.it

Siena to Ponte-d'Arbia — stage 79

Length: 25.9km

Ascent: 433m
Descent: 626m

Col Grand
St Bernard: 749km
Rome: 279km

Ponte-d'Arbia

Route: from Siena to Ponte-d'Arbia quickly leaves the centre of Siena on a small tarmac road. After a short section on the busy SS2, the route returns to the tracks over the beautiful, but exposed Tuscan hills. The route passes close to, but not through, a number of intermediate villages with cafés and shops.

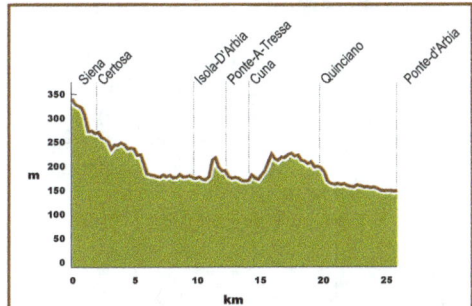

Ponte-d'Arbia is a very small town but with an excellent large hostel and a close-by restaurant offering pilgrim discounts.

The route takes you past Cuna Grange, an excellently conserved example of a fortified medieval farm and unusual for its size. There are also traces of a hospital established there in the 12th century by the Hospice of Santa Maria della Scala of Siena, to give assistance to pilgrims travelling on the via Francigena.

Ponte d'Arbia is notable for its exceptional bridge, from which it derives its name, with the 6th century stage post and portico at one extreme, and a mill at the other.

Chiesa di San Jacopo - Cuna

(0.0) From piazza del Campo facing Torre del Mangia, turn left and exit on via del Rinaldini and then turn right at the end of the street [Direction Porta Romana] **(1.1)** After passing through the **Porta Romana**, immediately turn left through the archway and down the steps **(1.2)** Cross the main road (SR2) and go straight ahead [Strada di Certosa] **(1.9)** Turn right, remain on strada di **Certosa** [Direction Renaccio] **(5.5)** Road becomes a gravel track, continue straight ahead [Pass house on your right] **(6.0)** At the foot of the hill, turn right on the cycle track [Water point on the left] **(6.4)** Turn left and join the road through the industrial zone [Roundabout at the start of the road] **(7.0)** At the roundabout with the main road, continue straight ahead on the cycle track beside the road **(8.6)** At the end of the track, cross the road and turn left over the bridge and continue beside the road **(9.0)**

stage 79　　　Siena to Ponte-d'Arbia

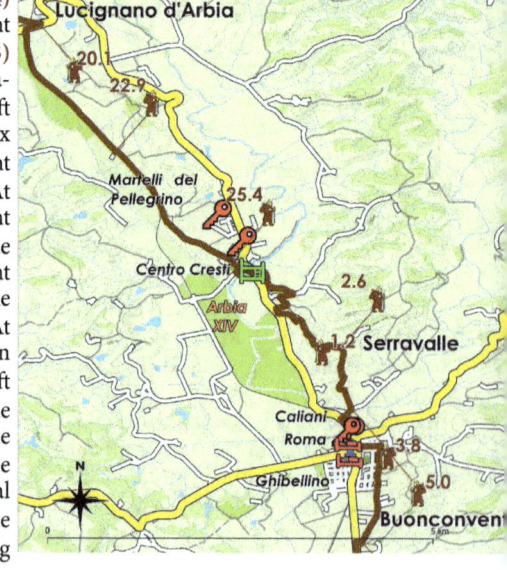

Beside the bar on the left side of the road in the industrial zone, continue straight ahead. Note:- the route formerly took the narrow passage at the side of the bar and then the subway under the railway station. However, the subway appears locked for security purposes. In the event that it reopens, turn right at the exit from the subway and continue to the main road, cross and continue on the road opposite to rejoin the current route**(9.4)**At the junction with the main road (SR2), turn left and carefully follow the busy road [Cross railway track] 🚶 **(9.8)**In **Isola-d'Arbia**, turn right beside the bar Il Pellegrino. Note:- the prior route joins from the left [Via della Mercanzia]**(10.0)**Bear left on the road – via della Mercanzia [Pass the shops on your right]**(10.3)**At the T-junction with the SR2, turn right**(10.4)** Immediately after passing the bar, turn right [Road passes under the railway] 🚶 **(11.3)** Turn sharp left towards Ponte-a-Tressa**(11.5)**At the top of the ridge fork left down the hill and away from the crucifix [Via del Poggio]**(12.0)**Continue straight ahead [Pass equestrian centre] 🚶 **(12.4)**At the Stop sign in **Ponte-a-Tressa**, turn right [Pass apartments on your left]**(12.6)**At the end of the housing development, fork right onto the gravel track and pass between the trees [Direction Il Canto del Sole]**(13.2)**At the T-junction on the top of the ridge, turn left on via di Villa Canina 🚶 **(13.4)**Turn left [Towards the village of Cuna]**(14.2)**At the entrance to **Cuna** turn right [Towards the arch] 🚶 **(14.5)**At the crossroads in the tracks, after leaving Cuna, bear left [Metal cross]**(14.9)**At the junction, continue straight up the hill**(15.2)**Fork left [Avoiding

Siena to Ponte-d'Arbia — stage 79

strada della Fornacina]**(15.3)**Track forks in three directions take middle track straight up the hill 🚶 **(15.6)**Just before reaching the top of the hill, fork right**(16.0)**Turn sharp left onto the ridge**(16.2)**At the T-junction, turn sharp right [Pond on the left]**(16.5)**At the T-junction with a minor road, cross straight over and turn immediately left and follow the gravel track. Cyclists should turn left on the road and then bear right on the track in 70 metres [Parallel to the road] 🚶 **(16.6)**Keep right on the track**(17.1)**Fork right up the hill 🚶 **(17.7)** Fork left [Pass farm on the right]**(17.8)**Continue straight ahead on the central track [Towards the top of the ridge]**(18.1)**Fork right [Towards the farm on the right] 🚶 **(18.8)**Continue on the tarmac section [Hamlet of Greppo]**(19.0)**Fork right [Direction Quinciano] **(19.7)**At the junction in **Quinciano** bear left on the road, downhill [Pass conifers on your right] 🚶 **(20.1)**Fork right down the hill on the track and then turn right [Towards the main road]**(20.3)**Cross the road at the pedestrian crossing and turn right [Continue behind barrier]**(20.3)**Bear left down a gravel track [Continue beside railway track] 🚶 **(22.9)**At the crossroads, turn left, cross the bridge and then turn right [Continue with the railway on the right] 🚶 **(25.4)**At the junction with a tarmac road on the edge of Ponte-d'Arbia, fork right on via degli Stagni towards river [Pass the sports field on your right]**(25.5)**At the T-junction turn right and cross the new bridge**(25.5)**At the T-junction with the main road, turn right [Pass over the river bridge]**(25.9)**Arrive at **Ponte-d'Arbia (XIV)** [Beside the pilgrim hostel]

Accommodation and Tourist Information

Isola-d'Arbia

🏠**Agriturismo - San Giorgio**,Località Colle Malamerenda, 53100 Isola-d'Arbia(SI), Italy; Tel:+39 0577 378147; +39 0577 375224; +39 3495 395933; Email:info@san-giorgio.net; san-giorgio.net; Price:A

Lucignano-d'Arbia

🛏**Hotel - Borgo Antico**,Via di Lucignano, 405, 53014 Lucignano-d'Arbia(SI), Italy; Tel:+39 0577 374688; Email:info@hotelborgoantico.com; www.hotelborgoantico.com; Price:A

Monteroni-d'Arbia

🏠 **Casa Privata** [Letizia Lusini],Piazza Gramsci, 7, 53014 Monteroni-d'Arbia(SI), Italy; Tel:+39 3382172483; Email:leti.fortunella@gmail.com; francigenatoscana.it/via-francigena-tappa-34-da-siena-a-ponte-darbia/#la-casa-del-poggio-a-ponte-a-tressa-vicino-a-isola-darbia

🛏 **Hotel - 1000 Miglia**,Via Cassia Sud, 654, 53014 Monteroni-d'Arbia(SI), Italy; Tel:+39 0577 372227; +39 0577 375251; Email:info@hotelmillemiglia.it ; hotelmillemiglia.it; Price:B

🔑 **Apartment - Antica Dimora**,Via Roma, 59, 53014 Monteroni-d'Arbia(SI), Italy; Tel:+39 0577 375115; +39 3388 737851; Email:roccmess66@virgilio.it; anticadimora-monteronidarbia.com; Price:B

Ponte-a-Tressa

🔑 **Apartment - La Casa nel Poggio**,Via del Poggio, 247, 53014 Ponte-a-Tressa(SI), Italy; Tel:+39 3479391048; Email:maxtanga71@gmail.com; francigenatoscana.it/via-francigena-tappa-34-da-siena-a-ponte-darbia/#la-casa-del-poggio-a-ponte-a-tressa-vicino-a-isola-darbia; Price:B

Ponte-d'Arbia

✉**Centro Cresti**,Via Cassia, 3, 53014 Ponte-d'Arbia(SI), Italy; Tel: +39 3277 197439; Email:centrocresti@libero.it; centrocresti.it; Price:C; **PR**

🔑 **Affittacamere - Martelli - Casa del Pellegrino**,via Cassia, 18, 53014 Ponte-d'Arbia(SI), Italy; Tel: +39 3348 464235; +39 348 7463634; Email:martelli.c@outlook.com; www.affittacameremartelli.it; Price:C; *Located between Centro Cresti and the road bridge*

🔑 **Camera - da Cri** [Cristina],Via Fratelli Cervi, 19, 53014 Ponte-d'Arbia(SI), Italy; Tel:+39 342 196 7918; Email:acasadacri@gmail.com; camere-da-cri.tuscanyitalyhotels.com; Price:B

stage 80 — Ponte-d'Arbia to San-Quirico-d'Orcia

Length:	26.3km
Ascent:	926m
Descent:	670m
Col Grand St Bernard:	775km
Rome:	253km

Collegiata di San Quirico

Route: the stage from Ponte-d'Arbia to San-Quirico-d'Orcia continues over the Tuscan hills interleaving long stretches on the *strade bianche* with shorter stretches on tarmac roads. The route passes through the bustling town of Buonconvento and the village of Torrenieri (XIII) before arriving in the attractive hill top town of San Quirico d'Orcia (XII).

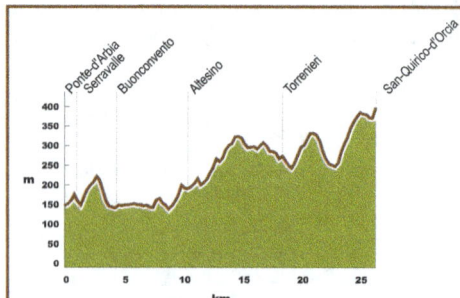

Beware following the signs to the left at the T-junction **(0.8)** this will add a 100 m climb and descent and 4 km to the day.

Though Etruscan in origin, the first explicit reference to San Quirico d'Orcia was when there was a dispute between the diocese of Siena and Arezzo over the possession of some parishes, among which was San Quirico in Osenna. The outcome of this was a decision, confirmed by King Liutprando, in favour of the church of Arezzo. The name Osenna was in use until the 17th century and probably referred to a watercourse, which has now disappeared. From the beginning of the 11th century, the name of San Quirico in Osenna is mentioned more frequently, especially in connection with travel along the via Francigena.

Today, the main street, via Dante Alighieri, is the heart of the town. At one end stands the Collegiata and at the other the church of Santa Maria Assunta, with its fantastical medieval bestiary adorning the portal. Further along via Dante Alighieri there is the main square and entrance to the Renaissance gardens, Horti Leonini. The Collegiate church of San Quirico. Once a rural church, was rebuilt into the current structure in the 12th century. The rear section was altered in 1663 to add the choir. It is built on the Latin cross plan, with a single nave and side chapels. Notable is the main portal, in Lombard style, with columns supported by lions. The arch includes ten columns, whose capitals are decorated with animals and vegetable figures, while the architrave features, bizarrely, two crocodiles facing each other.

🍴 **(0.0)** On leaving the main door of the Centro Cresti turn left on the small road **(0.0)** At the T-junction with the main road, turn left **(0.3)** At the junction with the gravel road, turn left **(0.8)** Just before reaching the cemetery, turn sharp right on the stony road. [Towards chiesa di San Lorenzo] **(1.0)** As the road turns right towards the **Serravalle** village centre, turn left on the path [Downhill and between the fields] 🍴 **(1.2)** At the T-junction with the broad track, turn right [Towards the main road] **(1.4)** At the T-junction with the gravel

Ponte-d'Arbia to San-Quirico-d'Orcia — stage 80

road, turn left, uphill and bear right [Main road immediately to your right]**(1.7)**At the T-junction, turn right (**2.6**)At the junction, turn right [Top of the hill] (**3.8**)At the T-junction, turn right [Pass under the railway bridge]**(4.0)**Pass the cemetery and at the T-junction with the SS2, turn left [Pass a petrol station on your left]**(4.3)**After, crossing the river bridge turn right [Direction Centro]**(4.4)**Turn left into the old town of **Buonconvento** [Pass through the archway, Porta Senese]**(4.6)**In piazza Matteotti, turn left on the narrow street [Pass a sign "Roma 201" on your right]**(4.7)**Cross the main road (SR2) and continue straight ahead [Over the level crossing] **(5.0)**At the junction, continue straight ahead [Apartments on your right]**(5.6)**Bear left on the track ahead**(5.6)**At the crossroads with via E. Berlinger, turn left [Between apartment buildings] **(6.8)**At the T-junction with the stony road, turn right towards the main road [Row of conifers to the right]**(6.9)**At the T-junction with the busy main road, cross over and turn left on the grass path behind the crash barriers [Via Cassia – SR2]**(7.2)**Turn right on the road [Direction Montalcino]**(7.8)** Take the pedestrian crossing over the road and follow track to the right up the hill **(7.9)** Turn left and right to remain on the track parallel to the road**(8.7)**Pass under the road and keep left to return to the track again on the left side of the road **(9.1)**Just before the road bends to the left, turn sharp left [Direction Castello Altesi] **(10.4)**After passing the castello take the left fork and follow the ridge [**Altesino** winery to the right] **(11.5)**Bear left to skirt the buildings on the right [Tree lined road] **(12.6)**Keep left on the white road**(13.2)**Just before reaching a large farm on the right, turn left [Follow the road to Torrenieri] **(18.3)**At the T-junction in **Torrenieri**, turn right on the main street [Via Romana**(18.7)**At the crossroads in the centre of Torrenieri (XIII), continue straight ahead [Church directly ahead]**(19.3)**Immediately after passing the cemetery on your right, continue straight ahead on the road [Conifers on the right] **(20.8)**Fork right and continue on the main road **(22.7)**After passing through the woods at the foot of the hill, turn right on the stony road [Towards the elevated highway]**(23.0)**Immediately after passing under the highway, bear left [Parallel to the highway] **(24.0)**Turn left [Avoid the entrance to the farm]**(24.6)**At the T-junction, turn left, uphill **(25.1)**Keep left on the track [Towards the town] **(26.2)**Continue straight ahead [Under the arch]**(26.2)**Continue straight ahead. Note:- to avoid the steps, turn left and then take the second left over the bridge to the town centre [Climb steps]**(26.3)**At the top of the steps, continue straight ahead on via Dante Alighieri [Towards the church]**(26.3)**Arrive at **San-Quirico-d'Orcia (XII)** beside the church [Piazza Chigi].

stage 80 — Ponte-d'Arbia to San-Quirico-d'Orcia

Accommodation and Tourist Information

Buonconvento

🛏 **Hotel - Ghibellino**, Via Dante Alighieri, 1, 53022 Buonconvento(SI), Italy; Tel:+39 0577 809112; +39 0577 809114; Email:Info@hotelghibellino.it; www.hotelghibellino.it; Price:A

🛏 **Albergo - Roma**, Via Soccini, 14, 53022 Buonconvento(SI), Italy; Tel:+39 0577 809112; Email:info@hotelghibellino.com; www.hotelghibellino.it/albergo-roma-gallery; Price:B

🔑 **Affittacamere - la Sosta a Casa Anita**, Via del Sole, 80, 53022 Buonconvento(SI), Italy; Tel: +39 3405 989804; Email:lasostacasanita@gmail.com; www.bedandbreakfast.eu; Price:B

🔑 **Affittacamere - Caliani**, Via Roma, 53022 Buonconvento(SI), Italy; Tel: +39 1347 5696; +39 3385 725294; Email:affittacamere.caliani@yahoo.it; traveleto.com/hotel/it/affittacamere-caliani.html; Price:B

ℹ **Comune di Buonconvento**, Via Soccini, 32, 53022 Buonconvento(SI), Italy; Tel:+39 0577 80971; Email:info@comune.buonconvento.si.it; www.comune.buonconvento.si.it

San-Quirico-d'Orcia

🛏 **Il Palazzo del Pellegrino**, Via Dante Alighieri, 33, 53027 San-Quirico-d'Orcia(SI), Italy; Tel:+39 0577 899728; +39 3791294369; Email:palazzodelpellegrino@gmail.com; Price:C; *Key available at the tourist office can be fully booked in the high season*; **PR**

🛏 **Collegiata dei Santi Quirico e Giulitta** [Lucrezia], Piazza Chigi, 4, 53027 San-Quirico-d'Orcia(SI), Italy; Tel:+39 328 1329899; +39 0577897587; +39347 7748732; Email:agogange@gmail.com; Price:C; *Credentials required*

🛏 **Hotel - il Garibaldi**, Via Cassia, 17, 53027 San-Quirico-d'Orcia(SI), Italy; Tel:+39 0577 898315; Email:ristoranteilgaribaldi@virgilio.it; www.ilgaribaldisanquirico.it; Price:B

🔑 **Affittacamere - l'Antica Sosta**, Via Dante Alighieri, 145, 53027 San-Quirico-d'Orcia(SI), Italy; Tel: +39 3406 491216; Email:info@anticasosta.eu; www.anticasosta.eu; Price:B; *Also listed on booking.com*

🔑 **Apartment - Casa dei Trenta**, Via dei Canneti, 7, 53027 San-Quirico-d'Orcia(SI), Italy; Tel: +39 3495 739818; Email:casadeitrenta@virgilio.it; booking.com; Price:B

ℹ **Ufficio Turistico**, Via Dante Alighieri, 33, 53027 San-Quirico-d'Orcia(SI), Italy; Tel:+39 0577 899728; Email:protocollo@comune.sanquiricodorcia.si.it; www.comunesanquirico.it/area-turismo

Torrenieri

🛏 **Pellegrinaio del Poggio**, Via Cesare Battisti, 37, 53024 Torrenieri(SI), Italy; Tel: +39 3487 372473; +39 3429 415024; Email:giuseppe.antichi@libero.it; Price:C; *Group accommodation*

San-Quirico-d'Orcia to Radicofani — stage 81

Length:	33.4km
Ascent:	1427m
Descent:	1030m
Col Grand St Bernard:	801km
Rome:	227km

Bagnio Vignoni

Route: there is a choice of routes both strenuous, with long and exposed climbs and with few en route opportunities to break the journey beyond Castiglione d'Orcia.

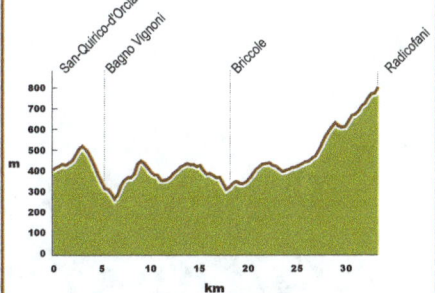

The "Official Route" from San-Quirico-d'Orcia to Radicofani passes to the east of the via Cassia to the very pilgrim aware hill-top community of Radicofani. The Alternate Route, which was perhaps more popular in medieval times, passes through Abbadia San Salvatore on the western side of the Val d'Orcia and beneath Monte Amiata. The 2 routes rejoin at Ponte-a-Rigo on the via Cassia. Many pilgrims choose to cover the routes in 2 days taking an over-night stop in Gallina.

The first known document mentioning the via Francigena, the Codex Diplomaticus Amiatinus–dated 876, is held in the Abbey of San Salvatore.

For centuries, the imposing Fortress of Radicofani, on the border between Tuscany and Lazio, has been the symbol of defence and control over the via Francigena. This powerful fortification, built on top of a high summit, was built over a long period of time, starting from 978 onwards, though its origins go even further back in time. The thick bastions were capable of resisting the most violent attack, even artillery fire, while the mighty tower, thirty-seven metres high and rebuilt in the last century, offers enchanting, endless views all over the Val d'Orcia park and the volcanic Monte Amiata.

The church of San Pietro Apostolo, with its beautiful Romanesque architecture, is the most important religious place in Radicofani. The interiors are wonderfully decorated with oil paintings, frescoes and a collection of terracotta pieces from the Della Robbia workshop, as well as wooden sculptures. The church of Sant'Agata is opposite the church of San Pietro in the same little square. Once a convent, it has been beautifully decorated inside and also houses a precious Madonna with Saints by Andrea Della Robbia.

San Pietro Apostolo

stage 81 — San-Quirico-d'Orcia to Radicofani

🏠(0.1)From the church in San-Quirico-d'Orcia on piazza Chigi continue ahead on via Dante Alighieri [Pass through piazza della Libertà](0.4)Turn right at the crossroads on the edge of the old town [Via Giacomo Matteotti](0.6)At the next crossroads, continue straight ahead on via Giuseppe Garibaldi [Direction Vignoni]🏠(1.3)Take the left fork on the gravel road, towards Vignoni🏠(2.6)Take the left fork [Towards Vignoni](3.5)Take the left fork, towards the village [Direction Vignoni]🏠(3.7)Pass through the archway and then turn right [Chapel on the left](3.8)At the T-junction with the broad track, turn left, downhill(4.1)Take the left fork, downhill [Agriturismo on the right]🏠(5.4)The signed route passes beside the thermal baths of **Bagno Vignoni**, where restaurants and cafes may also be found. If you wish to bypass this then some distance may be saved by continuing ahead and turning left on the main road. Else turn right on the pathway and continue directly to the thermal pool [Beside the parking area](5.6)On reaching the pool, turn left(5.7)At the T-junction with the road, turn left [Pass the car park on your right](5.9)At the roundabout,

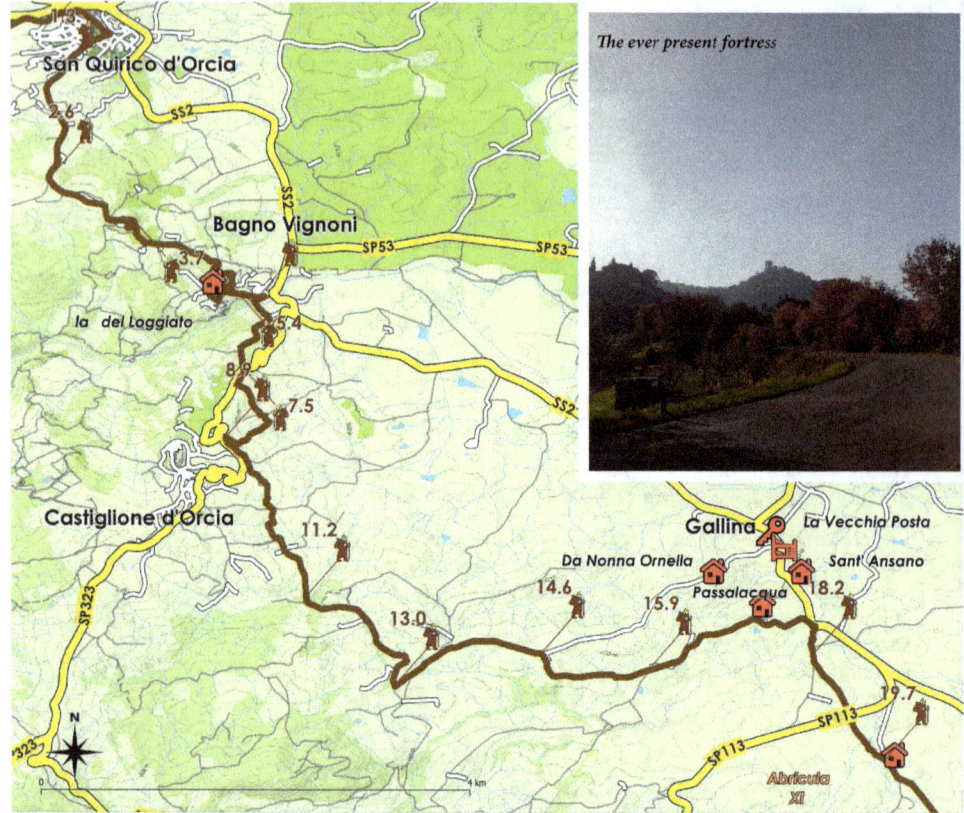

The ever present fortress

turn right [Pass the bus stop on your right](6.3)Turn sharp right on the gravel track🏠(6.4)Continue straight ahead [Cross the foot-bridge](6.6)Just after passing Osteria dell'Orcia, turn right [Keep the woods on your left]🏠(7.5)Cross the road and continue on the track with the vines on your left [Rocca d'Orcia visible on your right](7.7)At the T-junction with the gravel road, turn left [Olive trees on your left](8.2)Take the right fork [Beside farm-

San-Quirico-d'Orcia to Radicofani — stage 81

house, towards another farm]**(8.3)**Turn right [Beside farmhouse] **(8.9)**Shortly before reaching the main road, turn left on the track [Keep the road on your right]**(9.2)**Bear right up the hill on the short track and then keep left on the gravel road [Pass the vines on your right] **(11.2)**In the valley bottom, continue straight ahead [Cross the bridge] **(13.0)**At the junction, after passing the woods on the right, turn sharp left on the gravel road along the ridge [S] **(14.6)**On the crown of the bend to the left, turn right on the track. Note:- the agriturismos and village of Gallina is straight ahead at the junction [Pass farm on the left] **(15.9)**At the junction, continue straight ahead on the gravel road [Farmhouse on the left] **(17.1)**Turn right on the grass track beside the driveway [Pass an agriturismo on the left]**(17.7)**Bear right on the track and cross the stream [Main road close on the left] **(18.2)**At the junction with the white road, bear right [Uphill between the conifers]**(18.3)** Take the left fork beside the fencing and pass near the vestiges of **Briccole (XI)** [Pass farm on the left]**(19.0)**Take the pedestrian crossing over the main road and continue straight ahead on the track [Across the stream] **(19.7)**At the intersection with the old via Cassia, turn right on the road [Pass agriturismo]**(20.0)**Take the left fork [Tarmac road, uphill] **(22.2)**Take the left fork [Stone walled garden on your right] **(23.3)**At the end of the long bend to the left, continue straight ahead. Note:- the Alternate Route via Abbadia San Salvatore leaves to the right [Information board on the right]**(23.4)**Approaching the T-junction with the via Cassia (SR2), bear left on the descending grass track, pass under the road and then turn right on the track parallel to the main road [Keep the river bed on your left] **(25.1)**Pass under the highway and cross the river on the stepping stones and then bear right under the second road [Continue with the river close on your right]**(26.1)**At the crossroads continue straight ahead towards the farmhouse **(26.4)** Cross the foot bridge and turn left**(26.7)**Approaching the main road, turn right [Towards the farm] **(27.0)**At the crossroads in the tracks, continue straight ahead along the ridge [Pass farm buildings on your left] **(28.3)**At the T-junction with the road, turn right [Direction Radicofani]**(28.5)**Bear left on the road [Direction Radicofani] **(30.7)**After a bend to the left following SP478 mark 28.VIII, turn right on the track [At the

141

stage 81 — San-Quirico-d'Orcia to Radicofani

end of the crash barrier](30.9)Bear right on the grass track 🕮 (32.1)At the junction with the stony road, bear left(32.5)At the junction, bear left and continue uphill on the stony road(32.8)At the T-junction with the main road, turn right(33.0)Turn left towards the centre of Radicofani [Viale Odoardo Lucchini] 🕮 (33.2)At the crossroads, go straight ahead and then bear right on the ramp [Towards centres](33.3)Fork left, uphill [No Entry](33.4) Arrive at **Radicofani** centre [Church of San Pietro to the right]

Accommodation and Tourist Information

Bagno-Vignoni
🏠 **B&B - la Locanda del Loggiato**,Piazza del Moretto, 30, 53027 Bagno-Vignoni(SI), Italy; Tel:+39 0335 430347; +39 0577 888925; Email:locanda@loggiato.it; loggiato.it; Price:A

Castiglione-d'Orcia
🏠 **Agriturismo - Sant'Alberto**,Via Vecchia Cassia, 53023 Castiglione-d'Orcia(SI), Italy; Tel: +39 3405 043914; Email:info@santalberto.com; www.santalberto.com; Price:A
🏠 **Agriturismo Sant' Ansano**,Località Gallina, 53023 Castiglione-d'Orcia(SI), Italy; Tel: +39 36 6385 4655; Email:info@santansano.com ; www.santansano.com; Price:B

Gallina
🛏 **La Vecchia Posta**,Via Cassia, 43, 53023 Gallina(SI), Italy; Tel: +39 331 997 2594; Email:lavecchiaposta@yahoo.com; web.facebook.com/ostellolavecchiaposta; Price:C; *Kind owners 2 restaurants close by*; **PR**

🏠 **Agriturismo Passalacqua** [Elena],Via Cassia, 53023 Gallina(SI), Italy; Tel:+39 0577 880129; +39 3355 470868; +39 3398 620877; Email:info@agriturismopassalacqua.it; www.agriturismopassalacqua.it; Price:A; *Pre-booking preferred but not obligatory. Dinner can be provided if requested in advance. Closed January and February* ; **PR**
🏠 **B&B - Da Nonna Ornella**,Le Querciole, 9, 53023 Gallina(SI), Italy; Tel: +39 2808 4706; Email:diva.orfei@gmail.com; Price:B; *1km from Gallina* ; **PR**
🗝 **Affittacamere - Albafiorita**,Strada del Pozzo, 53023 Gallina(SI), Italy; Tel:+39 0577 880118; +39 3407 079401; +39 3408 388663; Email:fiorildafalciani@gmail.com; albafiorita.jimdo.com; Price:B

Radicofani
🛏 **Spedale di San Pietro e Giacomo**,Via Dello Spedale, 2, 53040 Radicofani(SI), Italy; Tel: +39 3387 982255; +39 3389 205540; Price:D; *Credentials required*
🛏 **Ostello di Radicofani** [Irene],Piazza Anita Garibaldi, 2, 53040 Radicofani(SI), Italy; Tel: +39 3760622460; +39 3315 291556; Email:radicofani@ostellifrancigena.it; ostellifrancigena.it; Price:C; *Open March to November*
🏠 **Agriturismo - la Selvella**,Strada Provinciale 478-Km29, 53040 Radicofani(SI), Italy; Tel:+39 0578 55555; +39 348 7201546; Email:selvella@selvella.com; www.selvella.com; Price:A
🛏 **Albergo - la Torre**,Via G.Matteotti, 7, 53040 Radicofani(SI), Italy; Tel:+39 0578 55943; Email:ristorantealbergolatorre.wordpress.com; Price:B; **PR**
ℹ **Ufficio Informazioni Radicofani**,Via Renato Magi, 59, 53040 Radicofani(SI), Italy; Tel:+39 0578 55684; Email:uffturadicofani@virgilio.it; web.facebook.com/profile.php?id=100075561446611

San-Quirico-d'Orcia to Radicofani stage 81

Route via Abbadia San Salvatore

Route: Abbadia San Salvatore offers a broader choice of commercial accommodation and eating places than Radicofani. This substantially off-road route will add 3 km to your overall journey, but also affords an opportunity to visit the abbey whose foundation predates the journey of Sigeric and perhaps view the *Codex Diplomaticus Amiatinus*.

Length:	25.7km
Ascent:	1227m
Descent:	1335m

(0.0) Turn right and immediately right again onto the gravel track [Pass sign board on your left] (0.9) At the T-junction with the broad track turn right [Pass agriturismo **Il Poderino** on your right] (1.9) At the junction in the tracks continue straight ahead [Pass farm buildings on your left] (3.0) At the junction with the tarmac road turn left beside the road [Pass bunker on your right] (3.8) On the crown of the bend to the left, turn right on the gravel track [Modern building complex on your left before the turn] (4.0) Take the left fork (4.4) Take the right fork (6.3) Bear left and remain on

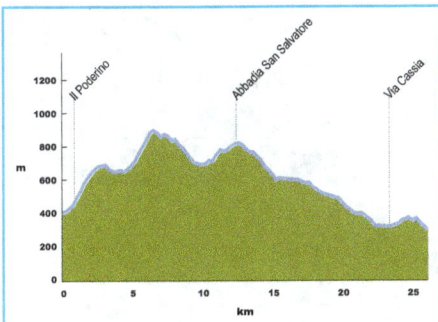

the track [Road parallel on the right] (6.4) Take the right fork (6.5) Cross the small bridge and turn right on the road. Take the first turn on your left [Conifers on you left at the turn] (8.0) At the T-junction with the narrow tarmac road, turn left [Downhill] (10.0) Continue straight [Avoid turning to the left] (11.0) At the T-junction, turn left (11.9) At the T-junction, turn left [Wooden garage in the garden on your right] (12.2) At the brow of the hill turn right. At the T-junction turn left into the medieval town of **Abbadia San Salvatore** and follow via Filippo Neri [Uphill, between houses] (12.5) Turn right on via Sant'Angelo and then immediately left on via Pinelli (12.5) Turn right on via Sant'Angelo and then immediately left on via Pinelli (12.7) Continue straight ahead between the medieval houses [Pass archway on your right] (12.9) Emerge from the houses and turn right (13.5) At the junction with the main road, turn left and continue beside the road [Pass

stage 81 — San-Quirico-d'Orcia to Radicofani

small shrine on your left] (15.8)Take the right fork and leave the main road [View of the Fortrezza di Radicofani on the hilltop to the left] (18.2) Take the left fork [Pond on the right] (21.3) Remain on the main track [Towards the industrial zone] (22.3)At the T-junction in the industrial zone, turn right [Continue with the via Cassia on your left] (23.0)On reaching the **via Cassia**, continue on the path with the road on your left, take the pedestrian crossing, turn left and immediately right on the gravel road [Pass between the farm buildings] (24.0)Bear right [Parallel to the via Cassia] (25.7)At the T-junction rejoin the main route, which turns towards the via Cassia. [Parallel to the via Cassia]

San Salvatore Abbey Crypt

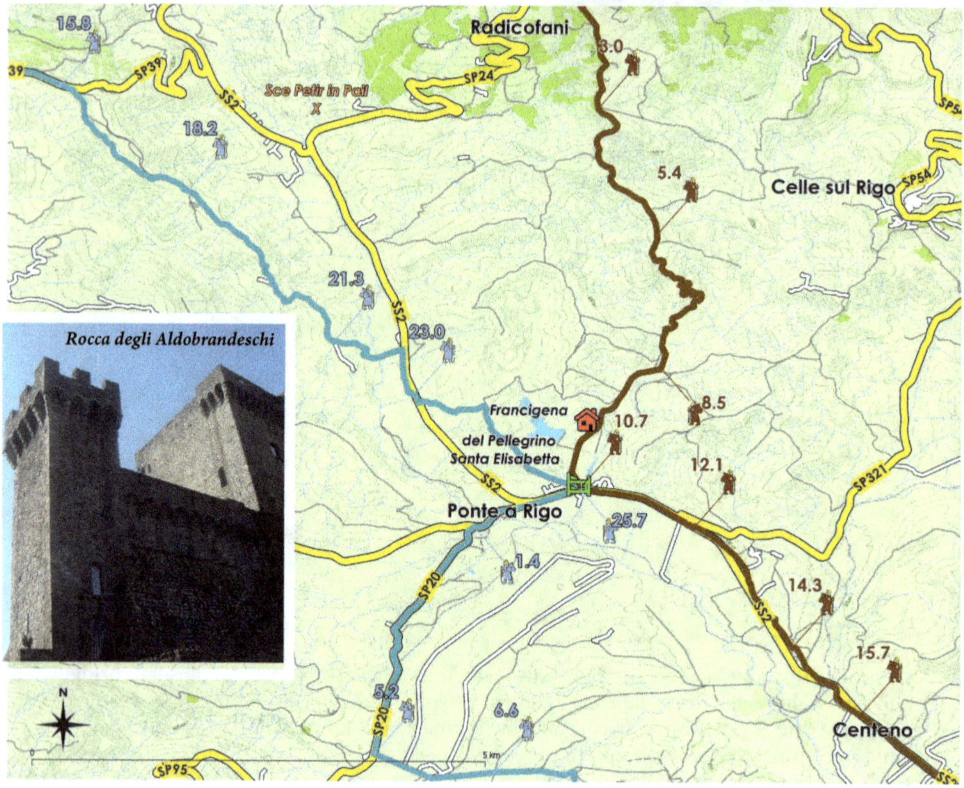

Rocca degli Aldobrandeschi

San-Quirico-d'Orcia to Radicofani — stage 81

Accommodation and Tourist Information

Abbadia San Salvatore

Abbazia di San Salvatore, Via del Monastero, 50, 53021 Abbadia San Salvatore(SI), Italy; Tel:+39 0577 777352; Email:dongiampaolo@virgilio.it; abbaziasansalvatore.it; Price:D; *Please call ahead credentials required*

Parrocchia di Santa Croce, Via Mentana, 31, 53021 Abbadia San Salvatore(SI), Italy; Tel:+39 0577 778310; *3 places*

Agriturismo Trefossata, Località Trefossata 196, 53021 Abbadia San Salvatore(SI), Italy; Tel:+39 0577 776204; +39 347 210 3923; Email: info@agriturismotrefossata.it; www.agriturismotrefossata.it; Price:A

Hotel - Fabbrini, Via Cavour, 53, 53021 Abbadia San Salvatore(SI), Italy; Tel:+39 0577 779911; Email:info@hotelfabbrini.com; hotelfabbrini.com; Price:B

Albergo Ristorante - Olimpia, Via Trieste, 22, 53021 Abbadia San Salvatore(SI), Italy; Tel:+39 0577 778250; +39 380 2383263; Email:info@albergoristoranteolimpia.it; albergoristoranteolimpia.it; Price:B

Osteria dei Locandieri, Via Trento, 37, 53021 Abbadia San Salvatore(SI), Italy; Tel:+39 0577 778198; +39 0577 552243; +39 3388298309; Email:trattorialocandieri@gmail.com; osteriadeilocandieri.it; Price:B

Bagni-di-San-Filippo

Agriturismo "Il Palazzo" [Barbara and Mimmo], Localita' Pietrineri, 8, 53023 Bagni-di-San-Filippo(SI), Italy; Tel:+390577872741; +393480457046; +393924652405; Email:ilpalazzobarbaraemimmo@gmail.com; ilpalazzobarbaraem.wixsite.com/my-site-2; Price:A; *Dinner and breakfast available*

Monte Amiata

stage 82 — Radicofani to Acquapendente

Length:	23.9km
Ascent:	728m
Descent:	1138m
Col Grand St Bernard:	835km
Rome:	193km

Descending from Radicofani–Val di Paglia

Route: a long stage from Radicofani to Acquapendente again with few opportunities for intermediate stops after reaching the valley bottom at Ponte a Rigo. However, the exit from Radicofani includes some of the most dramatic landscapes of the entire route.

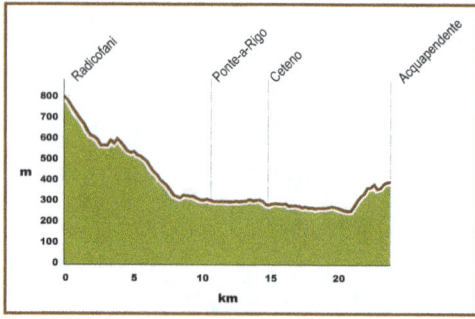

The descent from Radicofani on a gravel road is followed by a long section on the via Cassia which can be very busy with limited protection from the traffic for walkers. It is strongly recommended that you consider the longer (by 8km) Alternate Route via Proceno, where accommodation can be found. Aquapendente is a bustling town offering a broad range of facilities.

First settled by Etruscans, then Romans, Acquapendente was sacked and taken by the Longobards. In the Middle Ages it was established as a village and monastery by the Benedictine order, because of its position on the via Francigena. The town became known as the Jerusalem of Europe because of its cathedral dedicated to the Holy Sepulchre. The name of the city, meaning pending water, stems from the presence of several small waterfalls forming the Paglia, a stream setting the boundary between Lazio and Tuscany.

Acquapendente also maintains a long tradition called the Pugnaloni. The festival goes back to the 1100s, when the townspeople rebelled against the tyranny of Frederick I Barbarossa (otherwise known as Red Beard). Two farmers came across a miraculously flowering dead cherry tree and took it as a sign from the Madonna del Fiore, the town's protector saint, that they should rise up and seek liberty from tyranny. They did so, and started a procession to give thanks. Now, on the third Sunday of May, great masterpieces using flower petals and leaves, are displayed all over town as a symbolic recognition of Madonna of the Flowers and nature itself. The beautiful artworks follow a theme of liberty, nature and religious freedom. The festival also includes a parade, flag throwers and a religious procession.

Radicofani to Acquapendente — stage 82

🚶 **(0.0)** From the church of San Pietro turn right and continue along the main street [Via Roma] **(0.4)** Pass through the archway and leave the historic centre. Continue with care straight ahead on the pavement downhill [Viale Giacomo Matteotti] **(0.8)** At the crossroads, continue straight ahead [Direction Roma] 🚶 **(1.0)** On the apex of the bend to the right, continue straight ahead on the unmade road [Old via Cassia] 🚶 **(3.0)** Take the right fork [Uphill] **(3.9)** Take the left fork [Towards the "Pantano" agriturismo] 🚶 **(5.4)** Take the right fork [Farm on your left] 🚶 **(8.5)** Take the right fork, remaining between the trees [Keep river Rigo to the left] 🚶 **(10.7)** At the T- junction with the via Cassia in **Ponte-a-Rigo (X)**, turn left. Note:- the Alternate Route via Abbadia San Salvatore joins from the right. For the Alternate Route via Proceno initially follow the via Cassia to the right [Bar on the right] **(10.9)** Bear right to follow the track close to the road 🚶 **(12.1)** Rejoin the road

Entering Acquapendente

and cross to the left side **(12.5)** Bear left on the slip road [Direction Torricella] 🚶 **(14.3)** Just after passing through the hamlet, turn left and then immediately right on the track **(14.6)** At the junction with the broad track, keep right and then continue ahead on the tarmac **(14.9)** Rejoin the via Cassia and cross the river bridge. Then cross the road and bear right on the smaller road into the hamlet of **Ceteno** 🚶 **(15.7)** Rejoin the via Cassia and continue straight ahead with great care 🚶 **(21.0)** After crossing the long river bridge, take the first right turn and then immediately left on the small road. Note:- the Alternate Route joins from Proceno on the right 🚶 **(22.6)** At the T-junction with the via Cassia, turn right [Enter Aquapendente] **(22.8)** Turn left, across the car park, and take the track to the left of the Albergo ["Aquila d'Oro"] **(22.9)** Take the steps downhill and to the left **(23.0)** At the T-junction, turn right on the stony track, uphill [Gardens below on the left] **(23.1)** In front of the albergo "la Ripa" turn left and then bear right [Via Cesare Battisti and via Roma] 🚶 **(23.9)** Arrive at **Acquapendente (IX)**, beside the church of Santo Sepulcro [Piazza del Duomo]

stage 82   Radicofani to Acquapendente
Proceno Route

Route: this longer Alternate Route avoids the dangers of the via Cassia quickly joining quiet gravel roads and offers the opportunity to rest in the medieval village of Proceno. (0.0)At the T-junction with the main road, turn right, cross the road and continue to the right on the track parallel to the road [SR2, pass bar on the right](0.4)Leave Ponte a Rigo, and keep left on the track. In the event the track is overgrown or has been ploughed in proceed on the grass beside the road to the Sovana junction [Continue on the left side of the road towards Abbadia S.S.](0.9)At the end of the track turn right and then left to follow the road with care - crash barriers bound the road ahead [The road crosses the river] (1.4)Take the next road to the left [Direction Sovana] (5.2)Turn left onto a gravel track, direction la Valle(5.9)Fork right down the hill [The hamlet of **La Valle**] (6.6)Continue straight ahead, over the crossroads in the track(7.5)At the T-junction in the track, shortly after crossing the Torrente Siele, turn right (8.8)Take the left fork (10.1)Continue straight ahead [Towards la Casina] (11.1)At the T-junction in **La Cascina**, turn right (14.5)At the T-junction beside the cemetery, turn left up the hill on the road [Direction Proceno](14.7)Take the right fork towards the castello in Proceno(15.3)In the piazza in **Proceno**, bear left on viale Marconi [Pass Palazzo Sforza on your left](15.4)At the T-junction, turn left and continue downhill on the winding road [Skirting the village on via Belvedere] (15.7)On the crown of the sharp bend to the left, continue straight ahead on the small road, downhill [Via della Pace](16.1)Beside the sports ground, take the right fork, downhill(16.2)At the T-junction, turn right [Downhill](16.5)Just after entering the woods, turn left on the track and skirt the field (17.3)At the T-junction with the road, turn right [Cross the river bridge](17.4) Bear left on the strada Provinciale [After river bridge] (18.7)At the bottom of the hill, shortly before the T-junction with the via Cassia, turn right on the small road and rejoin the "Official Route" [Strada Viccinale di San Giglio]

Length:	18.7km
Ascent:	539m
Descent:	587m

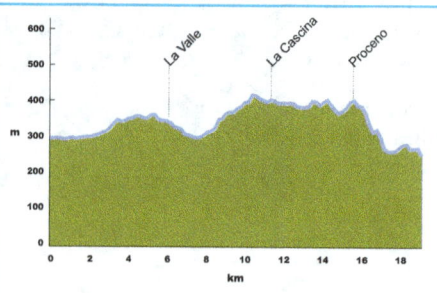

Castello di Proceno

LigaDue

Radicofani to Acquapendente — stage 82

Accommodation and Tourist Information

Acquapendente

Casa del Pellegrino San Rocco, Via Roma, 51, 01021 Acquapendente(VT), Italy; Tel: +39 3398 499965; +39 3471 662919; Price:D

Monastero di Santa Chiara di Acquapendente, Via Malintoppa, 10, 01021 Acquapendente(VT), Italy; Tel:+39 0763 734153; Email:info@monasterodiacquapendente.it; www.monasterodiacquapendente.it; Price:C

Albergo - il Borgo, Via Porta Sant'Angelo, 3, 01021 Acquapendente(VT), Italy; Tel:+39 0763 733971; +39 3471 366729; Email:ristoranteilborgoacquapendentevt@msn.com ; ristoranteilborgo-acquapendente-vt.blogspot.com; Price:B; *Warm atmoshpere good food central location* ; **PR**

Albergo - Toscana, Piazza N.Sauro, 5, 01021 Acquapendente(VT), Italy; Tel:+39 0763 711220; Email:info@albergotoscana.net ; www.albergotoscana.com; Price:B

Affittacamere - La Casa di Teo, Via Salvatore Allende, 7, 01021 Acquapendente(VT), Italy; Tel: +39 3279 281046; Email:Ivano.goracci@libero.it; Price:C; *Pilgrim friendly 1.5km from the historical centre*

Comune di Acquapendente, Piazza Girolamo Fabrizio, 17, 01021 Acquapendente(VT), Italy; Tel:+39 0763 73091; www.comuneacquapendente.it

Proceno

Casa del Pellegrino [Claudio Rossi],Piazza della Libertà, 23, 01020 Proceno(VT), Italy; Tel: +39 339 2586470; Email:rossiclaudio210@gmail.com; www.comunediproceno.vt.it

B&B - Castello di Proceno ,Corso Regina Margherita, 155, 01020 Proceno (VT), Italy; Tel:+39 0763 710272; +39 0335 373394; Email:castello.proceno@orvienet.it ; www.castellodiproceno.it; Price:A; *Pilgrim discount*

Comune di Proceno, Piazza della Libertà, 12, 01020 Proceno(VT), Italy; Tel:+39 0763 710092; Email:info@comune.proceno.vt.it; www.comunediproceno.vt.it

San Casciano Dei Bagni

La Casa del Pellegrino Santa Elisabetta [Alberto Guerrini],Via Cassia Vecchia - Ponte a Rigo, 53040 San Casciano Dei Bagni(SI), Italy; Tel: +39 3343 546142; Email:albertoguerrini04@gmail.com; Price:D

B&B - Francigena, Podere Pian del Celle sul Rigo, 252, 53040 San Casciano Dei Bagni(SI), Italy; Tel: +39 389 923 0556; booking.com; Price:B

| stage 83 | Acquapendente to Bolsena |

Length: 23.0km

Ascent: 676m
Descent: 743m

Col Grand
St Bernard: 859km
Rome: 169km

Lake Bolsena

Route: the route from Acquapendente to Bolsena meanders on farm tracks rejoining the via Cassia to pass through the town of Saint Lorenzo Nuovo where you will find shops and cafes. The route continues through woodlands before traversing the lower slopes of the caldera of the former volcano of lake Bolsena. The latter part includes paths over broken ground with some short steep ascents making for difficult progress for heavily loaded cyclists.

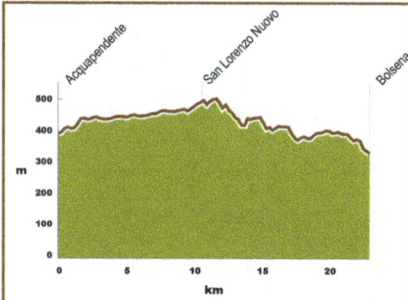

While it is fairly certain Bolsena is the successor to the ancient Roman town of Volsinii, scholarly opinion is sharply divided as to whether Volsinii was the same as the ancient Etruscan city of Velzna or Velsuna (sometimes termed Volsinii Veteres–Old Volsinii), the other candidate being Orvieto, twenty kilometres to the north-east. Other historians have pointed out that the town of Bolsena has no Etruscan characteristics. For example, Etruscan cities were built on defensible crags, which the castle is not. Pliny the Elder decided that a bolt from Mars fell and burned it down entirely. As a consequence, he maintained, the population moved to another site, which is thought to be Bolsena.

Of volcanic origin, Lake Bolsena was formed by the collapse of a caldera into a deep aquifer. Roman historic records indicate activity of the Vulsini volcano as recently as 104 B.C., since when it has been dormant. The two islands in the southern part of the lake were formed by underwater eruptions following the initial collapse.

Collegiata di Santa Cristina

Bolsena is also known for the Miracle of Bolsena, which occurred in 1263. A Bohemian priest, who was somewhat sceptical about the doctrine of transubstantiation, became convinced of its truth after seeing the miraculous appearance of drops of blood on the host he had just consecrated. The miraculous event was reported to Pope Urban IV, who instituted the feast of Corpus Christi in the following year, and planned the erection of the Cathedral of Orvieto, the town where he resided. The Duomo di Orvieto was eventually built to commemorate the miracle.

Acquapendente to Bolsena — stage 83

(0.0) From the Basilica del Santo Sepolcro, turn left on the main road [Pass Torre Giulia de Jacopo on your right] **(0.6)** Turn left, direction Torre Alfina [Shrine on the apex of the bend] 🚶 **(1.8)** At the top of the hill, bear right onto the narrow tarmac road [Pass silos on your right] **(2.2)** At the fork, bear right on the gravel track [Line of trees to your left] 🚶 **(3.0)** At the junction continue straight ahead on the gravel track **(3.5)** At the junction with the via Cassia, cross straight over onto the small road **(4.0)** Bear right on the gravel track towards the power lines and keep right at the next junction 🚶 **(5.3)** At the T-junction with a minor road, turn left and then immediately right [Farmhouse on your left] **(6.0)** Take the right fork [Strada del Podere del Vescovo] 🚶 **(7.4)** At the T-junction, turn left **(8.0)** At the next T-junction, turn left **(8.1)** Fork right on the track **(8.3)** Take the left fork 🚶 **(9.5)** At the T-junction with the main road, turn right on the via Cassia [Towards San Lorenzo Nuovo] 🚶 **(10.6)** At the traffic lights, in the centre of **San Lorenzo Nuovo**, continue straight ahead on the left side of the road [Direction Bolsena, Roma 124] **(11.0)** Bear left on the path to the rear of the houses **(11.1)** Cross the road and continue straight ahead on via degli Scoglietti and then bear right on via F Prada **(11.4)** As the road turns to the left, bear right on the track through the trees 🚶 **(11.8)** At the

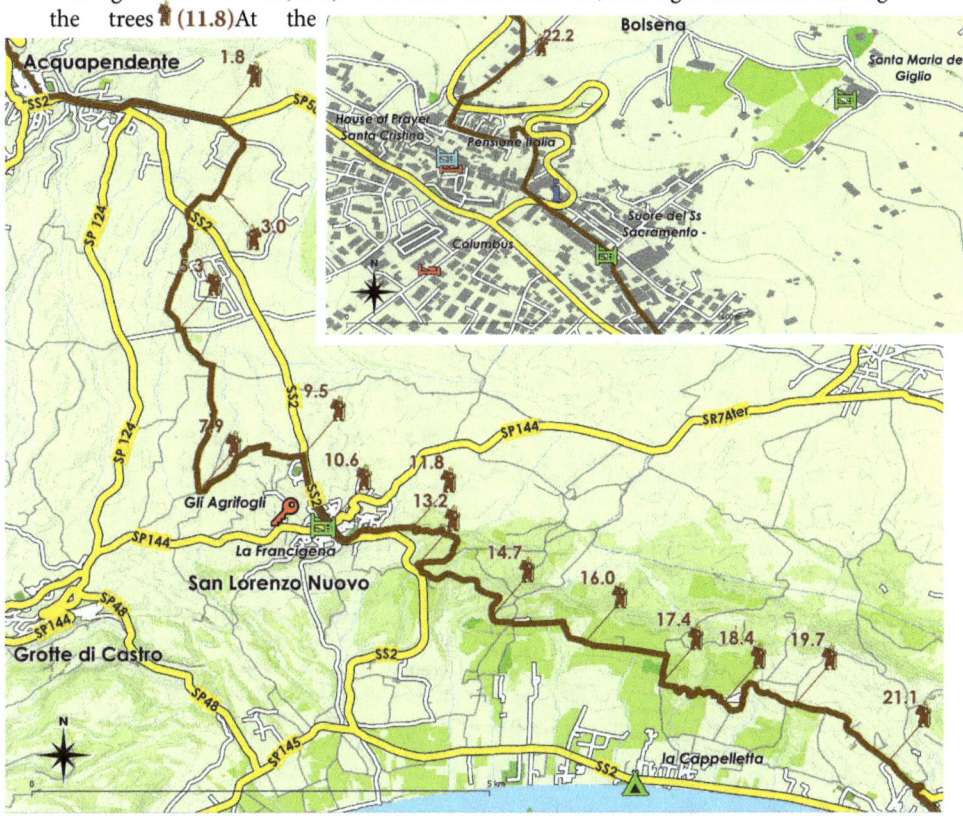

junction, turn sharp right **(11.9)** At the next junction, turn sharp left **(12.2)** Bear left and keep left up the hill **(12.3)** Bear right downhill **(12.8)** At the T-junction turn right 🚶 **(13.2)** At the next junction turn left **(13.3)** At the T-junction, turn left onto a gravel track 🚶 **(14.7)** At

stage 83 — Acquapendente to Bolsena

the fork in the track, continue straight ahead down the hill**(15.0)**Bear right and then fork left parallel to lake-shore**(15.6)**Fork right down the hill [Quarry on left] ⚑ **(16.0)**Keep left on the gravel track [Parallel to the lake shore]**(16.5)**At the fork, keep right**(16.9)**At the T-junction, turn right ⚑ **(17.4)**Turn left [Strada della Roccaccia]**(18.1)**Fork left up the hill [Line of posts directly on right] ⚑ **(18.4)**At the T-junction, turn right down the hill [Entrance to a large house on left]**(18.5)**Take the left fork**(19.1)**Fork right onto a smaller track ⚑ **(19.7)**Bear right [Parallel to lake-shore]**(20.1)**Fork left [Between a line of trees] ⚑ **(21.1)**Keep left on the track [Between olive groves]**(21.6)**At the T-junction, turn left and pass the "ostello"**(21.9)**At the Stop sign turn right down the hill ⚑ **(22.2)**Turn left across the parking area and then bear left on the small road [Pass close to the water trough]**(22.5)**Cross the main road and continue straight on the narrow street [Rocca Monaldeschi della Cervara on the right]**(22.5)**Take the first turning to the left on via degli Adami**(22.6)**At the end of the narrow street turn left and then right**(22.7)**Bear right down hill on the narrow street [Main road, below on your left]**(22.8)**In piazza Guglielmo Matteotti, at the foot of the hill, turn left and carefully cross the main road**(22.8)**Continue straight ahead on Corso della Repubblica [Pedestrian zone]**(23.0)**Arrive at **Bolsena (VIII)** centre in piazza Santa Cristina [The Basilica of Santa Cristina ahead]

Accommodation and Tourist Information

Bolsena

🛏**Foresteria Santa Maria del Giglio**,Via Madonna del Giglio, 49, 01023 Bolsena(VT), Italy; Tel:+39 0761 799066; Email:info@ conventobolsena.org; www.conventobolsena.org; Price:C

🛏**Suore del Ss Sacramento** -,Piazza Santa Cristina, 4, 01023 Bolsena(VT), Italy; Tel:+39 0761 586210; Email:rsssbolsena@ libero.it; www.rsssacramento.it; Price:C

🛏**House of Prayer - Santa Cristina** [Don Francesco],Corso Cavour, 70, 01023 Bolsena(VT), Italy; Tel: +39 3466 044158; Email:info@casacamporitiro.it; casadipreghierabolsena.com; Price:C

🛏 **Hotel - Columbus**,Viale Colesanti, 27 , 01023 Bolsena(VT), Italy; Tel:+39 0761 799009; www.hotelcolumbusbolsena.it; Price:A

🛏 **Pensione - Italia**,Corso Cavour, 53, 01023 Bolsena(VT), Italy; Tel:+39 0761 799193; +39 0761 798026; +39 3387 732831; +39 3498636499; Email:pensioneitalia@ libero.it; www.pensioneitalia.net; Price:B

⛺ **Camping Pineta**,Viale Diaz, 01023 Bolsena(VT), Italy; Tel:+39 0761 796905; +39 3387 329724; +39 3893 424601; Email:campingpinetabolsena@gmail.com; www.campingpinetabolsena.it; Price:C; Chalets also available

⛺ **Camping la Cappelletta**,Via Cassia Nord, 01023 Bolsena(VT), Italy; Tel:+39 0761 799543; Email:campinglacappelletta@hotmail.it; www.cappellettacampingbolsena.it; Price:C

ℹ **Comune di Bolsena**,Via Guglielmo Marconi, 01023 Bolsena(VT), Italy; Tel:+39 0761 7951; Email:info@comune. bolsena.vt.it; www.comune.bolsena.vt.it

San-Lorenzo-Nuovo

🛏**La Francigena Ristorante - Affittacamere**,Via Paese Vecchio, 01020 San-Lorenzo-Nuovo(VT), Italy; Tel:+39 0763 727936; +39 3339 531600; +39 3395 386654; Email:lafrancigena2013@libero.it; web.facebook.com/LaFrancigenaRistoranteAffittacamere; Price:B

🔑 **Apartment - Gli Agrifogli**,Via delle Grotte, 104, 01020 San-Lorenzo-Nuovo(VT), Italy; Tel:+39 340 345 8426; Email:gabriellabranca4@gmail.com; www. alloggioturisticoagrifogli.it; Price:B

Bolsena to Montefiascone — stage 84

Length: 16.5km

Ascent: 792m
Descent: 512m

Col Grand
St Bernard: 882km
Rome: 146km

Cattedrale di Santa Margherita–Montefiascone

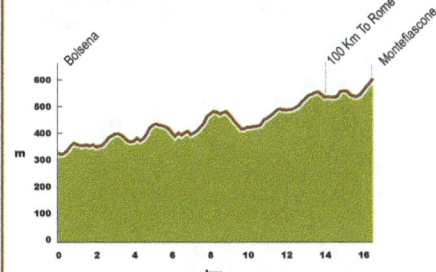

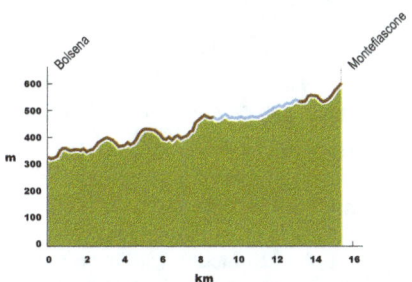

Route: the "Official Route" from Bolsena to Montefiascone climbs back into the hills overlooking the lake and progresses on farm and forest tracks before following a section of Roman road.

The route then makes a loop including a short section of the busy modern via Cassia before the final approach to the hilltop town of Montefiscone. A slightly more direct Alternate Route following the ancient via Cassia will avoid the loop.

The name Montefiascone is mentioned in 853 AD, as a possession of the bishop of Tuscania. The periods of highest splendour were the 13th and 14th centuries, when the castle was often a residence of Popes, and in the Avignon period it was the residence of Cardinal Albornoz, the Pope's representative in Italy.

Montefiascone Cathedral or the Basilica of Santa Margherita is one of the most important churches in the area, and has one of the largest domes in Italy, which is visible from most of the towns of the Viterbo area. When Pope Urban V established the Diocese of Montefiascone in 1396, the church that was the most popular and most central was chosen to be the cathedral of the new diocese, after which major reconstruction began. The building from the crypt up to the base of the dome dates from the 15th and 16th centuries and was undertaken by the Veronese architect Michele Sanmicheli, probably with the help of Antonio da Sangallo the Younger. At this time the lower church was created, and the plans for the upper church drawn up, but for economic reasons this phase of building stopped at the level of the roof, and the cathedral remained open to the elements until 1602. The bell towers and west front were designed and added in 1840 by the architect Paul Gazola, using very simple elements of decoration. In addition to a marble statue and some relics of Saint Margaret of Antioch, the cathedral contains the relics of Saint Lucia Filippini and the tomb of Cardinal Marco Antonio Barbarigo.

stage 84   Bolsena to Montefiascone

🚶(0.0)Leave piazza Santa Cristina by Porta Romana [Basilica and café on the left](0.2) At the crossroads with trees in the traffic island, turn left [Via Acqua della Croce](0.3)Turn right, pass car sales on the left, then take the left l fork(0.4)At the end of the road, turn left [School ahead at the junction](0.7)Fork right onto the track(0.9)Turn sharp right, over the stream 🚶(1.2)At the junction turn right and then left [Parallel to the lake shore](1.8)At the T-junction, turn right, uphill(2.0)Turn left, uphill on the long straight tarmac road [Pass between gardens and olive groves] 🚶(3.0)Take the right fork [Parallel to the lake-shore below](3.2)Bear right on the track and enter the woods 🚶(4.2)At the T-junction with the tarmac road turn right, down hill(4.3)At the T-junction turn left [Parallel to the lake-shore] 🚶(5.2)Fork right on the gravel track, direction Parco di Turona(5.8)Fork right, down the hill(6.2)Turn left on a gravel track, just before a small white chapel 🚶(7.2)Fork right through a band of trees [Into the clearing](7.3)After crossing the stream bear right [Derelict house to your left](7.3)At a junction of three tracks take the central track 🚶(8.7)At the crossroads, continue straight ahead. Note:- the "Official Route" descends again towards the lake before remounting the ridge. The Alternate Route proceeds directly to Montefiascone on a normally quiet road(9.6)At the junction with the road, turn right and carefully cross the SR-2 and take the track slightly to the right of the junction and bear left on the track [Pass through a gap in the crash barriers] 🚶(10.0)Rejoin the SR-2 and continue straight ahead behind the crash barriers(10.4)Bear left on the small road [VF milestone on the right] 🚶(11.6)Bear right, remain on the gravel road 🚶(13.0)At the road junction, turn sharp right [Large modern house to the right of the junction](13.5)At the T-junction, turn left on the tarmac road(13.9)At the junction with the via Cassia, turn left onto the pavement and follow the main road 🚶(14.1)**100 km to Rome** signpost [Beside Church of Corpus Christi](14.4)Bear right on the main road, direction Viterbo. Note:- the Alternate Route joins from the left [Hotel on the left at the junction](14.6)Turn left beside the modern office building on via Cardinal Salotti [Towards Orvieto] 🚶(15.3)Bear left on via Santa Maria delle Grazie [Towards Orvieto](15.6)At the junction with the SS71, turn

Bolsena to Montefiascone — stage 84

right [Direction Viterbo]**(15.8)** Take the left fork [Trees lining the left side of the road] **(16.0)** Turn right, uphill onto via San Flaviano [Keep the church on your right]**(16.1)** Bear left continuing uphill [High stone wall on your right]**(16.2)** Continue straight ahead across the road and up the ramp to enter the historic centre on Corso Cavour [Pass through the archway] **(16.5)** Arrive at **Montefiascone (VII)** centre [In piazza Vittorio Emanuele]

Direct Route to Montefiascone

Route: direct route to Montefiascone using the generally quiet ancient via Cassia and avoiding an unnecessary descent and climb. **(0.0)** Continue straight ahead on the ancient via Cassia(0.3) At the junction with the road, continue straight ahead [Pilgrim milestone] **(4.2)** Keep left at the junction [Stone VF sign](4.5) At the junction with the main road, continue straight ahead. Note:- the "Official Route" joins from the right

Length:	4.5km
Ascent:	142m
Descent:	81m

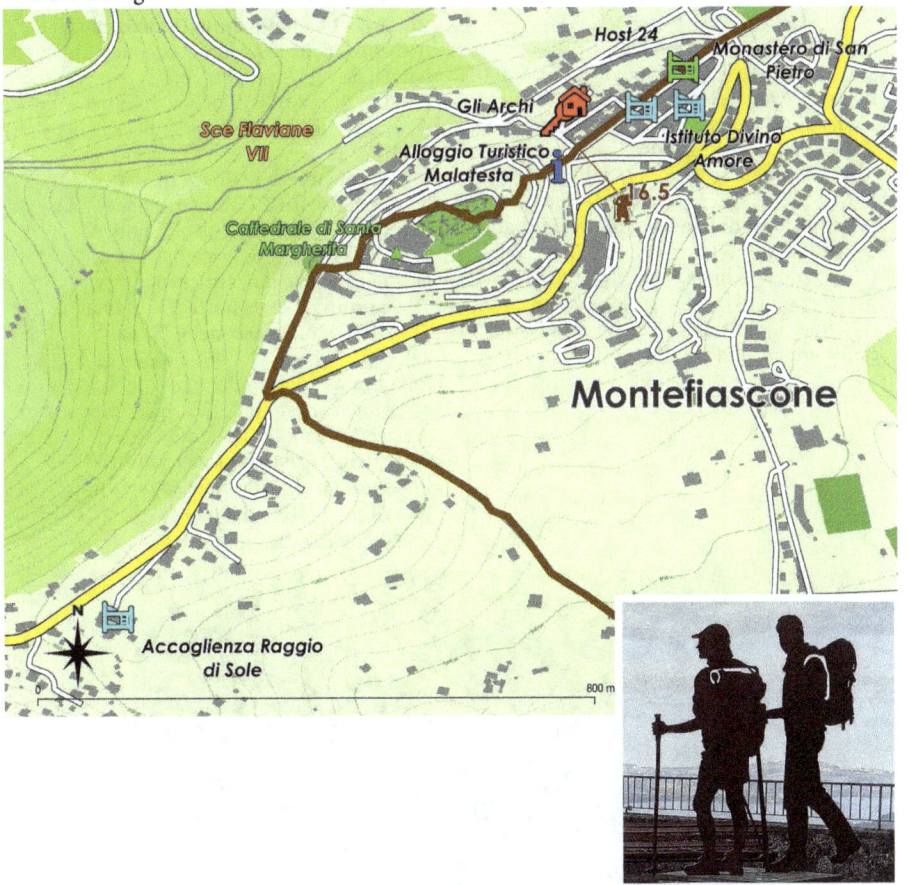

Pilgrim Monument–Montefiascone

stage 84 — Bolsena to Montefiascone

Accommodation and Tourist Information

Montefiascone

Host 24, Corso Cavour, 22, 01027 Montefiascone(VT), Italy; Tel:+39 3282818278; Email: cameresanflaviano@gmail.com; ilovehost24.it; Price:C

Domus Peregrini [Immacolata and Franco],Via Paoletti, 3, 01027 Montefiascone(VT), Italy; Tel: +39 3381 838216; +39 3207 772586; Email:immacolatacoraggio1958@gmail.it; Price:D; *Private house with 10 bunks close to the route 3km after Montefiscone centre*

Al Centesimo Chilometro, Via Asinello, 164, 01027 Montefiascone(VT), Italy; Tel: +39 3383032673; www.hostelz.com/hostel/484567-Al-Centesimo-Chilometro-100-Ristoro-del-Pellegrino; Price:C; *Small dormitory for men only. Good facilities at the ancient 100 km mark from Saint Peter's*

Istituto Divino Amore, Corso Cavour, 64, 01027 Montefiascone(VT), Italy; Tel:+39 0761 826089; Price:D; *Open April to October*

Monastero di San Pietro, Via Garibaldi, 31, 01027 Montefiascone(VT), Italy; Tel:+39 0761 826066; Email:benedettineap.mf@gmail.com; www.monasterosanpietromontefiascone.com; Price:D; *Dinner provided with home grown food*

Accoglienza Raggio di Sole [Signora Edy Bertolo],Via San Francesco, 3, 01027 Montefiascone(VT), Italy; Tel:+39 0761 820340; +39 0761 826098; +39 3475 900953; Email:edybertolo@libero.it; www.cappuccinilazio.com/viterbo/conventodi-montefiascone; Price:C; *Can arrange baggage transport to Viterbo*

B&B - Alloggio Turistico Malatesta,Via Malatesta, 35, 01027 Montefiascone(VT), Italy; Tel: +39 3286 123073; Email:marilena.dangelo@gmail.com; www.booking.com; Price:B; *Discount with credentials*

B&B - l'Asinello Sulla Francigena,Via Asinello, 56, 01027 Montefiascone(VT), Italy; Tel: +39 3471 894978; Email:lasinellosullafrancigena@gmail.com; web.facebook.com/asinellosullaFrancige-na; Price:B

Affittacamere - Gli Archi,Via Nazionale, 6, 01027 Montefiascone(VT), Italy; Tel: +39 2791 1230; gli-archi.bedsandhotels.com; Price:B; *Central location good facilities price and service*

Camping Amalasunta,Via del Lago, 77, 01027 Montefiascone(VT), Italy; Tel:+39 0761 825294; +39 345 23 94 462; Email:info@campingamalasunta.it; www.campingamalasunta.it; Price:C; *Caravans are available on the l;ake shore*

Ufficio Turistico,Piazza Vittorio Emanuele, 01027 Montefiascone(VT), Italy; Tel:+39 0761 820884; www.visitmontefiascone.it

Montefiascone to Viterbo

stage 85

Length: 17.9km

Ascent: 235m
Descent: 510m

Col Grand
St Bernard: 898km
Rome: 130km

Palazzo dei Papi di Viterbo

Route: the stage from Montefiascone to Viterbo descends from the Rocca dei Papi and becomes easier on farm tracks and clearly visible Roman roads. The route passes beside thermal pools before entering the city of Viterbo on very busy roads, and finally reaching the walled medieval town.

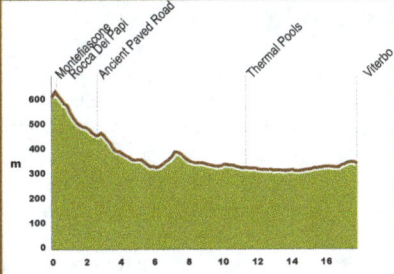

Viterbo has a good range of accommodation and excellent public transport connections to Rome and the intermediate towns. It is possible to buy drinks or a snack en route at the Parco Termale del Bagnacci.

Viterbo was an important Etruscan centre before falling to the Romans in the 4th century B.C.. In 1164 Frederick Barbarossa made Viterbo the seat of his Anti-pope governor, Paschal III. Three years later, he used his armies against Rome.

The Palazzo dei Papi or Papal Palace, hosted the papacy for about two decades in the 13th century, and served as a country residence or refuge in times of trouble in Rome. The columns of the palace were taken from a Roman temple.

Today, in spite of sustaining serious bomb damage during World War II, Viterbo's historic centre is one of the best preserved medieval towns in central Italy. Many of the older buildings (particularly churches) are built on top of ancient ruins, recognizable by their large stones. Viterbo is also often mentioned in the itineraries and chronicles of the journeys of illustrious people, who were not always motivated by veneration–for example, Charles the Great and Charles VIII. Although the old via Cassia did not pass directly through the city, the transit of pilgrims expanded the local economy and established Viterbo's role as a significant commercial centre for the region. In San Pellegrino, Viterbo's oldest and best preserved quarter, medieval houses with towers, arches and external staircases line narrow streets running between little piazzas decorated with fountains.

No pot holes after 2000 years of use

stage 85   Montefiascone to Viterbo

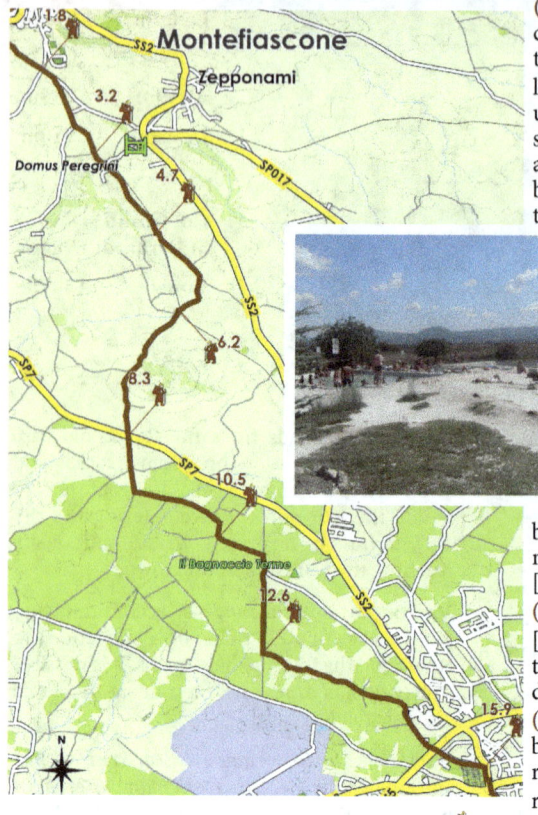

(**0.0**)In piazza Vittorio Emanuele, continue straight ahead through the arch [Uphill, clock tower on the left](**0.1**)Continue straight ahead up the steps. Note: - to avoid the steps, take via 24 Maggio to the left and rejoin the "Official Route" just before exiting the old town [Direction Rocca dei Papi] (**0.2**)Enter the gardens and go straight ahead [Between the trees] (**0.3**)Continue straight ahead through the gardens of **Rocca dei Papi** and descend on the steps before turning left [Pass beside the Torre del Pellegrino](**0.4**) From the parking area behind la Rocca, keep right in the narrow street - via della Rocca [View of lake Bolsena to your right] (**0.5**)At the T-junction, turn right [Towards the archway](**0.5**)Pass through the arch and turn left downhill [Town walls on your left] (**0.8**)At the intersection with the busy SP8, turn left and immediately right, downhill on the unmade road [VF map and sign](**0.9**)Take the left fork on the unmade road [Downhill] (**1.8**)At the crossroads, continue straight ahead, direction Viterbo [Towards pylons](**2.0**)Just after power substation, fork right onto a dirt track(**2.3**)Bear left on the paved section(**2.5**)Bear right [Olive grove on the left](**2.7**) Bear left onto the **ancient paved road** with a shrine directly to your right (**3.2**)Fork left down the hill [Via Paoletti] (**4.7**)Turn left under the railway and then right(**5.5**)Bear right to continue on the main track (**6.2**)Turn left after going under second railway tunnel and then bear right remaining on the main track(**8.3**)At crossroads with the major road (SP7), go straight ahead [Strada Casetta](**9.2**)Fork left after passing the house on the right (**10.5**)Fork left beside a fence and a line of trees(**11.1**)At the T-junction in the tracks, turn right towards the thermal pools(**11.4**)Bear right beside the **thermal pools** (**12.6**) With metal gates to your right, turn left (**15.9**)At the T-junction, turn right onto strada Cassia Nord [Large cemetery on your right](**16.3**)Pass under the fly-over and continue straight ahead [No Entry, towards petrol station](**16.4**)At the roundabout continue straight ahead [Direction centro](**16.6**)At the next roundabout, continue straight ahead, remaining towards Viterbo centre [Via della Palazzina, pass bank offices on the left] (**17.4**)Pass through the arched Porta Fiorentina into the old town of Viterbo (**17.5**)Turn right into piazza della Rocca(**17.6**)Continue straight ahead in the narrow street [Via S. Faustino] (**17.7**)In piazza San Faustino, turn left and then bear right [Via Cairoli](**17.9**)Arrive at **Viterbo (VI)** in piazza dei Caduti [Beside war memorial]

Montefiascone to Viterbo — stage 85

Accommodation and Tourist Information

Viterbo

Ospitale del Pellegrino - Santa Maria Nuova, Piazza San Pellegrino, 49, 01100 Viterbo(VT), Italy; Tel: +39 3346 960175; Email: ospitaledelpellegrino@gmail.com; www.santamarianuova-viterbo.it; Price:D; *Credentials required*

Convento Cappuccini, Via Crispino Beato, 6, 01100 Viterbo(VT), Italy; Tel: +39 0761321945; +39 3475 900953; Email: edybertolo@libero.it; Price:C; *Will arrange baggage transport from Montefiascone*

Il Villino - Casa Per Ferie, Viale 4 Novembre, 25, 01100 Viterbo(VT), Italy; Tel: +39 0761 341900; +39 3887 307841; www.ilvillinodiviterbo.it; Price:B; **PR**

B&B - Buon Camino Tuscia, Via Igino Garbini, 78, 01100 Viterbo(VT), Italy; Tel: +39 3287 462460; Email: buoncamminotuscia@gmail.com; web.facebook.com/tappa40; Price:A

B&B - Orchard [Valter Labate], Via Ortaccio, 01100 Viterbo(VT), Italy; Tel: +39 3400 664177; Email: info@bborchard.it; bborchard.it; Price:B; *Discount with credentials*; **PR**

B&B - Torre Medievale, Via delle Fortezze, 27, 01100 Viterbo(VT), Italy; Tel: +39 3388 358534; +39 3476 762363; Email: lauradiemme49@gmail.com; www.torremedievale.com; Price:B

B&B - Casa di Ale, Via Monte Cervino, 13, 01100 Viterbo(VT), Italy; Tel: +39 3200 112384; Email: alessandra.croci222@gmail.com; Price:C; *Pilgrim friendly*

Albergo - Viterbo Inn, Via San Luca, 17, 01100 Viterbo(VT), Italy; Tel:+39 0761 326643; Email: info@viterboinn.com; www.viterboinn.com; Price:B

Hotel - Tuscia, Via Cairoli 41, 01100 Viterbo(VT), Italy; Tel: +39 0761 345976; +39 0761 344400; +39 3756 239973; Email: info@tusciahotel.com; www.tusciahotel.com; Price:A; *Price group B in low season*

Hotel - Centrale, Via della Cava, 26, 01100 Viterbo(VT), Italy; Tel:+39 0761 227274; Email: info@hotelcentraleviterbo.it; www.hotelcentraleviterbo.it; Price:B

Tourist Office, Piazza Martiri d'Ungheria, 01100 Viterbo(VT), Italy; Tel: +39 0761 226427; Email: info@visit.viterbo.it; www.promotuscia.it

stage 86 — Viterbo to Vetralla

Length:	22.0km
Ascent:	751m
Descent:	776m
Col Grand St Bernard:	916km
Rome:	112km

Vetralla

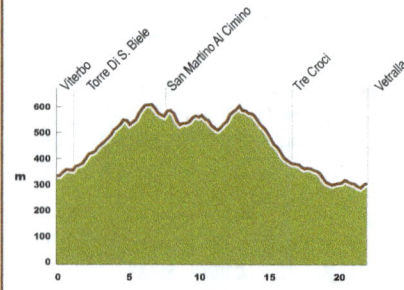

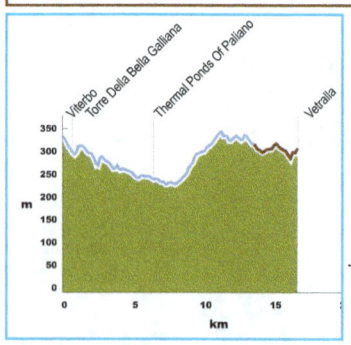

Route: the primary route from Viterbo to Vetralla follows minor roads and woodland tracks to the famed 13th century abbey (with parts dating from the 9th century) of San Martino Al Cimino. From San Martino Al Cimino there is a choice to continue to Vetralla or follow a more direct route bypassing Vetralla and passing by the rim of the volcanic Lago di Vico to rejoin the "Official Route" close to Capranica. A prior and shorter route is also possible passing through dramatic and ancient cuttings in the tuff stone.

Food and accommodation are available in San Martino al Cimino.

Local legend says that Vetralla dates back to the biblical figure of Noah, who ran the Ark aground on the heights of Valle Cajana, and availed himself of the excellent wines found there. The Etruscans left their mark in various tomb cities scattered throughout the entire region.

Vetralla sits on the slope of Mount Fogliano, at the crossroads of three important Roman roads–via Cassia, via Clodio, and via Aurelia. A relatively short distance from Rome, it became an important Roman outpost. Over the centuries, Vetralla was passed around as a trophy among the nobility of various epochs and was finally donated by Pope Julius II to England's ambassador of King Henry VIII, remaining under British protection for hundreds of years. Today's historic centre is a well-preserved example of medieval civic construction, retaining its sinewy alleyways and stone houses clustered together, interspersed with minute piazzas.

The Cathedral of Sant'Andrea is known for the Madonna of the Rosary, attributed to Ludovico Mazzanti and the Crucifixion of St. Andrew by Domenico Muratori. There is also an outstanding 12th century panel of the Madonna Intercessor (on the reverse, the Head of the Saviour). A small crystal shrine houses several reliquaries, including one in silver gilt by Giovanni Anastasio di Vitale, and a small silvered urn with the relics of St. Hippolytus.

Viterbo to Vetralla stage 86

🍴(0.0)Leave piazza dei Caduti and head south on via Filippo Ascenzi up the hill [Pass the church with the distinctive striped steeple on your left - Chiesa degli Almadiani](0.3)In piazza del Plebiscito take via Cavour [No Entry to vehicles](0.5)In piazza Fontana Grande, bear left on via Garibaldi [Pass to the left of the fountain](0.7)Cross piazza S. Sisto and exit the old town through the archway [Porta Romana](0.7)At the traffic lights cross the main road and then bear right on the small road, via San Biele [Railway on your right]🍴(1.2) Continue straight ahead up the hill [Pass through the archway of **Torre di S. Biele**](1.3)At the Stop sign, take the pedestrian crossing, turn right and follow the pavement beside the main road [Tree lined road](1.8)As the main road bears right, keep left on strada Roncone [Map on the left]🍴(3.4)Continue straight ahead, avoid left fork [Fence and metal gate on the right](3.8)At the end of the road, bear right on the pathway into the woods🍴(5.4)At the crossroads, turn left [Clearing on the right]🍴(6.5)Bear right on the track(7.0)At the junction with the tarmac road, take the middle road, straight ahead(7.7)At the T-junction, turn left [Uphill into **San Martino al Cimino**]🍴(8.0)Take the right fork [Strada Montagna

on the left](8.1)Bear left [Direction Roma](8.2)Turn right through the archway to Abbazia di San Martino al Cimino. Note: for the Alternate Route bypassing Vetralla turn left - direction Riserva Naturale Lago di Vico(8.4)At the crossroads, continue straight ahead through the parking area(8.6)Fork left on the narrow road [Strada Case Nuove]🍴(9.1) After leaving the final archway, turn left and left again [Via Lazio]🍴(11.2)At the T-junction turn left [Olive grove on your right](11.9)Beside the brick wall turn left up the hill🍴

stage 86 — Viterbo to Vetralla

(12.6)Take the left fork and follow the road as it turns left(12.9)At the crossroads with the tracks, turn right (13.7)Take the left fork into the woods(13.8)At the T-junction turn right(14.3)Fork left on the track (14.8)At the T-junction, turn right(15.1)At the crossroads, turn left on the path (15.8)Continue straight ahead opn the tarmac(16.8)In front of the church in the village of **Tre Croci**, turn right (17.4)Follow the road as it turns right(17.7)At thee crossroads with the main road continue straight ahead (19.0)At the junction, continue straight ahead on the white road. Note:- the Alternate Route joins from the right [Via Doganella](19.3)At the junction, bear right [Via Doganella](19.5)At the junction bear left on the road [Walled gardens on both sides at the junction] (20.0)Turn left on the grass track [House on the hilltop on the right just before the junction](20.2) Continue straight ahead on the broad track(20.5)At the T-junction with the tarmac road, turn right on the pavement beside the road (21.2)Take the left fork [Lower road between the trees](21.2)At the crossroads, continue straight ahead into Vetralla [Pass elevated road on your left](21.8)Bear left and then right [Cross piazza del Mattatoio](21.8)At the traffic lights, continue straight ahead [Via della Pietà, town walls to the right](22.0)Arrive at **Vetralla (V)** centre [T-junction with the via Roma]

Direct Route to Vetralla

Route: the Alternate and formerly "Official Route" from Viterbo to Vetralla passes along a narrow road cutting flanked by tuff stone cliffs on one of the most photographed sections of the route and close to an Etruscan burial site and the papal thermal baths and continues on farm and minor roads. (0.0)

Length:	13.6km
Ascent:	277m
Descent:	295m

From piazza dei Caduti head west towards the bus stand and tourist office [Piazza Martiri d'Ungheria](0.3)At the end of the parking area, turn left onto the broad paved area and enter Parco di Valle Faul [Towards the papal palace on the hill](0.4)Skirt the car park in Parco di Valle Faul [Car park to your left](0.6)At the T-junction with via Faul, turn right [Pass through the arch to leave the old town - Porta Faul](0.7)At the roundabout turn left [Pass **Torre della bella Galliana** on your left](0.8)Turn right and cross the main road and take the small road ahead [Strada Signorino](0.8)Take the left fork [Strada Signorino] (1.0)At the fork in the road keep to the right [Road continues between rock faces](1.2) Take right fork [Strada Signorino](1.9)At the crossroads, continue straight ahead [Between rock faces] (4.2)Fork left onto the gravel track, strada Risiere [Shrine on the corner](5.1) Take the right fork under the highway(5.2)Take the left fork [Parallel to the main road] (6.3)At crossroads in the track continue straight ahead with the main road remaining on your left. Note:- there are red and white signs that lead under the road and on towards the **thermal ponds of Paliano**. However, the signs quickly peter out. We advise those visiting the ponds to return here (7.4)After skirting the loop of the main road intersection, turn left to go under the road(7.5)At the T-junction in the track, turn right [Strada Primomo]

Lago di Vico

Viterbo to Vetralla   stage 86

(7.7)At the junction, continue straight ahead on the tarmac(8.1)Turn left on the grassy track (9.1)Bear right on the track [Uphill](9.5)Bear right [Pass the trees on your left] (9.8)At the T-junction, turn left [Strada Quartuccio] (10.3)At the junction, take the road bridge over the via Cassia and continue straight ahead [Strada Sasso San Pellegrino](11.1) Take the next turning to the right (11.9)At the T-junction, turn left on the road [Tree lined driveway ahead at the junction](12.2)Turn right on the track [Beside the olive grove] (12.5)Shortly after the track bends to the left turn sharp right on the path [Into the trees] (12.6)Turn left on the track [Uphill] (13.0)At the T-junction, turn right [Via Doganella] (13.6)At the T-junction, turn right and rejoin the "Official Route"

Direct Route from San Martino al Cimino towards Capranica

Route: if following the "Official Route" via San Martino al Cimino, this option will avoid a loop backtracking towards Vetralla (saving 12.5 km) and joining the next stage close to Capranica where accommodation can also be found. The route mainly follows woodland tracks before following a minor road to rejoin the "Official Route".(0.0)Take the road up the hill [Direction Riserva Naturale Lago di Vico] (2.0)At the T-junction, turn right [Direction Ronciglione, shrine on the left](2.5)As the road bends to the left, bear right on the unmade road and enter **Riserva Naturale Lago di Vico** [Milestone at the junction] (5.7)At the crossroads, continue straight ahead [Continue through woodland on volcano rim] (9.5)At the junction with the tarmac road, turn right and **exit Riserva Naturale Lago di Vico** [Farm ahead] (11.9)At the T-junction with the via Cassia, turn left and immediately right, then bear left on the unmade road. Rejoin "Official Route" [Signpost Vico Matrino]

Length:	11.9km
Ascent:	501m
Descent:	602m

Accommodation and Tourist Information

Cura

🔑 **Locanda - Dal Sor Francesco**,Via Blera, 28, 01019 Cura(VT), Italy; Tel:+39 0761 481185; +39 3495 155718; Email:info@dalsorfrancesco.it; www.dalsorfrancesco.it; Price:B

San-Martino-al-Cimino

🏠 **B&B - la Locanda Cistercense**,Piazza del Duomo, 3, 01100 San-Martino-al-Cimino(VT), Italy; Tel:+39 345 1763424 ; +39 3896 820037; Email:locandacister@gmail.com; www.locandacister.com; Price:B

Vetralla

Familarca,Via Cassia la Botte, 89, 01019 Vetralla(VT), Italy; Tel: +39 3347 868102; +39 3393 520365; Email:familarca@gmail.com; web.facebook.com/Familarca-APS-320596084753517; Price:C; *Credentials required*

Lento e Contento [Paolo Valotti],localitá Pontarello, 54, 01019 Vetralla(VT), Italy; Tel: +39 351 503 9074; Email:paolovalotti7@gmail.com; web.facebook.com/Lento-e-Contento-104848901818040; Price:C; *Dinner possible*

Ostello - Parrocchia San Francesco [Don Paolo],Largo San Francesco, 11, 01019 Vetralla(VT), Italy; Tel:+39 0761 477144; +39 0761477105; Price:D

Monastero delle Benedettine Regina Pacis,Via del Giardino, 4, 01019 Vetralla(VT), Italy; Tel:+39 0761 481519; Email:accoglienza@casareginapacis.com; casareginapacis.com; Price:B

🏠 **B&B - Casa Francigena** ,Strada Asmara, 76, 01019 Vetralla(VT), Italy; Tel: +39 351 810 9949; casafrancigena.com; Price:B

Albergo Da Benedetta,Via Francesco Petrarca, 3, 01019 Vetralla(VT), Italy; Tel:+39 0761 460093; +39 375 563 2231; +39 392 465 8290; Email:info@albergodabenedetta.it; www.albergodabenedetta.it; Price:B; *Discount with pilgrim credentials baggage transport can be arranged*

Ufficio Turistico,Via Cassia Sutrina, 01019 Vetralla(VT), Italy; Tel:+39 0761 460006; +39 3519169417; Email:prolocovetralla@libero.it; www.prolocovetralla.it

stage 87 — Vetralla to Sutri

Length:	23.3km
Ascent:	612m
Descent:	637m
Col Grand St Bernard:	938km
Rome:	90km

Early Morning Amphitheatre–Sutri

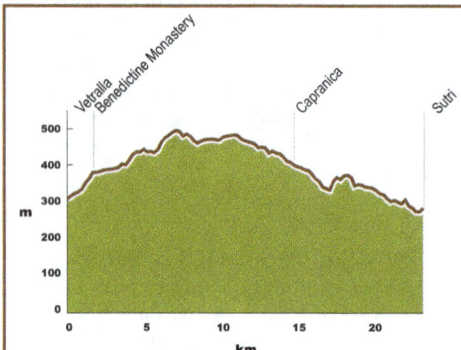

Route: the stage from Vetralla to Sutri begins on a small tarmac road before rejoining woodland tracks on the lower slopes of the Lago di Vico volcano and intersecting with the direct route from San Martino al Cimino. The route then winds through hazel nut groves to the town of Capranica where you will find cafes, shops and accommodation.

The stage continues along more small roads and woodland tracks to the fascinating town of Sutri.

Sutri, recorded as Suteria by Sigeric, but is also listed as a staging post by Nicola de Munkatveà, Philip Augustus, Abnnales Stadenses, Charles the Great, Hugh of Provence and Otto II. The town's prosperity is closely linked to its position on the via Cassia in Roman times and on the via Francigena in the Middle Ages. Titus Livius, known as Livy in English, was a Roman historian who wrote a monumental history of Rome and the Roman people, describing Sutri as being one of the keys of Etruria, Nepi being the other. The settlement came into the hands of Rome after the fall of Veii, and a Latin colony was founded in the 12th century, Sutri being ruled as a municipality and often allied with Rome against Viterbo. In 1236 the destruction of the city bridge prompted Pope Gregory IX to allow the town to impose tolls for the restoration of the bridge and the maintenance of the roads. But from the 15th century, the increased use of the alternative route to Ronciglione, brought about the decline of Sutri and Vetralla.

Picturesquely situated on a narrow tuff hill and surrounded by ravines, Sutri is best known for its Roman amphitheatre and Etruscan necropolis. These consist of dozens of rock-cut tombs and a Mithraeum (a place of worship for the followers of the religion of Mithraism), incorporated in the crypt of its church of the Madonna del Parto.

The amphitheatre is completely carved out of local tufa stone. Although it is fairly small, it faces the town as it did in ancient times and offers an enchanting, almost mystical atmosphere. Opinions vary as to exactly when it was built, ranging from as early as the Etruscan archaic period to the first decades of the Christian era.

Vetralla to Sutri   stage 87

🚶 **(0.0)** From the T-junction, turn left [Via Roma, cobbled street, uphill] **(0.4)** Shortly after the road bears right through piazza Marconi, take the left fork on the narrow road [Via San Michele, crucifix at the junction] **(0.7)** Take the subway to cross the via Cassia and continue straight ahead. Note:- to avoid the steps, turn right and then take the first turning to the left, via Dante Alighieri. Rejoin the "Official Route" by turning right at the crossroads [Via dei Cappuccini] 🚶 **(1.7)** At the T-junction, turn left on via del Giardino [**Benedictine Monastery**] **(2.0)** Bear right on the road [Pass an olive grove on the left] **(2.3)** At the junction,

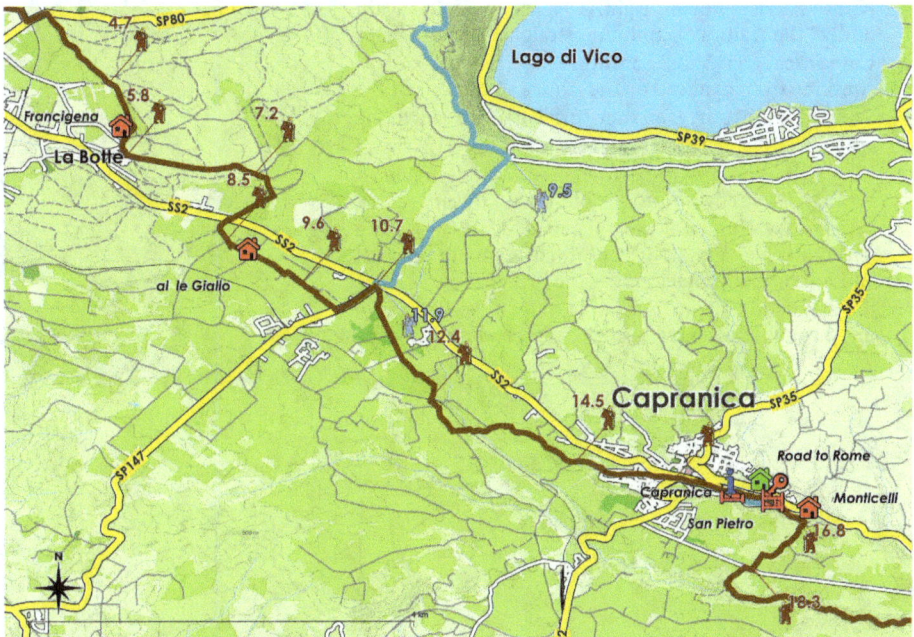

continue straight ahead on strada del Giardino 🚶 **(3.1)** At the T-junction turn right on the road [Railway track on your left] **(3.3)** At the T-junction, turn left [Over the railway crossing] **(3.5)** At the crossroads turn right across the car park onto the track towards the woods [Follow the edge of the woods with fields on the right] 🚶 **(4.7)** At the crossroads, continue straight ahead **(5.4)** Turn right on the track towards Botte [Strada Pian della Botte] **(5.7)** Turn left uphill on the road 🚶 **(5.8)** At the top of the hill and before entering Botte, turn left onto a gravelled track into the woods 🚶 **(7.2)** Take the right fork, down the hill **(7.7)** At the T-junction turn right **(8.2)** At the intersection with the via Cassia, turn right and immediately left down a small track. Note:- the path ahead crosses cultivated hazel nut groves and may make for difficult going for cyclists who can turn left on the via Cassia to rejoin the "Official Route" at the Vico Marino junction [Pass disused chapel on your left] 🚶 **(8.5)** At a large stone go straight ahead between the trees [Broken fence to the right] **(8.6)** At the end of the fence, turn left and immediately right [Parallel to the via Cassia] **(8.9)** At the T-junction turn left on the unmade road and immediately right through the gate [Continue across the fields parallel to the main road] **(9.4)** Turn left on the track and then immediately right [Grass track beside a fence] 🚶 **(9.6)** Continue straight ahead across the track **(10.1)** At the T-junction with a broad tarmac road turn left [Open field on your right] 🚶 **(10.7)** Just before reaching the via Cassia turn sharp right onto the unmade road. Note:- Alternate Route

stage 87 — Vetralla to Sutri

rejoins from the via Cassia ahead**(11.7)**At the crossroads in track continue straight ahead on strada Doganale Oriolese [Metal gates to the right] **(12.4)**Cross over the railway and continue straight ahead [Wire fencing beside the hazel nut grove on the left]**(13.0)**At the junction, bear left, downhill [Pass under railway track] **(14.5)**At the T-junction in the tracks, turn left [Crash barriers to your right]**(14.8)**After passing again under the railway, continue straight ahead [Enter **Capranica**, via Valle Santi]**(15.2)**At the crossroads, continue straight ahead on the Antica strada della Valle Santi **(15.6)**At the Stop sign, turn left[High wall to the left]**(15.8)**At the T-junction, turn right on via Nardini [Elevated road on the left]**(16.1)**Go straight ahead through the archway into the old town [Towards clock tower]**(16.2)**Continue straight ahead. Note:- the route ahead involves a flight of steps, cyclists should turn left and follow via Romana under the bridge to just before the T-junction [Ponte dell'Orolgio] **(16.8)**After passing through the centro historico, descend on the steps

Clock Tower - Capranica

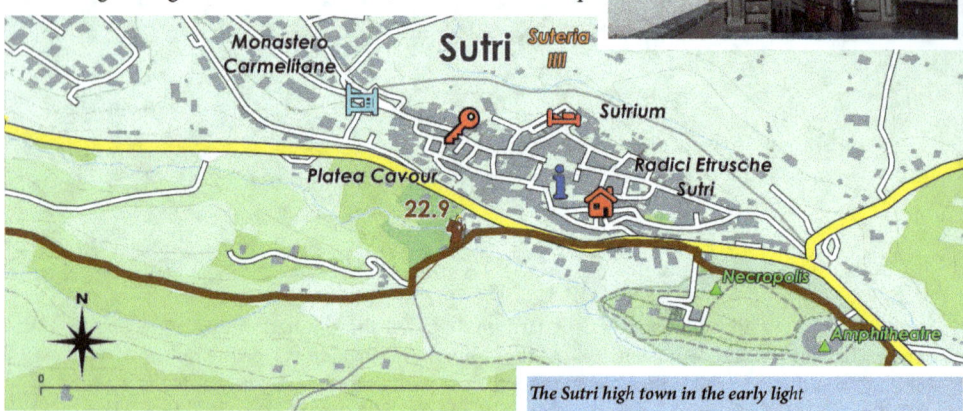

and turn right [Beside the town wall]**(16.9)**At the junction with the via Romana at the bottom of the steps turn left and immediately right on the gravel road, strade Pogliere [Factory on your left as you turn right]**(17.7)**Just before a bend to the left, fork right on the track **(18.3)**At the T-junction with the SP91, turn right [Hazelnut grove on the right]**(18.4)**Turn left on the track [Fencing on the left and right]**(18.7)**Take the left fork [Proceed in the valley bottom] **(22.9)**At the T-junction, turn left on the road. Note:- the "Official Route" has changed a number of times in this area and you may find conflicting signs. We will follow

The Sutri high town in the early light

Vetralla to Sutri   stage 87

the "Official Route" at the time of writing [Torre Arraggiati on the left]**(23.2)**Join the main road and continue behind the crash barriers on the right**(23.3)**Arrive at **Sutri (IV)** [Via do Porta Vecchia and the high town to your left]

Accommodation and Tourist Information

Capranica

🛏**Casa Vacanze Castrovecchio**,Vicolo del Garofano, 2, 01012 Capranica(VT), Italy; Tel: +39 3397 578403; +39 3281 911363; Email:Casavacanzecastrovecchio@gmail.com; web.facebook.com/Casavacanzecastrovecchio; Price:A

🏠 **Road to Rome** [Travis Criddle],Vicolo Del Ponticello, 39, 01012 Capranica(VT), Italy; Tel: +39 348 359 5971; Email:roadtorome.org@gmail.com; www.roadtorome.org; Price:D; *Dinner available*; **PR**

🏠 **B&B - al Casale Giallo**,Località Campo Spinella, 01012 Capranica(VT), Italy; Tel:+39 0761 660480; +39 3358 765277; +39 3381 099072; Email:info@alcasalegiallo.it; www.alcasalegiallo.it; Price:B

🏠 **B&B - Monticelli**,Località Monticelli, 1, 01012 Capranica(VT), Italy; Tel:+39 0761 669692; www.booking.com; Price:B; *Call direct for discounted price for pilgrims with credentials*

🛏 **Hotel - Capranica**,Corso Francesco Petrarca, 46, 01012 Capranica(VT), Italy; Tel:+39 0761 660245; hotelcapranica.it; Price:B

🔑 **Affittacamere - Casa San Pietro** ,Via Castel Vecchio, 54, 01012 Capranica(VT), Italy; Tel: +39 3474 511431; +39 3893 122518; Email:alloggiosanpietro@gmail.com; Price:B

ℹ **Comune di Capranica**,Corso Francesco Petrarca, 40, 01012 Capranica(VT), Italy; Tel:+39 0761 667900; Email:protocollo@comune.capranica.vt.it; comune.capranica.vt.it

Fonte Vivola

🛏**Oasi di Pace - Casa Per Ferie Suore Francescane**,Via delle Viole, 15, 01015 Fonte Vivola(VT), Italy; Tel:+39 0761 659175; +39 3920 9788; Email:info@oasidipace.it; www.oasidipace.it; Price:B; *The sisters will collect and return pilgrims by car from the via Cassia near Sutri* ; **PR**

Sutri

🛏**Monastero Carmelitane**,Via Garibaldi, 1, 01015 Sutri(VT), Italy; Tel:+39 0761 609082; Email:carmelo.s.concezione@gmail.com; www.carmelitane.org; Price:B

🏠 **B&B - Radici Etrusche Sutri** ,Via Tauro Statilio 35, 01015 Sutri(VT), Italy; Tel: booking.com; Price:B; *Kitchen available*

🛏 **Albergo - Sutrium**,Piazza San Francesco, 1, 01015 Sutri(VT), Italy; Tel:+39 0761 600468; Email:info@sutriumhotel.it; www.sutriumhotel.it; Price:B

🔑 **Affittacamere - Platea Cavour**,Piazza Cavour, 12, 01015 Sutri(VT), Italy; Tel: +39 3292 136615; platea-cavour-casa-vacanze.business.site; Price:B

ℹ **Ufficio Turistico**,Piazza del Comune, 34, 01015 Sutri(VT), Italy; Tel:+39 0761 609380; Email:turistico@comune.sutri.vt.it; www.sutriturismo.it

stage 88 — Sutri to Campagnano-di-Roma

Length:	24.3km
Ascent:	486m
Descent:	491m
Col Grand St Bernard:	961km
Rome:	67km

Chiesa di San Giovanni Battista–Campagnano di Roma

Route: the stage from Sutri to Campagnano-di-Roma initially passes beside the archaeological sites of Sutri before following sections of *strada provinciale*.

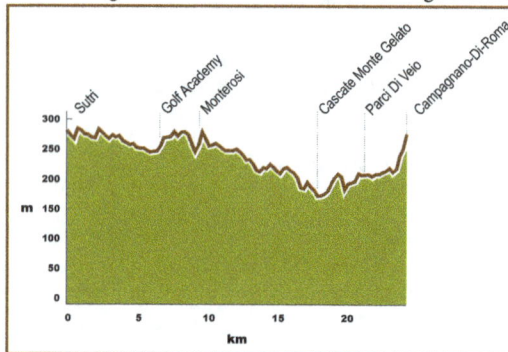

The stage continues on farm tracks through the hazel nut groves to Monterosi, where it is possible to find cafés and shops.

After crossing the bridge over the via Cassia (now a multi-lane highway) the route continues on minor roads before approaching Campagnano-di-Roma through the Parco del Treja.

Campagnano-di-Roma offers a good range of shops, restaurants and accommodation.

The first documentation of Borgo di Campagnano dates from 1076, when it was defined as a *castellum*, having been carved out of the great estate assembled on the Roman pattern by Pope Adrian I (ca. 780)–his *Domuscula Caprarorum*. It was cited again in 1130, among the properties of the monastery of San Paolo. Campagnano remained relatively autonomous until 1410 when it entered into the possession of the Orsini family. In 1662, the village passed to the Chigi, who between 1600 and 1700, enlarged the Medieval centre. In 1818, Campagnano became a municipality and participated actively in the birth of the Kingdom of Italy to which it was annexed in 1870. The current town is composed of three distinct sectors: the modern sector, the Renaissance-Baroque sector and the Medieval sector, which is located at the extremities of the plateau and is rich in towers, palaces and churches.

If you are there in April or May, you could enjoy the Palio delle Contrade, a costumed parade, which is followed by a race of dignitaries on donkeys representing the town's districts and battling it out for the prized Palio (a painted drapery). Alternatively, there is the Festa del Baccanale in May, a 55 year tradition of culinary, wine, and artisan highlights.

The church of San Giovanni Battisti built in 1515 has some fine frescoes.

Sutri to Campagnano-di-Roma — stage 88

🚶(0.0)Bear right on the cobbled road and enter the park through the gate. Note:- in the event that the gate is locked, continue to the next right turn(0.4)After passing the amphitheatre, continue on the stony path, cross the bridge, and bear right(0.6)Keep left up the hill 🚶(1.1)At the T-junction with the tarmac road, turn left and follow the road with care(1.1)Fork right on the track [Pass the metal barrier](1.8)At the junction with the via Cassia, take the second turning to the right [SP90, direction Bracciano] 🚶(3.2)On the apex of a bend to the right, turn left on the broad track [Strada Campo la Pera](3.8)At the T-junction, turn left on the gravel road [Hazel nut grove on your left and right] 🚶(6.5)At the T-junction, turn right to skirt the golf course on strada per Monterosi [Pass the **golf academy** entrance on your left](7.2)At the fork, bear left on the unmade road, remain beside the golf course 🚶(8.4)At the junction, continue straight ahead on

via strada Sutri Vecchia [Golf course on the right](9.2)Continue straight ahead through the car park and up the hill [Elevated road on the left](9.4)Continue straight ahead on the main road, via XIII Settembre [Towards the centre of **Monterosi**] 🚶(9.7)In piazza Garibaldi, turn left [Pass fountain on your right](9.9)Bear right behind the crash barrier [Bridge over the highway](10.3)Bear left on the footpath [Highway on the right] 🚶(10.8)Turn sharp left on the small road [Via della Salivotta](11.4)Take the right fork [House driveway on the right] 🚶(13.0)Cross over the road (SP38) and continue straight ahead on via Cascinone [Pass wire fence on the left] 🚶(15.2)At the T-junction with the tarmac road, turn right [Via Ronci](15.7)At the junction, turn sharp right [Field visible through the trees on the left] 🚶(16.9)At the crossroads with the SP37, continue straight ahead into Parco Regionale Valle del Treja [Strada Monte Gelato] 🚶(17.9)Shortly after crossing the bridge turn left on strada Monte Gelato [**Cascate Monte Gelato** on the left](18.4)Take the left fork on

stage 88 — Sutri to Campagnano-di-Roma

strada Monte Gelato [Exposed rock face on the left] ▌ **(19.3)** At the T-junction, turn right [Direction strada vicinale Bottagone]**(19.8)** At the junction, continue straight ahead towards the wooded hillside**(19.9)** Take the left fork remaining on the tarmac [Towards the houses] ▌ **(20.5)** At the T-junction, turn right**(21.5)** Bear left and continue straight ahead [Towards **Parci di Veio**] ▌ **(22.2)** Keep right at the junction ▌ **(23.2)** At the junction, bear right over the bridge [Via Santa Lucia]**(23.8)** Bear right onto the ramp leading up to the town**(24.0)** At the T-junction, turn left on the main street through the high town - via Sant'Andrea [Pass the bell tower on the left] ▌ **(24.3)** Arrive at **Campagnano-di-Roma** in piazza Cesare Leonelli [Beside the church]

Accommodation and Tourist Information

Campagnano-di-Roma
🛏 **Ostello Campagnano - Case nel Borgo**, Via Sant Andrea, 65, 00063 Campagnano-di-Roma(RM), Italy; Tel: +39 3316 004982; +39 3382 868402; Email:info@ostellocampagnano.it; www.ostellocampagnano.eu; Price:C; *Can arrange luggage transport BnB also available*

⛪ **Oratorio San Giovanni Battista** [Don Renzo],Via Dante Alighieri, 7, 00063 Campagnano-di-Roma(RM), Italy; Tel:+39 06 9041 094; +39 3339 381576; Email:donrenzotanturli@virgilio.it; Price:D

🛏 **Hotel Ristorante - Benigni**,Via della Vittoria, 13, 00063 Campagnano-di-Roma(RM), Italy; Tel:+39 06 9042 671; +39 334 5267735; Email:info@hotelbenigni.it ; www.hotelbenigni.it; Price:B

Monterosi
🔑 **Apartment - La Campana** [Alessandro Mirri],Via Roma, 5, 01030 Monterosi(VT), Italy; Tel:+39 3333999639; Price:C

Nepi
🏠 **B&B - Casale Vicino al Golf Nazionale**,Via di Monte Topino, 381, 01036 Nepi(VT), Italy; Tel:+39 335 770 4686; +39 334 3738566; Email:enricoguida@fastwebnet.it; casale-vicino-al-golf-nazionale.business.site; Price:A

Campagnano-di-Roma to La Storta   stage 89

Length:	23.1km
Ascent:	747m
Descent:	853m
Col Grand St Bernard:	986km
Rome:	42km

Looking towards Rome from Formello

Route: despite the proximity to Rome this section from Campagnano-di-Roma to La Storta remains surprisingly rural on farm and woodland tracks and small roads.

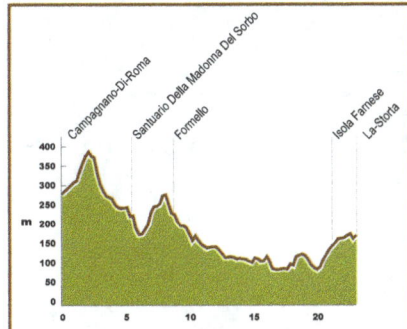

There remain some tricky descents and stiff climbs.

You can break your journey at Formello, where there is also an excellent hostel with a unique Sigeric staircase leading to your first sight of the eternal city.

La Storta has gained its notability thanks to Ignatius of Loyola, who was travelling the Via Cassia towards Rome in 1537, accompanied by Peter Faber and Diego Laynez. The group paused at a small church in La Storta to pray, and it was there that Ignatius is reported to have received a vision of God the Father and Christ holding the cross. Ignatius later said that Christ spoke the words Ego tibi Romae propitius ero ("I will be favourable to you in Rome"). The meaning of the sentence was not immediately clear to Ignatius, who thought it could mean that the three might be martyred in Rome, but thankfully Pope Paul III gave them a very friendly reception.

The location of the apparition is memorialized today with a small chapel dedicated to Saint Ignatius in the Piazza della Visione. The site of the vision was a place of pilgrimage from the early days of the Society of Jesus, but the current form of the chapel was restored and decorated by the Superior General Thyrsus González de Santalla in 1700. The Feast of the Vision of Saint Ignatius is celebrated on the second Sunday of November, and is marked by processions, bands, and a re-enactment of the vision.

(0.0) From the church in piazza Cesare Leonelli, continue straight ahead on the main street [Towards the arch, Corso Vittorio Emanuele]**(0.3)**Pass through the arch and turn left in piazza Regina Elena [Via San Sebastiano]**(0.5)**At the roundabout continue straight ahead 🛈 **(1.2)**On the apex of a sharp bend to the left, continue straight ahead on the more minor road - via di Maria Bona. Then take the pedestrian crossing and climb the steps on the left [Sports ground on the right]**(1.5)**Cross the road and continue on the path behind the barrier**(1.7)**Turn sharp right up the hill on via di Monte Razzano [Woodland on the

stage 89 — Campagnano-di-Roma to La Storta

right]**(2.0)**Take the left fork - strada delle Piane [House with roof terrace on the left at the junction] **(2.2)**Take the right fork - strada delle Piane **(3.3)**At the T-junction, turn left - strada delle Pastine [Towards Santuario del Sorbo]**(3.9)**Take the left fork on the tarmac road - strada del Sorbo **(5.1)**Take the left fork towards the sanctuary**(5.5)**Turn right on the road into the Valle del Sorbo [Pass the **Santuario della Madonna del Sorbo** on the left] **(6.6)**Cross the bridge and continue straight ahead [Uphill, towards the trees] **(7.9)**On entering Formello, bear right and right again [Via Antonio Angelozzi]**(8.1)**Take the left fork on the narrow road - via Enrico Bellomi [Downhill, No Entry]**(8.5)**At the crossroads, continue straight ahead [Pass house n° 132 on the left]**(8.8)**In the centre of **Formello**, bear right across the piazza [Pass through archway]**(8.9)**On entering the historical centre of Formello, bear left and then turn right on via 20 Settembre [Pass church of San Lorenzo on your left] **(9.1)**At the end of the road, bear left down steep steps**(9.2)**At the T-junction with

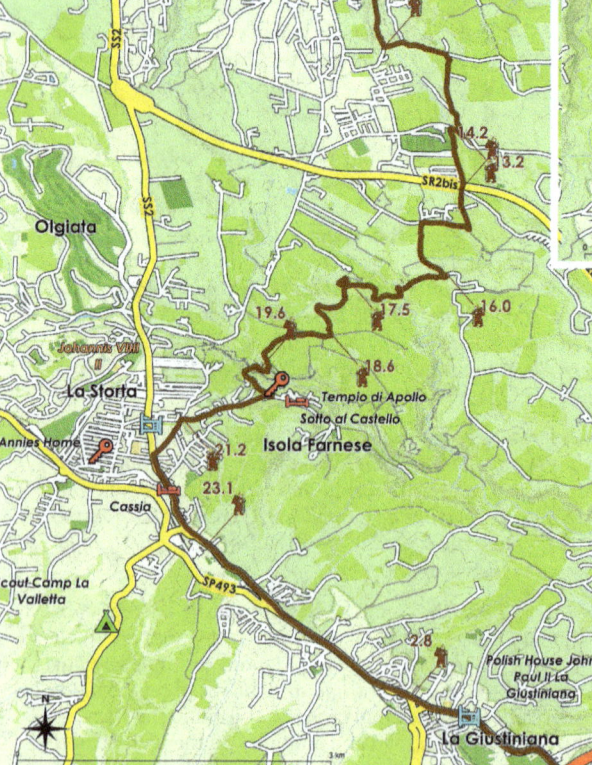

the main road, turn right downhill and then bear left at the bottom [Viale Regina Elena]**(9.6)**Take the right fork on the unmade road [Follow valley] **(10.3)**Turn left, through the trees [Pass an open field on the right] **(11.5)**At the T-junction with the tarmac road, turn left [Rock outcrop across the field on the left] **(11.7)**Turn on right on the gravel track between the fields**(12.1)**At the crossroads, turn right on the tarmac road [Between the fields] **(13.2)** Take the narrow path to the right and keep right behind the crash barriers**(13.4)**At the end

Campagnano-di-Roma to La Storta — stage 89

of the protected path, turn left [Via del Selvotta] 🔑 **(14.2)** After crossing the bridge over the highway, keep right [Via del Selvotta] **(14.4)** At the junction, keep left on the road [The road becomes a track] **(14.7)** Turn sharp right **(15.2)** At the crossroads, turn left on via Monte Michele [Between the fields] 🔑 **(16.0)** Turn right on the path signposted as the alternative route Ponte Sodo **(16.4)** Keep left beside the wooden rails 🔑 **(17.5)** Keep l, downhill beside the fence on your right 🔑 **(18.3)** At the T- junction, turn right on the gravel road **(18.7)** Turn left on the track across the field **(19.5)** Keep right and take the steps beside the wooden rails 🔑 **(19.6)** After the steps turn right on the concrete track towards the weir. Turn left over the footbridge and follow the road **(20.3)** At the T-junction turn right, uphill [Via dell Isola Farnese] 🔑 **(21.2)** At the junction, bear left up the hill [**Isola Farnese**] **(21.8)** At the T-junction on the brow of the hill, turn left on the via Cassia [Roma 17 km] 🔑 **(23.1)** Arrive at **La-Storta (II)** centre [Beside the elevated church on the right]

Accommodation and Tourist Information

Formello

🏨 **Hostel "Maripara"**, Piazza S.Lorenzo, 3, 00060 Formello(RM), Italy; Tel:+39 06 9019 4236; +39 349 1079088; Email:mansio@comune.formello.rm.it; Price:C; *Get your first view of Rome from the top of the Sigeric staircase* ; **PR**

🔑 **Affittacamere - Il Rosciolo Sulla Francigena** , Via del Rosciolo, 3, 00060 Formello(RM), Italy; Tel: +39 3337 895953; Email:Ilrosciolo3@gmail.com; il-rosciolo-sulla-francigena-casa-vacanza.business.site; Price:B

🔑 **Apartment - La Loggetta sul Borgo**, Via Xx Settembre, 9, 00060 Formello(RM), Italy; Tel: booking.com; Price:A; *Airport shuttle can be arranged*

ℹ **Comune di Formello**, Piazza San Lorenzo, 8, 00060 Formello(RM), Italy; Tel:+39 06 9019 41; Email:segnalazioni@comune.formello.rm.it; comune.formello.rm.it

Isola-Farnese

🛏 **Hotel - Tempio di Apollo**, Piazza della Colonnetta, 8 , 00123 Isola-Farnese(RM), Italy; Tel:+39 06 3089 0595; Email:info@tempiodiapollo.com ; www.tempiodiapollo.com; Price:A

🔑 **Affittacamere - Sotto al Castello** [Silva Sgalippa], Via dell'Isola Farnese, 175, 00123 Isola-Farnese(RM), Italy; Tel:+39 333 6727228; Price:C

La Storta

🏨 **Casa per Ferie - Nostra Signora del Sacrp Cuore**, Via Cassia, 1826, 00123 La Storta(RM), Italy; Tel:+39 06 3089 0863; Email:info@casanostrasignora.it; casanostrasignora.it; **PR**

🛏 **Hotel - Cassia**, Via Cassia, 1736, 00123 La Storta(RM), Italy; Tel:+39 06 3089 1772; +39 06 3089 0588; Email:info@hotelcassia.com; www.hotelcassia.com; Price:B; *Discount if you book through the hotel website*

🔑 **Apartment - Annies Home** , Via Arturo Rossato, 29, 00123 La Storta(RM), Italy; Tel: +393298832358; booking.com; Price:B; *Problems reported with making contact*

⛺ **Scout Camp - La Valletta**, Via della Storta, 783, 00123 La Storta(RM), Italy; Tel: Email:info@basescoutlavalletta.it; basescoutlavalletta.it

Roma

🏨 **Polish House John Paul II - La Giustiniana**, Via Cassia, 1200, 00189 Roma(RM), Italy; Tel:+39 0630 365181; +39 0630 10398; Email:dompolskijp2@gmail.com; viacassia.pl; Price:B; *To book call Monday to Friday 09.30-1.15 or 16.30-18.30*; **PR**

stage 90 — La-Storta to Saint Peter's Square

Length: 19.2km

Ascent: 509m
Descent: 651m

Col Grand
St Bernard: 1009km
Rome: 19km

Saint Peter's Basilica

Route: the final stage from La-Storta to Saint Peter's Square begins using pavements beside the very busy via Cassia. Relief from the traffic is found in the Reserva Naturale della Insugherata before following the equally busy via Trionfale to the Monte Mario park, where you have magnificent views of the city. Finally you will take the broad city boulevards for the approach to the Vatican. At the time of writing there has been a recurrence of Africa Swine Fever in the wild boar population that lives in the reserve and walkers are advised to avoid the park. It is advisable to check current status with the AEVF or the Rome tourist authorities. For those not wishing to deal with the Rome traffic or cross the reserve there

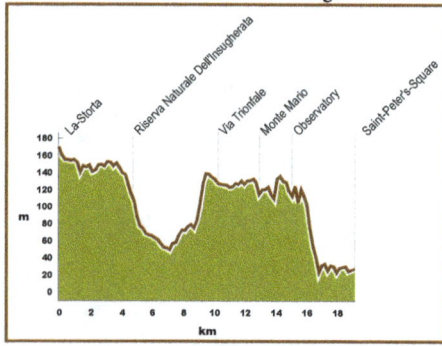

are frequent and inexpensive bus or train services from La Storta. Leaving the train at the Monte Mario station and following the final part of the signed route will allow you to enjoy the breath-taking views of the city below the Parco di Monte Mario.

For your Testimonium pass through the security barriers of the basilica (pilgrims with credentials do not need to join the long line) and make your way to the right side of the basilica facade where the document will be issued by the security staff inside the hat and coat check area.

St Peter's Basilica is Catholicism's most sacred shrine and draws pilgrims and tourists from all over the world. A shrine housing hundreds of precious works of art, some salvaged from the original 4th century basilica built by Constantine, others commissioned from Renaissance and Baroque artists. The dominant tone is set by Bernini, who created the baldacchino (a canopy over an altar or throne) twisting up below Michelangelo's huge dome. He also created the cathedra in the apse, with four saints supporting a throne that contains fragments once thought to be relics of the chair from which St. Peter delivered his first sermon.

The Vatican City is the world's smallest state, and occupies one hundred and six acres within high walls watched over by the Vatican guard. Here, where St. Peter was martyred (c. A.D. 64) and buried, is the residence of the popes who succeeded him. The Vatican is ruled by the Pope, Europe's only absolute monarch. About five hundred people live in this tiny country, which also has its own post office, banks, currency, radio station, shops, daily newspaper and judicial system.

La-Storta to Saint Peter's Square stage 90

(0.0)On the via Cassia, below the church in La-Storta, continue with great care on the road towards Roma [Church on the right and petrol station on the left] (2.8)Take the left fork, remain on the via Cassia (4.7)Pass over the highway and turn right enter the gate beside house 1081 [**Riserva Naturale dell'Insugherata**](5.0) Take the right fork and follow the track as it turns to the left (6.7)Turn right over the stream and immediately left(7.1)Turn sharp right on the track(7.6)Take the right fork and remain in the valley (8.6)At the junction turn sharp left(9.1)Exit the park and turn right on the tarmac(9.3)At the crossroads at the top of the hill, turn left on via Achille Mauri (10.3)Turn left on the busy **via Trionfale** and continue on the pavement on the left side of the road(10.8)Take the pedestrian crossing and cross to the extreme right hand side of the complex junction, and then continue straight ahead, remaining on via Tirionfale [Pass the entrance to the university on your right] (12.0)At the traffic lights shortly after passing the playground on your left, turn left on the broad street [Echography clinic to the right at the junction](12.3)In piazza Walter Rossi, turn right, left and then right again on via della Camilluccia [Metal railings to the left of the pavement](12.7)Turn left on via Edmondo de Amicis [Pass olive trees on your right](12.9)On the crown of the sharp bend to the left, turn right on the path and continue to keep right at the junction in the path [Pass through the metal gates in the **Monte Mario** park] (13.8)Turn right, uphill(14.3)Turn right, beside the school(14.6) Join a broader road and bear right [Metal gates on your left] (14.9)Exit from the park and turn left [Via Trionfale](14.9)Turn left up the steps and through the archway into the walled Monte Mario park. Note:- to avoid the obstacles in the park remain on via Trionfale to the crossroads with the tree lined via Andrea Doria, where you should bear right on via Leone IV to rejoin the "Official Route" in piazza del Risorgimento(15.0)Fork left on the path(15.1)Cross the road and continue on the path [Pass the **observatory** on the left, views of the city to the right](15.3)Keep right(15.7)Turn right and descend the hill (16.6)At the bottom of the hill pass through the gate and continue straight ahead(16.8)After leaving the park, take the pedestrian crossing over the road and continue straight ahead [Via Novenio

stage 90 La-Storta to Saint Peter's Square

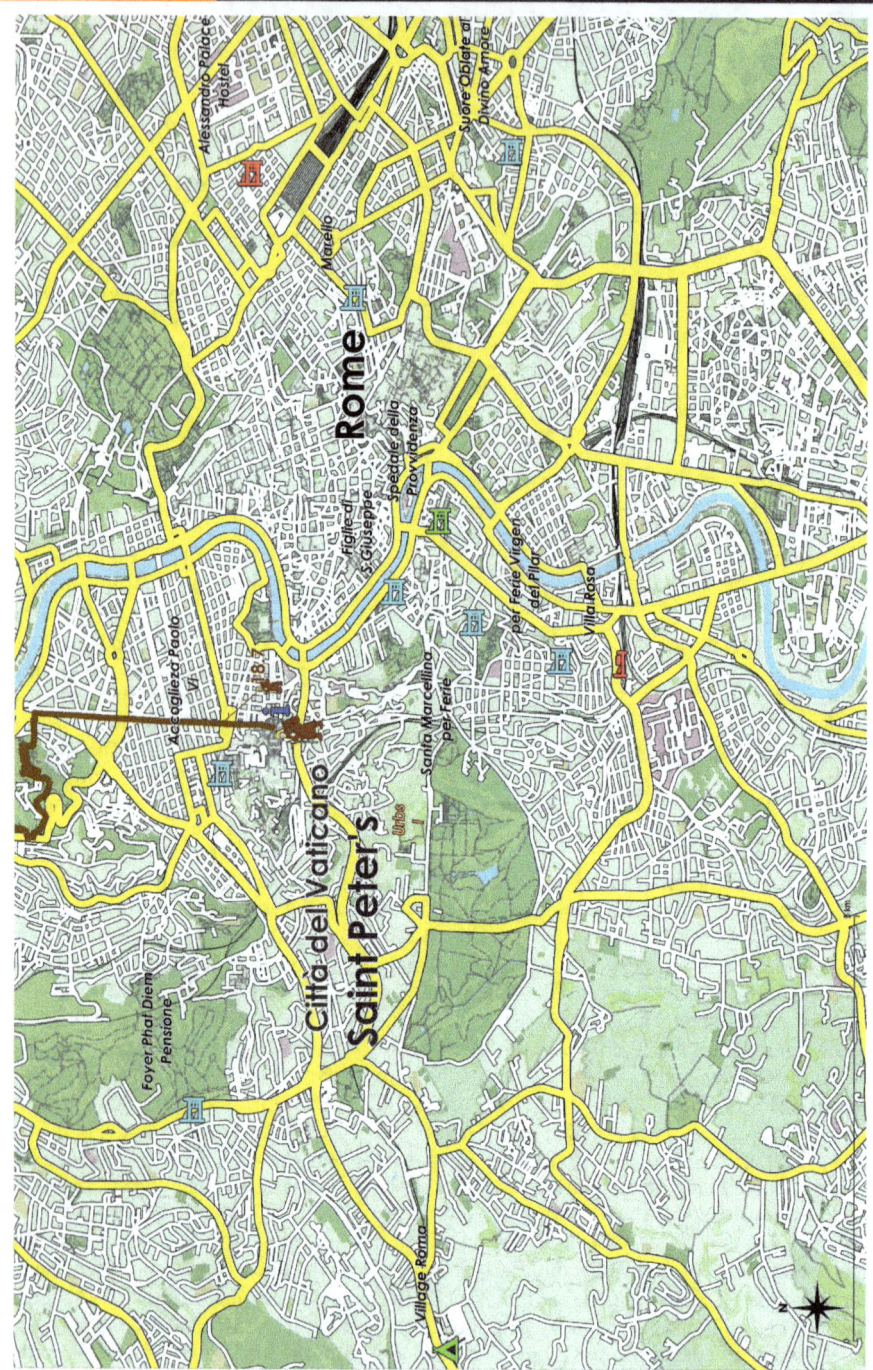

La-Storta to Saint Peter's Square   stage 90

Bucchi] **(16.8)** At the T-junction, cross the broad road and go straight ahead through the gardens in piazza Maresciallo and turn right [Viale Angelico] **(18.7)** Continue straight ahead across piazza Risorgimento towards the Vatican on via di Porta Angelica [Dome of St Peter's to the right] **(19.2)** Arrive at **Saint-Peter's-Square (I)**

Accommodation and Tourist Information

Fiumicino

⚿ **Guest House - Apple Old House**, Via della Torre Clementina, 8, 00054 Fiumicino(RM), Italy; Tel:+39 0664017243; +39 3401366324 ; Email:applehousesrome@gmail.com; www.applehousesrome.it; Price:B; *Free airport shuttle*

Roma

■**Spedale della Provvidenza** [Signora Lucia Colarusso],Via dei Genovesi 11B, 00153 Roma(RM), Italy; Tel: +39 3534 286139; Email:info@pellegriniaroma.it; www.pellegriniaroma.com; Price:D; *Credentials required*

■**Alessandro Palace Hostel**,Via Vicenza, 42, 00185 Roma(62043), Italy; Tel:+39 06 4461 958; Email:palace@hostelsalessandro.com; alessandropalace.com; Price:B

■**Ostello Marello**,Via Urbana, 50, 00184 Roma(62042), Italy; Tel: Email:hostelmarello@yahoo.it; booking.com; Price:A

■**Casa per Ferie - Virgen del Pilar**,Via Alessandro Poerio, 51D, 00152 Roma(RM), Italy; Tel:+39 06 5833 1508; +39 3273637770; Email:info@casavirgendelpilar.com; casavirgendelpilar.com; Price:A; **PR**

■**Foyer Phat Diem - Pensione**,Via della Pineta Sacchetti, 45, 00167 Roma(RM), Italy; Tel:+39 06 6638 826; +39 06 6633 636; Email:foyerpdr@gmail.com; foyerphatdiem.com; Price:B

■**Ostello Villa Monte Mario**,Via Trionfale, 6157, 00136 Roma(RM), Italy; Tel:+39 06 3540 641; Email:info@villamontemario.com; villamontemario.com; Price:B

■**Santa Marcellina - Casa per Ferie**,Via Dandolo, 59, 00153 Roma(RM), Italy; Tel:+39 06 5817 558; Email:casaperferie@marcelline.it; casaperferiesantamarcellina.it; Price:B; *Please book in advance*

■**Suore Oblate al Divino Amore**,Via Marruvio, 4, 00183 Roma(RM), Italy; Tel:+39 06 7047 4884; Email:oblatedivinoamore@yahoo.it; oblatedivinoamore.wordpress.com/dove-siamo/roma; Price:A

■**Casa Figlie di S.Giuseppe**,Vicolo Moroni, 22, 00153 Roma(RM), Italy; Tel:+39 06 9444 3884; +39 3927416640; Email:info@casasangiuseppe.it; www.casasangiuseppe.it; Price:A

■**Casa Accoglieza Paolo Vi**,Viale Vaticano, 92, 00165 Roma(RM), Italy; Tel:+39 0639732055; Email:info@casapaolosesto.it; www.casapaolosesto.it; Price:A

🛏 **Hotel - Villa Rosa**,Via Giovanni Prati, 1, 00152 Roma(RM), Italy; Tel:+39 065883643; Email:info@hotelvillarosa-roma.eu; www.hotelvillarosaroma.eu; Price:A

⛺ **Camping Village Roma**,Via Aurelia, 831, 00163 Roma(RM), Italy; Tel:+39 06 6623 018; Email:roma@huopenair.com; roma.humancompany.com; Price:C; *Chalets and apartments also available*

Vatican City

ℹ **Tourist Information Office**,Piazza San Pietro, 00120 Vatican City(RM), Italy; Tel:+39 06 6988 2350; +39 060608; Email:turismo@comune.roma.it; www.turismoroma.it

Via degli Abati

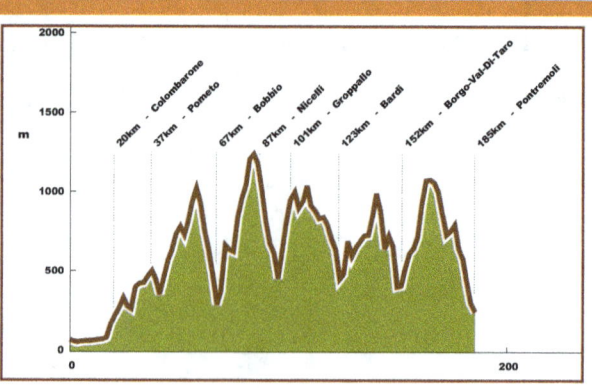

Via degli Abati

As with the *Camino* there was never a single route that was followed by northern Europeans pilgrims to Rome and beyond, but rather a network of trails each used depending on the pilgrim's starting point, prevailing weather, levels of brigandry or even warfare and the pilgrim's association with shrines dedicated to saints and martyrs along the way.

The modern via Francigena, generally described in this book as the "Official Route", owes its overall direction to the chronicle of a single pilgrim, Sigeric, though in truth the modern via Francigena rarely follows in his exact footsteps. During the period of rediscovery of the routes to Rome the promotion of a single modern route has helped focus investment in signposting, development of appropriate accommodation and renovation of important historic sites on a contiguous route, allowing committed pilgrims to make their journey with comparative ease.

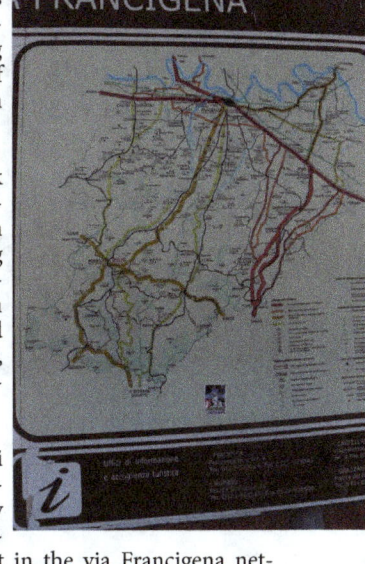

The via degli Abati (the Abbott's Way) may be viewed as another component in the via Francigena network, this is certainly the view of the Piacenza province tourist office and many signposts on the route, or it can be viewed as a pilgrim route in own right leading to the tomb of Saint Columban the Younger(*Columbanus/Colombanus/Colombano*) in the Monastery of Bobbio. Established in 613 AD the monastery was recognised as a leading European centre for culture and learning for more than 4 centuries.

The Irish Saint Columban travelled widely in Europe preaching against the revival of paganism following the collapse of the Roman empire. He was renowned for establishing earlier abbeys in Burgundy and Lombardy and for rigid views that put him in conflict with popes, kings, bishops and even Brunhilda.

There is evidence to suggested that the well marked route, of 185 km, from the outskirts of Pavia to Pontremoli predates Sigeric's chronicle by some hundreds of years. This rugged route has the potential to significantly reduce your overall journey and to exchange the flat tracts of the Po valley for the dramatic, wooded hills of the Apennines. Commercial and pilgrim accommodation is available along the route although less frequently than in the more populous Po valley.

stage 59a — Pavia to Colombarone

Length:	19.9km
Ascent:	437m
Descent:	265m
Pavia:	0km
Pontremoli:	185km

Woodland beside the Ticino

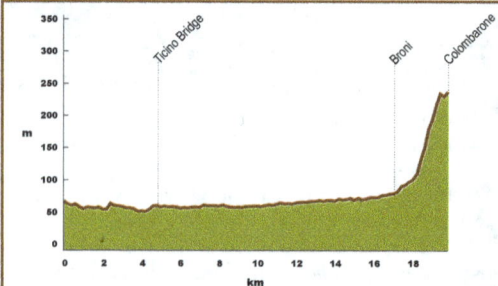

Route: from Pavia to Colombarone, the via degli Abati separates from the via Francigena after 5 km (for details of the exit from Pavia see Stage 59 and for Pavia accommodation refer to Stage 58) and then follows wooded paths beside the Ticino before a difficult crossing of both the Ticino and Po on a long heavily trafficked bridge.

The route crosses the Po floodplain on the *argines* and minor roads before reaching the town of Broni where there are numerous cafes and grocery stores. From Broni the route makes a stiff climb on a very minor road to enter Colombarone on the generally quiet SP45 beside which you will also find the main accommodation options.

 In 929 AD the monks of the Bobbio monastery carried the remains of San Colombano to Pavia, the then capital of Lombardy, in an appeal to King Hugo of Provence to protect the possessions of the monastery. The procession crossed the Ticino by boat a little downstream of the current bridge at Portum Peducolosum (today known as Portalbera). It is possible that it is from the passage of this procession that Colombarone drew its name. Portum Peducolosum is located where the Po narrows allowing a safe and swifter crossing and was used by Hannibal as early as 218 BC.

Leaving Pavia

Pavia to Colombarone

stage 59a

🚶(0.1)At the end of the crash barriers turn right [Towards the farmhouse](0.1)In front of the farmhouse turn left [Farm track](0.8) Where the primary track turns left, bear right [Between the trees] 🚶(1.2)At the junction beside the boat dock, continue straight ahead [Avoid track to the left](1.3)At the junction continue straight ahead [Keep the river close on your right] 🚶(2.5)At the T-junction turn right [Pass an electricity substation on your right] (2.6)At the crossroads, continue straight ahead [Plantation close on your left](3.4)In the parking area after crossing under the road bridge, turn left 🚶(3.5)Shortly before the stop sign, turn sharp left on a partially obscured path to the climb the embankment, cross the crash barrier and very carefully proceed to cross the long road bridge. Note:- in times of heavy traffic the bridge can be very dangerous - there is no pedestrian footway 🚶(4.9)After crossing the **Ticino bridge** and as the road begins to bear left,

Parting of the ways

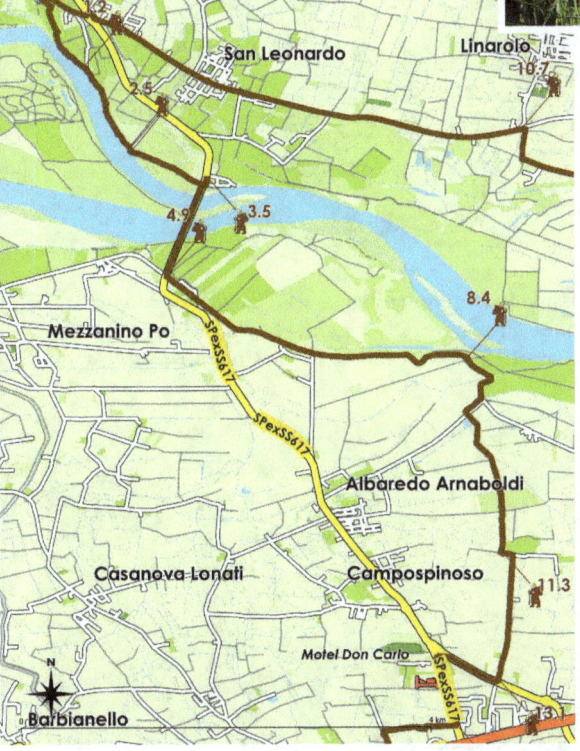

turn left on the small tarmac road road [Ciclovia del Po](5.0)As the tarmac road bears left continue straight ahead on the gravel track on the argine [Ciclovia del Po] 🚶(8.4)Leave the Ciclovia del Po and continue straight ahead on the argine [Towards the radio towers on the hill ahead](9.1)At the junction, bear right and remain on the argine(9.3)At the crossroads after crossing the small bridge, continue straight ahead on the gravel track 🚶(11.3) Turn left and immediately right on the gravel track [Towards the hills] 🚶(13.1)At the crossroads with a major road, turn right beside the busy road(13.7)Before reaching the roundabout turn left across the parking area and the left again on the left busy road 🚶 (14.8)At the foot of a small incline turn right on the gravel road [Cross the bridge](15.1)Turn left and then right [Skirt the large

stage 59a — Pavia to Colombarone

house]**(15.6)** At the T-junction with the gravel road turn left [Towards the electricity pylon]**(15.8)** Keep left on the tarmac road and take the bridge over the highway 🍴 **(17.1)** Cross the railway tracks and continue straight ahead into **Broni** [Towards the crossroads] **(17.2)** Take the pedestrian crossing over the main road and continue on the small street straight ahead**(17.4)** At the crossroads continue straight ahead [Traffic lights overhead] **(17.5)** Turn right [Via Cavour]**(17.7)** In the square, facing the Comune di Broni, turn left [Keep the church to your left]**(17.9)** Turn right on via Dante [Direction Canneto Pavese] **(18.0)** In the square bear right on via Montegrappa [Pass steps on your left]**(18.0)** At the crossroads continue straight ahead uphill [Via Montegrappa] 🍴 **(19.4)** At the T-junction with the tarmac road turn right**(19.7)** At the Stop sign continue straight ahead [Direction Canneto Pavese]**(19.9)** Arrive at **Colombarone** [At the road junction beside the trattoria]

Ticino - Po bridge

Pavia to Colombarone — stage 59a

Accommodation and Tourist Information

Broni
🏠 **B&B - Garden Hill**,Via Dante, 94, 27043 Broni(PV), Italy; Tel:+39 3332107156; Email:info@gardenhillbnb.eu; gardenhill-bnb.eu; Price:B

🛏 **Motel - Don Carlo**,Strada Bronese, 27043 Broni(PV), Italy; Tel:+39 0385 42115; Email:info@mhoteldoncarlo.com; www.mhoteldoncarlo.com; Price:A

Canneto Pavese
🏠 **Agriturismo - Casa Casoni**,Via Costiolo, 7, 27044 Canneto Pavese(PV), Italy; Tel:+39 038561251; www.casacasoni.it; Price:B; *Breakfast included*

🏠 **B&B - Alberodikarta** [Marta and Carlo],Via Casa Bazzini, 29, 27044 Canneto Pavese(PV), Italy; Tel:+39 347 088 9418; +39 328 3632 777; Email:marta.menditti@gmail.com; alberodikarta.com; Price:B; *Pilgrim discount available*

🔑 **Affitacamera - La Vecchia Cantina**,Via Colombarone, 36, 27044 Canneto Pavese(PV), Italy; Tel:+39 0385 88326; Email:info@lavecchiacantina.it; www.lavecchiacantina.it; Price:B

Cigognola
🏠 **B&B - Monteguzzo**,Strada per Monteguzzo, 6, 27040 Cigognola(PV), Italy; Tel:+39 0385 284143; +39 3475908750; +39 3474507683; Email:info@bbmonteguzzo.it; www.bbmonteguzzo.it; Price:A

Montescano
🏠 **B&B - La Casa Colonica**,Via Piane, 20, 27040 Montescano(PV), Italy; Tel:+39 349 561 2182; bb-la-casa-colonica.business.site; Price:A

Oltrepò Pavese Wine Region

stage 59b — Colombarone to Pometo

Length:	16.9km
Ascent:	884m
Descent:	588m
Pavia:	20km
Pontremoli:	165km

Roadside vineyards

Route: on the short stage from Colombarone to Pometo the route begins by following the generally quiet SP45 but unfortunately with no pavements/sidewalks, making occasional diversions through farming hamlets. The route then begins to climb on small tarmac and gravel farm roads. You will pass a number of wineries but there are no cafes, restaurants or food stores until close to Pometo.

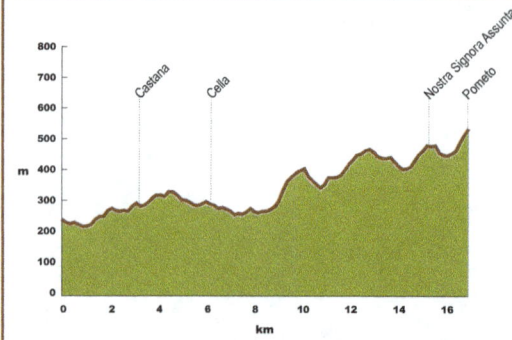

The Oltrepò (other side of the Po) Pavese, sometimes called the Tuscany of Northern Italy, is the largest wine growing area in Lombardy and specializes in the Pinot Noir grape (Pinot Nero). In addition to classical wines such as Buttafuoco both red and white sparkling wines are produced.

Food is a high priority also in the region featuring local produce including the famous Salame di Varzi. When passing the region with a Roman legion in 40 BC Pliny commented "good wine, hospitable people and very large wooden barrels".

Colombarone to Pometo　　stage 59b

🚶(0.0)From the junction beside the trattoria continue along the SP45 [Direction Castana] 🚶(2.2)At the junction bear right [Direction Castana] (2.4)Take the left fork [Uphill]

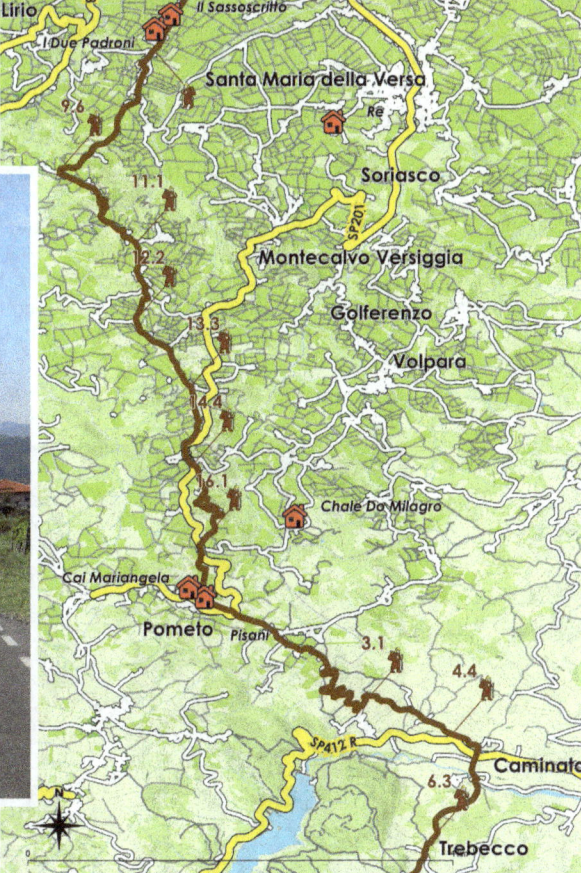

🚶(3.2)In **Castana**, take the right fork towards Montecalvo [Pass the church on your left side](3.7)Take the right fork on the smaller road [Direction Località Cà di Giacomo](3.9)Turn right at the T-junction to rejoin the SP45 🚶(4.3)Take the left fork, remaining on the SP45 [Uphill](4.6)Take the right fork on the small road [Pass close by wine producer on the right] (5.1)At the crossroads continue straight ahead [Towards the church bell tower] 🚶(6.2)In **Cella**, turn right beside the shrine towards Montecalvo [Pass wine makers on your left] 🚶(7.6)At the junction keep left [Direction Castelrotto](7.7)At the chapel take the right fork [Continue uphill](7.8)At the top of the hill bear left on the small road(8.0)At the T-junction, turn right on the SP45(8.2)Take the right fork [Direction Cà Tessitori] 🚶(9.4)At the junction, keep left in the principal road🚶(11.1)At the T-junction turn right and begin to go downhill [Concrete wall with vines above on the left](11.8)At the T-

Pinot Nero

stage 59b — Colombarone to Pometo

junction with the parking area on your left, continue straight ahead on the track up the hill ⚑ **(12.2)** At the junction with the tarmac road, continue straight ahead [Towards the brow of the hill] **(12.7)** At the top of the hill continue straight ahead on the gravel and grass track [Pass water tank on your left] ⚑ **(13.3)** As the tarmac road descends steeply to the left, bear right on the gravel track [Between the trees] **(13.5)** Take the left fork [Slightly uphill] **(14.1)** Join the tarmac road and continue slightly downhill [Pass large industrial building on your right] ⚑ **(14.4)** Beside the parking area turn left [Pass between the town hall and the restaurant] **(14.9)** Turn left up the hill [Direction Canevino Centro Storico] **(15.2)** At the T-junction with the cobbled road turn right up the hill. Note:- if you do not wish to make the climb to the church, turn left [Towards the church] **(15.3)** At the entrance doors to Chiesa **Nostra Signora Assunta** di Canevino backtrack down the hill on the cobbled road continuing to bear right **(15.4)** Continue downhill on the cobbled road ⚑ **(16.1)** At the T-junction turn left and keep right [Direction Ruino] **(16.2)** Beside the farm buildings bear right and then left to follow the grass track up the hill **(16.4)** Take the left fork up the hill **(16.7)** Fork left again continuing up the hill **(16.9)** Arrive at **Pometo** [Beside the town hall]

Colombarone to Pometo — stage 59b

Accommodation and Tourist Information

Canevino
🏠 **Agriturismo - Chale Do Milagro**, Frazione Piana Versa, 27040 Canevino(PV), Italy; Tel:+39 340 221 1652; Email:chaledomilagro@gmail.com; www.aziendamilagro.com; Price:A

Montecalvo Versiggia
🏠 **Agriturismo - Casa Re**, Frazione Cas Re, 1, 27047 Montecalvo Versiggia(PV), Italy; Tel:+39 338 408 7360; +39 0385241201; Email:info@casare.com; casare.com; Price:B

🏠 **B&B - I Due Padroni**, Frazione Spagna, 9, 27047 Montecalvo Versiggia(PV), Italy; Tel:+39 346 857 2343; +39 348 5595 064; www.duepadroni.it; Price:A

🏠 **B&B - Il Sassoscritto**, Fraz.ione Tromba, 16, 27047 Montecalvo Versiggia(PV), Italy; Tel:+39 0385836068; +39 347 8069995; Email:infoilsassoscritto@gmail.com; ilsassoscritto.it; Price:A

Montu' Beccaria
🏠 **B&B - La Colinesse**, Frazione Casa del Moro, 13, 27040 Montu' Beccaria(PV), Italy; Tel:+39 334 739 4077; +39 3347394067; Email:ornet61@gmail.com; Price:B

Pometo
🏠 **Agriturismo - Pisani**, Via della Chiesa, 12, 27040 Pometo(PV), Italy; Tel:+39 331 370 3508; Email:info@agriturismopisani.it; agriturismopisani.it; Price:B; *For small fee will lend car to visit restaurant*

🏠 **Agriturismo - Cai Mariangela** [Paola], Frazione Ruino, 27040 Pometo(PV), Italy; Tel:+39 3383268021 ; +39 038598813; Email:info@caimariangela.it; www.caimariangela.it; Price:B

Santa Maria Della Versa
🏠 **Agriturismo - Da Prati**, Via Aldo Moro, 4, 27045 Santa Maria Della Versa(PV), Italy; Tel:+39 333 403 6945; +39 335 5938577; Email:nfo@daprati.it; daprati.it; Price:A

The Po valley from Chiesa Nostra Signora Assunta di Canevino

stage 59c — Pometo to Bobbio

Length: 30.4km

Ascent: 1614m
Descent: 1858m

Pavia: 37km
Pontremoli: 148km

Abbazia di San Colombano

Route: the strenuous stage from Pometo to Bobbio will climb above 1000 m before descending into the Trebbia Valley and finding the bustling town of Bobbio with the abbey at its core. The route initially follows a tarmac road followed by grass tracks making a steep descent towards the village of Caminata. From Caminata the route follows tarmac, gravel and grass farm tracks and then ancient mule roads to make the long climb towards the summit of Monte Pan Perduto. Shortly before the summit you will cross the grounds of the botanical gardens of Pietra Corva where you can take a well earned meal break at their friendly restaurant. There are short stretches of *strade statale* interwoven with farm tracks on the long descent into Bobbio.

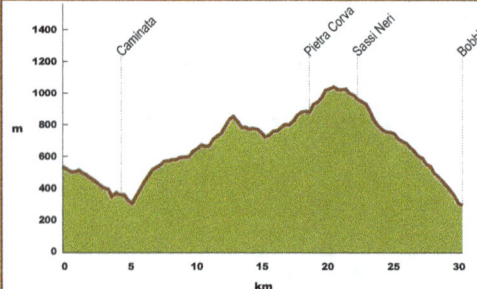

The Abbey was founded in 614 by Saint Columban whose books became the nucleus of the famous Abbey library.

The Abbey monks were to live a strict life of study and prayer as they worked to transcribe ancient texts by hand. The Abbey flourished and became known throughout Europe as a centre of learning. Between the 7th and the 10th centuries, despite one of the most turbulent times in the history of northern Italy, the Abbey and the monastic community kept growing in importance. In addition to boasting a productive Scriptorium and a remarkably large collection of manuscripts, Bobbio Abbey became a centre of resistance to Arianism and a base for the conversion of the Lombard people.

The Abbey and church were taken from the monks by French occupying forces in 1803 and subsequently the library was dispersed throughout Europe. Today visitors can still see the scriptorum, basilica, Columban's sepulchral ark and in the Abbey museum pilgrim flasks dating from the 6th century.

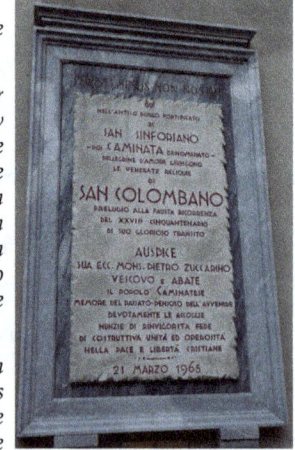

Caminata

Pometo to Bobbio — stage 59c

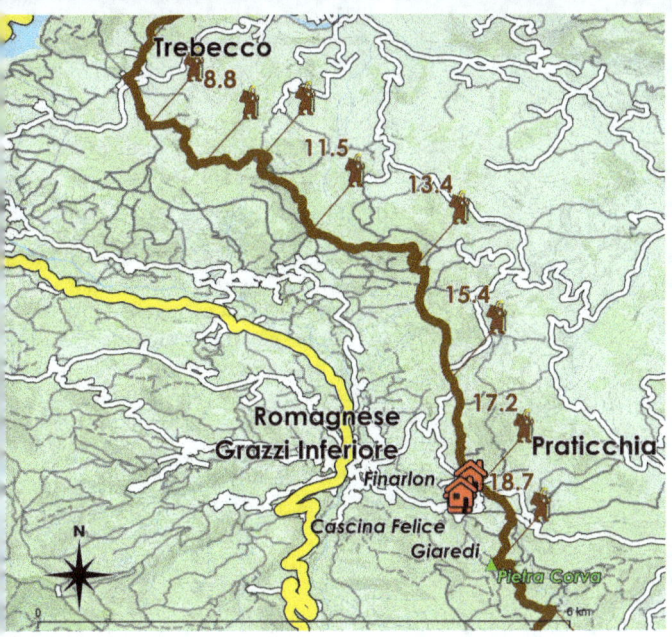

(0.0) With the entrance to the town hall behind you go straight ahead [Via dal Verme] **(0.3)** At the crossroads, continue straight ahead downhill [Direction Caminata] **(3.1)** At the apex of a hairpin bend to the right, bear left [Signpost via Abati - Pontremoli] **(3.3)** As the main track bears left, turn right on the grassy track [Downhill] **(3.6)** At the corner of the vineyard where the main track turns left, continue straight ahead down the hill **(3.8)** Bear right and cross the stream. Then bear left up the hill with the vines on your right **(3.8)** At the junction with the broad track, go straight ahead with the vines on your right **(3.9)** At the T-junction with the tarmac road turn right, uphill [Towards the hamlet] **(4.0)** At the crossroads, continue straight ahead **(4.4)** At the junction bear left towards the church in **Caminata (4.6)** At the T-junction turn left [Pass through a parking area] **(4.7)** In the square in front of the church bear right on the cobbled street down the hill [Pass No Entry sign] **(4.7)** Take the right fork and continue down hill on the narrow cobbled street **(4.8)** At the crossroads with a major road continue straight ahead [Via Tidone] **(5.1)** Bear right to cross the river bridge then immediately turn left **(6.3)** At the junction, bear left up the hill **(6.4)** At the crossroads, continue straight ahead on the narrow path through the trees **(6.7)** At the junction in Trebecco, bear right up the hill on the tarmac **(6.8)** At the crossroads, turn left and continue up the hill **(6.9)** Take the right fork [Direction Fontanasso] **(7.6)** At the junction in the tracks, turn left **(7.9)** Bear right and remain on the main track **(8.1)** At the entrance to the hamlet bear right and then left to pass between the houses **(8.8)** At the crest of the hill keep left on the stony path **(9.7)** At the T-junction turn right, uphil towards the woods [Pass a domed building on your right] **(9.9)** Beside the garage turn left on a grassy track **(10.0)** Bear right on the grass track into the hamlet **(10.0)** At the top of the hill in the hamlet, turn right on the broad gravel track **(10.1)** At the junction continue straight ahead on the gravel track [Pass a barn on your left] **(11.5)** At the junction on the brow, turn left and continue on the mule track [Shrine to your right] **(11.6)** At the junction turn left on the track **(12.0)** At the junction turn left **(12.4)** Take the right fork **(13.4)** At the T-junction, turn left and slightly uphill **(13.5)** At the T-junction turn right and slightly downhill **(13.9)** Continue straight ahead on the main track **(14.1)** At the junction again continue straight ahead **(15.4)** Continue straight ahead with the tarmac road close on your left **(15.6)** Turn left on the gravel track leaving the tarmac road [Slightly uphill] **(17.2)** At the T-junction with the tarmac road turn left [Red oversized bench by the junction] **(17.4)** Take the right

stage 59c — Pometo to Bobbio

fork [Direction Pietra Corva]**(17.8)** Keep right on the road [Direction Pietra Corva] **(18.7)** At the entrance to the car park beside the **Pietra Corva** restaurant and shop, turn left and begin to climb the hill through the woods**(18.9)** Take the left fork [Pass picnic tables on your right]**(19.0)** At the junction close by the fence, turn right [Sign for the Columban Way] **(19.0)** At the T-junction with a fence ahead, turn left [Between the fences] **(19.6)** At the junction beside the signboards bear right **(20.0)** At the T-junction turn right [30 minutes to Sassi Neri]**(20.4)** At the top of the rise bear left **(21.2)** In the clearing continue straight ahead [Avoid turn to the left]**(21.3)** In the following clearing bear left **(22.4)** At the T-junction with the tarmac road, turn left and then take the first turning to the right [**Sassi Neri**]**(23.2)** Immediately after a bend to the right in the road, turn sharp left on the gravel track [Pass a house close on your right] **(23.3)** After passing the house turn sharp right on the grass track [Steeply downhill]

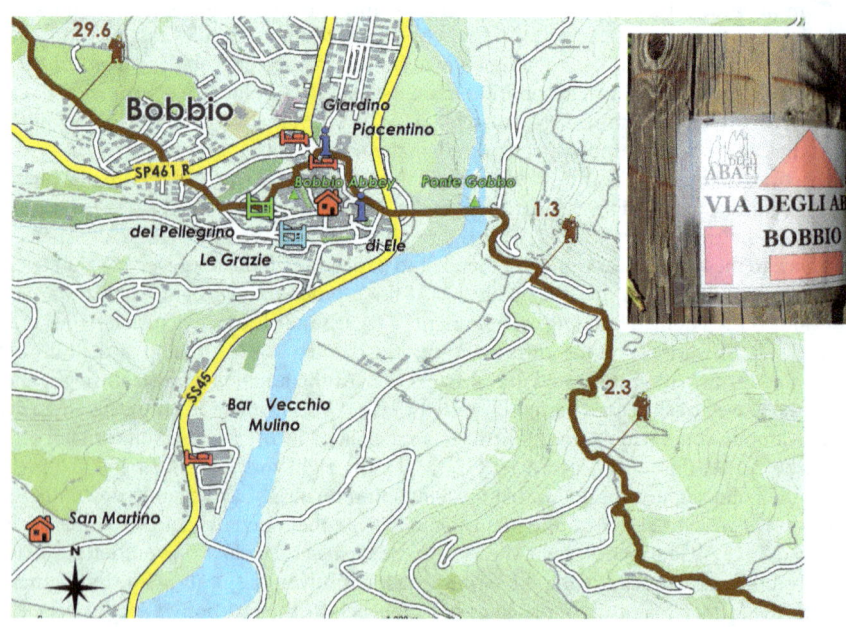

Pometo to Bobbio   stage 59c

(23.9) At the T-junction turn right on the stony track **(24.2)** At the T-junction with the tarmac road turn right 🏠 **(25.1)** At the T-junction with the road, turn left on the tarmac **(25.9)** At the T-junction with the tarmac road turn left 🏠 **(26.8)** At the T-junction turn right [Bobbio 5.2 km] **(27.5)** Shortly after a bend to the right, turn left to leave the road on a steeply descending gravel track **(27.8)** Beside the vines take the right fork on the narrowing track [Downhill] 🏠 **(29.2)** At the junction at the entry to Bobbio keep left [Trees on your left] **(30.0)** At the crossroads with a major road continue straight ahead [Direction Castello Malaspina] **(30.1)** At the junction continue straight ahead on Strada del Roso [Castle to your left] **(30.2)** Take the next turning to the left **(30.4)** Arrive at **Bobbio** [Piazza S. Colombano]

Accommodation and Tourist Information

Bobbio

🛏️ **Ostello - Casa del Pellegrino** ,Piazza S. Colombano, 3, 29022 Bobbio(PC), Italy; Tel:+39 0523 936236; bobbio.civitascolumbani.it/casa-pellegrino; Price:D

🛏️ **Ostello - Le Grazie** [Don Roberto],Piazza Santa Fara, 29022 Bobbio(PC), Italy; Tel:+39 347 5389566; Price:D

🏠 **Agriturismo - San Martino** [Emma and Marcello],Località San Martino, 5, 29022 Bobbio(PC), Italy; Tel:+39 0523 932287; +39 339 786 5868; +39 333 969 1991; Email:agrisanmartino@gmail.com; www.agriturismo-sanmartino.com; Price:C

🏠 **B&B - La Casa di Ele**,Contrada dei Donati, 3, 29022 Bobbio(PC), Italy; Tel:+39 3287548349; andandoporelmundo.com/italia/bobbio/bb-a-casa-di-ele

🛏️ **Hotel - Piacentino**,Piazza San Francesco, 19, 29022 Bobbio(PC), Italy; Tel:+39 0523 936266; Email:info@hotelpiacentino.it; www.hotelpiacentino.it; Price:B

🛏️ **Albergo Bar Ristorante - Vecchio Mulino**,Via Genova, 32, 29022 Bobbio(PC), Italy; Tel:+39 0523 932395; ristorante-albergo-vecchio-mulino.business.site; Price:B

🛏️ **Hotel - Giardino** ,Piazza San Francesco, 12, 29022 Bobbio(PC), Italy; Tel:+39 0523 936247; Email:info@albergobargiardino.it; albergobargiardino.it; Price:B

ℹ️ **Amici di San Colombano**,Piazza Duomo, 7 , 29022 Bobbio(PC), Italy; Tel:+39 0523 936124; +39 347 5389566; +39 339 6456086; Email:librettigianluca@gmail.com

ℹ️ **Ufficio Turistico**,Piazza San Francesco, 29022 Bobbio(PC), Italy; Tel:+39 0523 962806; +39 0523 962815; Email:iat@comune.bobbio.pc.it; www.comune.bobbio.pc.it

Farini

🏠 **B&B - Le Margherite**   ,Località Nicelli, 88, 29023 Farini(PC), Italy; Tel:+39 335 455 039; Email:margret.metz@libero.it; www.bnblemargherite.it; Price:B

Romagnese

🏠 **Agriturismo - Giaredi**,Frazione Grazzi Superiore, 27050 Romagnese(PV), Italy; Tel:+39 335 158 4358; Email:agriturismo.giaredi@email.it; www.facebook.com/Agriturismo-Giaredi-413700865422016

🏠 **Agriturismo - Finarlon**,Frazione Grazzi Superiore, 27050 Romagnese(PV), Italy; Tel:+39 335 812 1515; Email:eurobusiness@twtnet.com; terrealtedoltrepo.it

🏠 **Agriturismo - Cascina Felice**,Frazione Grazzi Superiore, 27050 Romagnese(PV), Italy; Tel:+39 3493233034; Email:cascinafelice2015@libero.it; web.facebook.com/profile.php?id=100057621783092

Santa Maria

🏠 **B&B - La Bicocca**,Via Casa Draghi, 35, 29022 Santa Maria(PC), Italy; Tel:+39 340 878 2503; booking.com; Price:B

stage 59d — Bobbio to Nicelli

Length:	20.1km
Ascent:	2068m
Descent:	1276m
Pavia:	67km
Pontremoli:	117km

Ponte Gobbo

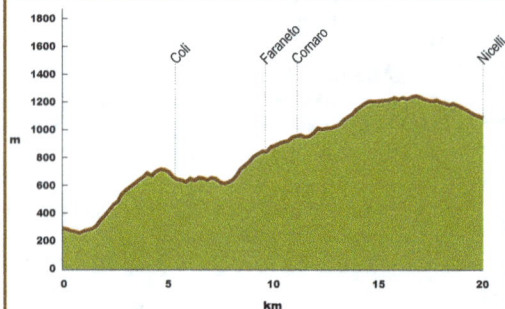

Route: the route from Bobbio to Nicelli leaves the town centre on the Ponte Gobbo over the river Trebbia. Once again the farm and mule roads will lead the trail back over 1000 m and reaching 1200 m at Sella dei Generali before continuing on the gravel ridge road and descending through the woods to Nicelli and the neighbouring Mareto. Coli has both a shop and bar/restaurant.

The "Ponte Gobbo" or hunchback bridge, owes its name to the 11 uneven arches that support the structure. In the Middle Ages, the construction of a bridge was a work of great ingenuity and for some it was seen to be almost magical and has given rise to many legends, which often had the devil joining two places that nature (and God) had wanted separate.

A legend tells that the devil contacted San Colombano, promising him to build the bridge in one night, in exchange for the first mortal soul to cross it. The saint accepted and during the night, various demons were summoned to help the devil with the masonry work holding up the arches of the bridge, but the demons were of different heights and so the arches of the bridge came out in different sizes. In the morning, the devil waited at the end of the bridge for his reward. However, `San Colombano sent him a little dog. The disappointed and angry devil took his revenge by kicking the bridge which has been crooked ever since.

In reality the river is subject to frequent floods and widening leading to repeated damage to the bridge that has been repaired by many different hands over the centuries.

From Ireland to Bobbio – the gardens of Bobbio Abbey

Bobbio to Nicelli

stage 59d

🚶(0.0)From Piazza S. Colombano take the narrow street on the left side of the abbey(0.1)At the end of the narrow street turn left and follow via S. Lorenzo [Pass in front of the doors of Chiesa di San Lorenzo](0.1)After passing the shops with the arched portico, turn right [Walled garden ahead at the junction](0.2)At the stop sign turn left and bear right [Pass between the restaurants on Piazza S. Francesco](0.3)Beside the fountain, turn right and pass the tourist office on your left(0.5)Bear left on the narrow walled road towards the river(0.6) At the junction with the main road at the foot of the hill, take the pedestrian crossing and cross the old river bridge(0.9)At the end of the bridge turn right and follow the road up the hill 🚶(1.3) Immediately after crossing the river bridge turn left on the gravel track(1.5)Take the right fork and then fork right again on the narrow track [Abbots Way](2.2)At the crossroads in the tracks continue straight ahead steeply up the

Descending towards Coli

rocky path 🚶(2.3)At the T-junction bear right and then left to follow the tarmac road(2.6) Leave the road and turn left on the steep track into the woods(2.9)At the crossroads with a broader track continue straight ahead [Uphill](2.9)At the T-junction beside the stone building, turn left(3.0)At the T-junction with the tarmac road, turn left and continue up the hill(3.2)Turn sharp right onto a stony track and continue uphill [Barn below to the left at the junction] 🚶(4.4)At the T-junction, turn left [Pass under the power lines](4.7)At the

stage 59d — Bobbio to Nicelli

Mule road leaving Bobbio

T-junction with the tarmac road turn right [Pass a house on your left]**(5.0)**Turn right on the narrow track downhill [Towards the village]**(5.1)**At the T-junction with the tarmac road turn right [Towards the water trough]**(5.4)**At the T-junction with a tarmac road, turn right [Towards the bell tower in **Coli**] 🚶 **(5.5)**Facing the church, turn left on the narrow road [Piscina Comunale]**(5.8)**Shortly before reaching the swimming pool turn left**(5.9)**At the fork take the major branch to the left**(6.1)**As the tarmac road starts to climb and turn to the left, take the gravel track to the right 🚶 **(6.6)**At the T-junction with the tarmac road turn right and keep right [Towards the village]**(6.7)**On the crown of the bend to left, bear right on the grassy track [Into the trees] 🚶 **(7.9)**Continue straight ahead on the less steep path. Then keep right at the following junction 🚶 **(9.0)**At the junction continue straight ahead on the mule track**(9.3)** At the junction continue straight ahead on the fairly level track [Avoid the track descending to the left]**(9.7)**At the T-Junction with a broad stony track, turn righ [Uphill]**(9.7)**In hamlet of **Faraneto**, turn sharp right on the stony track [Uphill]**(10.0)**Remain on the road as it turns to the left 🚶 **(11.2)**Take the right fork, slightly downhill [Towards the village of **Cornaro**]**(11.3)**At the junction, bear right again [Towards village centre]**(11.8)**At the junction, bear right on the tarmac [Pass rocky incline on your left]**(11.9)**Take the left fork, slightly uphill 🚶 **(13.2)**Turn sharp left up the hill [Pass corrugated barn on your left]**(13.3)**At the exit from the village turn sharp right on the stony track [Eroded hillside to your left]**(13.6)**At the junction in the tracks, bear left on the narrow track [Between the field and hedgerow] 🚶 **(14.4)**At the T-junction with the tarmac road turn right**(14.7)**As the tarmac road turns sharply to the left, turn right on the gravel road [Direction Mareto]**(15.4)**To cut the corner, turn right on the track, cross the brow of the hill and then turn right on rejoining the road 🚶 **(17.3)**Continue to bear right on the broader track [45 minutes to Nicelli]**(18.1)**Turn sharp right to leave the broad track and take the grassy track downhill**(18.2)**At the foot of the hill turn right [Pass water pumping station] 🚶 **(19.9)**A the T-junction turn left on the stony track**(20.1)**Arrive at **Nicelli**, at the road junction beside village sign board

Bobbio to Nicelli   stage 59d

Accommodation and Tourist Information

Coli
Albergo Ristorante - Poggiolo, Località Poggiolo, 118, 29020 Coli(PC), Italy; Tel:+39 0523 931063; Email:info@albergopoggiolo.it; www.albergopoggiolo.it; Price:B

Mareto
B&B - Le Margherite, Località Nicelli, 88, 29023 Mareto(PC), Italy; Tel:+39 335 455 039; Email:margret.metz@libero.it; www.bnblemargherite.it; Price:B

Agriturismo - Le Sermase, Località Nicelli, 58, 29023 Mareto(PC), Italy; Tel:+39 0523 915330; +39 533 4591186; Email:lesermase@libero.it; www.facebook.com/Agriturismo-Le-Sermase-234743833600733

Albergo - Dei Cacciatori, Località Mareto, 29023 Mareto(PC), Italy; Tel:+39 0523 915131; +39 0523 1820755; albergo-deicacciatori.it; Price:B

Ready for winter - Nicelli

stage 59e — Nicelli to Groppallo

Length:	13.2km
Ascent:	790m
Descent:	920m
Pavia:	87km
Pontremoli:	97km

Leaving Nicelli

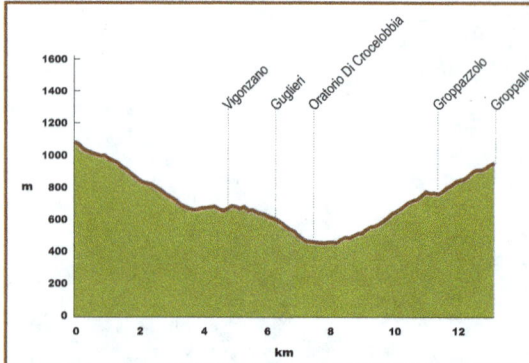

Route: the short but strenuous stage from Nicelli to Groppallo descends into the Nure valley taking the road bridge over the Torrente Nure and then fording the Torrente Lardana. The crossing of the Lardana is not well marked and could be dangerous following heavy rain - a longer Alternate Route via the Farini bridge is also described. After crossing the river, the route once again makes stiff climb back towards 1000 m on off-road tracks to reach the welcoming village of Groppallo where you will find shops, restaurants and accommodation. There are no eating places directly on the main route but Farini on the Alternate Route has both bars and a restaurant.

Monte Castellaro rises above the village of Groppallo and is surmounted by the church of Santa Maria Assunta. The church replaced the castle that gave rise to the name and which is known to have been owned by the Bishop of Piacenza in the 12th century. Feuding between the Genoese Ghibelline and Guelph families led to the burning of the castle in the 13th century. After rebuilding the castle was again seriously damaged by Count Pietro Scotti in 1515 and the church finally took over the site at the end of the 16th century.

Excavations at the site have revealed a soap-stone workshop, coins issued in Pavia in the 10th century and fragments of Bronze age pottery.

The centre of the village is known as Barsi with some people still speaking the distinct dialect of Gropalino.

The autumn fruit of the woodland

Nicelli to Groppallo   stage 59e

Oratorio di Crocelobbia

🚶(0.0)From the road junction beside village sign board, head south east and then turn left towards the village centre(0.1)In the centre of the village take the right fork and continue downhill(0.2)At the crossroads with a tarmac road, continue straight ahead on the grass track [Garage on your left](0.4)At the T-junction, turn left and left again and follow the tarmac road through the hamlet of Molinari(0.9)Turn right downhill on the gravel track [Pass barn on your right]🚶(1.3)At the crossroads in Borderoni, continue straight ahead [Post and rail fence on your left](1.6)At the crossroads in the track, turn right down the hill(2.0)At the junction continue straight ahead, downhill on the stony track(2.2)Keep left at the fork in the tracks🚶(2.7)Take the right fork downhill, continuing on the stony track(3.0)Continue straight ahead on the track, downhill in the woods🚶(4.0)At the junction continue straight ahead on the main track(4.1)Again continue straight ahead on the main track [Avoid turning to the right](4.8)At

the T-junction with the tarmac road on the edge of the village of **Vigonzano**, turn right🚶(5.3)Take the track to the right and leave the tarmac road [Enter the woods]🚶(6.3)At the T-junction with the tarmac road in the village of **Guglieri** turn right down the hill(6.4)As the tarmac road turns left, fork right on the stony track and keep close to the wall on the left(6.5)Take the left fork, downhill on the less steep track(6.8)Overlooking the hamlet below, take the left turn and continue between the trees(7.3)At the foot of the track, turn right on the tarmac road and take the bridge over the river. Note:- after crossing the initial bridge the primary route will ford the Torrente Nure. If you are unsure of the safety of the crossing then you can turn left at this point and follow the alternative route crossing the bridge in Farini🚶(7.5)At the end of the bridge immediately turn left on the stony track [Pass the small **Oratorio di Crocelobbia** on your right](7.6)Take the right fork [Keep the river - Torrente Nure - to your left](7.7)Keep right on the path in the field parallel to the

stage 59e — Nicelli to Groppallo

river [Tree plantation below on the left]**(8.1)**Leave the main track and turn towards the river and with due regard to the conditions, carefully cross the river [Direction Guado Nure]**(8.3)**Pass between 2 red and white signs and leave the river**(8.3)**Take the narrow path through the trees **(8.5)**Pass behind the house and turn right on the road**(8.7)**Turn left off the road and take the grass track through the trees**(9.0)**Continue through the meadows with the trees close on your right**(9.1)**At the T-junction, turn left with the bushes and broken wall on your right**(9.2)**After passing through a gap in the bushes and entering another meadow, turn left and climb towards the road and follow the tarmac to the right**(9.4)**Take the left fork [Direction Chiarabini] **(9.6)**Take the right fork [Between the barn and the house]**(9.6)**At the T-junction with the road, turn left, pass the arched building on your left then turn right on the grass track after passing the small stone built shelter**(9.7)**Take the left fork**(10.5)**At the junction bear right on the stony track [Farini bridge variant joins from the left] **(10.8)**At the T-junction in the tracks, turn left**(11.0)**At the T-junction with the stony track, turn right slightly downhill**(11.4)**In **Groppazzolo** at the T-junction with a tarmac road, turn slightly left and then right on the gravel towards the second tarmac road**(11.5)**At the T-junction, turn left on the tarmac road**(11.7)**At the T-junction, turn right up the hill **(11.8)**Take the right fork and continue uphill **(12.9)**At the T-junction with a more major road turn right**(13.2)**Arrive at **Groppallo** beside Albergo Centrale - Salini Fratelli.

Diversion via the Farini Bridge

Route: if you have doubts in crossing the Torrente Lardana the Alternate Route will lead you to the village of Farini which is downstream from the river confluence and where you will find a safe crossing on a road bridge over river. The diversion will add approximately 3km to your journey. (0.0)Turn left and follow the tarmac road, remain parallel to the river on your right (2.1)Turn left and then right to cross the river bridge(2.4)At the end of the bridge as the main road bear right, bear left on via Spinelli(2.5)As the road turns right, take the grass track straight ahead(2.6)Cross the road and continue uphill with the woods to your left(2.7)At the T-junction with the road, turn right(3.0)Shortly after a tight turn to the right, turn left on the grass track between the disused farm buildings (3.2)Cross the road and continue on the track through the trees(3.2)At the T-junction with the broad track, turn left(3.4)Rejoin the road and turn right(3.5)Take the right fork [Direction Ca' Nova](3.9)Turn left on the gravel road and skirt the hamlet(4.0)Bear left on the track into the trees (6.1)At the junction in the tracks, go straight ahead and rejoin the main track

Length:	6.1km
Ascent:	524m
Descent:	285m

Nicelli to Groppallo stage 59e

Accommodation and Tourist Information

Farini
B&B - Orto dei Semplici, Località Ceno, 11, 29023 Farini(PC), Italy; Tel:+39 335 625 5864; Email:mariateresapuliti@gmail.com; ortodeisemplicitalia.it; Price:A

Groppallo
Chiesa Santa Maria Assunta [Don Alfonso],SP51, 58, 29023 Groppallo(PC), Italy; Tel:+39 3386373955; Price:D; *3 beds summer only*

Albergo - Centrale Salini Fratelli, Viale Europa, 46, 29023 Groppallo(PC), Italy; Tel:+39 0523 916104; Email:prenotazioni@fratellisalini.it; www.fratellisalini.it; Price:B; *Pilgrim menu available*; **PR**

Albergo Ristorante - Italia, Viale Europa, 84, 29023 Groppallo(PC), Italy; Tel:+39 0523 916119; Email:info@albergoristoranteitalia.pc.it; www.albergoristoranteitalia.pc.it

Albergo Ristorante - Lo Smeraldo, Viale Europa, 128, 29023 Groppallo(PC), Italy; Tel:+39 0523 916108; Email:info@losmeraldoristorante.it; www.losmeraldoristorante.it; Price:B

The restored tower of San Antonio at Selva di Sotto on the outskirts of Groppallo

stage 59f — Groppallo to Bardi

Length:	21.8km
Ascent:	1101m
Descent:	1462m
Pavia:	100km
Pontremoli:	84km

Castello di Bardi

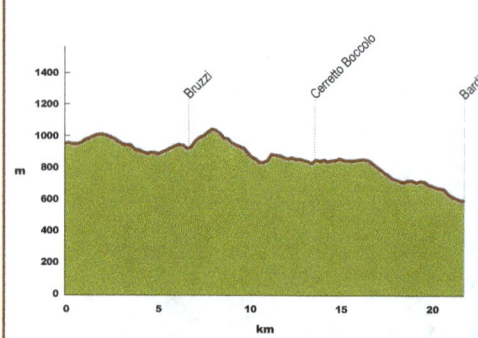

Route: the stage from Groppallo to Bardi generally parallels the *strade provinciale* on wooded mule and farm roads intermixed with short stretches on the tarmac. There is a restaurant in Bruzzi, but no other facilities until the outskirts of Bardi

The Castello di Bardi also called "Rocca di Bardi", is built on top of an outcrop of red stone and dominates the valleys of Ceno and Noveglia. It is first referenced in August 898 when it was purchased by the Bishop of Piacenza as a refuge from the Barbarian invasions.

In 1257 it was acquired by the Landi family who over centuries converted it into a luxurious residence.

From this base the Landi's grew a substantially independent state including the valley of the Taro and even with the right to mint their own coins.

The castle was sold in 1682 to the Farnese family and then passed to the Bourbons and began a fall into decline before eventually being acquired by the newly unified Italian state where for a period it served as a military prison.

The castle is open to the public throughout the year.

So many roads lead to Rome

Groppallo to Bardi — stage 59f

👤**(0.0)** From Albergo Centrale in Groppallo continue east on viale Europa **(0.5)** At the end of the road fork right remaining on the principal road [Pass "Monumento alle genti di montagna a Groppallo" on the outcrop to the left] **(0.7)** Immediately following a bend to the right, turn left onto the gravel track [Pass large house on your right] 👤**(2.0)** At the junction keep right on the main gravel track [Corrugated barn below] **(2.2)** At the T-junction with a gravel track, turn left [Pass yellow shipping container on your left] **(2.8)** At the T-junction in the hamlet of Riovalle turn left and then immediately right [Pass through the archway] **(2.9)** At the T-junction with the tarmac road turn left [Pass house No. 30 on your left] 👤**(3.2)** Bear right to leave the road on a gravel track [Direction La Croce] **(3.4)** Take the central grassy track, downhill [Embankment to your left] 👤**(4.3)** At the junction in the tracks turn left downhill into the

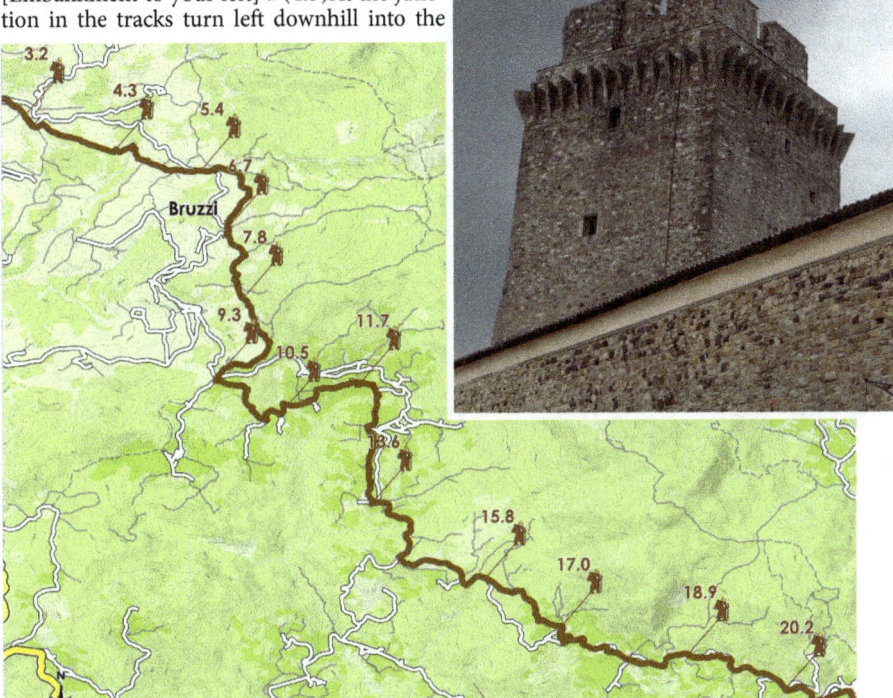

The central castle stronghold

woods [Wind generator on the horizon to the left] **(4.9)** At the junction bear right [Embankment on your left, field on your right] **(5.0)** At the T-junction at the entrance to the hamlet of Selva Sotto, bear right [Pass stone built barn on your right] **(5.1)** At the T-junction with the tarmac road turn left [Pass under power lines] 👤**(5.4)** At the T-junction with the tarmac road in Selva Sopra turn right **(5.5)** Just before the bridge turn left and then right [Direction Terruzzo] **(5.7)** At the junction, continue straight ahead on the stony track uphill [Meadow on the left, house on the right] **(5.9)** Fork right and uphill, continue in the woodland **(6.1)** Take the right fork, slightly downhill 👤**(6.7)** At the T-junction with the tarmac road, turn left. Note:- cafe/bar ahead in the village of **Bruzzi (6.7)** Take the left fork up the hill [Wall on your left] **(7.1)** Take the right fork, uphill **(7.6)** At the crossroads continue straight ahead on the stony track into the woods 👤**(7.8)** At the junction, continue straight ahead [Meadow on your right] **(8.5)** At the T-junction in the track, turn right [Towards the brow] 👤**(9.3)** At the

stage 59f — Groppallo to Bardi

road junction, with the cafe on your left, continue straight ahead towards the hamlet and then take the first turning to the left [Direction Chiastre]**(10.3)**At the T-junction, turn left down the hill [Towards the meadows] 🍴 **(10.5)**At the junction, turn left onto the tarmac road and continue downhill towards the trees**(10.9)**Shortly before reaching the concrete barn, turn left to leave the tarmac and take the right fork uphill on the stony track 🍴 **(11.7)** In the hamlet continue straight ahead [Pass a water trough on your right]**(11.9)**Take the right fork on the stony track towards the trees**(12.4)**At the crossroads, continue straight ahead on the grassy track [Direction Grezzo] 🍴 **(13.6)**At the T-junction with the tarmac road in the hamlet of **Cerretto Boccolo**, turn left and then turn right to follow the SP77 🍴 **(15.8)**Shortly after a bend to the right in the road, bear left on the track climbing gently up the hill in the trees**(16.3)**Take the left fork, remain in the trees 🍴 **(17.0)**At the crossroads with a tarmac road in the hamlet of Cogno Grezzo, turn right on the tarmac, pass a garage on your right and then bear left on the stony track**(17.4)**At the T-junction with the SP77, turn left on the tarmac towards the centre of Grezzo 🍴 **(18.9)**On the crown of the bend to the right, fork right on the gravel track and then immediately left [Embankment on your left]**(19.2)**Rejoin the SP77 and turn right 🍴 **(20.2)**Immediately before the road turns sharp left, bear right on the track, downhill [Towards the yellow house]**(20.5)**Return to the SP77

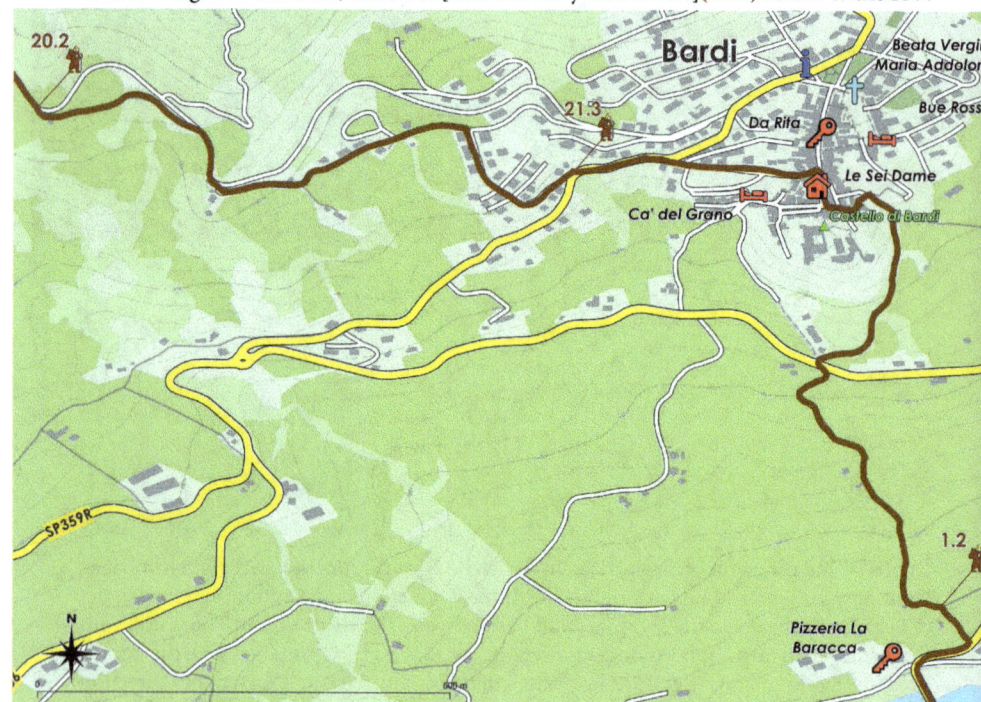

and turn right**(20.6)**Immediately after passing the church, bear right on the small tarmac road [Strada San Siro]**(21.1)**Turn right on the tree lined street [Via J.F. Kennedy] 🍴 **(21.3)** At the junction with the main road, turn left and then bear right [Castle on your right] **(21.7)**At the T-junction, turn right and pass the fountain on your left and take via Giodani [Direction Castello]**(21.8)**At the end of the street turn left into Piazza del Grano**(21.8)**Arrive at **Bardi** beside the ramp to the castle entrance [Piazza Bernardino Formigari]

Groppallo to Bardi — stage 59f

Accommodation and Tourist Information

Bardi

✝ **Parrocchia Beata Vergine Maria Addolorata**,Piazza Vittoria, 13, 43032 Bardi(PR), Italy; Tel:+39 0525 72350; Email:parrocchia.bardi@alice.it; Price:D; *3 beds*

🛏 **Albergo Ristorante - Bue Rosso**,Piazza Martiri D'Ungheria, 10, 43032 Bardi(PR), Italy; Tel:+39 0525 72260; Price:B

🛏 **Albergo - Ca' del Grano**,Via S. Francesco, 5, 43032 Bardi(PR), Italy; Tel:+39 327 732 2836; Email:info@cadelgrano.it; www.cadelgrano.it; Price:A

🗝 **Affittacamere Pizzeria - La Baracca**,Località Ponte Al Ceno, 208, 43032 Bardi(PR), Italy; Tel:+39 0525 71149; Email:labaraccaristorante@libero.it; ristorantepizzerialabaraccaabardi.wordpress.com

🗝 **Affittacamere - Da Rita**,Via Predella, 1, 43032 Bardi(PR), Italy; Tel:+39 052572238; www.parmawelcome.it

ℹ **Tourist Office**,Via Pietro Cella, 5, 43032 Bardi(PR), Italy; Tel:+39 0525 733075; Email:uitbardi@mail.com; www.turismobardi.it

Bardi from the castle

stage 59g — Bardi to Borgo-Val-di-Taro

Length:	28.8km
Ascent:	2375m
Descent:	2549m
Pavia:	122km
Pontremoli:	62km

Approaching Borgo val di Taro

Route: the stage from Bardi to Borgo-Val-di-Taro descends to take the road bridges over the rivers Ceno and Noveglia and then begins a long and demanding climb back to 1000m with brief descents including a section passing the monastery of Gravago. The stage is again largely undertaken on wooded former mule roads. Water can be found in most of the hamlets but there are no cafes or shops until the final kilometre of the stage.

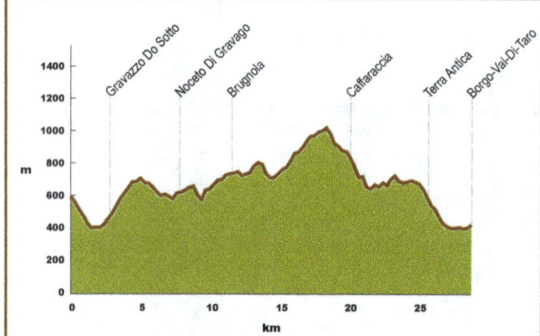

Borgo-Val-di-Taro or more familiarly Borgotaro is generally considered to be the capital of Alto Val Taro. In Roman times it was known as Turris gaining its current name in the 12th century, but with a long association with the via Francigena. The town was gifted to the Bobbio monastery and later dominated by the Landi, Farnese and Bourbons.

In WWII Borgotaro was a centre of resistance with allied PoW escapees smuggled through the hills to the Ligurian coast. However, in these more peaceful times much of its fame comes from the delicious Porcini mushrooms found in the wooded hills where much of the Parmigiano Reggiano is also produced. The town boasts a museum dedicated to mushrooms and an annual mushroom festival.

🚶 **(0.0)** From the ramp to the castle entrance take the path downhill to the east between the buildings and the castle boundary wall [Sign Borgo Val di Taro 9 hours] **(0.1)** At the foot of the concrete track, take the right fork [River below on your left] **(0.5)** Cross the tarmac road and continue downhill on the stony track 🚶 **(1.2)** Beside the shrine, turn right and continue downhill **(1.2)** At the T-junction with the tarmac road, turn right and continue downhill and across the bridge **(1.8)** Take the left fork and cross a second bridge [Direction Tosca] 🚶 **(2.4)** Shortly before the road bends to the right, turn right on the stony track, steeply uphill **(2.8)** At the crossroads in the tracks beside the hamlet of **Gravazzo do Sotto**, continue straight ahead on the stony track up the hill **(3.2)** With a farmhouse on your left, take the right fork and continue uphill **(3.4)** At the crossroads on the brow continue straight ahead

Bardi to Borgo-Val-di-Taro stage 59g

(**3.7**)Take the right fork and continue up the hill(**4.4**)At the crossroads beside the disused farmhouse, turn right and go downhill to join the road below(**4.5**) At the T-junction with the stony road, turn left on the road [Road turns right] (**5.4**)As the tarmac road turns sharp right, bear left on the stony track and immediately take the right fork [In the direction of the monastery of Gravago](**5.8**) Take the right fork, downhill (**6.7**) At the crossroads in the tracks, continue straight ahead, slightly uphill(**6.8**)Take the right fork, downhill [Avoid the more narrow track to the left](**7.2**)At the T-junction with the tarmac road, turn left [Pass the church on your right](**7.3**)Take the narrow track to the left, uphill (**7.8**)After emerging from the hamlet of **Noceto di Gravago** continue straight ahead on the broad gravel track(**7.9**)At the T-junction with the tarmac road turn left [Towards the bridge](**8.3**) As the road turns right, bear left on the small tarmac road [Direction Palazzo](**8.4**)Continue straight ahead on the grass path(**8.6**)Cross the road and continue on the path [Direction Pieve di Gravago] (**9.2**) After crossing the stream, bear right on the broad gravel track, uphill(**9.2**) Bear right on the grass track [Between the post and rail fence and the river below](**9.6**)Take the left fork and continue uphill [Football pitch on your right](**9.7**)At the T-junction with the broad track, turn left and continue with the woods on your left and fields on your right(**9.9**)At the T-junction beside the cemetery turn left [Towards the church] (**10.8**)Briefly join a tarmac road then bear left on the stony track towards the stone built house(**10.8**)Immediately after passing the house take the right fork, uphill(**11.2**)At the junction with a tarmac road turn right and immediately left to pass behind the buildings(**11.5**)Fork left on the grass track towards the hamlet of **Brugnola** (**11.8**)At the T-junction, turn right on the tarmac road, downhill(**12.3**) Beside the derelict building, turn left to leave the road and then right to gain a forest track. Note:- a longer variant of the route branches to the left (**13.1**)At the crossroads in the tracks, continue straight ahead(**13.5**)On the brow, continue straight ahead(**14.1**)At the T-junction with the broad gravel road, turn left (**15.6**)Beside the driveway entrance and the sign board, turn sharp left to leave the road and follow the stony track uphill(**15.6**)Take the right fork and continue uphill(**15.8**)Take the right fork [Direction Caffaraccia](**16.0**) Bear right on the broad track downhill [Direction Caffaraccia](**16.4**)Take the right fork into the trees (**18.1**)At the T-junction turn left(**18.2**)At the junction, bear left and then turn right at the crossroads. Note:- the track ahead at the crossroads leads to another

stage 59g — Bardi to Borgo-Val-di-Taro

longer variant. 🚶 **(19.1)** At the T-junction beside the stone house, turn right and continue downhill **(19.9)** Take the right fork to leave the road [Towards the houses] 🚶 **(20.1)** Cross the road and continue on the stony track through **Caffaraccia(20.2)** Cross the tarmac road and continue downhill on the stony track through the archway **(20.3)** Beside the cemetery, turn right and then left and join the downhill track with the church on your left **(20.6)** At the junction with the tarmac road, turn left and immediately following the hairpin bend take the road to the left [Direction Isola] **(20.9)** Shortly beform reaching a park bench, turn right downhill on the grass track 🚶 **(21.2)** Just after crossing the river with the rope guide rail, turn right on the path keeping close to the river 🚶 **(22.7)** At the T-junction with the tarmac road and with a church to your right, turn left on the road **(23.3)** Shortly before the road junction on the hairpin bend, take the wooded track to your right, downhill 🚶 **(24.3)** At the junction with the tarmac road, turn right and immediately reenter the woods [Via Francigena sign] **(25.3)** At the T-junction with the gravel road, turn right and immediately fork left on the grass track down the hill 🚶 **(25.7)** At the junction continue straight ahead [**Terra Antica** to the left] **(26.3)** At the T-junction with the tarmac road turn right [Continue parallel to the railway tracks] 🚶 **(27.0)** As the road bends to the right, bear let on the narrow grass track [Behind the stone house] **(27.2)** At the T-junction with the tarmac road turn right, cross the bridge and continue straight ahead on the pedestrian and cycle path **(27.9)** At the junction beside the parking area, turn left [Cycle path with post and rail fence] 🚶 **(28.1)** Turn left across the wooden bridge and then left again at the end of the bridge **(28.6)** At the T-junction with the main road, turn right [Petrol station opposite] **(28.8)** Arrive at **Borgo-Val-di-Taro** by the steps leading to the arched entrance to the old town.

Accommodation and Tourist Information

Bardi

🏠 **Agriturismo - Brugnola 1932**, Località Brugnola, 225, 43032 Bardi(PR), Italy; Tel:+39 320 813 0540; +39 348 3055736; Email:info@brugnola1932.com; brugnola1932.com; *Vegan Country House and animal sanctuary*

🏠 **Agriturismo - Il Castagneto**, Località Castagneto di Gravago, 43032 Bardi(PR), Italy; Tel:+39 347 850 4448; +39 052577141; Email:castagneto18@libero.it; www.parmawelcome.it/it/scheda/organizza-il-tuo-viaggio/dove-dormire/agriturismo/azienda-agrituristica-il-castagneto

🏠 **Agriturismo - Ca' d'Alfieri**, Località Predario, 29, 43032 Bardi(PR), Italy; Tel:+39 0525 77174; +39 347 6668071; +39 347 8927775; Email:info@cadalfieri.it; www.cadalfieri.it; Price:A

🏠 **B&B - Le Sei Dame**, Via Giordani, 18, 43032 Bardi(PR), Italy; Tel:+39 333 840 9000; Email:info@leseidame.it; www.leseidame.it; Price:A

🏠 **B&B - Albachiara**, Località' Osacca, 247, 43032 Bardi(PR), Italy; Tel:+39 347 323 4389; +39 3319155076; web.facebook.com/albachiara.osacca

🏠 **Agriturismo - Gennari Giuliano**, Località' Bergazzi, 194, 43032 Bardi(PR), Italy; Tel:+39 0525 77177

🏠 **B&B - Ca' del Lupo**, Località Bergazzi, 197a, 43032 Bardi(PR), Italy; Tel:+39 0525 77177; +39 347 2483601; +39 349 2566546; Email:info@cadellupo.com; cadellupo.com; Price:A

Borgo Val Di Taro

✝ **Parrocchia Sant'Antonino** [Don Angelo Busi],Via Cesare Battisti, 72, 43043 Borgo Val Di Taro(PR), Italy; Tel:+39 3357111444; +39 3332080963; Price:C; *4 beds*

🏠 **B&B - Il Portello**, Salita Nazario Sauro, 2, 43043 Borgo Val Di Taro(PR), Italy; Tel:+39 3271832647; Email:bbportello@gmail.com; www.bbilportello.it; Price:B

🏠 **Agriturismo - La Vigna di San Pietro**, Frazione San Pietro, 39, 43043 Borgo Val Di Taro(PR), Italy; Tel:+39 338 761 1996; lavignadisanpietro.it; Price:A

🏠 **B&B - Cristina e Giulio**, Via P V Manara, 2, 43043 Borgo Val Di Taro(PR), Italy; Tel:+39 0525 920082; Email:cistina.anelli@aliceposta.it; www.parmawelcome.it/it/scheda/organizza-il-tuo-viaggio/dove-dormire/bed-breakfast/bed-breakfast-22-twentytwo; Price:B

Bardi to Borgo-Val-di-Taro

stage 59g

🏠 **Agritiurismo - Antico Borgo**
[Paola],Località Vadonnino di San Pietro, 2, 43043 Borgo Val Di Taro(PR), Italy; Tel:+39 3474313826; +39 0525.90950 ; Email:info@agriturismovadonnino.it; agriturismovadonnino.it; Price:A

🏠 **Agriturismo - le Querciole**,Località Le Querciole Di San Pietro, 3, 43043 Borgo Val Di Taro(PR), Italy; Tel:+39 0525 96810; +39 338 8992569; Email:info@agriturismo-lequerciole.it; www.agriturismo-lequerciole.it; Price:A

🏠 **Agriturismo - Terra Antica**
[Laura],Località Cappella di San Martino, 31, 43043 Borgo Val Di Taro(PR), Italy; Tel:+39 0525 921179; +39 3409100361; Email:info@terra-antica.it; www.terra-antica.it; Price:A

🏠 **B&B - Liberty**,Via Montegrappa, 4, 43043 Borgo Val Di Taro(PR), Italy; Tel:+39 335 606 1246; booking.com; Price:A

🛏 **Albergo - Firenze**,Piazza Giuseppe Verdi, 3, 43043 Borgo Val Di Taro(PR), Italy; Tel:+39 0525 96478; Email:info@albergo-firenze.it; albergo-firenze.it; Price:B

🛏 **Albergo - Roma**,Largo Roma, 9, 43043 Borgo Val Di Taro(PR), Italy; Tel:+39 0525 402177; +39 339 542 7166; Email:info@nuovoalbergoroma.it; nuovoalbergoroma.it; Price:B

🛏 **Hotel Ristorante - Mistrello**,Via Europa, 2, 43043 Borgo Val Di Taro(PR), Italy; Tel:+39 0525 97444; +39 328 894 1748; Email:info@hotelmistrello.it; hotelmistrello.it; Price:A

⛺ **Camping - Europa**,Via Achille Stradella, 5, 43043 Borgo Val Di Taro(PR), Italy; Tel:+39 0525 99363; +39 327 13 53 463; Email:fblazzarelli@gmail.com; www.prolocoborgotaro.net/camping; Price:C

ℹ **Ufficio Informazioni Turistiche**,Piazza Prospero Manara, 7, 43043 Borgo Val Di Taro(PR), Italy; Tel:+39 052596796; Email:uit@comune.borgo-val-di-taro.pr.it; www.sostalborgo.it

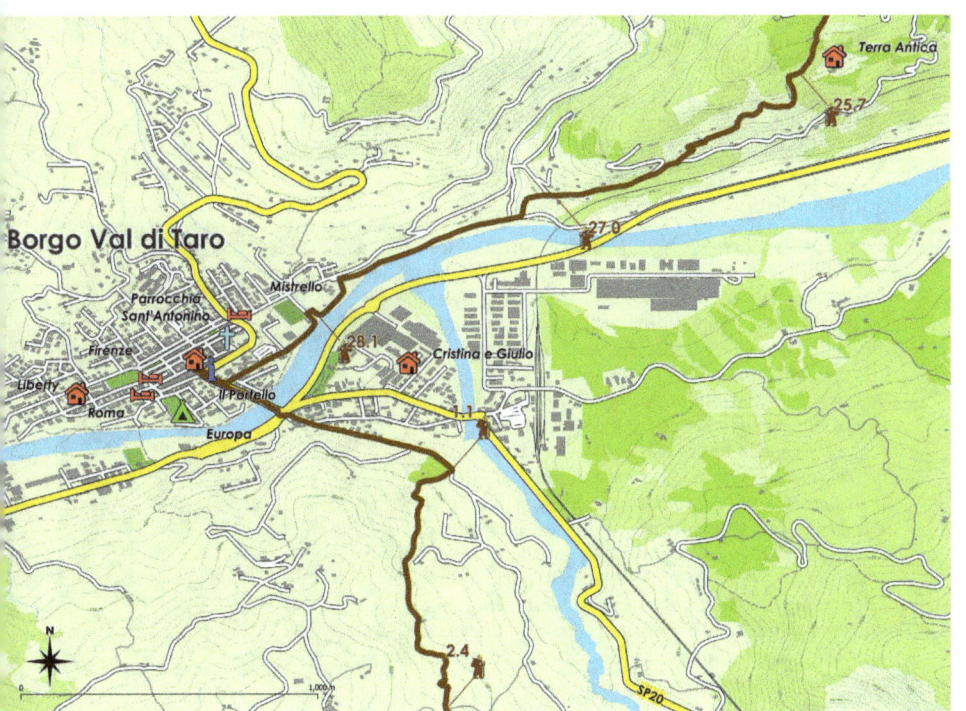

stage 59h — Borgo-Val-di-Taro to Pontremoli

Length:	33.7km
Ascent:	2640m
Descent:	2813m
Pavia:	151km
Pontremoli:	34km

Pontremoli wakes - view from Castello del Piagnaro

Route: the long final stage of the via degli Abati leads from Borgo-Val-di-Taro to Pontremoli where we return to the via Francigena of Sigeric. Once more the mule roads climb through woodland to cross the Passo del Borgallo and again reach 1000 m with dramatic views of Lunigiana and the Tuscan-Emilian Ridge before the long descent into the Magra valley and Pontremoli. For those wishing an early escape from the hills and valleys there is a good train service from Borgotaro to Pontremoli and beyond.

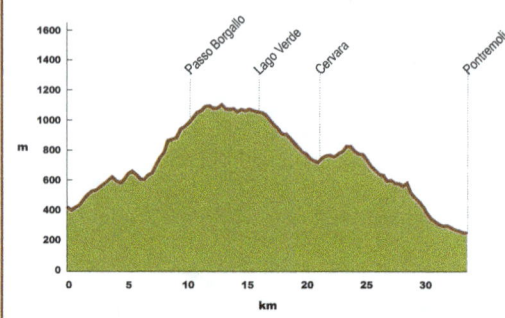

Accommodation is listed in this section for facilities on the approach to Pontremoli. Additional Pontremoli listings can be found under stage 67.

Major Gordon Lett, a WWII British Army officer, was a PoW escapee who became the leader of the International Brigade and a local hero. The Brigade comprised escapees of many nationalities and local volunteers who fought the German occupiers and their sympathizers along the Magra valley from late 1943 until the ultimate German withdrawal. They were so successful at harassing the German army that they were repeatedly resupplied by allied air drops and reinforced with SAS troops. Immediately after the declaration of peace, Lett was officially appointed to oversee the difficult transition of Pontremoli. Lett wrote that he was "humbled by the kindness, generosity and bravery of the local population. They had nothing to give but gave everything they had and, sometimes, paid for it with their lives. They had no political aspirations and fought only to protect their families and their way of life."

Creatures of the forest

Borgo-Val-di-Taro to Pontremoli   stage 59h

Resistance Monument - Passo Borgallo

(0.0) From the archway leading to the old town, retrace your steps on Via Taro and continue towards the river bridge [Direction Parma] (0.4) At the roundabout following the bridge, continue straight ahead on the narrow road [Pass a church close on your right] (1.1) Immediately after passing the cemetery turn right up the hill (2.4) At the junction with the broad track, continue straight ahead across the crossroads and follow the narrow footpath [Pass derelict building on your left] (3.0) At the junction turn right on the tarmac road [Pass house on your left] (3.7) At the junction, bear left on the main track [Remaining in the woods] (4.4) At the bend to the left in the road, following the hamlet of Valleto di San Vincenzo, bear right on the gravel track (4.8) At the T-junction with the tarmac road, continue straight ahead on the narrow track [Direction Passo Borgallo] (5.1) At the junction with the tarmac road, bear left and continue uphill on the road [Pass the church on your left] (5.6) As

stage 59h — Borgo-Val-di-Taro to Pontremoli

the road bears right on the exit to San Vincenzo, turn left on the concrete then grass track, downhill [Pass white house on your left] **(5.9)** At the foot of the grass path at the junction with a gravel road, turn left and then right [Cross the Tarodine river bridge] **(6.9)** Immediately before the sign board for Verdana, turn right on the narrow tarmac road [Direction La Galla] **(7.4)** At the top of the rise at a junction with a gravel track, bear left on the grass track, uphill **(7.5)** At the junction with the gravel track, turn left [Pass water tap on your right] **(7.6)** At the T-junction after the church turn left and immediately right [Direction Cimiterio] **(7.9)** On reaching the cemetery turn left on the stony track **(9.1)** Approaching

Vestiges of a muleteers rest house

the forestry track, turn left [Passo Borgallo 25 minutes] **(9.6)** Fork right on the narrow track slightly downhill **(10.3)** At the T-junction, turn left up the hill [Towards the skyline] **(10.3)** At the summit of **Passo Borgallo** turn sharp right **(11.5)** At the war memorial continue straight ahead on the broader track **(11.8)** At the junction with a gravel track from the left, continue straight ahead **(11.8)** At the next junction, turn left **(12.2)** At the T-junction, turn right **(13.7)** At the junction with houses to your right and wood carvings beside the track, continue straight ahead **(14.3)** Turn left to cross the river [Direction Lago Verde] **(14.4)** Keep left at the fork in the tracks, pass through a small dip and then a steep climb on the other side **(16.1)** Pass **Lago Verde** on your right and continue on the broad track between stone built chalets **(18.5)** Continue straight ahead on the descending trail [Water tap on the right] **(21.2)** On the exit from the village of **Cervara** take the right fork uphill **(21.3)** On the crown of the hairpin bend to the right, bear left on the woodland track [Pass garages on your left] **(23.6)** At the T-junction turn left and follow the road to the left **(24.1)** Beside a single garage keep sharp right on the road **(25.9)** As you descend the hill take a sharp right onto a stony track into the trees [Direction Vignola] **(26.6)** Take the

Rejoining Sigeric's path - Piazza del Duomo

Borgo-Val-di-Taro to Pontremoli — stage 59h

left fork (**29.3**) At the crossroads in the tracks, turn right downhill [Towards the sounds of the highway] (**29.8**) Shortly after the tarmac road turns left, turn right downhill on the stony track (**30.2**) At the crossroads with the tarmac road, continue straight ahead on the tarmac before quickly taking the stony track to the left (**30.3**) At the T-junction following the first arch, turn left and then immediately right to pass through an arched passageway, downhill (**30.4**) At the junction with a tarmac road at the foot of the cobbled passage, turn left on the road [Further arch ahead at the junction] (**31.2**) At the T-junction under the power lines, turn right (**31.3**) At the junction, keep right and follow the road into Pontremoli (**33.3**) At the complex junction bear left on vialle Fiorini and cross the river bridge (**33.6**) At the T-junction turn right (**33.7**) Arrive at **Pontremoli** centre in piazza del Duomo. Note:- the Sigeric via Francigena continues from this point [Duomo to your left]

Accommodation and Tourist Information

Cervara

✝ **Canonica San Giogio** [Michela and Fabio], Via Cervara, 146, 54027 Cervara(MS), Italy; Tel:+39 3289022700; +39 0187830177 ; +39 339 6203651; *Please call well in advance sleeping bag necessary no shops in the village*

Pontremoli

🏠 **Agriturismo - Il Glicine e la Lanterna** [Graziella], Via Casa Corvi, 220, 54027 Pontremoli(MS), Italy; Tel:+39 0187 460050; +39 339 8554222; Email:glicinelanterna@gmail.com; glicine-lanterna.it; Price:A

🛏 **Hotel - Ca' del Moro**, Via Giovanni Bellotti, 2, 54027 Pontremoli(MS), Italy; Tel:+39 0187 832202; Email:info@cadelmororesort.it; www.cadelmororesort.it; Price:A

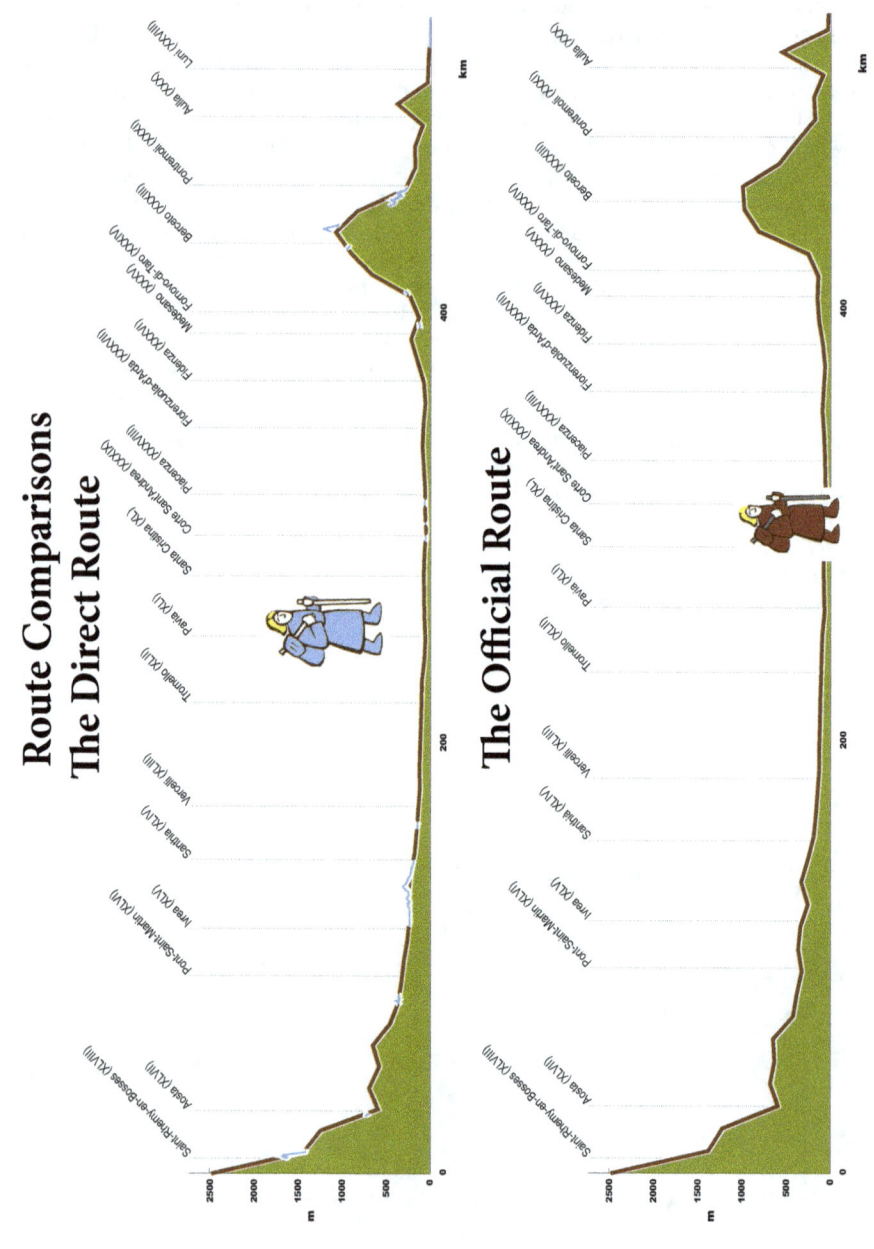

Route Comparisons
The Direct Route
The Official Route

Quo Vadis?
Where do you go now?

*Via Appia Antica leading south from Rome
passing the point where St Peter uttered the famous phrase.*

www.ingramcontent.com/pod-product-compliance
Lightning Source LLC
LaVergne TN
LVHW020137080526
838202LV00048B/3961